Contextualized Stylistics

STUDIES IN LITERATURE 29

Series Editors
C.C. Barfoot - M. Buning - A.J. Hoenselaars
W.M. Verhoeven

Associate Editors
P.Th.M.G. Liebregts - A.H. van der Weel

Contextualized Stylistics

In Honour of Peter Verdonk

Edited by Tony Bex,
Michael Burke
and Peter Stockwell

Amsterdam - Atlanta, GA
2000

The paper on which this book is printed meets the requirements
of 'ISO 9706:1994, Information and documentation
- Paper for documents - Requirements for permanence'.

ISBN 90-420-1491-1 (bound)

Printed in The Netherlands

CONTENTS

FOREWORD

This volume is intended to honour the legacy of Peter Verdonk, Professor of Stylistics at the University of Amsterdam, where he has worked in the English Department for the greater part of the last thirty years. All of the contributors, many of whom are prominent in their respective fields, have been influenced by Verdonk's painstaking criticisms, which elucidate the contextual elements of literature as an aid to interpretation. In the introduction to his *Academisch Proefschrift, How Can We Know the Dancer from the Dance? Some Literary Stylistic Studies of English Poetry* (1988), Verdonk commented on his general debt to what he called the "British school of stylistics" and his particular debt to Hallidayan systemic functional grammar which "enables the stylistician to account for variations in surface structure, that is to offer functional explanations of them, and ... furnishes the possibility of viewing a text as part of a complex social and cultural process" (6-7). Verdonk's own work (e.g., most recently, *Twentieth-Century Poetry: From Text to Context* (1993); *Twentieth-Century Fiction: From Text to Context* (1995), edited with Jean-Jacques Weber; and *Twentieth-Century Drama: From Text to Context* (1998), edited with Mick Short and Jonathan Culpeper) has amply repaid that debt, and it is fitting that a number of scholars, many of whom are centrally members of the British school of stylistics, should join together both to recognize his own contribution to the project and to develop it further.

As Verdonk's own words suggest, a fully contextualized stylistics is a daunting prospect. "Context" is a slippery word that covers both the co-text, which surrounds that part of the text that is being analysed, the social and cultural backgrounds, which bring a text into being, and the social, cultural and cognitive positionings of those readers who interpret the text and give it meaning. It is unlikely, therefore, that any single scholar will be able to deal comprehensively with all these areas. What distinguishes this collection is that the various contributors have, in their respective ways, enlarged our understanding of what may count as "context". What they share in common is a rejection of a purely formal description of linguistic features. Although such description may well furnish a starting point, there is no necessary connection between the formal features of a text and the interpretations and evaluations which may be brought to bear on the text. Such connections are contingent both upon the intended functions of such a formal description and the sensitivity of the stylistician.

We would stress that while this volume is representative of those scholars who have been influenced by Verdonk's work, it does not encompass them all. Many people we approached were unable to contribute because of other commitments and some who approached us had to be refused so as to keep the volume a manageable size. The present contributors are roughly divided between colleagues from the University of Amsterdam and other Dutch universities on the one hand, and colleagues from the international Poetics and Linguistics Association (PALA) on the other. They also cover all periods of Verdonk's academic career from one of his PhD supervisors to his most recent PhD supervisee.

Olga Fischer, a close colleague of Peter at the University of Amsterdam, is perhaps best placed to contextualize Peter from the perspective of this institution where he has worked for the past thirty years:

> Peter was a member of PALA from almost the very beginning and this was a natural outcome of the new direction he was taking in his teaching and research at the end of the 1970s. In the *Engels Seminarium* teaching programme there was at that time a grammar module in the English Literature postgraduate programme, which was basically a kind of remedial grammar course based on "Zandvoort" (the book which all students had already read from cover to cover in the three years leading up to their MA). As a result of this somewhat intensive interface the book was unsurprisingly no longer "appreciated" by the students. It was Peter who made a virtue out of necessity by turning this pure grammar course into a grammar course totally devoted to the language of literature, but with a very strong grammatical, and in fact implicitly remedial base. This then is how stylistics was born at the University of Amsterdam. Peter grew in his new-found interest and so did the students who now came to love this part of the curriculum, which had previously been considered tedious. As

a result a great number of MA stylistics theses were written under Peter's guidance.

I think I can speak for all my colleagues in the department when I say that we will especially remember Peter as a colleague who was always willing to take on the most difficult and arduous administrative tasks. In the past decade especially, Peter's presence in the department has been invaluable. As the chairman of the *Dagelijkse Bestuur* 1993-1997 (a committee burdened with the day to day running of the department) he has served us in such a way that ensured that there was peace and quiet in the department, that the department's links with the outside world and the higher authorities were smooth and well-organized, that the various tasks were well-supervised and sorted out (with Peter even doing them himself if push came to shove), that problems when they arose (as they too often did) were solved in the least painful way, that weddings and funerals, births, illnesses, birthdays were well attended to, that people knew where to find a listening ear in emotional times .... etc., etc., etc. It was for all the above reasons and more that we were very glad that we could persuade him to stay on as our head of department by standing unanimously behind his personal chair. His professorship was indeed well-earned. We sincerely hope that all the care that he has invested in us, in the students and in our *Engels Seminarium* has not taken too much out of him, and that he will continue to enjoy his love for his work and the new scholarly enterprises that he has set out on as emeritus professor. We feel it is fitting that we can celebrate his leave-taking with this book, whose coming into being owes everything to his current PhD supervisee Michael Burke. Peter, we wish you well, and we hope to see you often in the corridors of the fifth floor of the *Bungehuis* for a long time to come and to hear your soft knock on our office doors.

Similarly, in order to contextualize Peter from a PALA perspective, we found Katie Wales, his old friend and a former chair of the association more than willing to offer the following words:

For me, Peter and the Poetics and Linguistics Association are inextricably interwoven. In the early years of the association, in the 1980s, Peter volunteered to produce what turned out to be a comprehensive and carefully annotated annual stylistics bibliography, which proved a valuable research tool in its updating for several years. He also acted as secretary for PALA for several years, and organized a successful PALA conference in Amsterdam, the first to go "international" in 1990. More recently, he has been a member of the Editorial Board of the association's journal, *Language and Literature.*

But these are not the only, or even the most important reasons why Peter and PALA go together in my mind. At one of the very first conferences we had Peter organize a "workshop" on Sylvia Plath's poetry, based on his own self-wrought practices as a teacher of stylistics to his upper-intermediate and advanced students of English at the University of Amsterdam. The experience was so satisfying that from then on I was "hooked" on the value of stylistic analysis in the classroom, and at subsequent conferences never failed to listen to Peter on the poetry of Heaney, Larkin, Auden and others. For Peter's analyses never failed to deliver what must be one of his central beliefs, expressed in his Introduction to his edited volume *Twentieth-Century Poetry: From Text to Context* (Routledge, 1993): namely that "an effective and sensitive analysis of textual structure and its semantic implications provides a sound basis for a rewarding and aesthetic interpretation of literary texts". Peter's sensitivity to language, and his huge enjoyment of literature, shine through everything he writes, whether on classical rhetorical or cognitive poetics.

Because of the range of contributors and because of the focus offered by Peter Verdonk's interest in contextualized stylistics, this collection, in fact, represents the state of the art in literary linguistics. It is an indication of the strength and vibrancy of the discipline − much of which is a consequence of Peter's work and encouragement over the years − that the volume is as rich as it is. We told contributors only to focus on the notion of "contextualized stylistics", and that their papers would be edited into a Festschrift volume. As a consequence we have a wide range of theoretical and methodological approaches, applied to poetry, prose and drama, and covering the whole field of literature from the medieval to the contemporary. The book represents and exemplifies the diversity of different engagements with the literary context available to the modern stylistician. Chapters range from detailed practical analysis to far-reaching theoretical discussion.

While recognizing Verdonk's scholarly interests and developing them in ways that he would both understand and approve of, all the contributors would bear witness to Peter's human warmth and humour, which surfaces in the body of particular chapters (especially the opening and closing chapters of the volume). It is most publicly present in the poem on the following page which concludes this introduction. We hope you will agree with the kind words of Roger Fowler, one of the earliest explorers in contextualized stylistics, uttered just a few weeks before his tragic, early death, that this project is "an excellent idea".

Tony Bex, Michael Burke and Peter Stockwell

The Tale of the Transvaal Amsterdammerbird[1]

The white-headed owl[2] of the Transvaal
Gave out a long *tu-whoo*.
He wanted to start with a short *tu-whit*
But the *whoo* had forced itself through.

He wanted to give a wise lecture
Dressed in a jacket of blue,
To whit, a stylistic analysis
Of a poem 'bout a lad come to *woo*.

But his wise wit and hyper-intelligence
For a moment had quite 'scaped *awoo*.
His mind was invaded by Joke.[3]
He could only come out with *a woooooooo*!

He had stood on the Shield of Achilles,
But he'd drunk too much fine Potchy plonk.
Tu-whoo, tu-whoo, tu-whoo he cried
And then came to a complete Verdonk!

---

[1] With thanks to Mick Short for the transcript of this poem. The poem itself was first "performed" by Mick and Tom Barney, both of Lancaster University, in the presence of Peter Verdonk during a social function at the PALA Conference held in Potchefstroom, South Africa (April 1999).
[2] Peter, it transpires, is a keen collector of (imitation) owls. Hence the subject matter of this poem.
[3] "Joke" is the first name of Peter's partner. It is (roughly) pronounced *yoka*.

ACKNOWLEDGEMENTS

The editors would like to thank the series editor, C.C. Barfoot, for his kind encouragement and efficiency. The editors and publishers would like to thank Jane Gardam for copyright permission to reproduce an extract from her novel *Bilgewater* (Abacus, 1976). We are very grateful to Jetty Peterse and Mariëtte Guertz for all their secretarial help. Thanks to Joanna Gavins for the owl. The authors and editors have made every effort to identify copyright holders for permissions to use material where appropriate. We would be grateful to be notified of any errors or omissions and would be pleased to make the necessary amendments at the earliest opportunity.

THE WRITING ON THE WALL

WALTER NASH

Thanks, courteous wall: Jove shield thee well for this!
(A Midsummer Night's Dream, V.i,176).

"Kick the Pope", it used to say, in withered whitewash, on the wall by
the forecourt of an old Lube and Krypton Tuning garage that I
occasionally passed on my way to work. Further, this sweet and lovely
wall announced, "Chelsea are wankers", a disparaging comment on the
sporting successes of Chelsea's football club; and then − on a political
note − "Tories get stuffed", to which had been added, in a different
hand, "at the taxpayer's expense", followed by a subsidiary gloss, "but
not on the NHS".[1]

If this is the writing on the wall − if such stuff were all of the writing
on any wall − it could well go unnoticed and unremembered, and
certainly never be demurely transcribed into a passing scholar's mental
notebook. The common inscriptions of the garage wall, the underpass and
the bridge arch are drearily aggressive or malign, their language
obsessively faecal or sexual, the substance of their grudge against the
world presented in terms of primitive religion, Association Football, the

---

[1] Graffiti recollected can be as difficult to "date" as ancient manuscripts. The
accusation, on an East Midland wall, that Chelsea, a London team, are wankers
(practitioners of the solitary vice), may be dated to the early 1970s, when Chelsea
won the UEFA Cup, having previously beaten Leeds in the FA Cup Final (after a
replay). "Not on the NHS" suggests the Thatcherite revisions of the Health Service
in the early-to-mid 80s. "Kick the Pope" is not so much a graffito as recurrent knee-
jerk sectarian snarl. In this form it is a bowdlerized version of a brutal *Urtext*, "Fuck
the Pope", which our gentle graffitist might have considered a case of taking
theological differences too far.

organs of generation and the rudiments of political feeling. They have a
quarrel with life, but their quarrelsomeness is diffuse and curiously
confined. They rarely branch out, or vary their themes. One never meets,
for example, an injunction to "Kick the Lord Chancellor", or the
allegation that "Deconstructionists are wankers" (a proposition that might
be plausibly argued); or some footnote on bitter personal experience,
such as "Encyclopaedia salesmen get stuffed (in twenty-four easy
instalments)". Vulgar graffitists stick to a few topics. They are loyal in
their thick hatreds, consistent in their scorn of the same unbeloved things,
year in, year out. They are yobs, and yobs rule OK?

It is fortunate − my dear Peter − in this as in other respects, that we
have universities. The academy, as it happens, makes a natural home for
the select graffito, and academic graffiti nearly always exhibit some
degree of distinction, along with a sardonic humour that transcends the
cloacal and copulative, though it sometimes appears that faculty members
are no less splenetic, and no less crude in the venting of their spleen, than
football fans and religious bigots. Neat inscriptions in the executive toilets
of reputable colleges record the play of scholarly approval or malice:
"John Doe − The Professors' Professor" ("John Doe" being in this case
a person of grave demeanour and great learning, able to remain
eloquently impenetrable on a range of philosophical topics); or, in
dialogic style "What chair for N.N.? − One wired to the National Grid"
(N.N. being a person of large ambition and an appetite for power
somewhat in excess, perhaps, of what the graffitist considers seemly).[2]
The mural inscriptions composed by members of the academic staff do
not make up any great corpus, but one may learn from them at least
something of the scholar's inveterate capacity for suspicion, jealousy,
personal hatred and partisan rancour, the gamut of those dark affects that
for many gentlefolk − yourself no doubt among them − make early
retirement a not unattractive prospect. No one who has not lived among
university dons ("don" − a grotesque honorific once reserved for fellows
at Oxford and Cambridge but now freely accorded by journalists to
academics from everywhere) can understand how their temperaments are
as atrabilious as those of their Mafia counterparts.

---

[2]   Though discretion, and respect for the now departed, prevents me from revealing
the identities of John Doe and N.N., I am able to confirm that they are (or were)
actual and known persons. The cited examples are from reliable walls in the vicinity
of the Sch**l of Engl*sh at the Un*v*rs*t* *f N*tt*ngh*m. Asterisks rule, *K?
M*m's the w*rd, P*t*r.

Student wit, on the other hand, is broader, more genial, usually not so vindictive. It relishes the congress of the deft and the daft. On the wall of a locker-room, next to the contraceptive vending automat, it states: "The chewing gum in this machine tastes horrible". (This pleasantry is so well travelled, however, that by now it is probably to be found in every locker-room on every campus in the United Kingdom − a standard rubric, testifying to the ubiquity of the condom). Then there are curriculum jokes, the wild flowerings of rooted study. The student of Descartes writes "I drink, therefore I am", adding, in puzzled consequence "I'm drunk, therefore I was"; the Shakespearean writes "To be or not to be, that is the question; answer on one side of the wall only"; the physicist declares "Schrodinger rules the waves, OK"; the rebel in any cause proclaims "Down with early Byzantine church music"! − a piece of delicious whimsy difficult to explain to the puzzled observer, because in such instances the deconstruction of the text is a laborious undertaking that ultimately destroys the joke.[3] These are "high" graffiti. To produce them, and to appreciate them, it is at least necessary to think now and then, and to have read a little.

What these elevated specimens share with the meaner sort of wall-writing is a simple regularity of grammatical and rhetorical form. All graffiti are in some degree "primitive": primitive as syntactic structures, primitive as paradigms of discourse. Inquisitive and sufficiently informed foreigners might be entertained by them, but they could not begin to learn from them, for example, the ramifications, in tense, aspect, voice and modality, of the English verb system. How often does a graffito exemplify any tense other than the simple present? The world of the graffito is ostensibly the world "as of now"; it is not a realm of histories, possibilities and speculations. In what is assumed to be a context of immanent action and experience, the writing on the wall deals in directives (recommendations, commands) or in declaratives (assertions, propositions, definitions). In its "low" forms, it says "Kick the Pope", "Tories get stuffed" (directives); it says "Chelsea are wankers", or − a

---

[3] According to my *The Language of Humour* (London: Longman 1985, 40), the Byzantine music joke "is said to have been observed on a wall at the University of Edinburgh". That may well be; it is indeed more than plausible; much virtue in "is said"; though I forget now who said it. The other examples in this "campus" list are either quoted from personal observation and recollection, or drawn from Nigel Rees' collection *Graffiti 3* (London: George Allen & Unwin, 1981).

vaingloriously recurrent theme, inviting competitive challenge – "I have a big one" (declaratives).

In its "higher" manifestations it uses comparable syntactic structures, but in more elaborate forms, and to wittier effect. It can say "Stop the world, I want to get off", or "Help save our trees – eat more beavers" (directives); it can say "Abstinence is the thin end of the pledge" and "I think sex is better than logic but I can't prove it" (declaratives). These "high graffiti" may look more ambitious than their lowly counterparts, but share with them, nevertheless, a very simple grammar. The tense of the declaratives is almost always the present; in some cases there may be no verb, so that the inscription takes the form of a so-called "equational sentence", for example "Karl Marx's grave – another communist plot".[4] What is evident from the "high" graffito, however, is that the inscription no longer implies totally the "real", dull, brickdust world of fact and sense, but through word-play and punning and metaphor evokes domains of fantasy, speculation, lunatic logic, playful possibility.

Many graffiti are one-liners or brief definitions ("John Doe, the professors' professor"; "Chelsea are wankers"); out of the one-liner, however, develops a more significant form, the dialogic or responsive graffito. The scholiast who added the response "at the taxpayers' expense" to the directive text "Tories get stuffed", not only changed the semantics of the primary statement from directive ("go and do this, you Tories") to declaration ("Tories undergo this experience"); he (or not impossibly she) created a primitive semblance of dialogue, consisting of an initiating utterance and a follow-up. This is the process of many graffiti: proposition eliciting a response. Graffitic responses rarely fulfil the demands of "relevance" which govern ordinary exchanges, but are as a rule pointedly irrelevant, subverting, challenging, or otherwise sporting with the sense of a proposition.

This typical "dialogic" graffito, dates back to the late 1970s or early 80s:

---

[4] Because graffiti "travel" a good deal, by scripted repetition or by oral report, it is often difficult to establish the origin of a joke. In the case of Marx's grave, however, I am fairly certain that the graffito is an oblique comment on events of January 1970, when politically motivated (presumably "fascist") vandals, having daubed the philosopher's grave in Highgate cemetery with swastikas, attempted to demolish it with explosives.

Come home to a real fire − buy a cottage in Wales.

The *proposition* in that case − "Come home to a real fire" − was a slogan printed on the advertisements of the British National Coal Board, who hoped to sell more coal for domestic consumption, and hence to encourage their customers to enjoy a culturally-approved form of comfort. All true Britons, the assumption goes, commend a "real" fire. ("Real" as opposed to the sad, uncosy artifice of electric bars glimmering behind plastic logs). The added *response* − "buy a cottage in Wales" − alludes mischievously to the activities of Welsh nationalists, whose sporadic campaigns in the 1970s included the burning down of holiday cottages and "second homes" belonging to English people.[5]

This kind of graffito asks for immediate recognition of a quotation, a slogan or a catch phrase; essentially, for some knowledge of current talk and transactions. It is a familiar awareness of things-as-they-are-right-now, an awareness that can be summed up in our current phrase "street-smart", or simply in the one word, "street". The street-smart people of the 1970s may not have known that they were "street", but they certainly knew about political arsonists, and also about the Coal Board's advertising campaign, and could connect one thing with another. Things change, of course; the connection has slipped, the juncture of words and events is broken in this case, as it is always being broken in popular discourse. Fire-raising is now a mercifully rare expression of nationalist feeling; politics has moved on,[6] the world of words and business has moved on, and if people at large can no longer summon promptly to

---

[5] This graffito points to the convergence of two socio-economic themes: the travails of the British coalmining industry in the 1970s, when strikes and the increasing competitiveness of other domestic heating fuels (electricity, gas) led the National Coal Board to mount poster campaigns like the one quoted; and the nationalism of Welsh Wales, particularly after the referendum of March 1979, when the proposals for a Welsh Assembly were rejected. The "incendiarists" (as commentators called them, carefully steering round the words "terrorist" and "arsonist") took to burning holiday cottages belonging to absent Englishmen, on the questionably logical grounds that in buying these cottages the English were depriving young Welsh people of potential homes, thus driving a workforce out of its native country.

[6] "Politics" has indeed "moved on"; in May 1999, following a new referendum, a Welsh Assembly, with powers of regional government, sat for the first time in Cardiff.

mind, as a matter of "street-knowledge", the old Coal Board advertisement, this graffito becomes an apparently pointless text, requiring as much elucidation as any classical inscription or many-layered Shakespearean pun.

Graffiti are ephemeral, very much as catch-phrases, political slogans and "adlanguage", on which they frequently draw for wording, are ephemeral. It is in part an impermanence of the recording surface; when the wall is knocked down or cleaned, or the hoarding re-papered, the words disappear into the imperfect recollections of those who once observed them. More than that, however, it is a transience of the events or concepts to which they specifically relate. The words "beam us up, Scotty", written on a men's room wall, under a jagged and charred hole in the ceiling,[7] make an amusing graffito (and a pointed commentary on the hebetude of university maintenance departments) for just as long as the hole in the ceiling stays unrepaired and the clients of the men's room clearly recollect gruff old Scotty, och aye, the omnicompetent engineer who used to operate the teleportation machine in the TV space odyssey called *Star Trek*. Without the hole, you might as well scrub the wall clean; without the perceived allusion, you might as well forget the words. Words that relate to bygone events, outworn entertainments, sporting contests, *et hoc genus omne*, however witty in their day, obviously lose their charm when a new day comes.

There are, however, some graffitic comments that transcend a commonplace wit and manage to survive the vagaries of chance and changing circumstance. Try this:

> The meek shall inherit the earth
> – But not its mineral rights.

That little dialogue is founded upon a very familiar *proposition*, a verse from the Beatitudes (St Matthew, V.5) which is then cynically subverted; the completed text assumes the tone of the corporate ethos, the entrepreneurial tenor of yesterday, today and any day. Like the "cottage in Wales" graffito, this inscription presents in concise form a whole potential tract of ironic discourse. It would be possible to make a commentary paraphrase out of this, to expand it into an argument, to add supporting instances and cautionary qualifications, until the whole thing

---

[7] For the location of this, see note 2 above.

would swell like a footnote in a doctoral thesis, becoming longer and denser than the piece of text it was meant to clarify. Sensible people will of course leave commentary alone and let the graffito text speak briefly for itself; nevertheless, the point remains that a dialogic graffito can suggest a whole discursive process.

There is a rivalry of sorts between the one-line graffito and the dialogic form, reflecting a contrast of polemic attitudes. One-liners are always authoritative in intent; one-liners are put-downers or shut-uppers, "closed" assertions. The dialogic forms challenge the one-line authority; they answer back, they throw counterpunches, they go one better, they prise the discussion open. Some dialogic graffiti invite plural responses in playful debate:

> Be alert — England needs lerts.
> No, we have too many lerts — be aloof.
> No, don't be aloof, there's safety in numbers — be alert.

It would be pretentious to call that little piece of simulated backchat a "controversy",[8] yet this is how controversies unfold, or re-fold, in such repeated patterns of give and take, of proposition and counter-proposition. In this respect the dialogic writing on the wall evokes, or "shadows" much of the writing in the editorial or the political script, where cases are argued in often tedious elaborations of the repeated pro and the asserted con. And in many a leader column, to say nothing of headlines, there are statements confidently turned and packaged and almost ready to do duty as graffiti in the better sort of convenience. Such statements, however, do not as a rule suggest the writing on the wall. They are stray thoughts from the think-tank, pretending to be aphorisms. Printer's ink allows ambitions denied to mere chalk or aerosol.

Broadsheet aphorisms are seldom so very memorable, and even tabloid headlines fade by-and-by from the recollection;[9] whereas, despite

---

[8] What it most resembles is the "fooling" and pun-chopping of some moments in Shakespearean drama.

[9] A few, notably those generated by *The Sun* newspaper, retain a horrid hold: e.g. "Gotcha!", on the occasion of the sinking of the Argentine warship *Belgrano* in 1982, and "Up yours, Delors!", and "Frog Off"! in response to Jacques Delors' presidential conduct of the European Community. Such instances, however, are mere ejaculations, like "Kick the Pope"; they lack the gnomic playfulness of the superior graffito.

the ephemerality of the genre, nearly everyone can recall at least one "good" graffito, or at all events remember being told about one. How graffiti get into the verbal repertoire of the ordinary user-in-the-street is hard to say; but unless the user is a hermit living in a trance of self-absorption, there must always be some receptiveness to these folk-wisdoms and gnomic inscriptions. Some graffiti we notice in passing — or, so to speak, while we wash our hands. They are memorized and kept in mind for the benefit of the first acquaintance who might find them amusing. Graffitic literature (if that term is admissible) thus becomes "oral" literature; it gets passed on. In this way, the vast majority of memorable graffiti become known by report rather than personal observation; assurances of their existence, even notes on provenance, are passed round circles of acquaintances, each one of whom may then claim to have "come across" this or that specimen.

This presents a particular aspect of a general human weakness, that of pretending to first-hand knowledge. With time, pretence hardens into certainty. I cannot claim with confidence a direct, eyeballing acquaintance with some of my favourite graffiti; for example, the delightful "response" of "I love Margaret Holmes" — "Good Lord, Watson, so do I", or that notorious text which must rank as a classic instance of mural impudence, reputedly set high up on the wall of a men's urinal, almost in the angle of the ceiling, "If you can read this you are pissing on your boots". However, like many who enjoy such vulgar jokes, Peter, I am not unwilling to give the impression that I have observed these inscriptions *in situ*. I feel I must have done so. I can almost see in my mind's eye the relevant wall. There is a curious and compelling transition process of "I have been told about it" shifting to "I may have read it" then with a skip to "I have seen it". (If there were a next stage it would be "I probably wrote it"). Graffiti invite that kind of fiction, the personal attestation of having been there, observed the event, seen the relevant document; it is as though mere quoting by hearsay somehow deprived the sample of its validity and force. There is scholarship in these things; when we quote we must quote — or seem to quote — from the original wall.

But are original walls all tumbling down, what with bulldozers and cleaning agents? Walls may be less available now than heretofore, or better policed, yet no matter; cyberspace beckons the graffitist, and the World Wide Web with its numerous sites. In due course a graffito site must surely emerge, if one is not already in place, a virtually real wall in the wide waste of the universe, accessible to epigrammatists, rhymesters and minor parodists, available at the touch of a key to collectors who need have no scruples about claiming the discovery of things which are everyone's to discover. It will be enough to say that you saw it on the Net. In the meantime, the graffitists of the waste ground, the back alley and the factory yard are left to ply their trade, along with the superior practitioners who haunt the administrative staff ablutions and the library cloakroom.

Why do they persist in it? It must be uncomfortable, nervous, often dangerous, and on occasion provocative of the sternest retribution of the law. In the city of Sheffield, in January 1996, an unfortunate young man was sentenced to prison for *five years* for persistently leaving his "tag" — that is, for spraying colourful designs on derelict houses and old walls. True, he was not a graffitist in the sense of the present essay. He was a species of graphic artist, not a verbal practitioner. Nevertheless, he went out and wrote on walls, not once but again and again and again (like the young lady from Spain who was terribly sick on the train): and they jailed him for it. British law is very hard on offences against property. A sceptical observer could be forgiven for thinking that as a rule you might do better, penalty-wise, to batter your spouse, grossly abuse a child, or abscond with the life savings of a disabled senior citizen than be caught carrying an aerosol can of paint with the apparent intention of inscribing a few pointed socio-political comments on some grey eminence of civic masonry. Graffitists know how they run the risk of censure and worse: then why do they persist in — let us invent a word, a verb and a gerund — "graffitizing"?

There is, possibly, the delicious threat of detection in the naughty act, a mind-flooding "rush" that may impel the social maverick to reach again and again for his chalk, his paint pot, or his felt-tipped pen. But then, a stronger impulse than mere delight in misdemeanour could well be the egoism that needs the world to take notice of an existence. Wartime graffiti would announce, beneath the representation of a face peering over a wall, "Kilroy was here", or "Chad was here".[10] For many, a strong

---

[10] "Kilroy" was an American import into Britain; "Chad" was the native version, his appearances usually accompanied by a sketch of what looked like a bald man peering over a fence. One of his eyes was represented as a "plus" sign, the other as a "minus", leading to the conjecture that Chad was a parody of a rudimentary circuit diagram — an electrician's "tag", as it were.

motive to graffitizing may be simply to insist that the graffitist, like
Kilroy or Chad, "was here". Take notice of me — this writing testifies to
my presence. I print, therefore I am. Even that, however, may be too
narrow a view of the matter, doing scant justice to the laudable wish to
make a point and share a joke in the most immediately accessible forum.
Look, says the graffitist, I rejoice in my inventions, which do not require
the patronage of an editor or a publisher. Writing on the wall is just
another language game, played now, between you and me, before your
very eyes.

Occasionally, graffitists comment on the practice and nature of their
art, like critics reflecting on the nature of texts. Possibly the most
arresting, if grotesque, definition of the practice of graffitizing is supplied
by the unknown moralist who writes: "Graffiti are the skid-marks of the
soul". ("Skid-marks": *1)* Tyre marks on the road, and *2)* [vulgar slang]
faecal stains on clothing, or in a toilet bowl.)[11] The writing on the wall,
this pungent inscription apparently suggests, is an accidental token of the
soul's irregular *motions*. The conflated senses of "(uncontrolled) vehicle
movement", "(uncontrolled) bowel movement", and "(uncontrolled)
psychic impulse" are not wholly apparent in the wording of the text, but
the connections are left for the onlooker to construct. It is a ludicrous
reading, and one that requires from the reader an understanding tainted
by his own acquaintance with the lexicon of vulgarity, but it has
something of the conviction and persuasive impact of a true epigram, in
which the force of the saying lurks in potential, beneath the surface of the
text.

None of this furnishes a pretext for a scholarly and systematic study
of graffiti, such as might — my dear Peter — occupy the twilight years of

---

[11] The example suggests a particular value of graffiti, in documenting contemporary
usage and slang. As nearly as I can recollect, I first heard about it in the early 1980s,
as a graffito apparently commenting on a whole wall-full of submissions. I have
consulted eight reputable desk dictionaries of contemporary English, all published in
the mid-80s. None of them lists *skid mark* in its "decent" sense, though two – *Collins
Cobuild English Language Dictionary* and *The Longman Dictionary of Contemporary
English* cite it in examples from their corpora: "skid marks on every corner"
(Cobuild 1987) and "There were skid marks on the road where the van had crashed"
(Longman 2nd edition, 1987). It is perhaps not surprising that none of them lists the
"indecent" sense, though it may appear in dictionaries and registers published since
that time. Most dictionaries are a long way in arrears of current usage, particularly
usage of the *vulg.colloq.* variety.

a professor *emeritus*. Perhaps a millennium hence, when savants are gravely seeking to capture evidence for some grammatical or semantic feature of late twentieth-century Eurospeak, these mural scribblings will come into their own as valuable inscriptions, even as curriculum texts. Until then, they can be left to the weather and the scrubbing brush. Nevertheless, graffiti deserve just a little serious attention, along with other sportive elements of current popular usage. Apart from being furtive, fugitive, illicit, grubby, not infrequently obscene and occasionally funny, they represent a type of discourse, the *ludic*, which any philosopher of usage has to take into account. There are things done in play that have serious ends.

Furthermore, graffiti have resemblances with catch-phrases, popular sayings, proverbial utterances, wisdoms, saws, slogans, soundbites, with the whole squirming genus of declarations and directives, the modes through which public communications and interactions are increasingly conducted. Ours is the age of the catch phrase. One-liners rule, OK? We are maddeningly soundbitten, beset by the buzz of political saws; and since the writing on the wall is a part of this popular − or *populist* − activity in language, it has some value as a primary source for the student of modern rhetoric.

Graffiti are often disrespectful, jibing, combative − in a society that lacks respect (or rejects the very notion of respect), and is by nature derogatory, seeking always to pull the mighty from their seats, the stars from their heavens, the football managers from their jobs, the luvvies from their stages and silver screens. Mockery is the necessary business of the graffitist, who will turn to sardonic purpose the gravest writing on the public wall. "Jesus saves" is the legend on the noticeboard outside the Methodist church; but the graffitist has added, "in extra time" − a typical example of graffitic parody, the invoking of a style or variety of English (in this case the style of a headline from a newspaper's sports pages).

Political slogans, neatly packaged and pointedly formulated by the adman and his designing crew, are vulnerable to the graffitist − and hence to the graffitist's cousin, the cartoonist. One of Mr Steve Bell's cartoons in *The Guardian* (16.5.96) represents a view of London from the roof of the lawcourts, where stands the familiar blindfolded figure of Justice with her scales and sword, the round world under her feet. In the cartoon, however, the globe she stands on is the head of Mr Michael Howard, then Home Secretary, and her sword is a large needle, threaded from spools, which lie in the pans of her scale. (This is obviously a visual allusion to the name "Threadneedle Street", ie. the location of the Bank of England). It is not clear whether she is blind, but that hardly matters, since her proud head has been turned through 180 degrees. This image is a kind of rebus, or visual pun, its purport being that Mr Howard has "stitched up" British justice — or as Americans might say, "put in the fix" — through his proposals on criminal law, notably for legislation designed to transfer sentencing out of the discretion of judges and into the power of the state.

This is the principal, "foregrounded" message of a cartoon, which contains much carefully drafted background detail. One such detail is a rectangular hoarding, on which, in white letters on a dark ground, appears the legend:

> Yes, it smelt.
> Yes, we farted.

Beneath which, a smaller caption reads:

> British justice — The finest money can buy — Conservatives.

The hoarding is evidently a "party political" billboard of the kind that commonly appears in the period preceding a General Election. The robust — not to say scabrous — message of this cartoon billboard is in fact a parodic mime of hoardings actually put up by the publicity agents of the Conservative Party. These stated, in large white letters on the conventional conservative-blue ground:

> Yes it hurt.
> Yes it worked.

That slogan-text referred, without elaborative comment, to the social and economic policies of the Conservative administration, and in particular to "cuts" in public spending (which may have "hurt", but allegedly "worked" by controlling inflation) during the years of John Major's government (1990-97). The text is an unapologetic boast — a justification for what ministers of government have done. "You see now, it was all for your own good", it claims; or as athletes and their trainers put it, "No pain, no gain". The cartoonist's retort, on his pseudo-billboard set in a busy drawing of traffic hopelessly jammed in the streets of a city crammed with more and more vacant or half-constructed office blocks, is that "it" did not "work" at all; "it" was unpleasant — it was corrupt — it "smelt" — because "we" in the irrepressible crudity of our political nature, made it so. Bell's cartoon is thus an extended satirical comment on the failure (as he sees it) of the ruling party's policies. In the foreground is the Home Secretary's abortive attempt to impose his will on the judiciary; while in the background is the artist's comment on the general inadequacy of the Conservative administration.

The slogan "Yes it hurt. Yes it worked" is echoed in another cartoon by Mr Bell, published in *The Guardian* less than a week later (21.5.96). Here the Prime Minister, Mr John Major, and the then Chairman of the Conservative Party, Dr Brian Mawhinney, stand in Smith Square (where the party headquarters are located), counting banknotes which they have found in a bag marked *Republika Serpska* ("Serbian Republic", the current rumour being that the Serbs had an interest in contributing to Conservative Party funds). Mr Major, as always in Bell's cartoons through six ferocious years, is wearing his underpants outside his trousers — a mischievous allusion to the costume of Superman, who wears his figure-hugging red trunks over his fetching blue body-stocking.[12] Dr Mawhinney is saying "I think it came from the high ground over there — in a purely personal capacity of course", these phrases being expressions used by Dr Mawhinney during a controversy over the dubious and possibly compromised source of some of the party's political income. Behind the two men, in a very prominent position, though now the text is partly obscured by their figures, is an electoral billboard. It states:

> Yes it's stolen.
> Yes we spent it.

Once again, the original billboard text is parodied, in an accusatory comment on the behaviour of party managers.

---

[12] This jibe originated in the chance observation of some journalist (perhaps Mr Bell himself?) that John Major tucked his shirt into the underpants, which could be seen peeping over the waistband of his trousers. This was enough to furnish a satirist with a productive theme, which Mr Bell exploited, month after month, with the genial scurrility of a Gillray.

"Yes it hurt. Yes it worked" is an electoral slogan which
Conservative PR men may have expected to become a catch phrase. Mr
Bell, however, intervenes in the public progress of the electoral slogan by
inventing parodic forms, after the fashion of graffiti. They are not "real"
graffiti, of course. They are simulated graffiti, the writing on the wall in
a cartoon; if a name would help, we might call them graffitisms. But the
graffitisms on cartoon walls take effect in much the same way as the
graffitic challenges of the locker room or the pub toilet. They impose on
the unqualified assertion a dialogic challenge. They make war on official
one-liners and soundbites by treating them irreverently, sometimes even
irrelevantly, as though the authoritative pronouncement were too wide of
the real mark to be taken seriously. In this healthily subversive work the
casual graffitist is superseded by the cartoonist, who in turn is overtaken
by the political satirist mocking our willingness to be governed by
slogans and catchphrases. This is the useful end of the writing on the
wall; otherwise, it provokes a shrug, or raises a laugh, and fades from
the memory, like the work of all those sad ephemeral wits who practise
their craft on gable ends or canal bridges or − *eheu, fugaces!* − the
derelict brickfaces of areas and front yards, like the forecourt of the old
Lube and Krypton Tuning garage, which in former days I would
sometimes pass, my dear Peter, on my way to work.

(SUR)REAL STYLISTICS:
FROM TEXT TO CONTEXTUALIZING

PETER STOCKWELL

A little bit of context

The opposite of seeing things through rose-tinted spectacles is to look through a glass, darkly, and perceive in the distorting lens not what is there, but what the viewer is disposed to see. Practitioners of stylistics, in whose literary linguistic company I include myself, have tended to take the "rosy" view of our own discipline, its potential and achievements. Stylistics has been advocated as the solution to the double-bind of cultural readings and individual interpretation, offering neither an objective mechanism for meaning-recovery nor an entirely subjective solipsistic indeterminacy, but an "intersubjective validity".[1] This means that linguistic frameworks and concepts can be used explicitly by the critic to validate a plausible reading, which is offered to other readers for inspection and possible disagreement. As Verdonk and Weber put it, "with a stylistic methodology, ... indeterminacy is neither ignored nor allowed to go wild but is contained, for the stylistic methodology ensures that our reading is both explicit and replicable."[2]

For those sporting the latest distorting glasses, this pragmatic middle-ground is unsatisfactory. Any containment of the potential of meaning in a discourse is seen as inimical to the principle of the arbitrariness of the linguistic sign. For those raised on post-structuralist mysticism and Derridean sleight-of-pen, only the absolute freeplay of meaning is admissible. Anything less is a compromise sliding into determinism, buying into authority and linguistic colonialism along the

---

[1] Peter Verdonk and Jean-Jacques Weber, eds, *Twentieth-Century Fiction: From Text to Context*, London: Routledge, 1995.

[2] *Ibid.*, 3.

way. When linguists look at what critical theorists make of stylistics, there is often a sense of dismay. Simpson,[3] for example, quotes Abrams'[4] brief definition of stylistics and points out how most of it is inaccurate and misrepresentatative of the discipline. Within university departments of literary study, most colleagues have only a vague idea of what stylistics is, and it is either marginalized in the syllabus as "part of linguistics" or is tucked into a critical theory course as one component along with other ideological approaches to literature. Mostly, in academic practice, it is ignored. Though most modern critical writing engages with "language" as its theoretical focus, much of the discussion bears as much relation to linguistics, as does modern chemistry to alchemy. Curiously, the main misconceptions about stylistics are shared by established academics and beginning students. These misconceptions are that stylistics is entirely formalist, and aims towards objectivity by laying a discrete analytical model onto a text to wring out a single meaning, thereby invalidating any other interpretation.

While there might have been some slim justification for this in the dim past, such a charge does not seem to me to stick to any current or recent stylistic practice. Even the most decontextualized discussions of the Jakobsonians (in the 1950s and 1960s) and Hallidayans (in the 1970s and 1980s) were never entirely formalist nor functionalist to the exclusion of any other factors. Attacks on stylistics treat it as a monolithic project. Fish's famous jab[5] against some examples of published analysis simply fails to differentiate good stylistics from poorly thought-through stylistics, and then generalizes the local faults to the discipline as a whole. Even linguists from within the discipline have assisted in fossilizing this version of past stylistic practice. Burton[6]

---

[3] Paul Simpson, *Language Through Literature*, London: Routledge, 1997, 2-7.

[4] M.H. Abrams, *A Glossary of Literary Terms* (4th edition), New York: Holt Rinehart & Winston, 1981, 192.

[5] Stanley Fish, *Is There a Text in This Class? The Authority of Interpretive Communities*, Cambridge, Mass: Harvard University Press, 1980, 68-96.

[6] Deirdre Burton, "Through Glass Darkly: Through Dark Glasses — On Stylistics and Political Commitment — via a Study of a Passage from Sylvia Plath's *The Bell*

takes issue with writers up to the early 1980s for their "tacit assumption ... that presumes that it is the legitimate task of the stylistician to observe and describe phenomena in a 'neutral' and 'objective' way" (196), though she does not quote from or refer to a single example of this alleged shoddy practice. There is not even a single example of pure formalism in any of the other articles contemporary with Burton's in the same volume of Carter's collection of stylistics; and since then there has been an explicit move towards a contextualized stylistics, as the companion volume[7] illustrates.

If there has been any shift in emphasis at all between the inaccurately-named Russian formalists of the 1920s and the stylistics of the present, it is not that the complexities of context have suddenly been discovered, but that there is an explicit awareness that contextualization needs to be theorized as an integral part of the linguistic model. The series *From Text to Context*[8] is the best demonstration of this. Literary stylistics − unlike pure linguistics − has always necessarily integrated the effects of context into its discussion, to varying degrees of explicitness. Toolan takes the "text-context binarism" of linguistics to task in order to advocate an integrationist approach to language study, but it is noticeable that almost all of the work that he criticizes for falling into the binary trap is pure or theoretical rather than applied linguistics.[9] Literary stylistics tends, at some point, to engage with literary criticism and affective interpretations of readers, and thus very few pieces of literary stylistics are purely decontextualized.

Jar", in Ronald Carter ed., *Language and Literature: An Introductory Reader in Stylistics*, London: George Allen & Unwin, 1982, 195-214.

[7] Ronald Carter and Paul Simpson, eds, *Language, Discourse and Literature: An Introductory Reader in Discourse Stylistics*, London: Unwin Hyman/Routledge, 1989.

[8] Peter Verdonk, ed., *Twentieth-Century Poetry: From Text to Context*, London: Routledge, 1993; Verdonk and Weber *op.cit.*; Jonathan Culpeper, Mick Short and Peter Verdonk, eds, *Exploring the Language of Drama: From Text to Context*, London: Routledge, 1998.

[9] Michael Toolan, *Total Speech: An Integrational Linguistic Approach to Language*, Durham, NC: Duke University Press, 1996.

The problem between literary criticism and literary linguistics lies in being clear about what counts as the context of a text. Toolan asserts that "ultimately there is no absolute separability of text from context; text (language) is never autonomous, and context is never permanent or stably linked to but distinct from text .... In other words, text and context finally do not exist at all, except situationally."[10] Toolan lays part of the blame for such binarism on the fact that writing (which includes transcriptions of uttered speech) makes it easy, conceptually, to separate the materiality of text from the contextual circumstances of its production, situation and reception. Furthermore, when context has traditionally been separated from text it has been, because context has usually been regarded as meaning primarily *historical* context. This narrow view of context has been evident in almost all literary criticism, which has focused mainly on production, partly on situation, and rarely on reception until fairly recently. Consequently, literary criticism, as practised through most of the twentieth century, has been primarily a specialized branch of history.

Against this appropriation of the historical context for literary criticism, literary linguistics has appeared to be ahistorical and therefore (so the faulty reasoning goes) decontextualized. A false division of labour has arisen from this polarization: literary criticism has assumed responsibility for insight into *what* texts mean; stylistics has assumed responsibility for *how* they are meaningful. Since there are many more possible interpretations of specific literary texts than there are semantic and pragmatic models to account for meaning in general, it has seemed that the former activity is much more interesting than the latter. Historicized forms of scholarly interpretation have become the central paradigms of literary study, leaving literary linguistic and rhetorical analyses marginalized. There are a series of misconceptions and false logical turns here, and the rest of this paper will attempt to unravel some of them and provide an illustration of the importance of contextualization in stylistic analysis.

---

[10] *Ibid.*, 5.

A variety of contexts

It is simplistic and easy to equate context with history. In my recent critical reading into the literature of surrealism, for example, almost all of the studies have concerned themselves with historical matters. Surrealism is often described as a narrative with sources, influences and parent-figures in late nineteenth-century French Symbolism, early century Fauvism, and First World War Dadaism.[11] There are often chronologies of key events in the history of surrealism[12] and the critical material is loaded with names and places and dates and times all associated with the period of production of surrealist texts. All of these studies privilege the historical description of the inter-war years with surrealism as the focus. When the literary output of surrealism (in the form of actual poetic texts) is described, the discussion tends to relate the specific text to the general historical context: surrealist literature as a response to the militaristic logic of the war, as being in alliance with communism, as a movement developing alongside cubism, futurism, or early psychoanalysis.

The only other type of context represented as having any importance is the biographical context. Studies describe the backgrounds, conversations and lives of the surrealist writers and artists,[13] either recounted first-hand in the form of memoirs, journals or diaries, or as studies in the historical reconstruction of a life-story. Perhaps inevitably, given the nature of this documentary evidence, biography is

---

[11] In, for example, David Gascoyne, *A Short Survey of Surrealism*, London: Cobden-Sanderson [reprinted 1970, London: Frank Cass], 1936; Anna Balakian, *Literary Origins of Surrealism: A New Mysticism in French Poetry*, London: London University Press, 1967; W.S. Rubin, *Dada, Surrealism, and Their Heritage* (exhibition catalogue), New York: Museum of Modern Art, 1968; D. Tashjian, *Skyscraper Primitives: Dada and the American Avant-Garde 1910-1925*, Middletown, Conn: Wesleyan University Press, 1975; and Robert Short, *Dada and Surrealism*, London: Laurence King, 1980.

[12] Rubin, *op.cit.*, 197-216.

[13] Herbert Read, ed., *Surrealism*, London: Faber & Faber, 1936; R. Motherwell, *The Dada Painters and Poets*, New York: Wittenborn Schulz, 1951; P. Waldberg, *Surrealism*, London: Thames & Hudson, 1965; and Anna Balakian, *Surrealism: The Road to the Absolute,* (revised edition, original 1959), London: George Allen & Unwin, 1970.

presented chronologically and as an aspect of history. Where related contexts are mentioned, such as the psychology, philosophy, and artistic sense of the surrealist writers, these are subsumed into more general historical factors. Aspects of the writers' lives are selected for recounting, for example, only when they seem to have a relevance to the broader historical narrative.

There are all sorts of different relevant contexts embedded in this general historicism, which are obscured by the overall view. Of most interest for me are the various *linguistic* contexts surrounding surrealism. Surrealist writing and speech (at staged events such as meetings and exhibitions, early versions of performance art) involve a range of techniques. The surrealist principle of "objective chance" led to the use of collage, where two or more disconnected elements were brought together in a shocking and unexpected juxtaposition. In poetry this produced "automatic writing", in which the writer would try to set sentences down with as little rational thought as possible. Sometimes this was genuinely random, as in the surrealist practice of writing "chainpoems" involving different people composing a line each, or in the game "the exquisite corpse" in which a piece of paper is passed around and each new writer adds a word, phrase or sentence while only seeing the last contribution (an early composition produced the game's name). Sometimes the irrationality was a little more studied and deliberate:

> There would be a verb, a subject, a complement, adverbs, and everything perfectly correct, as such, words; but meaning in these sentences was a thing I had to avoid .... The verb was meant to be an abstract word acting on a subject that is a material object, in this way the verb would make the sentence look abstract. The construction was very painful in a way, because the minute I *did* think of a verb to add to the subject, I would very often see a meaning and immediately I saw a meaning I would cross out a verb and change it, until, working for quite a number of hours, the text finally read without any echo of the physical world.
>
> (Marcel Duchamp)[14]

---

[14] Quoted in A. Schwarz, *The Complete Works of Marcel Duchamp*, New York: Harry M. Abrams, 1969, 457.

The psycholinguistics of automatic writing would involve a discussion of both composition and reception, and would require a complex consideration of how a reader might try to reconstruct the apparent intention behind the text. Other psycholinguistic contexts for investigation might include a discussion of how far the explicit ideology of surrealism was encoded in actual verbal practice, and how individual writers varied in their output and mind-styles; or how the cognitive mappings involved in striking dissonant images are worked out in the process of readerly meaning-construction. The surrealists valued the language of children, lunatics and "primitive" cultures as being untainted by bourgeois civilization, and there are obvious dimensions for study here in the match between these forms of language and surrealist writing. An exploration of verbal-visual cognitive mappings in the surrealist word-image (where painting and text are fused) would be another potential psycholinguistic context.[15]

Similarly, there are a variety of possible sociolinguistic dimensions to surrealism that are not exclusively or primarily historical in orientation. The register of much surrealist writing is learned and literary, born of the fact that in their own social origins the surrealists tended to come from the bourgeoisie rather than the working class. The register of surrealist slogans and manifestos is quite different from the poetry proper, owing more to the style common to communist discourse of the 1920s. There is sociolinguistic work to be done on the representation of gender in surrealism, given the movement's cult of the feminine, in which the projected voice of surrealist writing is almost always masculine. A sociolinguistic analysis would also have a lot to say about the ideological view of race and colonialism in surrealism. Issues of dialect and standardization are relevant contexts for exploration, and there are many complex problems in the fact that much writing originally in French or Spanish has been translated. Finally, a sociolinguistic perspective can challenge some of the eccentric critical opinions on surrealism and linguistics, such as Balakian's view that the

---

[15] Mark Turner, *The Literary Mind*, New York: Oxford University Press, 1996; Ray Gibbs, "Researching metaphor", in Lynne Cameron and Graham Low, eds, *Researching and Applying Metaphor*, Cambridge: Cambridge University Press, 1999, 29-47.

French language was impoverished before surrealism and underwent a change as a result of the movement alone.[16]

In the literary criticism of surrealism (as in that of most genres and works) a whole range of contexts are subsumed within the historical overview. Biographical, cultural, linguistic, artistic, purposive, receptive, idiosyncratic and pedagogic contexts are all considered (if at all) as parts of the historical reconstruction of the text's meaning. It seems to me that a receptive approach is particularly illuminating with surrealism, for example, since the techniques of surrealism have been used throughout the century for all sorts of non-revolutionary purposes, and readers' reactions to surrealist texts vary enormously. What a stylistic exploration can achieve is a constant refocusing on the various forms of context. The pragmatic technique of working back and forth from text to linguistics serves to create a process of contextualizing, in order to avoid the trap of text-context binarism. I will illustrate this in the rest of this paper.

A whole-context example
Here is a poem by Hugh Sykes Davies, of the London Surrealist Group, originally published in *London Bulletin* (No. 2) in May 1938:

Poem

It doesn't look like a finger it looks like a feather of broken glass
It doesn't look like something to eat it looks like something eaten
It doesn't look like an empty chair it looks like an old woman searching in a heap of stones
It doesn't look like a heap of stones it looks like an estuary where the drifting filth is swept to and fro on the tide
It doesn't look like a finger it looks like a feather with broken teeth
The spaces between the stones are made of stone
It doesn't look like a revolver it looks like a convolvulus

---

[16] Balakian, 1970, *op.cit.*

It doesn't look like a living convolvulus it looks like a
dead one
KEEP YOUR FILTHY HANDS OFF MY FRIENDS
USE THEM ON YOUR BITCHES OR
YOURSELVES BUT KEEP THEM OFF MY FRIENDS
The faces between the stones are made of bone
It doesn't look like an eye it looks like a bowl of rotten
fruit
It doesn't look like my mother in the garden it looks like
my father when he came up from the sea covered with
shells and tangle
It doesn't look like a feather it looks like a finger with
broken wings
It doesn't look like the old woman's mouth it looks like a
handful of broken feathers or a revolver buried in cinders
The faces beneath the stones are made of stone
It doesn't look like a broken cup it looks like a cut lip
It doesn't look like yours it looks like mine
BUT IT IS YOURS NOW
SOON IT WILL LOOK LIKE YOURS
AND ANYTHING YOU SEE WILL BE USED
AGAINST YOU[17]

The initial reaction of most readers I have ever discussed this poem
with is one of confusion. The fact that it has no title, other than a baldly
descriptive one, to offer a contextualizing meaning often prompts them
to the usual literary critical default strategy: tell me when it was written
and who Hugh Sykes Davies was. However, it takes quite a lot of
historical and biographical context to make that sort of sense out of the
poem (as will emerge below), and there is another ideological context
(of surrealism), which produces an interpretation at odds with a purely
historically-founded relevance. Instead, in the rest of this paper, I am
going to blend a basically stylistic analysis with a consideration of
various contexts.

---

[17] Collected in E.B. Germain, ed., *Surrealist Poetry in English*, Harmondsworth:
Penguin, 1978, 104-5.

Surrealism and lexical semantics

The most obvious form that the poem presents (apart from being set out conventionally like a poem) is the syntactic arrangement of the first few lines: "It doesn't look like X, it looks like Y." This arrangement is composed of a negated assertion, followed by an assertion framed positively. Unlike my prototypical form two lines above, the poem does not separate the two clauses with a comma; in fact there are no punctuation marks used in the poem at all. This syntactic parallelism of negation and assertion is most often generally used by a speaker grasping to pin down a definition of something that is difficult to describe, and which has no precise lexical item to refer to "it". The repetition of the indeterminate "it" throughout the poem reinforces this perception.

In general usage, the elements in each clause are usually semantically linked: for example, "It's not a tree, it's a bush", "It doesn't look like a boat, it looks like a motorbike with water-jets", and so on. In these examples, the two elements share some features in common (trees and bushes are both general terms for plant-types, have leaves and branches, grow in soil, are common garden sights) but, crucially, have one or a few features of difference that make the utterance meaningful and purposive (bushes are usually smaller and more compact than trees). The purpose of the utterance is to represent a refinement of precision in definition.

A closely related set of semantic relations in general usage takes the form: "It's not a computer strictly, more a complex adding machine", or, "He's a farmer, or more exactly, a stockman", or, "It's not exactly raining, more drizzling." In all of the forms mentioned so far, there is an aspect of *synonymy* of various types. While absolute synonymy of different lexical items is very rare (if not impossible), it is possible to speak of *cognitive synonymy*, which can be defined:

> X is a cognitive synonym of Y if (i) X and Y are syntactically identical, and (ii) any grammatical declarative sentence S containing X has equivalent truth-conditions to another

sentence S^1, which is identical to S except that X is replaced by
Y.[18]

The syntactic form used in the poem sets up a negation, followed by an
assertion, which looks at first as if the two elements are being presented
as opposites (*cognitive antonyms*). However (as my own examples
above illustrate) the two terms are more usually in a relation of
plesionymy.

> Plesionyms are distinguished from cognitive synonyms by the
> fact that they yield sentences with different truth-conditions:
> two sentences which differ only in respect of plesionyms in
> parallel syntactic positions are not mutually entailing ....
> There is always one member of a plesionymous pair which it
> is possible to assert, without paradox, while simultaneously
> denying the other member.[19]

The examples Cruse then goes on to cite begin to look very like those
above: "It wasn't foggy last Friday − just misty", "It wasn't a tap I
heard − more of a rap", "He was not murdered − he was legally
executed." The point is that the syntactic arrangement presented
initially by the poem is apparently the same used in general to present
the semantic relation of plesionymy. This goes some way to explaining
my initial intuition that the poem frames itself as an act of definition
and refinement.

However, the poem is problematic at this point, since the two
elements in each of the first few lines of the poem are not in a clear
plesionymic relation with each other. The poem uses the customary
syntactic form of the plesionym, but presents elements that are
semantically incompatible, or at least not easily compatible. The nature
of the incompatibility varies: shift of material, species and manufacture
(finger − feather of broken glass); shift of the direction of the verb (eat
− eaten); shift from object to action (empty chair − old woman
searching); and so on. In each case, the semantic distance can be said to

---

[18] David Cruse, *Lexical Semantics*, Cambridge: Cambridge University Press,
1986, 88.

[19] *Ibid*, 285.

increase. Despite the syntactic presentation, the semantic relation
between the two elements seems to move towards non-synonymy.

> The line between plesionymy and cognitive synonymy can be
> drawn with some precision. However, the limits of
> plesionymy in the opposite direction along the scale of
> synonymity are more difficult to specify; as the semantic
> distance between lexical items increases, plesionymy shades
> imperceptibly into non-synonymy.[20]

In fact, the first few lines of the poem appear to be similar to the "odd"
examples which Cruse then goes on to give to illustrate the area in
which plesionymy "shades imperceptibly" into non-synonymy:

> ? My father's a policeman − or, more exactly, a butcher.
> ? Our dog − or, more exactly, our cat − died yesterday.

Where these two examples are close to non-synonymy, I would put the
lines from the poem firmly into the shady area closer to plesionymy.

The important thing in the poem is that there is the form of
plesionymy but the actual denial of it. However, in setting up this
apparent form, the poem disposes the reader to make an identification
of sorts between the uneasily compatible elements. The selection of
elements, by their semantic distance from each other, works with the
opposite force to disrupt any readerly attempt at identification. In the
reader's world, there is little common identifiable semantic ground
between what empty chairs look like and how old women searching in
heaps of stones might appear. Nevertheless, it is very difficult for
readers to abandon a text as absolutely incomprehensible; we all prefer
to *make sense* of things.

At this point Cruse's work on lexical semantics runs out of
usefulness: deviant combinations (very like those that appear in the
poem) are simply labelled as "odd" and used to circumscribe the
definitions of semantic well-formedness. What any given readers make
of the plesionymic forms of the poem is likely to form a range of
idiosyncratic interpretations. However, there are some cognitive
constraints on these interpretations, such that most readers with whom I

---

[20] *Ibid*, 286.

have discussed the poem tend to grapple with similar features in the first line, for example. The syntactic form and the non-use of a comma encourage a readerly construction of identity across the elements, and the blend between plesionymy and non-synonymy can only lead such an interpretation into unreality. That is, whatever "it" is, it is almost impossible to settle on a referent in our real world that both "doesn't look like a finger" in a specific way worth mentioning, and also "looks like a feather of broken glass". On the way to this realization — which is compounded by the repetition of the strategy in succeeding lines — the reader struggling for meaning inevitably passes through a range of idiosyncratic resonances. Some of these that I have recorded in discussion with readers include noticing that fingers and feathers can be seen to operate as digits, and an identification of humans and birds is made. Of course, the "feather" is not literal here but is a metaphorical figuring of a sliver of broken glass, and readers have said that this places images of cut and bleeding fingers into their minds, or fingers that are broken, or broken wings on birds with dead glassy eyes, and other resonant images.

Further lines increase the difficulty of such interpretations. While there are conceivably some conceptual similarities between fingers and feathers, the points of contact between "an empty chair" and "an old woman searching in a heap of stones" is less direct. One reading connected the empty chair with an absent husband or son, and a desperate search for the missing person or his grave. Similarly encouraged by the syntactic parallelism in succeeding sentences, readers often generalize the strategy across lines, and this is supported by the repetition of phrases across lines in the poem. So, for example, the grave which is the "heap of stones" turns out to be the watery grave of one killed at sea, swept into the filthy estuary and echoed later in the image of "my father when he came up from the sea covered with shells and tangle".

Dissonant semantic relations begin to find their way into phrases as well. Again, "it doesn't look like a finger", but now "it looks like a feather with broken teeth". Here the figurative feather of the first line has entered the unreal world of reference, but is further given teeth, which have been broken. Cruse[21] calls lexical items which create such dissonance *xenonyms*; where such odd or incompatible lexical semantic

---

[21] *Ibid*, 106.

relations are arranged across and between sentences we might call the overall effect *cognitive xenonymy*. In order to negotiate these effects, readers have to hold several possible rich interpretative paths at once. None of my readers were ever assertive enough to say, "This means x." Most of their readings presented several different possibilities and they refused to settle on any one of them.

Having reached this point stylistically we can approach it through the historical context. Surrealism came late to Britain and the English language. The magazine, *transition*, published from Paris in English, welcomed surrealism in April 1927. The third edition in June of that year contained poetry by Kurt Schwitters ("Blue is the colour of thy yellow hair / Red is the whirl of thy green wheels"). Notices of surrealist activity appeared in the early 1930s in *The Spectator, New Statesman and Nation*, and *The Criterion*. However, the central core of the "London Surrealist Group" did not form until the mid-1930s around David Gascoyne, Roland Penrose and Hugh Sykes Davies.

The semantic arrangement that Hugh Sykes Davies employs involves the dissonant combination of elements that are conceptually dissimilar in our familiar real world. This is an advanced form of one of the earliest of surrealist techniques, usually called "collage", since in painting it involved gluing scraps from disparate sources onto a canvas. Collage was used widely both in (the precursor movement) Dada and in early surrealism. It was originally devised as a means of closing the gap between art and reality by borrowing objects themselves. Artists such as Braque, Picasso and, most successfully, Schwitters put metro tickets, newspaper cuttings, concert programmes and other *objets trouvés* into their paintings. Like such "found objects" in sculpture, collage resists the glorification of the artist.

The most (in)famous example of the "ready-made" found object was the urinal that Marcel Duchamp produced at an exhibition of 1917, signed "R. Mutt" and entitled "Fountain". He defended this object to the selection committee of the exhibition:

> Whether Mr. Mutt with his own hands made the fountain or not has no importance. He CHOSE it. He took an ordinary article of life, placed it so that its usual significance

disappeared under the new title and point of view — created a new thought for that object.[22]

The collage technique in poetry manifests itself in the strangeness and difficulty of juxtapositions that resist literal interpretation. Most readers try to make sense of phrases such as "see the pulse of summer in the ice" (Dylan Thomas), "blue bugs in liquid silk" (Philip O'Connor), "The worlds are breaking in my head" (David Gascoyne), and "With the forks of flowers I eat the meat of morning" (Charles Henri Ford) by attempting to apply a metaphorical interpretation. However, subsequent sentences often disrupt any line of coherence that the reader might establish. With the collage technique, there can be little appeal to authorial intention: the last of the examples, by Ford, is the first line of a chainpoem blindly written by nine authors.

In surrealist thinking, the best image or phrase involved the greatest possible semantic distance between elements, the most extreme xenonym, in other words.

> The image is a pure creation of the spirit. It cannot be born of a comparison but of the bringing together of two realities, which are more or less remote. The more distant and just the relationship of these conjoined realities, the stronger the image — the more emotive power and poetic reality it will have.[23]

Hugh Sykes Davies' technique can be seen as a complex development of this basic compositional device. For the surrealists, such cognitive disruptions provided an opportunity for the reader to enter into a creative relationship with the surrealist text, allowing access to a reality undistorted by bourgeois rationalism or authority. The strategy is a dialectical one, as Herbert Read (in the introduction to *Surrealism* in 1936) states:

> In dialectical terms we claim that there is a continual state of opposition and interaction between the world of objective fact — the sensational and social world of active and economic

---

[22] Translated and quoted in Short, *op.cit.*, 25.

[23] Pierre Reverdy, translated and quoted in Waldberg, *op.cit.*, 22.

existence – and the world of subjective fantasy. This opposition creates a state of disquietude, a lack of spiritual equilibrium, which it is the business of the artist to resolve. He resolves the contradictions by creating a synthesis, a work of art which combines elements from both these worlds, eliminates others, but which for the moment gives us a qualitatively new experience.[24]

Collage and "automatism" (unplanned and undrafted unconscious writing) produced artistic works based on chance rather than conscious manipulation. Chance ambiguities, puns, coincidences, improbabilities, slips of the tongue and other random accidents were seized on by surrealists as having a reality of their own. Duchamp's painting of a moustache on the Mona Lisa was entitled "LHOOQ", which, pronounced in French, happens to sound like *"Elle a chaud au cul"* (loosely translated, "she has a hot arse"). Roger Vitrac vandalized public notices to generate multiple possibilities: *"Défense de fumer les fusées des femmes"* (Don't smoke/light the rockets/groupings/musical scale of women). The ravings of lunatics were reprinted. All of these were demonstrations of the "objective chance" in collocations of words.

Automatic writing is no more than the re-introduction of objective chance into language, whereas objective chance is the automatic writing of fate in seemingly raw facts (272).[25]

As an example, the artist Victor Brauner was hit in the eye and blinded in 1938 by a glass thrown by the Spanish surrealist Oscar Dominguez. Years previously in 1931, Brauner had painted a self-portrait with one eye crushed and his face bloody. In 1932, another self-portrait showed him with his eye pierced by a sharp instrument with the letter "D" on the handle. The surrealist notion of objective chance ideologizes all such material, conceptual and linguistic congruences.

In the Hugh Sykes Davies poem, there are multiple seemingly significant patterns and parallelisms at several different levels of

---

[24] Quoted in Germain, *op.cit.*, 25-6.

[25] Michel Carrouges, *"Le Hasard Objectif"*, in F. Alquié, ed., *Le Surréalisme*, Paris: Mouton, 1968, 269-78.

linguistic organization. One of the organizing principles of xenonymic elements seems to be simply phonological coincidence, linking "finger − feather", "revolver − convolvulus", "spaces − faces", "stones − bone", and the velar and labial plosives and liquid sound repetition in "It doesn't look like a broken cup it looks like a cut lip". Repetition of sounds and particular words across the poem give the illusion of a tight cohesive structure. There are several related semantic fields across the poem: "eaten", "broken teeth", "rotten fruit", "old woman's mouth", "broken cup", "cut lip"; and "estuary", "the tide", "the sea", "shells and tangle". These lend a sense of cohesion, but without much real coherence. Nevertheless, it is difficult to avoid the habit of trying to link up all the connections and see significance in them.

The poem seems centrally to be concerned with specification and categorization. Yet there are several points at which it seems to disrupt the whole principle of categorization. In the spaces between the lines "It doesn't look like X it looks like Y", are the lines:

> The spaces between the stones are made of stone ....
> The faces between the stones are made of bone ....
> The faces beneath the stones are made of stone.

The first of these can easily be interpreted as calling into question the idea of separate categories: if even the space beyond the boundary of the stone is itself stone, then the notion of the boundary loses all meaning. The second of the lines invokes skeletal images (and reminded one reader of the heap of stones she read as a grave). The last of these lines seems to have resonances of carved effigies, or petrified people (in both senses), or is a play on "stony-faced". By this point towards the end of the poem, the paranoid world of the poem has become so firmly established that definite reference can be made to "the faces" and "the stones". Similarly, phrases which began as suggested similes have by the end become definite references ("the old woman's mouth") or have appeared as real elements in the newly-constructed world ("broken feathers", "a revolver").

Even the apparently determined assertions of identity in the attempts at definition are subject to embedded qualification. Most lines are subordinated to the verb of appearance ("looks like"), which introduces doubt in what you are able to see and whether you can trust what you see. These also render the definitions as similes and negated similes.

Unlike a metaphor, the last thing "it" can *be* if it only looks "like" a
"feather of broken glass" is a feather of broken glass. The non-simile
assertions of the three "spaces and stone" lines extracted above are
made to seem even more definite and literal by this contrast.

The binaries of negation and assertion, "living" and "dead",
"mother" and "father", and "yours" and "mine" are paralleled by the
collage of register. Twice the register of definition is interrupted by
what seems like another "voice", graphologically indicated by
capitalization and a variation in syntactic form. The first of these, with
the imperative, the evaluative adjective "FILTHY", the reference to self
and the abuse-term "BITCHES", makes the capitalization appear to
represent angry shouting. The final section of the poem cohesively
takes up the last "negation-assertion" pattern, and ends with the
warning: "AND ANYTHING YOU SEE WILL BE USED AGAINST YOU". This
alludes, of course, to the old police caution on arrest ("anything you
say may be used against you") but the change of verbal modality alters
it from a caution to a threat, and the involuntary nature of the word
"see" (as opposed to voluntarily "watching" or "looking") makes real
the final sense of paranoia that has been accumulating throughout the
poem.

Reading reception and cognition

Within surrealist ideology, the technique of juxtaposing contraries and
xenonyms will dispose the reader to dialectical overload. The notions of
automatic writing and objective chance were later developed into
Salvador Dali's theory of the "paranoiac-critical method". This was
propounded by Dali and translated into English by David Gascoyne
shortly before Hugh Sykes Davies wrote his poem.

> Paranoiac-critical activity organises and objectivises in an
> exclusivist manner the limitless and unknown possibilities of
> the systematic associations of subjective and objective
> phenomena, which appear to us as irrational solicitations,
> exclusively in favour of the obsessive idea. By this method
> paranoiac-critical activity discovers new and objective

"significances" in the irrational; it makes the world of delirium pass tangibly onto the plane of reality.[26]

In this surrealist view, the surrealist object (whether a sculpture, painting or poem) is a concretized and *real*ized dream-image. The surrealist image is literal and has to be taken seriously. Furthermore, the experience of reading surrealistically effects the disposition of the reader to escape the confines of rationality, civilized order, repression and the fetters of institutions and authorities. The process of reading surrealism is claimed to be as creative and liberating as the production of automatic writing, hallucination or dream.

To illustrate this effect, I can return to the discussions of the poem I have had with various readers. Unanimously, the lexical choices of the poem produced a general sense of broken-down, post-apocalyptic squalor, decay, death, burial and violence. However, readers reached this general sense through various different experiences of the poem. The repeated xenonymic patterns in each line seemed to have a cumulative effect that in most cases served to draw the unreal elements of the poem into an apparent and thus troubling reality. The details of the resonant images, though, were different among readers. The two noun-phrases in each line always refer to concrete objects, rather than abstractions, and the verb-phrase ("looks like") which governs them foregrounds their *appearance*. These then produce *image-schemas* as readers progress through the text. In general, we use image-schemas to negotiate our way through life, to be able to deal with new and unfamiliar experiences metaphorically in terms of familiar patterns, and to help structure our cultural view of reality figuratively.[27]

---

[26] Salvador Dali, *Conquest of the Irrational* (trans. David Gascoyne), London/Paris: Julien Levy, 1936, 17.

[27] See George Lakoff and Mark Turner, *More Than Cool Reason: A Field Guide to Poetic Metaphor*, Chicago: University of Chicago Press, 1989; George Lakoff, *Women, Fire and Dangerous Things: What Categories Reveal About the Mind*, Chicago: University of Chicago Press, 1987; Mark Turner, *Death is the Mother of Beauty: Mind, Metaphor, Criticism*, Chicago: University of Chicago Press, 1987; and Mark Turner, *Reading Minds: The Study of English in the Age of Cognitive Science*, Princeton, NJ: Princeton University Press, 1991.

However, the two image-schematic noun-phrases in each line of the poem are not brought together in a straightforward metaphorical relationship. The cognitively prototypical form of presentation of a metaphor is to set out the conceptual mapping between two image-schemas as "A is B" ("Juliet is the sun", "LIFE is a JOURNEY", "a finger is a feather of broken glass"). Applying a bit of informal algebra in order to match this to the poem, I might say that this formulation can be expanded to: "A is not exactly A but is in fact B". This looks a little more like the lines of the poem. However, the poem is not even this simple, since the two image-schemas are stylistically related not directly to each other but to the unspecified "it". So instead we have something like: "A is not B, A is C". Of course, negatives can still function metaphorically, though they might be, literally, outrageously true (think of Donne's "No man is an island", which has troubled metaphor theory for years). We are still not algebraically there, though, since each side of the line in the poem is presented as a simile ("looks like") and so the final formulation is actually: "A is not exactly like B, A is in fact more like C". This is more like the "shady" area of a plesionymic form; it now matches the poem, but it is about to cause us all sorts of theoretical problems.

Even in being careful to set out the steps from prototypical metaphoric presentation to the form of the poem, I have been playing fast and loose with theories of metaphor and simile. Traditionally, a simile has simply been defined as a comparison that is explicitly stylistically signalled by "like" or "as", or an equivalent. Metaphors have been variously theorized as comparisons, substitutions, or interactions.[28] Determining the *cognitive* or underlying conceptual relationship between metaphor and simile has been fraught with discussion. There is an argument that treats them as conceptually similar, with a metaphor underlying a surface simile.[29] Much cognitive

---

[28] See David S. Miall, ed., *Metaphor: Problems and Perspectives*, London: Harvester Wheatsheaf, 1982; David Cooper, *Metaphor*, Oxford: Blackwell, 1986; Max Black, *Perplexities*, New York: Cornell University Press, 1990; and Andrew Goatly, *The Language of Metaphors*, London: Routledge, 1997.

[29] Eve Kittay, *Metaphor: Its Cognitive Force and Linguistic Structure*, Oxford: Oxford University Press, 1987.

linguistic work treats simile more like metonymy,[30] as a mapping within a single conceptual model rather than a mapping between models. Cameron makes a useful distinction between stylistic similes that introduce a conceptual incongruity and resolution ("My love is like a red red rose") and simple comparisons ("Apple juice is like cider"), and she calls the former *metaphorical similes*.[31] It seems to me that what we have in the surrealist poem are metaphorical similes.

Modelling such similes as provisional metaphors which are stylistically signalled allows me to talk about the readerly effects evident in discussion in terms of image-schematic mappings and the interanimating features involved.[32] In the poem, choosing to point out that "It doesn't look like a finger" nevertheless invokes the image-schema of fingers as a salient piece of knowledge, since it is not worth even mentioning that "it" doesn't look like a million other things, from a cat to a computer mouse. Certainly the cognitive effect in readers seems to be that this image-schema (B), once in mind, and even though it is negated, then in a rather ghostly way interacts with the "C" element ("a feather of broken glass"). B and C might be said to be in a *cognate* relationship with A. The result is an uneasy interanimation (or dialectic) of images, which produces a range of resonant readings.

For example, the old woman in the third line of the poem is imagined by most readers to be spindly as the empty chair, and there was a consensus that the image of a chair invoked was old, brown, worn and wooden, brittle and aged as the woman. The heap of stones is pictured as rubble or a makeshift grave in this line, but the interanimation with the tidal estuary in the next line relocates this heap of stones as wet barren rocks in the polluted seawater. By the next line, the idea of injured fingers, feathered with multiple cuts, is already in mind from the first line, so by this point several readers found it easy to identify birds and humans, and allow the idea of a feather to apply

---

[30] See Friedrich Ungerer, and Hans-Jorg Schmid, *An Introduction to Cognitive Linguistics*, London: Longman, 1996, 114ff.

[31] Lynne Cameron, "Operationalising 'Metaphor' for Applied Linguistic Research", in Cameron and Low, *op.cit.,* 131.

[32] For a theoretical statement of this see my "The Inflexibility of Invariance", *Language and Literature* 8/2 (1999), 125-42.

metaphorically to a human face with broken teeth. In "a feather with broken teeth", the image of real teeth seemed more common among readers than a reading which saw the fibres of the feather metaphorically as teeth. In many of my discussions of surrealist texts with readers, and particularly with other Hugh Sykes Davies poems, this notion of metaphors becoming literalized in readers' minds during the reading experience is common: in surrealist terms, this is the poem effecting access into unconscious paranoia.

The line, "It doesn't look like a revolver it looks like a convolvulus", involves readers knowing what a convolvulus is. All guessed it was a plant, and some knew that it was a twining species including bindweed. Those who associated these with guns and flowers made thematic connections with war and peace, though the next line with the dead convolvulus led them to interpret this as ongoing war with no peace. One reader connected bindweed with a corpse's winding sheet, with the stony grave of the first few lines, and the tangle around the drowned father later in the poem.

These patterns seem to train readers into accepting the interplay of surrealist images, so that my readers were more readily able to treat the lines in the second part of the poem as real rather than metaphorical. For example, responses to the line, "It doesn't look like an eye it looks like a bowl of rotten fruit", invoked an image of fruit with open eyes, or plums and peaches blinking, or a bowlful of eyeballs, or a corpse's eyes dead and soft as rotting fruit. There are clearly features of eyes and rotten fruit being mapped back and forth across the image-schemas in the line here. Similarly, accumulated mapped features of feathers, fingers, birds, faces, and broken bones all seemed to dispose readers to read the image "a finger with broken wings" literally, generating a collaged surrealist image in most of their minds. The following line sets up alternative metaphorical cognates: "It doesn't look like the old woman's mouth it looks like a handful of broken feathers or a revolver buried in cinders". All the elements of three new image-schemas here have been used previously; now they are combined into a new, shifting blend. All of this increasing interanimation of image-schemas throughout the poem reinforces the blurring of presence and absence, or reality and dream, in the three "spaces – stones" lines, making the paradoxes they enact even more readily acceptable.

Readers tried to construct global explanatory narratives to assimilate all of the images, but none were entirely satisfactory. Some of these narratives arose purely from the textual response: a battered woman in a war-zone searches for her dead husband and sons as carrion birds pick over badly-buried corpses; a woman's interior monologue represents her world turned around when her husband's drowned body is pulled from the estuary; a condition of endless war and hardship can only be experienced silently and visually in the face of state repression, in which truth and propaganda are interchangeable and uncertain, and nothing is allowed to be what it seems. Some of these narratives were connected by some readers to their own personal experiences, though they felt that these connections were not "allowable" proper responses to a literary text. Several readers wanted to find out more about surrealism in order to understand the poem "better". The historical date of composition (published in 1938) generated interpretations that gave the poem an ideological turn, seeing it as a striking pre-war snapshot of impending all-enveloping doom ("SOON IT WILL LOOK LIKE YOURS"), or as an attempt to convey the Kafkaesque absurdism of authoritarian Nazism and categories turned upside-down.

The discussion integrated and contextualized

In the discussion above I have not been very disciplined in the traditional sense. I have wandered around from critical theory to linguistic theory, included lexical semantics, a note on some bits of phonology and graphology, some cognitive linguistics, and skipped from history to sociology to reception theory along the way. However, it seems to me that this is the only thing to do if I am not simply to treat literature as data, nor to produce too partial a reading of a poem, nor to invalidate the interpretations of real readers, nor to produce an "explanation" that explains nothing but its own terminology, nor to miss out on the myriad branching possibilities that readings of surrealism offer.

Together with Verdonk and Weber, I prefer to see this "creative interaction between writer, text, reader and context"[33] as integrated analysis, working from text to context, back to text, back to context, in order to understand both textuality and contextualizing processes (for in the end they are the same thing), in order to enrich in this sort of analytical reading, out loud on paper, the resonances of the literature.

---

[33] Verdonk and Weber, *op.cit.*, 2.

The approach is not simply a matter of the freeplay of meaning. Of all literature, even surrealist texts are not indeterminate, but can be seen to generate a range of different though related interpretations. I have not been the only reader here; my practice has tried to be reader-informed and inter-subjective. The discussion is open to all contextualizations, but is constrained by the actuality of the text and by our current best understanding of linguistics and cognition.

Placing a surrealist text − and particularly this Hugh Sykes Davies poem − in the middle of this discussion is not entirely coincidental, of course. To this extent, chance may well be objective, as the surrealists supposed:

> It is the avowed aim of the surrealist movement to reduce and finally to dispose altogether of the flagrant contradictions that exist between dream and waking life, the "unreal" and the "real", the unconscious and the conscious, and thus to make of what has hitherto been regarded as the special domain of poets, the acknowledged common property of all. So far as the surrealists themselves are either writers or painters, it is also at the same time their aim to extend indefinitely the limits of "literature" and "art" by continually tending to do away with the barrier that separates the contents of the printed page or of the picture-frame from the world of real life and of action.[34]

The surrealist technique was the dialectical route of passing beyond false binary oppositions of life and art, reality and dream, or even text and context. The disciplined act of contextualizing, explicit, aware, scientific, receptive, and moving between text and context, is the future ground of real stylistics.

---

[34] Gascoyne, *op.cit.*, x.

HIDDEN MEANINGS

WILLIE VAN PEER

Hermeneutics and Stylistics

The central point about the interpretation of literary texts that I would like to defend is that interpretation is driven by two factors: on the one hand, it is driven by uncertainty over the meaning of a text, on the other hand it is driven by a wish for more certainty over that meaning, and by the possession of some elements that hold a promise to reach such higher certainty.[1] Many such elements may contribute to the search for a better interpretation (e.g. information from an author's biography, established lexical meanings as registered by the OED, or symmetries in a text's composition). Many elements may also contribute to the reader's uncertainty. In this essay, I will briefly consider one such element, namely "hidden meanings". As is well-known in hermeneutics, hidden meanings may play a significant role in literary texts. All too often, however, such hidden meanings are taken as a pretext to engage in quasi-profundity or mystification. Instead, I propose to treat such cases of hidden meanings as interpretative problems that researchers should try to solve. Hermeneutics would gain, I believe, if it were to consider itself as a problem-solving discipline. I will try to show in this essay how such a hermeneutics could be conceptualized. The underlying argument will be that a problem-solving hermeneutics requires (and profits from) stylistic analysis, without which it will remain powerless.

That raises the problem of how one should deal with cases of hidden meaning. It will be clear that anything "hidden" contributes to readers' uncertainty over a text's meaning. But how can one deal with this uncertainty? I will illustrate the matter with a concrete case. The

---

[1] This view is further worked out in my *Standards of Interpretation* (in preparation).

example concerns Auden's famous poem "Musée des Beaux Arts", about which Peter Verdonk has written one of the finest analyses:[2]

> About suffering they were never wrong,
> The Old Masters: how well they understood
> Its human position; how it takes place
> While someone else is eating or opening a window or just
>   walking dully along;
> How, when the aged are reverently, passionately waiting
> For the miraculous birth, there always must be
> Children who did not specially want it to happen, skating
> On a pond at the edge of the wood:
> They never forgot
> That even the dreadful martyrdom must run its course
> Anyhow in a corner, some untidy spot
> Where the dogs go on with their doggy life and the
>   torturer's horse
> Scratches its innocent behind on a tree.
>
> In Breughel's *Icarus*, for instance: how everything turns
>   away
> Quite leisurely from the disaster; the ploughman may
> Have heard the splash, the forsaken cry,
> But for him it was not an important failure; the sun shone
> As it had to on the white legs disappearing into the green
> Water; and the expensive delicate ship that must have
>   seen
> Something amazing, a boy falling out of the sky,
> Had somewhere to get to and sailed calmly on.

---

[2] Peter Verdonk, "'We Have Art in Order that We May Not Perish from Truth': The Universe of Discourse in Auden's 'Musée des Beaux Arts'", *Dutch Quarterly Review of Anglo-American Letters* 17 (1987), 78-96. The text of the poem is taken from W.H. Auden, *Collected Shorter Poems 1927-1957,* London: Faber and Faber, 1963, 529-31.

An interpretative problem

The poem seems to reflect on the art-works in a museum, presumably at the occasion of Auden's visit to the Museum of Fine Arts in Brussels, where Peter Breughel's painting *The Fall of Icarus* is displayed. At first sight, the poem provides an impression of what can be seen on several canvases of the Old (Flemish) Masters when they depict human suffering. The speaker of the poem presents an account of what emerges from these pictures; apparently a casual view of suffering, since neither animals nor human witnesses seem to care much for the sufferers' fates.

Note that this view is itself already an interpretation (of the paintings in the museum), linked to a generalization, which presumably runs roughly along the following lines:

(1) Some paintings in this museum represent human suffering.
(2) These representations seem (to the speaker/persona in the poem) to indicate its insignificance in human life.
(3) I conclude from this that the Old Masters who painted them expressed the insignificance of pain and suffering in the totality of human life.

This generalization may be unwarranted − perhaps other paintings in the museum, or works in other museums might show a different attitude toward suffering, but that is beside the point of the poem's meaning. Also, the interpretation of the paintings themselves may be unwarranted − perhaps the point of these paintings was quite different. Suppose, for instance, that Breughel's *Fall of Icarus* had a political meaning in its original context. Perhaps Icarus stands for the Spanish king Philip II, who sent his armies into the Netherlands to crush Protestantism. Perhaps Breughel wanted to depict the futility of Philip's enterprise, the futility of wanting to reign a people through terror. Perhaps, like Icarus in Breughel's painting, his efforts will come down with a splash and leave no traces behind. This is only an interpretation, but one that differs from the one advanced by Auden. But again, this matter is also irrelevant to the interpretation of Auden's poem itself, and I am only pointing this out to show how at yet another level the reader runs into the uncertainty surrounding the activity of interpretation.

In the master-works of these painters, the poem seems to say, suffering was but a side issue of life, something that formed part of it, albeit a banal part, not something to attach too much importance to, and certainly not something tragic. The colloquial, *parlando* tone of the speaker's voice further strengthens this impression. In this vein, Miguel Berga argues that the "overall effect of these stylistic strategies is, of course, to reinforce Auden's main point stated in the opening lines of the poem: the general lack of concern about an individual's tragedy."[3] Thus the text's casual organization and the apparent linguistic nonchalance underlines the agreement between the poem and its models, the paintings in the museum. Or does it? Is it not possible to think of this *parlando* tone as building a distance between the speaker and the ideas he wishes to communicate? The contrast between the seriousness of the subject matter and the lightness of the speaker's tone may indicate irony. Perhaps in talking so indifferently about suffering, the poet wants to give us a hint that he does not share the view that he finds in the old paintings. If so, then why does he (or his persona) not openly disavow them? Maybe Auden did not wish to reveal his reasons for this. Or maybe he wanted to respect the devotion to high artistic achievement of these fellow artists. Or he may have agreed with their views.

We may remain ignorant about the precise reasons Auden may have had (not) to distance himself openly from the view of the Old Masters as it is presented in this poem. Now obviously, for the interpretation of the poem it matters a lot whether Auden agrees or disagrees with the view of human suffering as it is purportedly observed in the old paintings. Clearly these are two incompatible interpretations, and thus we cannot hold them both to be true. At least, I agree with Robert Stecker, who rules out the possibility of two incompatible, i.e. contradictory, interpretations to be both true:

> I am not sure that anyone holds the view that there could be two incompatible interpretations of the same work, both of which are true. Anyone who did claim this would necessarily be mistaken. The reason is completely straightforward. If two interpretations are incompatible, they make mutually

---

[3] Miguel Berga, "Fallen Angels: On Reading Landscape and Poetry", *Language Awareness*, 8/1 (1999), 51-61.

contradictory statements. If both interpretations are true, then
both the mutually contradictory statements they make are true.
That means that a contradiction is true, and contradictions are
never true.[4]

If then the two interpretations of Auden's poem cannot both be true,
which one should we choose? And how do we know when and whether
we have made the right choice? The casual tone may be used as
evidence in favour of either interpretation. What other indications are
there to resolve the dilemma? It will be clear that there are no explicit,
overt ones, for if there were, the interpretative problem would not arise
in the first place. Hence the search is for more hidden cues. But what
could these be?

Some stylistic observations

A possibility that could be probed relates to the poem's formal
structure.[5] A first and superficial reading creates the impression that the
poem is written in blank verse without too much traditional poetic
structuring. That impression hides the fact, however, that the verse
lines rhyme. Although the rhyme scheme is not conspicuous, nor very
regular, it is nevertheless identifiable on close inspection, and may be
rendered as follows: a b c a d e d b f g f g e // h h i j k k i j . Every
single line of the poem rhymes with one other line, with the exception
of one, namely line 3, which does not rhyme with any other line in the
poem.

But what does this mean? Is it a mistake? Perhaps an oversight on
Auden's part? But if he so skillfully hid the rhyme design from a
reader's first impression, and if all lines strictly adhere to the rhyme
structure, must we not conclude that he must have been aware of it?
The probability that all the lines came to rhyme through pure chance is

---

[4] Robert Stecker, *Artworks. Definition, Meaning, Value*, University Park, PA:
The Pennsylvania State University Press, 1997, 122.

[5] I am indebted to Hans-Dieter Gelfert, *Wie Interpretiert Man eine Novelle und
eine Kurzgeschichte?*, Stuttgart: Reclam, 1993, 100-3 for the following analysis.
See also P.V. Le Page, "Some Reasons for Rhyme in 'Musée des Beaux Arts'",
The Yearbook of English Studies, 3 (1973), 253-8.

many times lower than the probability that some design is behind it all. However, if there is a design, why is one line so clearly out of step? If it is not by chance, then this must have been part of the grand design itself. But why? Is it perhaps difficult to find rhyme words in English for the last word of line 3? Was this merely an oversight? Was he too tired to find an appropriate rhyming-word? Had he lost interest in the game? Some of these questions can be ruled out with near-certainty. For instance, there are many rhyming-words in English for "place", the final word of line 3, such as, "face", "mace", "base", "case", "lace", and many others. Some other questions are harder to deal with, but, in general, it would seem highly improbable that the absence of a rhyme in one line was simply a case of oversight. With a poet of Auden's standing it is difficult to imagine that he would not have noticed the omission, or that he would have let it pass.

But if error or sloppiness are unlikely candidates for the problem's solution, the design must have been intentional. The case may be described in terms of *internal deviation*: the poet sets up a regular structure (for instance, of meter, rhyme, or syntax), and then unexpectedly deviates from the pattern established before. Internal deviations are rather common in poetry, and they have been studied, both in the stylistic analyses of individual poems and from a theoretical point of view.[6] Thus it would seem that we are not dealing with an idiosyncratic case, but with some well-known device that poets regularly employ to convey a specific idea, message, or impression. From the study of such internal deviations it is known that they generally carry extra interpretative weight: if an author first sets up a pattern and then deviates from it, this usually carries a special meaning. Usually, the poet wants to alert the reader to something in the pattern that is significant yet overlooked or unexpected. As Leech observes: "Particularly through the concept of tertiary or internal deviation, the

---

[6] See Samuel Levin, "Internal and External Deviation in Poetry." *Word*, 21 (1965), 225-37; Geoffrey N. Leech, "Stylistics", in Teun A. Van Dijk, ed., *Discourse and Literature*, Amsterdam/Philadelphia: John Benjamins, 1985, 39-57; Willie van Peer, *Stylistics and Psychology: Investigations of Foregrounding*, London: Croom Helm, 1986; Mick Short, *Exploring the Language of Poems, Plays and Prose*, London/New York: Longman, 1996, 59-61.

method [of stylistic analysis] enables us to see a linguistic basis for such critical concepts as 'climax', 'suspense', 'unity'."[7]

With this background knowledge in mind, let us now return to the question of what effect Auden could have aimed for through the absence of rhyme in line 3? It would appear that we are in the middle of an interpretative puzzle here. Obviously we are not in a position to be certain about its meaning, but then again we are not completely uncertain of possible meanings either. As a rule, cases of internal deviations are resolved by taking into account wider issues of a semantic nature, such as the text's theme or motive, the concrete subject matter or its socio-cultural context.

That context is the nature and the position of human suffering. The poem evokes a particular attitude toward that suffering. This attitude is conveyed through a colloquial register. The discovery of a half-hidden rhyme schema beneath that register may signify that Auden had in mind something that he wanted to convey to the reader, only if that reader was prepared to look at the text in considerably more detail. Evidently, most readers will not notice the rhyme scheme (nor its internal deviation). Now that you have found out, so the author seems to be saying, I'll tell you what I think of these paintings. Obviously this concerns torture, suffering, tragic downfall and how we locate these in our lives: "its human position", as it is called in line 3. But what "position" does suffering have? That is the central question that the poem addresses, but this is foregrounded precisely in line 3, the only line that does not fit the general rhyme pattern. In other words, what Auden thinks about the place of suffering in human life does *not* fit the general pattern that the rest of the poem has established. This is the ironic signal that conveys the different attitude that the speaker surreptitiously communicates to the reader: Suffering is *not* something about which I can write with the ease and self-evidence that the Old Masters brought to it.

The problem's solution
This, then, is the solution to the problem of the two incompatible interpretations. I propose that the persona in Auden's poem (in all likelihood an extension of the poet himself) does *not* agree with the

---

[7] Leech, *op.cit.*, 56.

view on human suffering that the paintings of the Old Masters
purportedly communicated. The *parlando* voice is not an indication of
agreement with the Old Masters, but of a distance to their position.
This conclusion is arrived at on the basis of a more detailed observation
of a half-hidden rhyme-scheme and an even better hidden internal
deviation from this scheme. The deviation marks a fundamental point in
the poem's structure, namely that precisely in the verse that speaks of
the "human position" of suffering (thus delineating the central theme of
the poem) an irregularity occurs that demands an explanation. This
explanation comes in the form of an analogy. Similar to line 3, in its
deviance from the general structure of the text, my views on suffering
and "its human position" deviate from the general views emanating
from the paintings of the Old Masters. By accepting this interpretation,
one can significantly decrease the amount of uncertainty about the
meaning of the poem. If I am not mistaken, we have hereby resolved an
interpretative problem that has existed for a while, and which has never
to my mind received satisfactory treatment. I would argue that it is
much harder to interpret the internal deviation of line 3, to bring it in
accordance with the opposite interpretation, namely that it signals
Auden's fundamental agreement with the view of suffering, as depicted
in the Old Masters' works.

Although I will refrain from doing so, one could move on from here
to see whether other pieces of evidence support the interpretation. One
could look for other texts in Auden's work where he speaks of
suffering, or we could try to find out his general ideas on this topic
from other documents like letters, memoirs, or notes. I think it is likely
that such a search would indeed corroborate the hypothesis advanced
here. Certainly Auden was not the kind of poet who revelled in
aesthetic representations of human suffering, and his personal attitudes
reveal a much deeper existential involvement with the problem of
suffering. This interpretation may be a much better approximation to
the truth than its opposing one, while most rival interpretations (e.g.
oversight) are relatively easy to dismiss. What the exercise shows is
that hidden meanings are often − contrary to much mystification going
on in hermeneutics − amenable to reflection and resolution, though
they require a careful textual and contextual analysis.

But why?

But if that is the meaning of the poem, then why didn't the poet say so? What prevented Auden from communicating his view on human suffering more explicitly in this poem? It can hardly be some limitation in his linguistic abilities, for verbal skill is what poets are mostly admired and praised for. There may be many reasons why authors provide their texts with "hidden" meanings. One may be some kind of game they play with their readers, comparable to the game of solving riddles.[8] As a game, it provides pleasure. A cognitive puzzle has to be solved, boosting attention and arousal; finding the solution sets free energy and produces hedonic release and feelings of accomplishment and satisfaction. Meanings that are half hidden (but retrievable) offer the reader cognitive attraction and emotional gratification.

These psychological processes may be summarized under the classical theory of "aesthetic delight". There are certainly other, more direct ways of communicating what Auden's poem is trying to say, but not with the same intensity and intelligence, nor with the same degree of sensuous energy. Interpreting the poem is unquestionably no substitute for a reading experience involving these energies, which may be one of the main reasons why readers are attracted to literature. All that an interpretation may do is to render the pattern of meaning insightful. To the intense oscillation of sense and sensibility it cannot really do full justice and must necessarily remain poor and superficial in comparison to the text and its reading experience. That is why readers feel they have to return to the text itself and experience its richness over and over again. There is nothing in the above interpretation of Auden's poem that can equal the precise quality of experience that reading the text brings. What an interpretation *can* do, however, is to render the reasons for enjoying a text, and returning to it, more transparent. Thus allowing us to enjoy its exquisite beauty even more.

---

[8] The *locus classicus* of the view of art-as-game is, of course, Johan Huizinga, *Homo Ludens: A Study of the Play Element in Culture*, Boston: The Beacon Press, 1955 [First edition 1939]. For a more general analysis of the games authors may play with their readers, see also Peter Hutchinson, *Games Authors Play*, London: Methuen, 1983.

THE TIP OF THE ICEBERG:
REAL TEXTS, LONG TEXTS AND MENTAL REPRESENTATIONS

KEITH GREEN

Much of cognitive linguistics, discourse analysis and text-theory proceed from a most basic axiom, that analysis cannot be sufficient unless some form of "mental representation" or "mental space" is posited. A mental representation may be a number of different things: it may be simply a store of previous encyclopaedic knowledge; a trace memory of previous elements in the text; or a kind of semantic and logical "waiting room" where elements are held until disambiguated. In this last sense it entails the notion of "mental space", following the work of Fauconnier.[1] Investigations into the nature of meaning, whether "literary", "literal", "semantic" or "linguistic" are increasingly using notions of mental representation and space to account for text processing, to solve logical difficulties, and to generally bring the work of linguists and psychologists closer together. Meaning, it seems, cannot be explained in terms of language alone, or in purely formal terms such as those based on mathematical models,[2] but must be seen in terms of human cognitive processes within a particular cognitive environment and context. Harris' notion of language, that elements can be treated as "purely logical symbols, upon which various operations

---

[1] Gilles Fauconnier, *Mental Spaces*, Cambridge: Cambridge University Press, 1985.

[2] As suggested variously by, among others, Bertrand Russell, "On Denoting", in R. Marsh, ed., *Logic and Knowledge,* London: Allen and Unwin, 1956 [1905], 39-56; Rudolph Carnap, *Meaning and Necessity,* Chicago: Chicago University Press, 1947; and Zelig Harris, *Methods of Structural Linguistics,* Chicago: University of Chicago Press, 1951.

of mathematical logic can be performed",[3] is ultimately unworkable. This conception of linguistics, which Lakoff equates with the tradition of objectivist semantics,[4] has, it seems, been overtaken by recent cognitive models. Much of the work in this area has been seen as a welcome relief from the dry and sterile analyses of "pure" linguistics and of those working within logical models such as Harris'. Similarly, to many it has helped to solve certain perennial logico-linguistic problems, such as those to do with co-reference, elegantly and simply. Yet its common-sense sheen and sheer workability cover a multitude of philosophical and linguistic problems. In this chapter I shall question the very idea of mental representations and spaces as the discourse-analysts' panacea it seems to have become.

The modern cognitivists' notion of mental *representations* is quite different from that of the philosophers'. Oddly, the latter's notion is more linguistic than that of many of their linguist counterparts and for those working with psychological models of discourse. For the philosophers of mind, a mental representation is an example of mental content, and content is captured quite systematically by *that*-complement clauses. In order not to give way too much to linguistics, however, philosophers have preferred the term "content clauses" rather than "complement clauses". This is partly because in general they do not want to suggest that thought is wholly linguistic. However, the linguistic representation is partly constrained by a syntactic feature i.e. that it be encoded in a clause. My belief that England will lose the Test series is represented precisely by the clause "(that) England will lose the test series", and whose condition of satisfaction is fulfilled if and only if England lose the Test series. We also tend to speak of the clauses "capturing" the belief. In this sense the clause is not the belief itself, but represents it in some crucial way.

The cognitivists' idea of mental representation is not like this at all. In the first place it is not captured by any linguistic form. Indeed, in many models it is a way of transcending linguistic form, a superordinate cognitive activity governing language and thought. In some cases, the mental representation is a heuristic device for resolving

---

[3] Harris, *op.cit.*, 18.

[4] George Lakoff, *Women, Fire and Dangerous Things,* Chicago: Chicago University Press, 1987.

interpretative and logical difficulties (particularly in the work of Fauconnier, see below), in others, a way of accounting for the mechanics of text processing. In Fauconnier's case there is not so much a representation as a cognitive space housing semantic potential, which is drawn on in the act of interpretation. Philosophers' mental representations are closely tied to propositional attitudes, which are typically manifested linguistically in, unsurprisingly, verbs of propositional attitude. For a person to have such an attitude is for him or her to stand in an appropriate relation to a kind of internal state: a mental representation. What these mental representations share with those of the cognitivists is the fact that they are theoretical postulates designed to explain certain behaviours. Philosophers have largely restricted themselves to the problems of opaque contexts, naming, referring phrases and descriptions, while the cognitivists have extended the analysis to cover pronominalisation, implicatures and "processing effort" in general,[5] although the distinction between the two groups is not a clear one. But what is the nature of these representations? One theory, derived from the work of Jerry Fodor,[6] is that propositional attitudes such as beliefs simply inherit their semantic properties from the semantic properties of the associated representations. But there is a fundamental problem here: words must get their meanings from somewhere other than from the words themselves (they do not have some innate Adamic meanings); but if they get them from mental representations or higher-order elements, where do *they* get their meanings from? My belief *that England will lose the Test series* is somehow correctly captured by the *that*-clause: it is correct because the words have inherited the semantic properties from my belief, which is some kind of internal relational state (but between which elements is extremely difficult to define correctly). The structure of the belief is similar to the structure of the clause.

The "naturalism constraint" on mental content dictates that semantic properties arise out of more basic non-semantic properties. Precisely what these properties are (and where they are to be found) is far from

---

[5] Dan Sperber, and Deirdre Wilson, *Relevance: Communication and Cognition,* Oxford: Blackwell, 1986.

[6] Jerry Fodor, *The Language of Thought,* Sussex: Harvester, 1975; and *Psychosemantics,* Cambridge, Mass: MIT Press, 1987.

easy to establish. There are several possibilities. The first is that they come from concepts that are innate. The second is that they come from a pre-existing, autonomous realm of meaning, which, though abstract, is as real as the philosophers' "table" and other manifestly physical objects. The third is that they come from a higher level "language of thought". The fourth is that they come from the body and the immediate physical environment, where meanings are mapped from the physical to the mental, from the concrete to the abstract (for example, deontic modal meanings are said to precede epistemic meanings, and metaphors typically originate from the physical environment).   The naturalism constraint would naturally rule out all but the last of these, the others being too abstract and ultimately untestable.[7] But in one sense it is clear that both philosophers and cognitive scientists are looking somewhere else for meaning — somewhere other than the words themselves, that is. Cognitive science is introspective in that this "somewhere else" is characterized as a function of some higher-level cognitive ability, but it is also outward-looking in its attempt to locate meaning, typically, in physical space, biology and evolution.

That the idea of mental representations is increasingly commonplace is demonstrated by Sperber and Wilson, who state:

> We assume that mental representations have a structure not wholly unlike that of a sentence, and combine elements from a mental repertoire not wholly unlike a lexicon. These elements are mental concepts: so to speak, "words of mentalese." Mental concepts are relatively stable and distinct structures in

---

[7] These positions are held, respectively, by: Noam Chomsky, *The Logical Structure of Linguistic Theory,* Chicago: Chicago University Press, 1955 [1973], *Syntactic Structures,* The Hague: Mouton, 1957, "Review of Skinner's *Verbal Behaviour*", in J. Katz, and J. Fodor, eds, *The Structure of Language,* New Jersey: Prentice Hall, 1964 [1959], *Language and Responsibility,* New York: Pantheon, 1977, *Knowledge of Language,* New York: Praeger, 1986; by J. Katz, *Realistic Rationalism,* Cambridge, Mass: MIT Press, 1995; by Fodor, *op.cit.* 1975; and by Lakoff, *op.cit.* and Eve Sweetser, *From Etymology to Pragmatics: Metaphorical Aspects of Semantic Change,* Cambridge: Cambridge University Press, 1990.

the mind, comparable to entries in an encyclopaedia or permanent files in a data-base.[8]

They go on to argue that "there are many more concepts in our minds than words in the language we speak." None of this is particularly remarkable. It draws most naturally on the rationalist tradition, and presents a common-sense mid-way position between linguistic determinism and concept rationalism. It draws, too, on the work of both Chomsky and Fodor, while the authors ultimately reject both positions. In any case, although concepts seem to have the upper hand here (there are more of them), they are linguistically dependent at least by analogy. Concepts must have lexicon-like qualities, while representations as a whole, being combinations of concepts, in some ways resemble sentences (although it is not clear what kinds of sentences they resemble and in what ways). Mental concepts are characterized by their similarity to language fragments and are analogous both to parts of the lexicon and, in a shift of analogy, to permanent computer files. The computer metaphor is both handy and contemporary,[9] and it is clear that if we did not suggest some isomorphism with language itself, we simply would not know how to further describe mental structures. In discussing the word "open" in a number of different communicative contexts, and with different direct objects (*open the bottle*, *open the washing machine*) Sperber and Wilson conclude:

> .... a word like "open" can be used to convey indefinitely many concepts. It is impossible for all of these to be listed in the lexicon. Nor can they be generated at a purely linguistic level by taking the linguistic context, and in particular the direct object, into account.[10]

---

[8] Dan Sperber, and Deirdre Wilson, "The Mapping Between the Mental and the Public Lexicon", *UCL Working Papers in Linguistics* (1997), 107.

[9] For problems with the computer model of the mind, see John Searle, "Minds, Brains and Programs", in J. Haugeland, ed., *Mind Design,* Cambridge: Cambridge University Press, 1980.

[10] *Op.cit.*, 109.

A number of issues present themselves here. Is the number of possible concepts "indefinitely many"? Why do we need the notion of concepts – can we not say that these possibilities are part of the "meaning" of the word "open", revising or extending our definition of "meaning" to accommodate Gricean pragmatic meaning? For Sperber and Wilson, whatever is going on with "open" cannot be wholly down to the word itself. Because concepts are "outside" the word, analysis must, in part, also focus on that which the word does not "possess", but may indicate: hence the concentration on referential and processing procedures. The semantics of "open" lies neither in the word itself nor in its co-text. In summary, words do not stand in a one-to-one relation with concepts, and do not possess core or invariant meaning. In one sense language acts like an indexical writ large: it indicates rather than encodes. Linguistic items are only prompts for certain cognitive activities.

There is no doubt that the idea of a mental representation, in the cognitivists' sense, has produced much fruitful analysis of hitherto troublesome linguistic issues, and in some cases (for example, co-reference) appears to have resolved them. However, the whole issue of whether mental representations are any *more* than a useful heuristic device is far from being resolved. Catherine Emmott suggests that the whole idea of mental representations is taken for granted in psychology (though she also notes that some psychologists do not take sufficient account of language) – but linguists, particularly those working within the empirical tradition, have by no means fully accepted them.[11] Mental representations, it seems, can be a number of different theoretical postulates which are mobilized depending on the particular problem considered. In cognitive linguistics, the move has been to counter the fixed, logical notions of meaning of earlier semanticists and logicians, including Chomskyan grammars (although Chomsky is well aware of the limitations of any mathematical model). In one sense, as I have already suggested, the cognitivists are less "linguistic" than the philosophers. As Mark Turner states, enthusiastically quoted by Lakoff and Sweetser in the preface to Fauconnier's *Mental Spaces*:

---

[11] Catherine Emmott, *Narrative Comprehension: A Discourse Perspective*, Oxford: Oxford University Press, 1997.

Expressions do not mean; they are prompts for us to construct meaning by working with processes we already know. In no sense is the meaning of [an] ... utterance "right there in the words"...; the words themselves say nothing independent of the richly detailed knowledge and powerful cognitive process we bring to bear.[12]

This argument represents the retreat from linguistic meaning seen over the past decade or so. Here again, words are attenuated, rather paltry things, when compared with the cognitive processes that underpin them.

Sweetser and Lakoff go on to brush aside the ontological problem of mental spaces, declaring that "we need not debate the 'reality' of them" (xxxii), while Lakoff reminds us that mental spaces "have no ontological status outside of the mind."[13] A number of developments have led to this non-problematic ontological status of mental spaces (and representations), which are worth pausing to consider. First, linguistic philosophy, that is, the solving of logical problems through close analysis of the language in which they are expressed, ran out of steam in the late nineteen fifties and early sixties, following half a century of development from Frege, Moore, and Russell through to Carnap, the logical positivists and the Oxford ordinary language philosophers. In one sense, ordinary language philosophy, particularly in the work of J.L. Austin,[14] was neither systemic nor abstractly theoretical. Its inspiration came from the close, meticulous analyses particularly of G.E. Moore, and is based on the view that meanings are fundamentally *linguistically* encoded. By the end of the fifties the problems of verification, logical and propositional form remained, despite the considerable optimism about the successes of ordinary language philosophy. Austin's painstaking analyses pushed a certain

---

[12] Mark Turner, *Reading Minds*, Princeton: Princeton University Press, 1991, 206, quoted in this form by George Lakoff and Eve Sweetser in the "Preface" to Fauconnier, *op.cit.*, xxii.

[13] Lakoff, *op.cit.*, 282.

[14] J.L. Austin, *How to Do Things with Words,* Oxford: Oxford University Press, 1962, *Sense and Sensibilia,* Oxford: Oxford University Press, 1962.

type of philosophical thinking into a kind of linguistic *cul-de-sac*. Yet another, perhaps more well known, aspect of Austin's work, speech act theory, led to pragmatic analysis, Gricean theory and ultimately Relevance Theory. What was abstracted away from Austin's work was not the methodology of close analysis, but the pragmatic or performative aspect. Thus even Austin's work ultimately led away from language to some other interpretative domain. In the reconstruction of "speaker's meaning" the hearer infers a rich set of possibilities. The classic statement of this position is to be found, of course, in Grice's account of "and". The temporal and logical meanings of "and" exists not at the linguistic or semantic level, but at the level of pragmatics and speaker-meaning derived inferentially within a particular context.[15]

Of course, other linguistic theories began to have influence in the closing years of the fifties. In some ways Chomsky, too, was influenced in particular by Russell and the early analytic philosophers. This was not of course in the area of language acquisition, but in his conception of language and its relation to logical form.[16] His first full-length study of language was not *Syntactic Structures* (1957), but *The Logical Structure of Linguistic Theory* (1955), a work that by its title alone clearly suggests Chomsky's metalinguistic aims. In short, Chomsky was not trying to knock language into shape, as the linguistic philosophers had attempted; his target was linguistic theory itself. His early work, which Chomsky himself was not convinced was "linguistics" in the traditional sense, pushed the study of language in a very specific, formal and abstract direction. But as Moore and Carling have argued, he did not wholly reject the work of the American descriptivists, such as Martin Joos,[17] but merely reorientated the focus from the a-systemically descriptive to the formal, algorithmic and mathematical.

---

[15] H.P. Grice, "Meaning", *Philosophical Review,* 64 (1957), 377-88.

[16] Chomsky had attacked Skinner's behaviourism in a famous review of *Verbal Behaviour* in 1959.

[17] T. Moore and C. Carling, Understanding Language: Towards a Post-Chomskyan Linguistics, London: Macmillan, 1982. Joos' *Readings in Linguistics: The Development of Descriptive Linguistics in America 1925-56,* Chicago: Chicago University Press, 1957, was published in the same year as Chomsky's *Syntactic Structures.*

Many followed, and linguistics once again was seduced by the idea of a formally secure system, what Lakoff and Sweetser refer to as "math envy", sometimes more jocularly known as *pi*-ness envy. To a certain extent, by the mid-1950s both descriptive linguistics and linguistic philosophy (in its Oxford form) had exhausted themselves. Coupled with a rise of knowledge of computers, neural networks and cognitive capabilities in general, and the dramatic rise of pragmatics, this led to a move away from the focus on language as *sui generis*.

Just as Gødel in the 1930s showed the impossibility of deriving mathematics from a finite number of logical axioms (as Russell and Whitehead had believed) and that mathematics itself was not the secure, formal system it had seemed, so cognitive scientists began in the 1970s to doubt the possibility of there being a truly generative grammar. However, in both cases it is not to say that because a system could not be finally secured, it was not to be abandoned. Here again there are similarities between Chomsky and Russell. Replying to his critics in the late 1960s, Russell stated that he saw no reason to abandon the work of *Principia Mathematica* (1910-13) merely on the grounds that in any formal system there will be statements that can neither be proved nor disproved. For Russell in this late stage of his work and thought, a formal system is considered as good as the work it can do, and Russell's certainly enabled a great deal of work to be done, extending our knowledge of mathematical processes. Similarly with Chomsky, many would admit that his programme has given us an elegant and mostly workable formal system, even if it is based ultimately on something "non-formal", i.e. the intuitions of idealized native speakers.

As experiments in AI have continued, so the idea of language as a formal system − and by that we mean one potentially realizable by a computable machine − has begun to be really tested. Chomsky's theories and methods are ready-made to answer questions such as "How can we program the computer to locate the antecedent x of pronoun y". This is possible because the operation is formal and predictive, with certain rules of syntax and distribution describable. In traditional grammars, that x is related to y is a formal rather than semantic description, computable in a strictly mechanical way. Certain kinds of logical operations were seen as being so close to the workings of natural language that Quine had stated not that the pronoun acted like a variable, but that the variable acted like a pronoun.[18] Anaphora, the relation between x and y, can be seen as the quintessential relation of this kind. The metalinguistic terms "pronoun" and "antecedent" are assigned and the relation treated as that of a bound variable to a constant. But Chomsky, who has often been wrongly accused of wishing to exclude semantics from linguistic inquiry (a misreading of the so-called "autonomy of syntax" argument), realizes that the relation is not straightforward. Indeed, it is not really even part of grammar. He states:

> ... it ... seems reasonable to suppose that the fundamental properties of quantifiers ... and anaphora (the relations between antecedents and pronouns, for example) can be expressed in part on the level of semantic representation, separate from extralinguistic considerations.[19]

At first glance this might seem as though he wishes to reduce anaphoric relations to formal mechanisms; but this is not so, for he considers them part of *semantic* representations. He further states:

> It is not grammatical principles which govern the relationship of [these] pronouns to their antecedents or intended referents. .... The actual reference of linguistic expressions in real life involves the interaction of cognitive systems. And grammar is only one of these.[20]

Pronouns and co-reference, seemingly the most stable and logical areas of linguistic computability, could not be tamed, or bound, quite so readily. Whether explicitly deictic or not, they are the most fundamental, subjective and complex linguistic elements, central to studies in artificial intelligence, psychology and text processing. But what is the nature of the "semantic representation" to which Chomsky refers? Emmott cites the following example of a seemingly non-

---

[18] W.V.O. Quine, *Word and Object,* Cambridge, Mass: MIT Press, 1960.

[19] Chomsky, 1977, *op.cit.*, 142.

[20] *Ibid.*, 147.

computable pronoun-antecedent relation, from Brown and Yule's *Discourse Analysis*:

i) Kill an active, plump chicken. Prepare it for the oven.[21]

Now, according to the traditional theory, "it" should refer back to the most salient NP left of the pronoun (unless it is a cataphoric or "forward-looking" pronoun) — that is, "an active, plump chicken".[22] But it is clearly not an active and plump chicken that is then being placed in the oven. Hopefully, it is a dead and plump one. Brown and Yule, though they do not develop the idea, suggest that pronouns refer to a "mental representation" of the appropriate antecedent. But what is the nature of this representation? Clearly it cannot be of an "active and plump chicken" — that is, some superordinate idea that imparts its semantic properties onto the phrase "an active and plump chicken" — because the problem would still be there, but transposed to a supposedly higher "cognitive" level. The problem of course is with the verb in this imperative clause. The verb oversees the NP in a way that modifies it. What we seem to have is a carrying-over to the next clause (containing the pronoun) some construction in which the verb has modified the noun and transformed it into a dead chicken. In a way, there must be some kind of nominalization going on. The pronoun refers to the post-modified noun, "the previously alive but now dead chicken."

  In a typical analysis, one or two sentences such as these are abstracted away from any further co-text. Because of this initial move the analyst is led to look either for strictly formal or distributional relations between elements or some higher-level order to secure coherence and unity. Thus in order for "it" to safely co-refer, the antecedent moves up a rank and becomes a "mental representation" that does not have to be fully representative of the whole antecedent phrase. The linguistic expression "an active and plump chicken" becomes the mental representation "a plump, dead chicken" (which was previously

---

[21] Emmott, *op.cit.*, quoting from G. Brown, and G. Yule, *Discourse Analysis*, Cambridge: Cambridge University Press, 1983.

[22] M.A.K. Halliday, and R. Hasan, *Cohesion in English*, London: Longman, 1976.

lively). There is another way of looking at the text, however, without moving into the quasi-Platonic realm of mental representations or spaces. We can more simply say that given the context, which in this case is largely generic in that it is part of a recipe (recognized by its formal elements), we simply "read past" the description, taking it to a different time, fairly secure in our knowledge that we do not normally put live creatures in the oven. More formally, the "plump, lively chicken" is the same chicken referred to by "it" but not at time T_1, but T_2.

Actually, the case is even simpler. We could even dispense with the imperative "kill" and still solve the problem, for in fact there is no problem. The clause "prepare it for the oven" already carries with it a guarantee of agreement because to prepare something for the oven is indeed to ensure that it is dead. This is ensured by our understanding of the words and not by some higher level cognitive ability. Without any need to call on the idea of mental representations the pronoun can and does refer to an active and plump chicken, which in being prepared for the oven remains plump but becomes decidedly dead.

Perhaps it is a poor example, but it does show how the notion of mental representations can be invoked on a piecemeal basis. Usually, these kinds of examples are constructed in a manner which makes the analysis come out just right. As I have argued elsewhere, Sperber and Wilson's short exemplifying dialogues, for example, embody what I have called the "Peter and Mary Principle": the protagonists in their small exchanges already seem to know each other just well enough for the contextual effects to work.[23] Like Sperber and Wilson, mainstream cognitive linguists are keen on the "richness" of cognitive abilities. This view, I think, also partly accounts for the kinds of texts analysed by some of the cognitive linguists, including Relevance theorists. Because the focus is on the cognitive apparatus "behind" the text, the text itself should not be too dense. Although some headway has been made in the analysis of literary texts by the cognitivists, the theoretical apparatus and methodology are more likely to be exercised on small, discrete chinks of discourse. Emmott wishes to see longer stretches of

---

[23] See my "Relevance Theory and the Literary Text: Some Problems and Perspectives", *Journal of Literary Semantics,* 13/3 (1993), 207-17, and "Butterflies, Wheels and the Search for Literary Relevance", *Language and Literature,* 6/2 (1997), 133-8.

text being analysed, but the problems confronting any analysis of significantly long text, say a novel, are manifold.[24]

One of the important things such an analysis demonstrates, then, is the significance of the actual texts analysed. It is curious, too, that the problem has rarely been considered through an analysis of more obvious difficulties. I am thinking here particularly of the classic gender-specific pronoun problem of English, as in a sentence such as "The reader must construct a mental representation. He then finds words to match it." In this example it is not a case of non-agreement, but rather of exclusion of possibility. The point here, made succinctly by Emmott, is that nominals, like pronouns, also need to be interpreted. In this example "the reader" is not marked for gender (but entails the idea of "one who reads"), but the following pronoun is. Are we to say that we have a mental representation of a reader who is both (or either) male or female, which we put in the mental waiting room until the pronoun can fix it?

The above examples draw both on mental spaces and mental representations. Fauconnier's notion of "mental spaces" has also been influential in the move away from a wholly linguistic focus. Logical problems such as co-reference are, according to Lakoff and Sweetser's introduction to his seminal text, "easy in the theory of mental spaces."[25] To avoid logical contradictions, referential structure is indicated by these spaces. The following example is discussed by Lakoff and Sweetser in their Foreword:

In this painting, the girl with the brown eyes has green eyes.

If the clause "the girl with brown eyes has green eyes" is embedded in a clause with a propositional attitude verb, it can be analysed in the Russellian manner. Thus "x believes that the girl with brown eyes has green eyes" is solved through an analysis of the scope of the verb. A more blatant contradiction is possible in similar opaque contexts: "*x believes* that *black is white*". However, in Fauconnier's example there is no verb of propositional attitude and hence the context is transparent,

---

[24] As demonstrated by Paul Werth, *Text Worlds: Representing Cognitive Space in Discourse*, London: Longman, 1999.

[25] In Fauconnier, *op.cit.*, x.

not opaque. Fauconnier's answer is to make the adverbial phrase "in this painting" equivalent to a verb producing an opaque context. To do this he simply lodges the phrase in the mental waiting room. The two parts of the sentence occupy two separate "mental spaces". In this sense it is clear that such logical problems are indeed "easy" within the theory of mental spaces. But can it be that for much of the twentieth century philosophers and logicians simply missed the point? This cannot be the case; what triggers the seeming simplicity of the analytical model is a fundamental shift of concern and perspective. Fauconnier's method suggests something about cognitive processes; Russell's (for example) suggested something about the structure of the world. Once you turn ontological problems "inwards", they can very easily disappear. This is not to deny the validity of Fauconnier's approach. However, to say that it has solved such logical problems is wrong; what it has done is present them within a context in which they are no longer problems. That context is mental and epistemological, not ontological.

There is a further move to go beyond these short, artificially constructed examples and to focus on "real" language, that is, language occurring "naturally" in its particular genre or context. Although this move is generally to be welcomed, it is not without its own problems. It is not simply the case that in looking at "real" language we automatically have a better understanding of how language works, despite the obvious common-sense nature of the proposal. There is, to begin with, the whole issue of what exactly constitutes "real" language. However, for the present, analysts such as Emmott put a great deal of faith in context, longer texts and real language. The question we need to ask is to what extent this focus will give us a different perspective on the material. Fauconnier is much less interested in the notion of real language, for his theory of mental spaces is designed to cope with classical logico-linguistic problems. Emmott, on the other hand, states:

> One of the major arguments [of this book] is that research on text comprehension must take account of full, real texts, since they are fundamentally different from the artificially constructed sentence pairs and "text" fragments that are often used in work on inference-making.[26]

---

[26] Emmott, *op.cit.*, 74-5.

Emmott offers the following list of "properties" of real texts. In summary they are:

Hierarchical structure: According to Emmott, within any discourse segment "certain sentences may be of more central importance than others, and there may be a typical ordering of components" (76).

Meaning partly derived from surrounding sentences: This is the classic call for attention to the context, particularly within literary studies. Here, the *context* is equated with *co-text*.

Requires reader to draw on stored information: This information can be of a number of different types, including memory of the text and so-called "encyclopaedic" knowledge of concepts.

Connectivity: The focus on connectivity broadens the scope of analysis from the traditional sentence-isolate to discourses. In the past, it was assumed that this connectivity could be captured by purely mechanical and formal means.

These can be reduced to general properties of context and prompts to processing. For an approach that takes such properties into account, the kinds of questions concern the amount of text needed. How much co-text of a novel, or a poem, for instance, do we need in order for our analysis to work? As much as it takes to find the antecedent in the text, even if it is long-distance? Just a surrounding chunk? Whatever it takes to make it work? These are not flippant questions, but ones that get to heart of the whole "real discourse" approach to text processing. Is there really any difference in looking at "real" conversation, or a passage from a D.H. Lawrence novel, as opposed to looking at the King of France, colourless green ideas, Peter and Mary's tiredness or plump chickens, in terms of issues, problems and their solutions? Many conclude that it is a *sine qua non* of analysis to posit some notion of mental representation within a "real" discourse.[27] This is partly because, as Emmott notes, the concerns of the philosophers and those of the cognitivists are different. The former tend to be interested in truth and existence, the latter in the mechanics of language and

---

[27] Including Emmott, *op.cit.*, Paul Werth, *op.cit.* and his "Extended Metaphor: A Text-World Account", *Language and Literature* (1994), 3/2, 79-103.

processing procedures. This of course is largely true, but it does not mean that those concerns do not overlap. Russell's theory of Descriptions, which remained virtually unchallenged for the first half of the twentieth century, was primarily a theory of ontology, but it also told us something about the way that natural language fragments work. Indeed, his model has been extended, rather than ultimately reduced, to account for not only definite descriptions, but also indefinites and other forms of descriptive phrases – even though Russell's initial impulse, to make a metalanguage fit for the description of mathematical processes, is no longer the reason for the analysis.

Essentially what Emmott and others are calling for is attention to be paid to the appropriate linguistic context. As Emmott's work in particular is primarily on pronouns and reference-chaining, her focus is on representation-strings, rather than individual concepts. However, if Sperber and Wilson are to be believed, the linguistic co-text can only go so far in specifying the "meaning" of a particular word. Interpretations have to be based not only on the correct assignment of references in a chain, but also on initial mental representations. As Emmott's examples are largely literary, we might expect such work to lead naturally to a contextualized stylistics, a stylistics, that is, which is fully embedded in the cognitive and which deals with "real" texts in their full contexts. The extent to which literary texts are "real" in any sense conceived of by philosophers is a problem in itself. The question remains, however, as to whether there is any real difference between "whole" texts and text fragments or artificial sentences in terms of both the results of the analyses and the implications for any descriptive theory of the machinery of texts. It seems that the decision to concentrate on longer texts is quite different from that of the decision to use "real" texts; and that in turn is a separate issue from that of the desirability of mental representations or spaces.

i) *Real texts*: For the purposes of demonstrating the explanatory power of a theory, some sort of idealization of data seems unavoidable, and perhaps desirable. Chomsky states:

> Opposition to idealization is simply objection to rationality; it amounts to nothing more than an insistence that we shall not have meaningful intellectual work. Phenomena that are complicated enough to be worth studying generally involve the

interaction of several systems. Therefore you must abstract some object of study, you must eliminate those factors which are not pertinent.[28]

The problem here is that in the process of idealization it is possible to "eliminate" those factors, which would threaten the coherence of the theory. I have already suggested that this in part is the difficulty with Sperber and Wilson's Peter and Mary dialogues. I have been chided for not providing a suitable alternative to these exchanges.[29] There is no easy alternative, for even if examples from "real" conversation were analysed, they could just as easily be *selected* for their convenience as constructed for it. In that case there is no reason to prefer "real" texts to imaginative and challenging artificial ones. Indeed, the properly constructed text may be able to suggest problems and their solutions that a real one cannot. This is possible because at a certain level of processing language is highly reliable; it is not endlessly ambiguous or utterly indeterminate at the level of comprehension. Following the work of Ruth Millikan, Origgi and Sperber state that "the direct proper function of a linguistic device is what keeps speakers and hearers using and responding to the linguistic device in a reliable way, thus stabilising the device in the community".[30] Part of the task of cognitive linguistics is to reconcile the stability of comprehension with the richness of cognitive systems which underpin it.

ii) Longer texts: Emmott's focus on narratives demonstrates that certain presumed formal mechanisms of co-reference, for example, cannot hold over longer texts. "Real" narratives such as those of literary texts, provide a rich corpus on which to draw. Further, they have been traditionally ignored by philosophers and cognitive scientists (although Sperber and Wilson do look at the nature of literary tropes). Emmott's work shows us the reliability of processes of comprehension,

---

[28] Chomsky, 1977, *op.cit.*, 57.

[29] Adrian Pilkington, Barbara MacMahon and Billy Clark, "Looking for an Argument: A Response to Green" *Language and Literature,* 6/2 (1997), 139-48.

[30] R. Millikan, *Language, Thought and Other Biological Categories,* Cambridge, Mass: MIT Press, 1984; and M. Origgi, and D. Sperber, (to appear) in D. Sperber, ed., *Metarepresentations,* Oxford: Oxford University Press.

while providing a non-linguistic account of reference-chaining: it shows us how we come to know what we know when we read.

iii) Mental representations: The idea of narrative or text comprehension is only tangentially linked with the idea of mental representations. These are invoked to account for co-reference ambiguities and disjunctions between referents, *at the level of comprehension*. Both Fauconnier and Emmott use them to resolve logical and referential difficulties, rather than to suggest something about the nature of the mind or of language.

At the level of comprehension then, Fauconnier and Emmott have shown that a notion of mental representation provides the basis for an adequate metalanguage for the solution of interpretative problems. What needs to be added to this account is a way of accounting for the affective features of texts, particularly literary texts. What is generally overlooked by philosophers, cognitive scientists and even linguists, is that *language* causes feelings, produces emotions and moves people. When we read a work of literature, for example, it is not some mental representation that enables us to feel the way we do, it is the power of the words. We may need some sort of mental representation to orientate ourselves around the world of the text, but something else is going on in terms of more complex cognitive activities. If words are only prompts for the construction of meaning, how is it that they can affect me even if I do not "understand" them? How can I construct a mental representation given the appropriate inferential context when my comprehension is only partial?

AUGUSTAN BALANCE AND COGNITIVE CONTEXTS: AN APPROACH TO THE STUDY OF POPE

TONY BEX

In a chapter on Seamus Heaney's poem "Punishment", Verdonk makes the point that "the actual reader of the text is an element of its context, i.e., the whole complex of factors affecting its meaning and interpretation."[1] He continues by arguing that "once readers are drawn into a text's contextual orbit, so to speak, they not only decode or interpret meanings but also encode or create them."[2] More recently, Lecercle has developed similar ideas in greater depth. He suggests, with Verdonk, that readers do indeed "decode or interpret meanings", but that these meanings are never fully under their control.[3] One reason for this is that utterances always echo earlier utterances, and that their meanings are reinscriptions, which carry the traces of earlier meanings. He also agrees with Verdonk that readers "encode or create" meanings, arguing that these "creative" meanings derive from the individual's encyclopedic knowledge and knowledge of language. Meaning, according to Lecercle, is therefore inherently unstable being subject both to socio-historical and personal contexts, and this leads him to propose four theses:

---

[1] Peter Verdonk, "Poetry and Public Life: A Contextualized Reading of Seamus Heaney's 'Punishment'", in *Twentieth-Century Poetry: From Text to Context*, London: Routledge, 1993, 117.

[2] *Ibid.*, 118.

[3] Jean-Jacques Lecercle, *Interpretation as Pragmatics,* London: Macmillan, 1999, 31.

Thesis 1: All interpretations are possible.
Thesis 2: No interpretation is true.
Thesis 3: Some interpretations are just.
Thesis 4: Some interpretations are false.[4]

The first of these theses has been disputed by Verdonk[5] and, while it may be trivially true to argue that individual readers are free to adopt a Humpty Dumpty position so that, for them, a text "means just what I choose it to mean — neither more nor less",[6] in practice such interpretative anarchy tends not to occur. Nevertheless, interpretative disagreements about texts in general, and particularly about literary texts, are extremely common which suggests that Lecercle's other three theses are worth investigating in a little more depth.

The claim that no interpretation is true I take to mean that no interpretation can be a complete account of the text under scrutiny. Some aspects of a text's meanings will always escape individual readers' attentions simply because their encyclopaedic knowledge is both incomplete and different from that of either the creator of the text or of other readers. Any particular interpretation will therefore always be partial and incomplete. Theses 3 and 4 do not follow logically from this, but pragmatically it would seem that the more partial and incomplete an interpretation is, the more it is likely to be false. And, conversely, the more complete and less partial an interpretation is, so the more "just" it will be.

My purpose in this chapter is to investigate how we might achieve incomplete, but just, interpretations through an analysis of the kinds of "work" we engage in when confronted by a complex literary text. To do this, I am presupposing that the producers of complex texts are acting "responsibly", i.e. that they have made linguistic selections that, to the best of their ability, are intended to have intellectual and emotional effects on their readers, and that they expect their readers to react "responsibly", i.e. that they will read the text assuming that such effects are intended but that these effects are unlikely to be achieved

---

[4] *Ibid.,* 31.

[5] Verdonk, *op.cit.,* 118.

[6] Lewis Carroll, *Through the Looking Glass,* London: The Folio Society, 1962.

without some effort on their part. I am certainly not suggesting that readers can engage in a reconstruction of the writers' intentions and meanings since this is clearly impossible,[7] but I am arguing, with Lecercle, that it is possible to construct interpretations that are congruent with such intentions and which are therefore "just". To refine the initial quotation from Verdonk, the actual reader of the text is, indeed, an element of its context, but such a reader can position him or herself either responsibly or irresponsibly within that context.

To explain how this can be done requires an understanding both of the fundamental cognitive bases of language which constrain interpretation, and the specific cognitive contexts which readers bring with them when they engage in interpretative acts. These areas have come under increasing scrutiny by cognitive stylisticians[8] who draw from recent developments within cognitive linguistics. Their work is both exciting and well-informed at the analytical level, but it is essentially explanatory of how readers achieve interpretations rather than an exploration of how "just" interpretations can be achieved. I suggest that this is because cognitive linguistics describes language as representational rather than as a social tool designed to have effects in the social world.[9] As Ungerer and Schmid point out:

---

[7] See, among others, Dan Sperber, and Deirdre Wilson, *Relevance Theory* (2nd edition), Oxford: Blackwell, 1995.

[8] Peter Crisp, "Allegory: Conceptual Metaphor in History", *Language and Literature* (forthcoming); D.C. Freeman, "'According to my Bond': *King Lear* and Re-cognition", *Language and Literature*, 2/1 (1993), 1-18; M.H. Freeman, "Grounded Spaces: Deictic -*Self* Anaphors in the Poetry of Emily Dickinson", *Language and Literature*, 6/1 (1997), 7-28; Mark Turner, *Death is the Mother of Beauty,* Chicago: University of Chicago Press, 1987, *Reading Minds: The Study of English in the Age of Cognitive Science,* Princeton: Princeton University Press, 1991, *The Literary Mind,.* Oxford: Oxford University Press, 1996.

[9] See the criticism of D.C. Freeman *op.cit.* by William Downes, "Reading the Language Itself: Some Methodological Problems in D.C. Freeman's "'According to my Bond": *King Lear* and Re-cognition'", *Language and Literature,* 2/2 (1993), 121-8.

> In cognitive linguistics the use of syntactic structures is largely
> seen as a reflection of how a situation is conceptualized by the
> speaker, and this conceptualization is governed by the
> attention principle. Salient participants, especially agents, are
> rendered as subjects and less salient participants as objects;
> verbs are selected which are compatible with the choice of
> subject and object, and evoke the perspective on the situation
> that is intended; locative, temporal and many other types of
> relations are highlighted or "windowed for attention" by
> expressing them explicitly as adverbials. Although languages
> may supply different linguistic strategies for the realization of
> the attention potential, the underlying cognitive structures and
> principles are probably universal.[10]

Although this claim is slightly hedged (e.g. "largely"), the view taken
here suggests a being who perceives a "state of affairs" in the world
and then selects from a lexicogrammar to represent a congruent "state
of affairs" linguistically. However, such a characterization of language
presents problems both for literary critics and stylisticians, since it
involves a significant reduction in their interpretative role by ignoring
the ways in which writers use language to influence and change the
views of their readers and to stimulate aesthetic and emotional
responses. By concentrating on one of language's functions, it means
that the others tend to be ignored.

While such linguists acknowledge the deep creativity of language,
focusing on how metaphor, metonymy, and other tropes are constitutive
of language in use, they argue that such tropes derive from our
experiences as grounded organisms. So Johnson, discussing the
ubiquity of the MIND AS BODY metaphor, comments:

> ... it is important to see that claiming that the MIND AS BODY
> metaphor is not optional does not entail that it is somehow an
> a priori structure of rationality, or a so-called "innate" idea.
> What it means, instead, is that given the kinds of bodies and
> brains we have, given the biological, social, and cultural

---

[10] Friedrich Ungerer, and Hans-Jorg Schmid, *An Introduction to Cognitive
Linguistics*, London: Addison Wesley Longman, 1996, 280.

environments we inhabit, and given our basic human needs, the MIND AS BODY metaphor is a highly motivated structure that partly defines our purposes and also helps to achieve them.[11]

If this is true, and the cognitive linguists produce an impressive array of evidence in support of such claims,[12] then it has important consequences for linguistic meaning in general and literary reading in particular. At worst, it suggests that the individual reader, struggling to make sense of a complex literary text, is airbrushed out of the picture to be replaced by some kind of universal organism structured in such a way as to create just those interpretations that are congruent with its make up.

I realize that this is a caricature, and that it fails to take account of Johnson's mention of the "social and cultural environments we inhabit", but the universalizing tendencies behind the cognitive project have to date tended to ignore the local variations of time and social structure which enable us to engage in mutually comprehensible discourse.[13] These tendencies can also be seen at work in some of Turner's earlier writings, and Turner is significant in being one of the most influential cognitive linguists who has worked on literary texts. In *Death Is the Mother of Beauty* he asserts:

> My intention is not to change the fundamental job of the literary critic, which is to hold worthwhile conversations about literature, but rather to give him or her the tools to do it responsibly and to do it better. At present, most literary critics

[11] Mark Johnson, "Philosophical Implications of Cognitive Semantics", *Cognitive Linguistics*, 3/4 (1992), 345-66, 353.

[12] E.g. George Lakoff, *Women, Fire and Dangerous Things,* Chicago: University of Chicago Press, 1987; and Ungerer and Schmid, *op.cit.*

[13] There is some evidence to suggest that scholars are beginning to historicize their critical analyses. So, Crisp, *op.cit.*, observes: "To understand any historically specific expression of conceptual metaphor, one must understand how the cognitively universal properties of metaphor interact with the particular social and cultural content." For reasons that would take too long to argue here, this claim seems to contradict Johnson in that it implies that conceptual metaphors may well be an "a priori structure of rationality."

do not know what is and is not known about cognition and language. Such awareness is required for a literary critic to gauge the implications of his assertions, to know whether his presuppositions are controversial or safe or plainly mistaken.[14]

Later, in *Reading Minds*, he continues:

I propose, roughly, that what is missing from the profession of English is *English*, but I do not mean by this that the curriculum should be richer in language courses, or that lucid prose style should be the anthem of our profession, or that we should all teach composition, or any of the other familiar proposals for changing the profession. Instead, I will argue that what the profession lacks is a grounding, integrated approach to language and literature as acts of the human mind. My argument constitutes a critique of the present state of the profession, based upon a vision of what the profession of English could be.[15]

These are astonishing claims, but they need to be taken seriously.

It is clear that Turner is not suggesting that critics should become experts in a new linguistics. But he is arguing, and his argument is developed at greater length in the works cited, that the study of language gives us insights into the nature of cognition; that literature's medium is language; and that discussing literature independently of its linguistic base and, by extension, its cognitive impulses, leads to an impoverished criticism. At one level, Turner's demands are non-controversial. The literary critic, whatever his or her ideological and intellectual allegiances, needs to be as well-informed as possible about all aspects of science and philosophy. But it is unclear to me whether the kinds of specialist knowledge that Turner is demanding from the literary critic (or, indeed, the stylistician) will necessarily lead to the insights he anticipates.

---

[14] Turner, 1987, *op.cit.*, 8.

[15] Turner, 1991, *op.cit.*, 7.

This is partly because some of the grounding arguments of the cognitivists seem muddled. The general concept that natural languages represent embodied experience and cannot be indexical of some external "reality" seems to me relatively non-controversial.[16] However, the two related claims: 1] that all language is therefore metaphorical; and 2] that these metaphors reveal something about the structure of the mind, need careful scrutiny. The first of these has the effect of emptying the term "metaphor" of all signification. Gibbs himself seems to recognize this when he argues that "My urgent plea is that we recognize the different ways that the term *literal* is used and develop better accounts of what is *not* figurative about thought and language."[17] The sense of frustration here suggests that he is concerned that we are in danger of becoming enmeshed in a new kind of Whorfianism: i.e., that all language is inevitably metaphorical and that any attempt to discuss the world "out there" in non-metaphorical terms is doomed to failure. Admittedly, elsewhere, in an interesting discussion of Whorf, Gibbs argues[18] that Whorf is constrained by the concept of an autonomous language faculty whose categories influence our cognition and contrasts this with the alternative view in which our cognition (which will be culturally variable), conceived of as metaphorical in nature, influences our language use. But even here we are left with an abstract entity, "cognition", whose workings can only be observed at second-hand (i.e., through specific uses of language).

Lakoff attempts to get round this problem by arguing: "Our every day folk theory of the world is an objectivist folk theory. We create cognitive models of the world, and we have a natural tendency to attribute real existence to the categories in those cognitive models."[19] Again, the borders between "objective reality" and metaphorical existence are blurred and the distinctions between those kinds of writing

---

[16] It is important to recognize that this does not conflict with my earlier view that cognitive linguists tend to see language as "representational". A perceived "state of affairs" may not correspond to an actual "state of affairs".

[17] Ray Gibbs, *The Poetics of Mind*, Cambridge: Cambridge University Press, 1994, 79.

[18] *Ibid.*, 438-42.

[19] Lakoff, *op.cit.*, 209.

that we deem to be "objective" and those that we treat as literary cease
to apply. But if this is the case, an account of how literature works
becomes very difficult to construct.[20] My point is that in reading
literature responsibly, we are engaging in a particular activity which
pays close attention to language and which engages in the construction
of precise and local meanings as far as this is possible. As Stockwell
has argued: "Literary reading is what makes literature literary: we
develop a generic propensity to read particular text-types in particular
ways."[21]

Of course, this is not to suggest that the kinds of universalizing
metaphors that the cognitivists have uncovered are not also part of the
organizing principles within a literary work. Indeed, to the extent that
Turner *et al* are correct, they cannot avoid being present. But for my
"responsible" critic, they are no longer the focus of attention. Language
may indeed be embodied in the ways that Turner stresses in *Reading
Minds*, but we must also recognize that the users of language in
particular exchanges wish to construct particular embodiments or, to the
extent that they wish to assert the "literal truth", disembodiments. And
a literary text tends to be interesting precisely because it is, in some
sense, unique. From this perspective, the very interesting work which
reveals underlying and organizing patterns of cognitive metaphor within
particular literary texts[22] does not need to appeal to universals, since it
can be read as an attempt to uncover the local and specific work which
has gone into the construction of a particular discourse process. Above
all, it involves recognising that "'membershipping' (categorization) is
contingent, varying from case to case according to criteria that may
differ from case to case".[23] Put very simply, the metaphor (or category)

----

[20] My views of what constitutes a literary text are set out in *Variety in Written
English,* London: Routledge, 1996, 176ff.

[21] Peter Stockwell, "The Inflexibility of Invariance", *Language and Literature,*
8/2 (1999), 125-42, 138.

[22] Such as D.C. Freeman, *op.cit.*

[23] Michael Toolan, *Total Speech: An Integrational Linguistic Approach to
Language,* London: Duke University Press, 1996, 88.

LIFE IS A JOURNEY is treated very differently by Bunyan in *Pilgrim's Progress* and Fielding in *Tom Jones* because Bunyan and Fielding had different designs on their readers and therefore employed different criteria to achieve their ends.

One approach which yields interesting insights into how meanings are constructed is being developed by Potter. He engages in a critique of cognitivism which problematizes the notion of mental representations, and suggests, more forcefully than I have done above, that there is an element of circularity in the ways that they have been conceived.[24] More to my point, however, is his view that:

> representations become separated from the practices in which they are viewed and start to be conceptualized as static entities which individuals carry around with them. Put another way, the cognitive focus draws attention away from what is being *done* with representations and descriptions in the setting in which they are produced.[25]

Potter has the same anti-objectivist position as the cognitivists, but is concerned with investigating the discoursal and rhetorical strategies that are used which allow people to refer to "facts". Although he focuses on spoken language, the kinds of line-by-line analyses he undertakes can be usefully employed by the responsible stylistician to ascertain how writers achieve incremental meanings. The virtue of this approach is that it reintroduces readers making them both part of the context of the work and creators of the meanings in the ways that Verdonk suggests. It also has the advantage of enabling us to show exactly how we come to the interpretations that we achieve without having to appeal to psychological constructs such as frames or schemata, since the discourse is being analysed in its own terms as part of a process in real time. Further, to the extent that we are being "responsible" in the sense I have been using the term, it forces us to historicize the text in an

---

[24] "... inner representations are inferred from various representational practices involving talk and writing, and such inferences tend to circularity with the inner representations being used, in turn, to explain those representational devices", in J. Potter, *Representing Reality: Discourse, Rhetoric and Social Construction,* London: Sage, 1996, 103.

[25] *Ibid.*, 103-4.

appropriate way by relating it to the concerns of the period to which it belongs.

I have chosen to try and develop this argument with reference to Pope for a number of reasons. On the one hand, he has sometimes been criticized as among the more prosaic of the great poets of the English canon. We are therefore less likely to be distracted by the metaphorical construction of mental states as perhaps happens with Romantic and post- Romantic poets. I would suggest that Pope typically attempts to represent a balance between Reason and the Passions (or rather Reason and the unfettered imagination) partly through the euphonious use of prosody, and partly by a developing intellectual argument. Pope is also particularly interesting, because he was deeply rooted in the Lockeian conception of empiricism, which asserted that the mind starts as a *tabula rasa*[26] devoid of ideas. The ideas that we subsequently conceive are either simple or complex, and true or false. He asserts that simple ideas are necessarily real, arguing in a manner similar to the cognitivists that such ideas "being in us the effects of powers in things without us, ordained by our Maker to produce in us such sensations, they are real *ideas* in us whereby we distinguish the qualities that are really in things themselves."

For Locke, then, objectivity presented no real problem, but it is a very reduced objectivity which depends entirely on our senses. More interesting is his discussion of the development of complex ideas and their validity. Although I have not space to discuss this here, Locke recognized that complex ideas

> being combinations of simple *ideas* put together and united under one general name, it is plain that the mind of man uses some kind of liberty in forming those complex *ideas* ...The question then is which of these are real and which barely imaginary combinations? What collections agree to the reality of things and what not?[27]

---

[26] Or, in Locke's own words: "Let us then suppose the mind to be, as we say, white paper void of all characters, without any *ideas,*" in John Locke, *An Essay Concerning Human Understanding* (ed. J.W. Yolton), London: J.M. Dent, 1961 [1706], Vol.1, 77.

[27] *Ibid.*, Vol.1, 315.

And it was this that particularly concerned Pope. As a poet, he was conscious of the risks he took in representing complex ideas and much of his poetic career was spent in distinguishing between those ideas that were merely fanciful and those that were real in a Lockeian sense. He reserved a particular venom (cf. *The Dunciad*) for those contemporary poets whom he considered to be merely fanciful for their poetry was not only bad, it was also immoral, because of its ability to mislead its readers.

His explorations of this theme occur in a number of his poems. Relatively early in his career in *An Essay on Criticism* (c.1709) he advises would-be critics to:

> First follow NATURE, and your Judgement frame
> By her just Standard, which is still the same;
> *Unerring Nature,* still divinely bright,
> One *clear, unchang'd,* and *Universal* Light.
> Life, Force, and Beauty, must to all impart,
> At once the *Source*, and *End*, and *Test* of *Art*.
> (ll. 68-73)[28]

Nevertheless, this rather bald advice fails to explain either the structural organization of good poetry, or the functions of rhetoric. These are discussed in the following lines:

> Those RULES of old *discover'd*, not *devis'd*,
> Are *Nature* still, but *Nature Methodiz'd;*
> *Nature*, like *Liberty*, is but restrain'd
> By the same Laws which first *herself* ordain'd.
> (ll. 88-91)[29]

and further elaborated in the following passage:

---

[28] J. Butt, ed., *The Poems of Alexander Pope,* London: Methuen, 1963, 146.

[29] *Ibid.*, 146.

> *True Wit* is *Nature* to Advantage drest,
> What oft was *Thought,* but ne'er so well *Exprest,*
> *Something,* whose Truth convinc'd at Sight we find,
> That gives us back the Image of our Mind.
>   (ll. 297-300)[30]

Given that these characterizations of nature appear in the same poem, they are clearly intended to be treated in a unitary manner, but to do this successfully requires engaging in the kind of work referred to by Potter. It could be plausibly argued that the first extract offers us as a ground the cognitive metaphor LIFE IS A JOURNEY, but this would be an impoverished reading which misses the complexities of argumentation employed by Pope. For the intending critic, the pursuit of judgement may be a journey, but it is one that takes place out of time and space. Although we are exhorted to follow nature, nature is a light that is all around us. It is also both the starting point and end of this journey. Further, it is the standard by which the success of the journey is judged. Appeals to the (cognitive) metaphorical nature of Pope's descriptions here will, therefore, only take us so far. However, to capture the philosophical intricacies of Pope's ideas, we need a richer, more "stylistic" and situated reading which notices that he uses recurrent triple expressions: "Nature, Judgement, Standard"; *"clear, unchang'd, Universal"*; "Life, Force, Beauty"; *"Source, End, Test."* By tracing the equivalencies in these triplets, we can ascertain how Pope is engaging in a rhetorical ploy which links abstract ideas to perceptions, then to more general experiences and finally to the concerns which should activate the critic. The second extract can then expatiate in greater detail on the relationship between the rules which govern poetry and those which operate in nature, but against a background which has been fully explored and explained. Interestingly here, however, Pope subtly shifts his characterization of nature, introducing an element of personification which is then exploited in the third extract. The third extract completes these rhetorical shifts by introducing nature as something that can be dressed, but interestingly the personification is incomplete since the clothing is that of words which are the instruments of the mind. And it is here that Pope brings us back to Locke's view of the "reality" of ideas.

---

[30] *Ibid.,* 153.

I have argued so far that Pope's arguments do not work by the simple accretion of metaphorical detail, but are the result of a series of complex rhetorical moves in which nature, judgement and artistic creation are constantly recontextualized so that their relationships are both changed but also clarified intellectually. Although responsible readers will pay close attention to these details, their task is not exhausted by them.

I can best illustrate this by analysing another passage from Pope's later great philosophical poem *An Essay on Man* (1730-32). Having discussed the potential dangers of an unfettered imagination, which is likely to lead us astray, Pope continues:

> Yes, Nature's road must ever be prefer'd;
> Reason is here no guide, but still a guard:
> 'Tis hers to rectify, not overthrow,
> And treat this passion more as friend than foe:
> A mightier Pow'r the strong direction sends,
> And sev'ral Men impels to sev'ral ends.
> Like varying winds, by other passions tost,
> This drives them constant to a certain coast.
> Let pow'r or knowledge, gold or glory, please,
> Or, (oft more strong than all) the love of ease;
> Thro' life 'tis followed, ev'n at life's expance;
> The merchant's toil, the sage's indolence,
> The monk's humility, the hero's pride,
> All, all alike, find Reason on their side.
>
> (*Epistle II*, ll. 161-174)[31]

Here we are confronted with a slightly different rhetorical strategy. Pope starts with a general principle, which is then followed by specific examples. Each couplet builds on what has gone before so that the reader moves from a general truth about nature and reason to an examination of their specific effects. As with my first example (see above), the ground metaphor is LIFE IS A JOURNEY but, although it is exploited more thoroughly in this passage, the nature of the journey is not kept constant. It starts on a road likely to be infested with highwaymen (or, at least, temptations on either side), but is soon

---

[31] *Ibid.*, 521.

transported to an ocean. What is interesting in this passage, then, is not the cognitive metaphor *per se* but the uses Pope makes of it.

Nature, in this passage, has been characterized in similar ways to those that I have investigated above, i.e., as the supplier of simple, real ideas (i.e., the preferred road) and that what is being explored is the function of reason in restraining the exercise of the passions. To understand this adequately requires a deeper understanding of Pope's use of poetic rhetoric than I have so far investigated. The section opens with a direct address to the reader and the use of "Yes" implies that Pope is offering some kind of summing up. This impression seems confirmed by the end of the first couplet, but the reader is then drawn to the second couplet, which acts as a gloss on what has apparently been clearly stated. In l. 161, Reason is personified nominally in terms, first negatively and then positively, whereas in l. 162, the personification is seen in terms of two processes, first positively and then negatively. A balance is thus achieved between these negative and positive polarities, but this balance is created on either side of the caesuras of the two lines. A complicating factor is the alliteration of "guide" and "guard" which invites the reader to treat l. 162 as relatively self-contained. And l. 164 starts with a conjunction, which ties it grammatically to the previous line. It can be argued then that the careful reader is being invited to engage in a complex process of interpretation, which links nature, reason and the imagination in a balanced but potentially unstable condition.

A prosodic analysis would tend to reinforce this impression. A possible reading of the first four lines produces the following patterning:[32]

---

[32] I have based this on my own vocal reading. I realize that other readers may choose to stress other syllables and that no such analysis can be definitive. Further, any particular reading will always be produced in such a way as to indicate the interpretation already reached by the reader. However, if I have followed my advice and been a "responsible" reader, my reading will at least be a plausible one. Taking this into account, it is clear that the reciter of a poem is, in the ways that Verdonk mentions (see above), very much "an element of the context" of the text.

```
 /    / x   x   x   / x x   x   /
Yes, // Nature's road must ever be prefer'd;
 /  x x   /   x   /      x   /  x   /
Reason is here no guide, // but still a guard:
  x   /   x   / x x    /  x x    /
'Tis hers to rectify, // not overthrow,
  x   /   x   /  x     /   x  /   x   /
And treat this passion // more as friend than foe:
```

Interestingly, only the final line reproduces the base metre (iambic pentameters), and this is fitting if we assume that this is where Pope draws his argument together. The positioning of the caesuras and their relative prominence is also significant. The first one highlights the affirmation, while the second and third balance the polarities that are Reason's functions. The final one is only weakly present, inviting us to treat the final clause as a single unit. The strongly accented syllables allow us to ascertain the significance of the elements that are stressed. Thus, although in general terms Reason may be a guide "here" it is not. Equally, the stress on "not" manages to give it the force of an injunction.

The remainder of the quoted passage exemplifies the argument achieved in these four lines. Again, there is a movement from the general to the particular typically realized by parallel instances, which knit the passage together. The "sev'ral Men" and "sev'ral ends" are particularized (albeit as "types") as the merchant, the sage, the monk and the hero, and the "mighty Power" (i.e. the ruling passion) is realized as love of gold, power, knowledge or glory culminating in the final line, which draws us back to the beginning. [33]

My argument, then, is that Pope's poetry typically proceeds by a rhetorical strategy that first establishes a complex general principle and then proceeds to exemplify it by exploring its operation in the world, and finally recapitulates the argument by showing how these particulars confirm the principle. In this respect, he was typical of the dominant modes of thought in the eighteenth century and the responsible reader needs to follow these strategies closely as they develop to create

---

[33] It may seem odd that "power" should be an end for the "sage", but power typically allows one to indulge in "indolence".

coherent and "just" interpretations of his work. Although Pope may share the same cognitive bases as other writers in the language, uncovering these does not necessarily lead to the kinds of discoveries that Turner hopes for.

So far, I have commented on the kinds of work required of the reader to produce interpretations of Pope's didactic verse, and suggested that it involves a process of following a developing intellectual argument, rather than one based on the relation between the emotional or sensory states. This is equally true of his satiric verse, but this typically requires extra work. The *Epistle to Arbuthnot* (1731-4) is interesting in this respect:

> Shut, shut the door, good *John!* fatigu'd I said,
> Tye up the knocker, say I'm sick, I'm dead,
> The Dog-star rages! Nay 'tis past a doubt.
> All *Bedlam* or *Parnassus*, is let out:
> Fire in each eye, and Papers in each hand
> They rave, recite, and madden round the land.
> What Walls can guard me, or what Shades can hide?
> They pierce my Thickets, thro' my Grot they glide,
> By land, by water, they renew the charge,
> They stop the Chariot, and they board the Barge.
> No place is sacred, not the Church is free,
> Ev'n *Sunday* shines no *Sabbath-day* to me:
> Then from the *Mint* walks forth the Man of Ryme,
> Happy to catch me, just at Dinner-time.
>   (ll. 1-14)[34]

The arresting opening invites us directly into Pope's study. We are offered two voices at once: that of Pope instructing his servant to shut out the world, and that of Pope writing to his friend. These dual voices are an essential element of Pope's strategy since he is making public his dissatisfaction and hurt with a recent attack made on him by Lord Hervey and Lady Mary Wortley Montague. He states in the *Advertisement*:

---

[34] Butt, *op.cit.*, 597-8.

I had no thoughts of publishing it, till it pleas'd some persons of rank and fortune ... to attack in a very extraordinary manner, not only my Writings (of which being publick the Publick judge) but my Person, Morals, and Family, whereof to those who know me not, a truer Information may be requisite.[35]

Thus it is clear that Pope wishes to refer to his private life as well as his public persona as poet.

However, the elements that particularly interest me here are the allusive terms which have to be processed successfully for the poem to achieve meaning. "The Dog-star", "Bedlam" and "Parnassus" all require a degree of glossing, but simple reference to the concrete entities that are meant by these terms will not capture the richness of meaning intended by Pope. "Parnassus" is probably easily recoverable as the sacred mountain dedicated to Apollo, "Bedlam" refers to the famous London lunatic asylum, but the "Dog-star" is more obscure in that it may refer simply to the time of year, although here it also alludes to the time when poetry was rehearsed in ancient Rome. These separate references are apparently contradictory in that poetry and madness are somehow being yoked together, but I would suggest that Pope is not inviting us to treat poetry and madness as equivalent, or even as two sides of the same coin, but is rather encouraging us to treat the references as though they were orbiting around each other as individual atoms.[36] We are, in other words, invited to construct a world in which apparent contradictions can co-exist.

The contradictions are then put to work in the second section, where Pope describes himself as subject to intrusion. The "Bedlam" of the first section is inhabited by the insistent seekers after Pope's patronage, while Parnassus has a tentative existence as Pope's home in Twickenham. Although there is a contradiction between the poetasters and the genuine poets, this contradiction is held in balance within the poem. Such ambiguities are illustrated very clearly in the penultimate line of the extract: "Then from the Mint walks forth the Man of

---

[35] *Ibid.*, 597.

[36] This would also mesh in with the prevalent Newtonian scientific ideas.

Ryme." Mint can refer both to the physical entity in London, or the study where the Man of Ryme is coining his verse. My argument is that Pope is rhetorically inviting us throughout the poem to construct sets of apparent oppositions which we refer to simultaneously, and that these oppositions both do work in the ways we continue with the poem. It is in this way that Pope achieves what I have called Augustan balance.

I have suggested, then, that responsible readers make themselves part of the context of the text by engaging in interpretative work. This work involves recognizing that literary texts are not merely representational. As Verdonk has memorably stated:

> It is the reader's response or pragmatic stage, in which the reader, as a verbal creature, displays his habitual communicative behaviour by responding to the poet's verbal structure as if it were an utterance or discourse in which a speaker invites him, and sometimes even provokes him, to create conceivable contexts for it.[37]

While agreeing wholeheartedly with this, I would go further and argue that the recognition of literature as a particular kind of discourse requires us to respond fully to every linguistic feature that is present within the text, and to use these features as clues to the arguments being advanced by the writer. In the case of Pope, I have suggested that we need to engage with the ways in which he develops an argument with incremental meanings, and how these meanings are frequently composed of opposites, which are held in balance. In the course of this argument, I have suggested that some of the positions held by the cognitive linguists tend to undermine such an engagement. I would stress, though, that I have no major disagreements with many of their arguments. I am primarily concerned at the ways in which their ideas have been developed within stylistics, believing that they risk interfering with the kinds of close critical reading which is the hallmark of Verdonk's work.

---

[37] Peter Verdonk, *How Can We Know the Dancer from the Dance: Some Literary Stylistic Studies of English Poetry,* Amsterdam: Amsterdam University Press, 1988, 107.

DISTANT VOICES:
THE VITALITY OF YEATS' DIALOGIC VERSE

MICHAEL BURKE

Introduction[1]

It was the literary theorist Mikhail Bakhtin who first conceived of the dialogic nature of literary discourse. In his theory he spoke of "orchestrations of voices", and coined such productive phrases as "polyphony" and "heteroglossia". The overriding weakness, however, in this otherwise enticing theory, was that it only applied to the prose form. Poetic discourse, in Bakhtin's view, was deemed single-layered, and hence unequivocally monologic in nature, and as such redundant to studies into the dialogic nature of literary language.[2] Until quite recently, both literary and literary-linguistic studies have tended to follow this line of argumentation and view the language of poetry as strictly monologic, characterized by a simple, single-layered discourse situation, involving a solitary voice, usually that of the poet. However, in view of the precarious nature of such an assertion this situation could not remain intact *ad infinitum*, and not too surprisingly a number of

---

[1]   As is appropriate for this collection, this chapter is a reworking of an old essay I once wrote for Peter Verdonk in his stylistics class, as an undergraduate student. I would like to thank Tony Bex, Olga Fischer and Simone Langley for their helpful comments regarding this revised version of that original text.

[2]   Mikhail Bakhtin, *The Dialogic Imagination: Four Essays* (ed. M. Holquist and translated by M. Holquist and C. Emerson), Austin: University of Texas Press, 1981. This contains translations of four of Bakhtin's essays from the 1930s which were collected and published after his death as *Questions of Literature and Aesthetics,* 1975: "Epic and Novel", "From the Prehistory of Novelistic Discourse", "Forms of Time and Chronotope in the Novel" and "Discourse in the novel". In fairness to Bakhtin it has been said that he grudgingly recanted his one-dimensional point of view towards the end of his life, and conceded that poetic discourse, in some cases, might also be considered dialogic.

contemporary stylistic scholars have recently seized on the manifest inaccuracies of Bakhtin's initial claim concerning poetry. The result of this has been the publication of several laudable studies. Two of these, which have been of influence to this particular study, are those by Widdowson and Semino. However, the study which has arguably been the greatest motivation for the writing of this one is that by Verdonk.[3] This work investigates a number of discoursal topics, including the spatial, temporal and interpersonal approaches to both context and deixis; the shifting identity of the poet's persona; and the egocentric nature of deixis. The assertion that poetry is dialogic may, I believe, benefit, in general, as a result of such additional stylistic analyses. It is therefore with the twin aims of extension and substantiation in mind that this paper shall focus on two poems from the rhetorically rich *oeuvre* of W.B. Yeats. It is this reader's conviction that this is appropriate ground in which finally to lay the ghost of the monologic nature of poetic discourse to rest. Indeed, with its melancholic tones and resplendent sonority, the poetry of W.B. Yeats appears ideally suited for an investigation into the true polyphonic nature of verse.

The two poems selected for analysis are "Leda and the Swan" (1923), taken from the collection *The Tower*, published in 1928, and the much earlier "The Song of Wandering Aengus" (1893) from the collection *The Wind Among the Reeds* (1899).[4] In addition to the reason given in footnote, the decision to employ these two particular poems has also been motivated by a number of somewhat practical criteria. The first of these concerns the actual physical time difference between

[3] Henry Widdowson, *Stylistics and the Teaching of Literature,* London: Longman, 1975; Elena Semino, "Deixis and the Dynamics of Poetic Voice", in Keith Green, ed. *New Essays in Deixis: Discourse, Narrative, Literature*, Amsterdam and Atlanta GA: Rodopi, 1995, 145-60; Peter Verdonk, "Poetry and Public Life: A Contextualized Reading of Seamus Heaney's 'Punishment'", in *Twentieth-Century Poetry: From Text to Context*, London: Routledge, 1993, 112-33.

[4] The decision to analyse "Leda and the Swan" was not an arbitrary one. It has been done to acknowledge Widdowson's immensely influential stylistic analysis (*op.cit.*, 7-13), which in turn shadowed a literary-linguistic investigation conducted by Michael Halliday, "Descriptive Linguistics in Literary Studies", in Angus McIntosh and M.A.K. Halliday, *Patterns of Language: Papers in General Descriptive and Applied Linguistics,* London: Longman, 1966, 67.

the writing of the two works, which allows one to observe elements of chronological consistency. A second is motivated by the similarity of the subject matter, inasmuch as both poems refer to mythical worlds, one Greek and one Celtic. A third is that one of these poems appears to be potentially dialogically "richer" than the other: an observation that shall be investigated in greater detail in the course of this study. However, before proceeding with these analyses it may be beneficial to take a brief look at the linguistic tool often referred to as *deixis*, which, together with the earlier mentioned Bakhtinian *dialogics*, will constitute the methodological mainstay of this paper.

Deixis: a brief overview

One of the many functions of deixis is to highlight the specific discourse role of the persona within a poem, and also any variations or alterations of a more multi-layered or complex nature which may occur in this aforementioned persona. On the subject of the shifting identity of the poet's persona Verdonk has spoken of "a sliding scale of correspondence" in the author/persona relationship, adding further that this can range from a position of almost total implausibility, to a distance that can be considered "practically negligible".[5] From a linguistic point of view, deixis has been defined by Wales as generally referring to "all of those features of language which orientate or 'anchor' our utterances in the context of proximity of space."[6] This involves such notions as "here and there", "this and that", and "now and then" relative to the speaker's viewpoint. In addition to this, Wales also stresses the importance of the multidimensional nature of discourse, and how it is heavily dependent on the situation or context. This position is further reiterated in Simpson's observation that deixis is

---

[5] Verdonk, *op.cit.*, 112-33. These convictions can, in fact, be traced to a previous article (Peter Verdonk, "Poems as Text and Discourse: The Poetics of Philip Larkin", in R.D. Sell, ed. *Literary Pragmatics*, London: Routledge, 1991, 94-109), and arguably even further back to Peter Verdonk's *How Can We Know the Dancer from the Dance? Some Literary Stylistic Studies of English Poetry*, Amsterdam: Amsterdam University Press, 1988.

[6] Katie Wales, *A Dictionary of Stylistics,* London: Longman, 1989, 112.

concerned with "orientational features of language, which function to locate utterances in relation to speakers' viewpoints."[7]

It is rightly claimed that deixis is not just semantic, but also pragmatic. Broadly speaking, it involves communication relying on the notions of co-operative, goal-directed action. What this basically means is that we appear to follow strategies in order to communicate messages, which will hopefully result in action. This is the case in everyday language where a speaker will anchor the discourse in his or her centre, which is sometimes referred to as the *origo*. This *origo* will be a kind of common frame of reference, so that both speaker and listener can start from the same point. For instance, when the definite article is employed by the speaker he or she assumes that the hearer is in possession of the facts of the conversation. This has the effect of creating a shared world of discourse understanding. However, it should be pointed out that the presence of a definite article is by no means always deictically anchored in the speaker's world. It can also be employed generically to reflect a universal truth or co-referentially, allowing it to be anaphorically anchored in the discourse world. Additionally, many deictic expressions may also be simultaneously both deictic and anaphoric. In a purely literary context, however, the effect that deixis is capable of producing is not something that is entirely unique. In previous theoretical approaches to poetry and prose it has been generally regarded as the alteration, or even manipulation, of viewpoint, and as such has thus been anchored firmly within the domain of narratology.

In the analysis that follows, I shall be concentrating on aspects of deixis similar to those highlighted in the aforementioned Semino article, which has served as an inspiration to inform this particular work. In doing so, I hope to succeed not only in supporting, but also enhancing her astute claim, based on Levinson that "poems do not necessarily project unique and stable voices located within fixed deictic contexts, but may involve variations of deictic centre."[8] It is fair to conclude that these deictic aspects are based on Green's six categories of deixis.

---

[7] Paul Simpson, *Language, Ideology and Point of View*, London: Routledge, 1993, 13.

[8] Semino, *op.cit.*, 145, after S. Levinson, *Pragmatics,* Cambridge: Cambridge University Press, 1983, 63-4.

Following Bex, I shall employ a number of these in my analysis. Unlike Bex, however, my application shall be, to a certain extent, implicit, and will be concentrating primarily on just two of these categories, namely, referential deixis (which includes articles and demonstrative pronouns) and *origo* deixis (which includes first and second person pronouns).[9]

Two examples of contextualized analysis

As previously stated, Yeats' work has been purposely selected for this dialogic investigation. However, despite the overriding theoretical nature of this study, the motivation for choosing these particular works for analysis was grounded in unashamed emotive involvement. This being the case, it would, I believe, be inappropriate to proceed without some mention being made of the fact. There can be little doubt that it is the presence of the mesmerizing symphony of melodious voices that one encounters flowing spontaneously from the page and into the deeper realms of our conscious and sub-conscious memories, which brings us time and time again back to the indescribable beauty which is the hallmark of much of Yeats' verse, and which can be intuitively described as enigmatic. Fascinating conundrums, however, invariably attract inquisitive minds, and as a result a theoretical attempt shall be made here to elucidate the dynamism of the poetic voice present within the two poems.

Leda and the Swan

A sudden blow: the great wings beating still
Above the staggering girl, her thighs caressed
By the dark webs, her nape caught in his bill,
He holds her helpless breast upon his breast.

---

[9] In addition to the two mentioned here, there are also four other categories of deixis that Green has suggested: "spatio-temporal deixis", "subjective deixis", "discourse deixis" and "syntactic deixis" (in Keith Green, "Deixis and the Poetic Persona", *Language and Literature*, 1/2 (1992), 121-34). See also Tony Bex, "Keats and the Disappearing Self: Aspects of Deixis in the Odes", in Keith Green, ed., *New Essays in Deixis: Discourse, Narrative, Literature*, Amsterdam and Atlanta GA: Rodopi, 1995, 161-78.

How can those terrified vague fingers push
The feathered glory from her loosening thighs?
And how can body, laid in that white rush,
But feel the strange heart beating where it lies?

A shudder in the loins engenders there
The broken wall, the burning roof and tower
And Agamemnon dead.

                    Being so caught up,
So mastered by the brute blood of the air,
Did she put on his knowledge with his power
Before the indifferent beak could let her drop?[10]

The theme of this sonnet has its roots firmly fixed in Greek mythology.
Zeus is said to have visited Leda in the form of a swan, and as a result
of the union, Leda gave birth to two daughters, Helen and
Clytaemnestra.[11] It has been suggested by one of Yeats' multitudinous
biographers that he may have got his inspiration for this poem from
seeing Michelangelo's painting of *Leda and the Swan*, which is to be
found hanging in a Venice museum.[12] Such an assertion corresponds to
a certain extent with Widdowson's study in which he asserts that the
discourse in the poem is indeed structured around the idea that Yeats is
describing either an actual picture which is physically before him, or
one whose content is clearly delineated in his mind.[13]

    If one were to take the poem at face value and adopt a traditional
monologic approach to the discourse situation, then it can be presumed

---

[10] W.B. Yeats,   *The Collected Poems of W.B. Yeats,* London: Macmillan (2nd
edition, 1950), 1933.

[11] In addition to the two daughters there were also two sons, Pollux and Castor
(also know as Dioscuri). These other siblings, however, are not of further interest
to this particular study.

[12] R. Ellmann, *The Identity of Yeats*, London: Macmillan, 1954.

[13] Widdowson, *op.cit.*

that the speaker is "merely" Yeats himself, at his rhetorical best. However, I am of the opinion that such a restricted perspective cannot possibly offer a satisfactory answer to account for the rich, multi-layered discourse complexity which is undoubtedly present in this poem. Hence, notwithstanding the simplicity of the rhetorical voice encountered in an initial reading, it will be argued here that there are most definitely subtle adjustments in the speaker's mode that are present in this work. Moreover, and more importantly, it shall be shown that the effect that is created by these inconsistent speakers has been motivated not simply by the action of an individual apprehending a painting, but rather by the irrefutable shifts in the deictic centre of the speaker.

In the opening quatrain the speaker appears to be in the process of giving an eye witness account of the assault and rape. This beholder, I believe, is male. This conviction is based on the corporeal memories of the onlooker, who only appears capable of recalling such body parts as "her thighs" and "breast". It is thus only these, essentially sexual, objects that have remained vivid in his mind while recounting the story. In addition, the verbs "caressed" and "holds", which are used to describe the act, seem totally inappropriate in such a context. This male-orientated argument is further strengthened by the fact that the female body-parts in the text are often positioned in the passive, while the (male) swan is often presented actively. These observations do, of course, by no means rule out a female onlooker, but in view of the above evidence it arguably seems less likely that this is the case. The nature of this eyewitness account immediately confronts the reader with the compelling line of argumentation that the speaker might be from antiquity. This automatically hampers any initial suggestion that the speaker might "simply" be Yeats himself. The actual answers to these questions are, however, far more complex than these preliminary musings might have one believe, as will be illustrated in the analysis that is to follow.

Upon closer inspection it appears that each of the four sections in this poem contains a different speaker, or, to be more specific, different transcendental "states" of a speaker. It can further be claimed that even within the sections themselves there are complex discourse situations present. This is in direct opposition to a number of recent claims on the subject matter of this poem. One such perspective concludes "that we must remember that the supposed point of view is Leda's."[14] In similar fashion, a second claim insists that "Yeats ... describes the rape from Leda's perspective."[15]   These points of view are to my mind too simplistic, and one might even venture infelicitous. The main motivation behind this contextualized stylistic investigation shall thus to be to highlight why I take this point of view.

It has already been suggested that the speaker in the first quatrain is quite probably a Greek male from the mythological world of distant antiquity, who is in the process of retelling his eyewitness account of the rape and assault. Yet the reiteration of an eyewitness account automatically, and quite logically, implies the presence of a listener or listeners. In view of this, it can be presumed that these addressees are primarily part of the text-world itself. This being the case, a scenario now becomes visible in which a solitary speaker is seen recanting his observations of the rape to people who are hurriedly arriving at the scene just moments after the event has taken place. This, as will become clear, is supported by the deictic elements in this quatrain.

It is often claimed that in order to attain maximum significance literary-linguistic analyses should begin at the very beginning, and not just where the main body of the text commences. It is with this in mind then that we immediately turn to the poem's title. The use of a proper noun "Leda" in conjunction with the definitive article "The" in "The Swan' has the effect of immediately drawing those individuals in the text-world into the shared-universe discourse situation.[16] This seems logical, because those individuals in the immediate vicinity of the rape would arguably know who Leda was, and also which god was capable of appearing in the guise of a swan. The reader, however, despite the apparent shared universe created by deictic elements such as the use of

---

[14] M.L. Rosenthal, *Running to Paradise: Yeats' Poetic Art*, New York and Oxford: Oxford University Press, 1994, 254.

[15] Clara Calvo and Jean-Jacques Weber, *The Literature Workbook,* London: Routledge, 1998, 47.

[16] In a similar fashion to Widdowson's analysis of "Leda and the Swan", mine will also pay close attention to both definite and indefinite articles. Indeed, it can be said that Widdowson's stylistic study was one of the first to show that articles can indeed be employed deictically in poetic discourse, rather than just being used anaphorically, cataphorically or homophorically.

proper nouns and definite articles, might initially be denied full access
to the poem as direct addressee. This, of course, may not always be the
case, as an individual reader may be in possession of a good working
knowledge of Greek mythology, and as a result might immediately be
capable of recognizing which mythological character was able to appear
in the guise of a swan. However, given the nature of modern
educational needs, it is perhaps more prudent to assume that, unlike the
poem's initial readers, many current-day ones may be excluded from
this knowledge. The shared universe among the scene's participants is
reinforced by a continuation in the use of the definite article. This can
be seen in the examples, "the great wings", "the staggering girl", "the
dark webs", etc. This phenomenon can also be observed in the use of
the possessive pronouns "her thighs", "her nape", "her helpless
breast", 'his breast", etc., which function both deictically and
anaphorically.

The temporal deixis in the first quatrain is also much more
complicated than it initially appears.[17] Despite the use of the present
participle "beating" and the present tense verb "holds", which could
imply a situation in which the persona's act of discourse is co-terminus
or contemporaneous with the scene described in the poem, it is most
improbable that this is, in fact, the case. The reason for this assumption
is that the events of an eyewitness account must by their very nature be
related to a third party after those said events have taken place. They
cannot be related co-terminously to the event itself. If this were to be
the case, then the discourse would basically be a live, running
commentary, akin to that of a football or rugby match that one might
hear on the radio. Although not totally improbable, such a scenario is
highly unlikely given the historical time and setting of the poem, not to
mention the unexpected nature of the attack itself.[18]

---

[17] The term "temporal" is employed here, and indeed throughout the body of this
text, to refer simply to "tense". It should not be confused with Green's category of
"spatio-temporal deixis".

[18] Although expressing a different perspective here, I believe that my line of
argumentation does not refute the validity of a popular current claim, which argues
that it is possible for reports to have a dual voicing. This allows the speaker to
move from a "historic" position to a present tense one, in order to convey the
immediacy of the events described. Such a perspective suggests that language is

By the end of the first quatrain though, a reader may quite feasibly still consider the speaking voice of this poem to be monologic. However, the drastic change at the onset of the second quatrain will mean that such a standpoint will have to be quickly discarded. The viewpoint now can no longer be considered a mere eyewitness account, because the "observations" relayed by the speaker are no longer purely visual, in an external sense, but seem now to be fundamentally of an inner nature. It therefore follows that, in view of this change in speaker, the addressee(s) in the discourse situation of the first quatrain can also no longer be the same one(s) as in the second. Stepping back from his freshly delivered oral account, it would seem that the previous speaker appears to have now descended into a deep reflective mode of being, in which his own consciousness has become both addresser and addressee. Evidence in support of this claim can be located in the text itself. The quatrain is made up of two main questions:

> How can those terrified vague fingers push
> The feathered glory from her loosening thighs?

and

> And how can body, laid in that white rush,
> But feel the strange heart beating where it lies?

Here one can observe a further ambivalent twist in the nature of normal face-to-face discourse exchange. As is the case with an imperative, a question usually involves a hearer/reader to whom it is being addressed. These particular questions though are of a deep rhetorical, self-reflective nature, and, as such, tend to exclude the presence of a second party. This claim is supported further by the repetition of the phrase "how can" in "how can those ... fingers push", and "how can body, ... feel". Here we see the speaker wrestling with himself in deep philosophic contemplation regarding the manifest horror of the act of rape. In fact, a marked shift in the speaking voice can be observed evolving here as the quatrain develops. This variation in the state of the

---

polyphonous in that it always includes "traces" of other voices and of other speakers.

speaker continues steadily along the cline of personae until the last line, where he quite literally "feels", together with Leda, "the strange heart beating where it lies". Once again though, as in the previous quatrain, there is perhaps a little disorientation. This time it is created by the use of the distal deictic of spatial proximity "those", which, despite the obvious spiritual coming together of experience that is taking place between victim and onlooker, endeavours to keep this developing emotional union from flourishing.[19]

The third section sees the speaker move even further along the aforementioned cline of personae. In this guise all traces of the eyewitness to this mythological molestation have been left behind, as we behold an all-knowing, all-powerful, omniscient quality taking hold of the speaker, as he rises seer-like to profess the impending death and destruction, which is to result from this amalgamation. As previously mentioned, there were two daughters that resulted from the unwanted union in the mythological story of Leda and the Swan. Helen, abducted by Paris, was the catalyst to the Trojan War and ultimately the destruction of Hector and his father's city of Ilium. Clytaemnestra was the wife of Agamemnon, the man who led the Greeks against the Trojans and who, upon his triumphant return, was to be murdered by her while bathing. So the vistas now "perceived" by the speaker of:

> The broken wall, the burning roof and tower
> And Agamemnon dead

are, in fact, future projections of violence that is to come as a result of the initial brutal act. The suggestion is thus that the callous rape and the moral destruction of Leda will ultimately lead to yet more death and destruction in the future. The event itself has been described by one of Yeats' biographers as "an annunciation of a historical cycle beginning in 2000 BC."[20] Such an observation implicitly alludes to a second

---

[19] The important role that deixis can play with regard to emotional distance and empathy has not gone unnoticed in contextualized approaches to language and literature studies, as can be observed in Levinson, *op.cit.*, 81. This phenomenon has also been referred to as "empathetic deixis" by John Lyons, *Semantics,* Vols. 1 and 2, Cambridge: Cambridge University Press, 1977, 677.

[20] F. Tuohy, *Yeats: An Illustrated Biography*, London: The Herbert Press, 1976, 186.

Annunciation: that involving the Virgin, which takes place some 2000 years after Leda's unrequested visitation. And if one were to continue this theme and in turn remain equidistant, then this cyclic notion of visitation brings one to our present year, 2000 AD. And one does not need reminding what sort of demonic beast Yeats envisaged "slouching toward Bethlehem" as a result of a third annunciation.[21]

The fourth and final section, like its three predecessors, once again experiences a shift in the discourse role. The two verbs in the opening sentence, "caught" and "mastered", are back-shifted. This contrasts quite distinctly with the present tense "engenders" in the previous section. This change in temporal deixis once more moves the deictic centre of the discourse situation, and shows how the speaker, even in these quite abstract rhetorical situations, can alter his role from that of a narrator of present events to one of past events. The poem ends with a rather profound question:

> Did she put on his knowledge with his power
> Before the indifferent beak could let her drop?

It is here, I believe, that the cline of (possible) speakers is at its closest yet to the essence of the poet himself. In this piece we are strongly drawn into the speaker's discourse world. This is achieved linguistically by the stability of a number of devices including the past tense, the proximal deixis of the definite articles, and the familiarity of the personal pronouns, which, although obviously anaphoric at this stage of the poem, could still have been replaced with their proper nouns by the poet, thus recreating deictic distance. A further feature of these last lines that also has the effect of pulling readers into the discourse situation of the poem itself is the use of the word "indifferent", which is employed to describe the swan's beak. In the case of this particular lexical item it can be suggested that only the poet himself, as speaker, would venture to use such an adjective in conjunction with this noun. The result of this near-personal juxtaposition is that it forces readers to

---

[21] In suggesting this I am touching on something that is widely acknowledged among most Yeats critics: that the two poems "Leda and the Swan" and "The Second Coming" produce a kind of mirror image.

open themselves up, in effect, coercing them to offer a personal response.

It can be thus concluded that in this particular poem it has been primarily the shifts in tense, together with the ambiguity of the shared discourse situation, and essentially the mutability of the speaker's position that have allowed meaningful evidence to be put forward, arguing a case for the true polyphonic nature of poetic discourse. In addition, it has been shown that although the predominant argument that the speaker is someone who is observing a painting is both valid and, to a large extent productive, it does perhaps become somewhat destabilized, and hence problematic, once the speaker has moved into a more internalized and therefore complex state of being. Fundamentally though, it can be argued that to presume that this poem is "merely" a Yeats monologue or that the speaker is a single constant voice, for instance that of Leda, as has been recently suggested by a number of scholars, would not only degrade the work itself, but would also impoverish the interactive, intellectual reading experience as a whole. However, although this appears to be the case in this poem, what is sauce for the goose may not necessarily be sauce for the gander. It is with this in mind that we now turn to our second text.

It can be ventured that the poem "The Song of Wandering Aengus", which centres on a Celtic god of love and his quest for his long lost sweetheart Edaine, seems to constitute the very embodiment of all of Yeats' phases of mysticism and symbolism. This impassioned pursuit, however, is not one that is predetermined to succeed. Rather it is one that is invariably fated to end in disappointment, as indeed the vast majority of amorous intentions in the real world also do. In the context of this theme Ellmann has suggested that Yeats himself claimed that whenever he was in love, it was not really his heart that was enraptured, but rather that of Aengus, who was engaged in his ineffectual quest for his cherished yet intangible Edaine.[22] There have though been other strongly differing critical views regarding the subject matter of this poem that cannot go unmentioned here. One such view is provided by Jeffries, who convincingly argues that the primary concerns of this poem are with nationalist desires that are expressed

---

[22] Ellmann, *op.cit.*, 313.

through the medium of Celtic mythology.[23] However, despite the
attractiveness of such a perspective I shall argue here that the
overriding theme is one of flagrant romanticism, rather than embittered
patriotism.

The Song of Wandering Aengus

I went out to the hazel wood,
Because a fire was in my head,
And cut and peeled a hazel wand,
And hooked a berry to a thread;
And when white moths were on the wing,
And moth-like stars were flickering out,
I dropped the berry in a stream
And caught a little silver trout.

When I had laid it on the floor
I went to blow the fire aflame,
But something rustled on the floor,
And some one called me by my name:
It had become a glimmering girl
With apple blossom in her hair
Who called me by my name and ran
And faded through the brightening air.

Though I am old with wandering
Through hollow lands and hilly lands,
I will find out where she has gone,
And kiss her lips and take her hands;
And walk among long dappled grass,
And pluck till time and times are done
The silver apples of the moon,
The golden apples of the sun.

---

[23] Lesley Jeffries, *The Language of Twentieth-Century Poetry,* London:
Macmillan, 1993, 9.

The employment of the definite article "The" in "The Song" together with the proper noun "Aengus" in the poem's title has a similar effect as in the first analysis, inasmuch as it appears to immediately draw the reader into the shared discourse world of the speaker, despite the fact that the actual nature of the object and the individual mentioned are, as yet, unknown to the reader. The title itself, coupled with this effect, gives the impression that the reader is about to be treated to a narrative, albeit a melodious one. From a psychological perspective this prepares us to hear a tale recounted by a single, steady, reliable narrator. It can be postulated that the proposed subject matter of "wandering" together with the notion of "song" may indeed suggest that this teller might very well be of Irish extraction. In addition, and in view of the ingrained nature of folk knowledge, Yeats himself, as an Irishman, would seem to be a clear candidate for this narrative role of imminent self-reflection. And indeed the expectations of the monologic reader would appear to be being met as the poem begins with a combination of the personal, rhetorical "I" form, and the past tense "went" (even though there may be a little confusion in the mind of the careful reader, because the third person noun in the title, Aengus, has suddenly been transformed into the first person singular, instead of the expected third person male singular). However, in spite of this slight discrepancy it is doubtful whether it will cause the reader to suspect the credibility of Yeats himself as the one "true" monologic voice, a conviction that is strengthened once the poem is in full flow.

The two opening stanzas, comprising of eight lines each, remain in the past tense with the use of numerous past participles and past tenses, e.g. "went", "peeled", "hooked", "dropped", "caught", "had laid", "rustled", "called", "had become", etc. The lack of temporal deictic shifts has the effect of reinforcing the belief that this particular text is but a rhetorical address from Yeats to his readers. This presumption is further supported by the lack of all too disturbing deictic variation. As is to be expected in coherent discourse, new entities are introduced in the text by the use of indefinite articles, and are thereafter tracked anaphorically for purposes of textual cohesion by the deployment of their definite counterparts. This can be seen in the example "a berry" / "the berry", etc. The one exception, however, to this discourse uniformity is the use of the definite article in "*the* hazel wood" in the opening line. This single instance though, it can be argued, is unlikely to cause too much disorientation in the reader. In addition, it is also apparent that Yeats has consciously chosen to use certain strong rhetorical figures. The most striking of these is the syndetic co-ordination in the opening stanza, "And cut ...," "And hooked ...", "And when ...", "And moth-like ...", which is employed to open successive lines. This highly rhetorical, highly emotive instance of syndeton has the effect of once more coaxing the reader into a frame of mind in which he or she accepts Yeats as the one true speaker. The plausibility of the claim is further supported by both the nature of the acts that are being described in the poem, together with the actual place and time, inasmuch as the text-worlds that are being referred to are feasibly realistic ... or so it would appear. This, one may recall, was not the case in the mythical lost worlds present in the previous poem. But despite the apparent harmony and equilibrium of the discourse situation, the voyager who has set sail on this particular poetic sea is headed for turbulent deictic waters, where the prospect of a safe and stable "anchorage" will be, at best, minimal.

The first line of the third and final stanza begins with the words "Though I am old with wandering". This will cause the engrossed reader to stop immediately in his or her tracks and contemplate the new discourse situation. Firstly, the temporal deixis has shifted from the past to the present tense, which will alone result in a shift in speaker. But this is re-enforced a hundred-fold by the extra-linguistic information at hand, namely, that the poem's speaker has been reflecting, but reflecting on the days of his youth from the perspective of his present state as an old man. The possibility now arises that the speaker may indeed be someone else, because at the time of the poem's actual conception Yeats was not at all elderly, but a young man in his twenties. Paradoxically then, it is the mythical aspect of this poem, initially rejected as erroneous, which now comes to the fore. This particular reader's perception of the text-world sees the aged Aengus encircled by inquisitive villagers. In this scenario, however, it is not only these spellbound fictional listeners who are the addressees of the poem, but also the individual readers who are drawn into the discourse by the persuasive desire to reach an emotive state of deep literary repose.

It is, however, only the opening two lines of the stanza that are in this present tense. Almost immediately the reader is confronted with yet another temporal shift in deixis as the tense changes to a future mode, and the reader is again forced to readjust his or her opinions concerning who is speaking. In the course of this future projection a linguistic mirror image is held up to the earlier discourse as we are again entreated to the syndetic trope of co-ordination in the sequence "And kiss", "And walk", "And pluck", which once again increases the rhetorical effect. But as the poem draws to a close the question must be posed as to whether or not this mythical nomadic speaker can still realistically be considered the persona behind the voice, or, in similar circumstances to the previous poem, has the voice now moved once more along the cline of personae, and is now at its closest yet to the essence of Yeats himself – where, in Verdonk's own words, the distance between author and speaker has become "practically negligible". Although compelling, the question as to whether or not this final mode of speaker represents a position close to the poet himself is perhaps not what is of primary interest here. What is, however, is that the wandering nature of the poem's protagonist is clearly reflected in the mirror image of the wandering quality of the speaking voice.

In sum, in the course of these two analyses it has been my intention to highlight the vitality of Yeats' dialogic verse, a polyphonic dynamism that I believe to be present in almost all poetry. In the first poem we saw that the discourse situation was unequivocally dialogic. In addition, we also saw that a strong case can be made against the prevailing yet problematic notion that the speaker is simply Leda. Further, this analysis also sought to question the, in many respects, still analytically constructive view that the deictic situation is a reflection of an individual either physically or mentally perceiving a painting. Likewise, in the second poem, we also saw that the discourse situation was profoundly dialogic. The shifts in speaker in this poem, however, were far less pronounced, and not as complex as those in the previous one (a situation, if we recall, which was anticipated at the outset of this literary-linguistic investigation). As a result, this second analysis may appear to be the weaker of the two. However, I would argue that this is not in fact the case, since what I have actually done here is to highlight an overtly rhetorical, and hence monologic, poem, and then with some success show that instead of it being principally monologic, as one might have presumed at the outset, it is in fact undeniably dialogic.

To conclude this discussion, it should be emphasized that these stylistic analyses were not merely textual, but unconditionally and unashamedly contextual, since stylistic approaches to prose and poetry that remain purely text-based may now, at the beginning the twenty-first century, be deemed both anachronistic and infelicitous. Throughout his academic life as a stylistician, Peter Verdonk has always advocated an interpretative approach that takes the reader on a personal journey *"From Text to Context"*. It is with hindsight then, that we may now reflect and state that we are not simply indebted to him for all the work that he has already done in the domain of contextualized stylistics, but also for the great inspiration he has been, and indeed continues to be, to younger stylisticians not too unlike myself, in encouraging them to test the boundaries of stylistic scholarship, and push the notion of context even further into the increasingly significant cerebral realms of cognition and emotion.

THE WOE THAT IS IN MARRIAGE

BOUWE POSTMUS

> But when the meaning assigned is too clearly formulated, then
> one reader who has grasped *a* meaning of a poem may happen
> to appreciate it less exactly, enjoy it less intensely, than another
> person who has the discretion not to inquire too insistently ....
> [O]ur impulse to interpret a work of art ... is exactly as
> imperative and fundamental as our impulse to interpret the
> universe by metaphysics.[1]

Patricia Coughlan in her influential essay, "'Bog Queens': The
Representation of Women in the Poetry of John Montague and Seamus
Heaney",[2] has argued convincingly that in his portrayal of women
Heaney not infrequently tends to subordinate the actuality of individual
women to a stereotypical ideal of femininity, thus turning them into
submissive, domesticated creatures. On the face of it the poet sets out to
celebrate certain traditionally feminine qualities, which on reflection
primarily seems to result in a severely limiting definition of women and
their roles. In her analysis of the representation of gender roles in
Heaney's work, Coughlan distinguishes two opposing and possibly
complementary representations of gender interaction. The poet either
tends to construct an "unequivocally dominant masculine figure, who
explores, describes, brings to pleasure and compassionates a passive
feminine one", or he "proposes a woman who dooms, destroys ... and
encompasses the man, but also assists him to his self-discovery: the

---

[1] T.S. Eliot, introduction, *The Wheel of Fire*, by G. Wilson Knight, 4th edition,
London: Methuen, 1972, xvi-xvii.

[2] Patricia Coughlan, "'Bog Queens': The Representation of Women in the Poetry
of John Montague and Seamus Heaney", in Toni O'Brien Johnson and David
Cairns, eds, *Gender in Irish Writing*, Milton Keynes: Open University Press, 1991,
89-111.

mother stereotype, intriguingly merged with the spouse."[3]

Other recent critics, like Seamus Deane[4] and Jonathan Allison,[5] have commented on the centrality of the marriage trope in Heaney's poetry. Deane points to Heaney's repeated attempts, in and through his art, to achieve the reconciliation of male power and female tenderness, in a ritual appeasement of their opposition. Allison, while admitting the central importance of the marriage metaphor, emphasizes how "it ceases to represent resolution and harmony. Instead, it represents unstable, anxious, and even forced union, and is associated with constriction and even destruction."[6]

In this paper, which attempts nothing more ambitious than clearly formulating *a* reading of Heaney's early poem "The Wife's Tale",[7] I should like to demonstrate the relevance of both Coughlan's and Allison's approaches to my interpretation of this early poem, which provides such a typical instance of marital anxiety, instability and lack of mutual understanding.

In the wake of the feminist revolution of the last quarter-century a great many sociologists and poets have of late concentrated their efforts on an analysis of the effects of gender on the social behaviour of men and women. The role of marriage in particular, and the roles of marriage-partners have come in for so much critical and imaginative scrutiny by so many contemporary thinkers and poets, laymen and specialists alike, that the fact that the institution of marriage was critically examined as early as the fourteenth century by the poet Chaucer in his *Canterbury Tales*[8]

---

[3] *Ibid.*, 99.

[4] Seamus Deane, "Seamus Heaney: The Timorous and the Bold", in *Celtic Revivals*, London: Faber, 1985, 174-86.

[5] Jonathan Allison, "Acts of Union: Seamus Heaney's Tropes of Sex and Marriage", in *Eire-Ireland*, 27/4 (1992), 106-21.

[6] *Ibid.*, 106.

[7] Seamus Heaney, *Door into the Dark,* London: Faber and Faber, 1969, 27-8.

[8] *The Complete Works of Geoffrey Chaucer*, ed., F. N. Robinson, 2nd edition, London: Oxford University Press, 1957, 1-265.

and by innumerable other poets and novelists in later centuries, tends to be unduly ignored and forgotten.

In fact, Chaucer's "The Wife of Bath's Prologue and Tale"[9] seems to be the very source and inspiration of two major modern poets, one American, the other Irish. Both Robert Lowell's "To Speak of Woe That Is in Marriage",[10] and Seamus Heaney's "The Wife's Tale" are clearly indebted to Chaucer's poem, and it may be interesting and instructive to dwell on some of the ways in which Heaney modifies and redefines the views on marriage articulated by the Wife of Bath.

If we assume that Heaney's title is an allusion to Chaucer's "The Wife of Bath's Tale", it may be helpful to refer briefly to the thematic focus of that tale. It was argued by G.L. Kittredge in his influential article "Chaucer's Discussion of Marriage",[11] that it belongs to a fairly close sequence of stories in *The Canterbury Tales* which deal in one way or another with the problem of marriage.

The American critic R.E. Kaske, following in Kittredge's footsteps, states that "the Marriage Group is organized thematically around a pair of intimately and complexly related questions: first, the question of which partner should rule, and second, the problem of the role of sex itself in marriage."[12] The Wife of Bath in her "Prologue and Tale" bluntly expresses her views on these subjects. She is openly impatient of the idea that virginity is to be preferred by all to matrimony. Her theory, confirmed by practice (she has had five husbands already!) is that happiness in marriage depends on the acceptance of the wife's mastery, and the story she tells of the knight who is guilty of rape and the loathly lady is meant to illustrate and enforce this view. Ironically, the Wife of Bath opens the prologue to her tale with these words:

> Experience, though noon auctoritee
> Were in this world, is ryght ynogh for me
> To speke of wo that is in mariage. (ll. 1-3)

---

[9] *Ibid.*, 76-88.

[10] Robert Lowell, *Life Studies* and *For the Union Dead,* New York: The Noonday Press, 1969, 88.

[11] G. L. Kittredge, "Chaucer's Discussion of Marriage", *Modern Philology*, 9 (1912), 435-67.

[12] R. E. Kaske, "Chaucer's Marriage Group", in Jerome Mitchell and William Provost, eds, *Chaucer the Love Poet*, Athens, Ohio, 1973, 45-65.

Ironically, because it transpires from her frank and revealing prologue that it was her husbands rather than herself who suffered their unmitigated share of woes and hardships in marriage. Nevertheless, it is clear that the Wife of Bath's message could by no means be considered representative of the medieval notions of marriage, which entailed submission to the point of serfdom on the part of the wife.

Lowell, in his "To Speak of Woe That Is in Marriage" from the collection *Life Studies*[13] demonstrates by dire example that the radical inequality between partners in marriage in the majority of cases has persisted until quite recently. The wife in Lowell's dramatic monologue is unlike the Wife of Bath in that she obviously does not have mastery over her husband and it is the injustice which results from their inequality, which lies at the heart of her complaint.

It is all very well for the Wife of Bath in her Tale to ask the question, "What thyng is it that wommen moost desiren"? (l. 905) and to provide the answer herself with

> Wommen desiren to have sovereynetee
> As wel over hir housbond as hir love
> (ll. 1038-9)

yet we can only begin to make sense of her answer if we realize that women in many centuries to come were not unwise enough to express this and similar sentiments openly, for fear of an intensification of their habitual suffering and repression, if not worse.

But how does all this bear upon Heaney's "The Wife's Tale"? In this poem, which to all intents and purposes answers to the conventions of the dramatic monologue − as it is told in first-person narration, at a dramatic moment in the speaker's life − the speaker, a farmer's wife, describes a particular event to a silent listener (perhaps another equally articulate, suppressed farmer's wife of her own age?), in the process revealing a great deal about herself.

From the opening lines on, the wife's world and her role in it are compared and contrasted with her husband's, or rather that of the men he is working with. The essential opposition is that of the lonely wife and the men as members of a group. The men seem to live in a world of their own, entirely different from the wife's, who is unable to cross the border

---

[13] Lowell, *op.cit.*, 88.

which separates their respective "countries". Her feelings are
ambivalent, because her desire to enter the men's world and to share
their sense of belonging and contentment is vying with a proud
conviction of her "otherness", which makes her entry into the world of
the men impossible, as it involves the betrayal and sacrifice of the very
feminine qualities that she is clinging to. Although much of the wife's
frustration and silent anger is blamed on the husband's insensitivity, it is
arguable that the blame is attached to him as a representative of the male
world rather than as an individual in his own right.

The wife's monologue centres on an event that apparently recurs
every year at harvest time. During a break for lunch, which she has
prepared and set out on a linen cloth in a corner of the field, she is asked
by her husband to inspect the quality of the newly-threshed corn. While
the farmer and his hands enjoy "the thick slices" (l. 15) as they like
them, she leaves them for this yearly ritual, which is beyond her
comprehension, yet for her unconsciously epitomizes and symbolizes her
husband's unthinking assertion of his "sovereynetee" or domination.

Through the poet's effective and careful selection of elements
referring to, and at the same time characteristic of, his wife's world, the
reader comes to realize the personality of the speaker. She stands
revealed as a woman who cares for neatness and cleanliness (cp. the
white, linen cloth, which she folds carefully before returning to the
farm); who is concerned with the proper way of doing things; who is
relieved when the awful noise of the thresher stops and there is a return
of rural peace and quiet; but above all she reveals herself as someone
who is completely out of her depth in this world of male companionship
and solidarity, its sweaty toil and its "grateful ease" (ll. 34-5). Her most
significant and revealing action is one of withdrawal: "And [I] went" (l.
34). Her exclusion from a world where fellowship and relaxation seem to
be male prerogatives is clearly one of the central insights that the poem
communicates. If the wife is seen as a prim, house-proud and lonely
woman, her husband and the men who help him bring in the harvest are
presented as inhabitants of an entirely alien world. The word
"unbuttoned" (l. 35) evokes an image of a carefree, informal enjoyment
of life and one wonders, apropos of the undoing of buttons, whether the
possible sexual incompatibility of the farmer and his wife may here be
hinted at as well. Their life-styles, after all, appear so diametrically
opposed: the one free, easy, and "unbuttoned", the other prim and
repressed.

The tone of disapproval that is evident in "the thick slices that he likes" (l. 15) is another indication of the wife's fastidiousness: she herself would not dream of compromising her sense of what is fit and what is not by eating thick-sliced sandwiches. Her lady-like preference is for the thin-sliced kind, and her concern for civilized and proper eating habits is expressed once more by the tone of dismissive contempt when she says of the men that "they lay in the ring of their own crusts and dregs" (l. 27).

Although the wife's view of her husband and his helpers as a bunch of uncivilized yobs, whose interests she could never share, let alone understand, may be regarded as sufficient ground for her feelings of disenchantment and alienation, one feels that a deeper, more hidden motive for her barely controlled anger and frustration may be discovered through a further analysis of a clearly related set of images, all of which in one way or another reflect an unmistakable sense of violence and conflict.

To begin with, in the opening section of the poem (ll. 1-7) a central place is occupied by the description of the threshing-machine in terms of a gigantic, straw-devouring monster, whose coarse feeding habits − its "humming and gulping" (l. 3) − anticipate the primitive eating habits of the men. We are meant to see how closely related the men as tool-using "animals" are to the thresher, a product of advanced technology, which seems to have been primarily designed as an extension of and aid to male aggression. The notion of a violent struggle is perhaps most explicitly present in the third part of the poem (ll. 20-26): the various denotative and connotative meanings of "hooked", "shot", "gaped" (cp. gaping wounds), "drum" and "fork", culminating in the crucial line 25: "As javelins might mark lost battlefields", all either overtly or covertly point to an almost obsessive perception of the harvest scene in terms of battle and war, ending in defeat. The wife's point of view is all the more effectively communicated because it clashes with the evident ease of the peaceful ring of men resting from their labours. We realize that in the course of their confrontation her unease (or should we say *dis*ease?) becomes increasingly unbearable, as her husband and his "fellows" do not even begin to suspect it, remaining blissfully unaware of it, safely ensconced as they are in a world of their own.

At this point the importance and centrality of the word "lost" in line 25 deserves to be commented upon further. Initially, we may feel at a loss to account for it; after all, what could be more like a celebration of victory than bringing a harvest home? Surely, that battle has been safely won by the farmer and his men? Notice how at the end of the poem the men are in complete possession of the field and how the poet has emphasized their gratified sense of victory through the only instance in the entire poem of full, masculine rhyme in the final couplet. Yet, in the most literal sense the field is lost. "The field of gazing grain", of abundant natural growth, has been brutally attacked and raped by the combined force of man and machine.

The farmer's wife, in her (conscious?) identification with the world of fertility, growth and procreation, does not only shrink away from the maltreatment of the corn, but equally from the maltreatment and neglect she herself suffers, and to which she instinctively feels to be related. Her natural sympathy for the fallen ears of corn, threshed by the joint efforts of the men and the machine, is directly linked to her own lifelong suppression and subjection for which there is no obvious or immediate remedy. Her husband's insensitivity, the poem implies, is not so much the product of individual injustice as of time-honoured social conditioning.

It must be the wife's despair at ever remedying her own condition that makes for the tone of crushed resignation, so characteristic of this unspoken complaint. In a world governed by tradition (it would be hard to find a world more traditional and conservative than that of an Irish farming community) it would indeed seem likely for the wife's woeful lament to go unnoticed, and, as such, hers is the voice of one crying in the wilderness. That the poet should have chosen the dramatic monologue as the vehicle for the wife's lament is quite appropriate, as it emphasizes the radical isolation of the woman in a man's world. Apparently, her isolation is such that she feels she could not even share her feelings with her female friends and fellow-sufferers, and therefore the best she can do is to give vent to her emotions in this silent monologue.

Traditionally the state, law, morality, religion and the sciences have been the creation and prerogatives of men. Similarly, the duties of providing for the family, including the growing of food and harvesting, have in the western world largely been the province of man. Based on these facts, it is not surprising therefore that until quite recently the inferiority of women was taken for granted. The wife's unsuccessful attempts to break through her husband's smug sense of superiority and her inability to enter the magic circle of self-satisfied maleness, illustrate, in their own telling way, that to a large extent our own civilization is a masculine bastion from which women are still effectively barred.

"The Wife's Tale" is the story of a woman who has adapted herself for too long to her husband's wishes:

> Always this inspection has to be made
> Even when I don't know what to look for
>   (ll. 18-19).

Consequently she finds it almost impossible and certainly very painful to ignore her rebellious instincts, since giving in to them would not only gain her the freedom and independence she has been pining for all her married life, but it would simultaneously involve the surrender of an identity based, for longer than she cares to remember, on being and doing what her husband decides and desires.

On the other hand, the poem records a dramatic and critical moment in the wife's life, as she appears on the verge of an unprecedented act of rebellion and the shedding of her yoke. The husband's apparent unawareness of his wife's plight may at least be partly understood by bearing in mind that historically the relation of the sexes may be crudely defined as that of master and slave. In these circumstances it is one of the privileges of the master to take his mastery for granted, while the position of the slave is such that (s)he can never forget it. Acting from a position of (as yet) undisputed male supremacy, the husband can afford not to think of it, thus remaining oblivious of his wife's bondage.

Finally, the wife's identification with the process of natural growth, as emblematized by the growing wheat, is probably based upon her capacity for motherhood, a quite indisputable and uniquely female function. In a way, she is a (re)incarnation of the classical goddess Demeter/Ceres, who protected the fruitfulness of the soil and all the stages the corn passes through from the moment it is sown. She presided over the harvest and all the agricultural labours which attend it. In this context it is interesting that in classical mythology Demeter should also frequently be depicted in her capacity of the goddess of marriage. Would it be too fanciful then, in view of this identification, to read "The Wife's Tale" as the lament of a displaced goddess, who yearns for the worship she was once entitled and accustomed to, and who is outraged by the behaviour of those very males who once were her worshippers, but who have since usurped her divine rights by turning themselves into gods with the aid of technological power? At any rate, the wife's vehement and explicit denunciation of her husband's pride in line 29 — "as proud as if he were the land itself" — is probably best understood if we realize that the husband's brutal invasion and occupation of the harvest field is felt by her to be not just a violation of the soil's essential female identity (and by extension of her own), but at the same time as an utterly unacceptable usurpation of this identity by her husband.

In the last four lines the poet, through a careful manipulation of the possibilities inherent in the basically decasyllabic line, succeeds in emphasizing the wife's isolation. Through the brief but distinct pause after "cloth" at the end of line 34 he hints at the briefest of hesitations, before the aggrieved wife finally makes up her mind to withdraw into her own world, after another unsuccessful foray into the domain of her husband and his men. The two strong caesurae in the next line (1. 35), the first after the decisive "went" and the second at the end of the line, more than make up for the shortage of two syllables. The men's expansive feeling of ease is reinforced by the emphatic pauses and the strong stresses on "they", "still" and "ease". And finally, there is the wonderfully effective and exceptional use (there is no other instance of rhyme in the whole poem) of full rhyme in the last two lines, which not only establishes a vital harmony between the men and their natural environment, but also suggestively seems to claim a connection between the wife's unease (or *dis*ease) and her habitual expulsion from the annual harvest scene.

One way of summarizing the events of this lunch break is to say that the husband's satisfaction about a job well done is at least partially derived from looking upon it as (another) proof of his virility and, consequently, that the wife's existential unease may be the result of the men's failure to appreciate her efforts and her needs, which amounts to the rape of her personality. Chaucer's Wife of Bath may have been close to the truth in claiming that in and out of marriage women desire above anything else to have mastery over their husbands and lovers. Heaney's Wife, however, demonstrates that it is virtually impossible to achieve that mastery in the sort of society that does not take kindly to experiments with the roles of men and women as they have been prescribed by tradition. In closely-knit agricultural communities (but the phenomenon is by no means restricted to these localities) the efforts of wives to assert their individuality and independence would therefore seem to be doomed from the start to turn into tales of the woe that is in marriage.

WHAT WAS JOHN DONNE HEARING?
A STUDY IN SOUND SENSE

E. M. KNOTTENBELT

Even after the Romantics had discovered the lyrical poet in John Donne, the rhythm of his poetry has been a point for debate amongst his readers. In most cases, his "not keeping of accent", for which Jonson said Donne should be hanged, has been seen to be commensurate with an abstruseness in thought.[1] Thus, in contrast to Marvell's "smooth song", Izaak Walton used the term "strong lines" (Donne's being "much better than the strong lines that are now in fashion in this critical age"), and quoted another contemporary on the *Anniversaries:*

> Indeed so farre above its Reader, good,
> That wee are thought wits, when 'tis understood.

Dryden focussed on the *Satires* and did not use the term "strong lines"; but he recognized the traits, which denoted metaphysical puzzles: "rough cadence" and "deep thoughts". Samuel Johnson, who based his criticism on poetry as an "imitative art", also thought that the shortcomings of the Metaphysicals pertained to both style and content: "they neither copied nature nor life; neither painted the forms of matter, nor represented the operations of intellect."[2]

What was Donne hearing, that his poetry should have appeared to

---

[1] "That Done's Anniversarie was profane and full of blasphemies: that he told Mr. Done, if it had been of the Virgin Marie it had been something. That Done, for not keeping of accent, deserved hanging", in William Drummond of Hawthornden, *Notes of Ben Jonson's Conversations with William Drummond of Hawthorden* (ed. F. Patterson), London: Blackie, 1923, 3.

[2] See George Williamson, *A Reader's Guide to the Metaphysical Poets: John Donne, George Herbert, Richard Crashaw, Abraham Cowley, Henry Vaughan, Andrew Marvell*, London: Thames and Hudson, 1968, 5-7.

diverge markedly in both matters of style and content from that of his contemporaries? It has nonetheless proven to be attractive enough for imitation, not only in his century but also in the first half of our own.[3] To be sure, Donne was experimenting; experimentation was *de rigueur*, but uniformity was being sought after especially in versification. Thus Wyatt's earlier metre, though often still tending toward the old Teutonic four-stress line, contains the five-stress number of syllables. Similarly, although Surrey's verse, as in his poulter's measure, occasionally approximates medieval forms, he aims at writing a regular line with Puttenham's corrective instructions in mind, those of Drummond of Hawthornden or of Gascoigne. As Nethercot has noted, "English poetry was still in its childhood, precocious as that childhood was, and the desire to direct and stabilize it by experiment was manifest everywhere."[4]

Not so with Donne. As Walton saw, following Carew who called Donne his "master" for drawing "a line of masculine expression", Donne's experimentation differed essentially from that of his contemporaries precisely because it was not restricted to matters of prosody and certainly not if this meant toeing the line for its own sake. We need only recall Donne's frequent worrying over the tyranny of "opinion" and "fashion".[5] But, if Donne's experimentation was of two

---

[3] See John T. Shawcross, "The Case of Donne" and Heather Dubrow, "Tradition and the Individualistic Talent" in *The Eagle and the Dove: Reassessing John Donne*, ed. Claude J. Summers and Ted-Larry Pebworth, *Essays in Seventeenth-Century Literature*, 1, Columbia: University of Missouri Press, 1986; Rosalie Colie, *The Resources of Kind: Genre-Theory in the Renaissance*, Berkeley: University of California Press, 1973. See also Louis I. Bredvold who, in his attempts to answer this question, gives an overview of others who have attempted to do the same: "The Naturalism of Donne in Relation to Some Renaissance Traditions", *Journal for English and German Philology*, 22 (1923), 193-232, and "The Religious Thought of Donne in Relation to Medieval and Later Traditions" (repr. *Studies in Shakespeare, Milton and Donne*, 1923/24, 193-232). See also T.S. Eliot, *The Varieties of Metaphysical Poetry*, London: Faber and Faber, 1993.

[4] A.H. Nethercot, "The Reputation of John Donne as a Metrist", *Sewanee Review*, 30 (1922), 470.

[5] Donne rebukes those who depend on what "are ordinarily received and accepted for truths: so that the end of knowledge is not truth, but opinion, and the way, not inquisition, but ease", in *Sermons* (ed. George R. Potter and Evelyn Simpson), Berkeley: University of California Press, 1953-62, 22. Compare this with his concern about the arbitrariness of "opinion" in matters that involve the individual

kinds, one of material, the other of style and versification, then the "rug-gedness", whether against the grain of current needs and opinions in taste or not, was more directly an intimation of the thought he had to convey. Donne's anticipation of his critics, since he spoke of his "harsh verse" and the "lame measure" of his "coarse lines" in various cases, suggests his awareness of this: it was not so much that he was hearing what others were not hearing as that he was not thinking with only half an ear. Coleridge, acutely sensitive to the discontinuities within the self and the individual's sense of his own moment within the continuity of history, understood it thus:

> To read Dryden, Pope, &c., you need only count syllables but to read Donne you must measure the time, and discover the time of each word by the sense of the passion .... In poems where the writer thinks, and expects the reader to do so, the sense must be understood to understand the metre.[6]

Donne presents his reader with a sounding of thought, with thought under the pressure of being thought out and felt through. The pressure, disruptive, smooth, or otherwise, is the movement of thought. If we are to make sense of the thought, we must listen to it in its inimitable, often conflicting, moments of pressure. "For God's sake, hold your tongue, and let me love." To read this as a straight iambic line is not to have heard the possibly less even, idiocentric, stresses of the living, colloquial, voice, the pitch of the speaker's voice asserting itself, through the assonantal stresses, at the height of desire frustrated by impatience: all the arguments in the world are not going to mitigate the strongly-felt desire to make love with the possibility of doing so there and then. The sense of immediacy in these lines is indisputable. The following lines, with the play on the three different possessive pronouns, also show the speaker's determination to be heard on *his* terms:

---

conscience as in *Biathanatos* (ed. Ernest W. Sullivan), London: University of Delaware Press, 1984, 69: "Controuerters often say on both sides, This is your Common opinion; And certaynely that is the common opinion in one Age which is not in another, though both be Catholique."

[6] "*Coleridgiana II*", *Literary World*, 12 (April 30, 1853), 349-50. See also Pierre Legouis, *Donne the Craftsman*, Paris: Henri Didier, 1928 (repr. New York, 1962); M.F. Moloney, "Donne's Metrical Practice", *PMLA*, 65 (1950), 232-9.

.... Or chide my palsy, or my gout,
My five gray hairs, or ruined fortune flout,
With wealth your state, your mind with arts improve,
Take you a course, get you a place,
Observe his honor, or his grace,
Or the king's real, or his stamped foot
Contemplate; what you will, approve,
So you will let me love.

The punctuated urgency of the speaker's condition is revealed,
technically, in the meted rhythm, in the trochaic inversions, in how the
feet and the individual syllables resist elision. In contrast, there is none of
that resistance to elision in lines by Gascoigne, which, however urgent
and close to natural spoken speech, are without question iambic:

For God's sake let us sit upon the ground
And tell sad stories of the death of Kings.

There is no such predictability in Donne, or if there is, then this is
because, as Dryden, Johnson and others have noted, the thought in its
movement is often argumentative: it follows the logic, which is often
unpredictable, of the argument. Only a tone-deafness, synonymous with
not having understood the pressure of a thought, will consistently read
iambic measures into a five-footed line, especially in the fifth foot, which
is rather a trochaic inversion (and which, notably in the *Satires*, is more
usually preceded by a stress-shift in the third or fourth foot).[7] In "Breake
of day", for instance, the mistress' quarrel with her lover is that he
behaves as if their love and love-making are the same as the business of
anything else:

Must businesse thee from hence remove?
Oh, that's the worst disease of love,
The poore, the foule, the false, love can
Admit, but not the busied man.

(ll. 13-16)

---

[7] On Donne's metre, see Arnold Stein's extensive studies, "Donne and the
Couplet", *PMLA*, 57 (1942), 676-96; "Donne's Prosody", *PMLA*, 59 (1944), 373-
97; "Meter and Meaning in Donne's Verse", *Sewanee Review*, 52 (1944), 289-301.

She laments her lover's deafness to the out-of-the-ordinary rhythms of their being together. She argues that love has no truck with time; it should be valued differently, because, unlike anything else, it has its own peculiar measure. This is conveyed in the play on "love" through repetition and in the disruption of the regular iambic metre in the stress on "love" and not on "can", so that, as is encouraged by the enjambment, the negative in the following line gains in emphasis. It is normally the case in Donne that a line can be read iambically − the iamb is closest to the rhythms of natural spoken speech in English. But it is often better if it is not; according to the sense of the argument, line 15 asks to be read with the trochaic inversion. The specifics of meaning reside in the rhythm. The rhythm is as important as the words, because the rhythm can change the actual meanings of the words. That, more often than not and certainly in contrast to the bulk of contemporary poetry, Donne's poems are not just conversations or dialogues but more markedly instances of colloquial speech, also bears witness to this same idea that attention has noticeably been paid to the implications of a thought in terms of how it sounds.[8] This sensitivity to the movement of thought in terms of what is being said and how the poet imagines the listener makes sense of what he is hearing also occurs in the rhythm of Donne's prose, early, middle or late. Consider these famous lines from the *Devotions*:

> No Man is an *Iland*, intire of it selfe; every man is a peece of the Continent, a part of the *maine*; if a *Clod* bee washed away by the *Sea*, *Europe* is the lesse, as well as if a *Manor* of thy *friends* or of *thine owne* were; any mans *death* diminishes *me*, because I am involved in *Mankinde*; And therefore never send to know for whom the *bell tolls*; It tolls for *thee* ("Meditation XVII").

Here the rhythm in its slow quiet gathering force is so obviously the sense of the thought, also aurally, that one need comment no further.

In or out of stride, for Donne could write a "smooth" line as well as anybody else, a thought or an idea is what it means through its movement within and across a verse line. Questions of metre are questions of sound sense, of thought sounded out by the always fluctuating rhythms of experience. A mind in the throes of thinking and feeling through what it

---

[8] For Donne and "the talking voice", see F.R. Leavis, *Revaluations*, London: Chatto & Windus, 1936, 18.

"knows" on the pulses is recorded; as well as the thrill of having found the right phrase, the musing at the intensity, the cynicism or doubt as to whether what is being felt is ratified truth. All are the upshot of a critical mind listening to itself with an inner ear which is simultaneously turned outward. Hence, according to the rules of prosody, Donne's tendency to be out of bounds, to work a line to breaking point.

Effective in Donne's rhythm is not only how a mind thinks but also *his* and no-one else's thought. Questions of rhythm are questions of thought, in the most particularized and exacting sense. It is the poet's knowledge, his truth, that we are discovering as he is in the throes of discovering it himself. In the case of Donne we are always aware of a thought, thought itself, undergone by the poet's sense of who he is and of what he is capable. A search for knowledge is a search for truth, which, only to be arrived at through experience, must of necessity be bound up with ascertaining what is perplexedly true and false within the experiencing self. It is a process of authenticating.[9] Indeed, the vexed rhythms − the stress-shifts in the middle of an iambic line through the repetition or association of words, the falling metre of a trochaic inversion rather than the rising metre of an iambic foot at the end of a line − these formal aspects of the verse, typical of a Donne poem,[10] are Donne exacerbating his thought into truthfulness:

> Gracchus loves all as one, and thinks so
> As women do in diverse countries go
> In divers habits, yet are still one kind,
> So doth, so is Religion; and this blind-
> ness too much light breeds; but unmoved thou
> Of force must one, and forced but one allow;
> And the right; ask thy father which is she,
> Let him ask his, though truth and falsehood be
> Near twins, yet truth a little elder is;
> Be busy to seek her, believe me this,
> He's not of none, nor worst, that seeks the best.
> To adore, or scorn an image, or protest,

---

[9] See Anne Ferry, *The "Inward" Language: Sonnets of Wyatt, Sidney, Shakespeare, Donne*, Chicago: University of Chicago Press, 1983; and Stephen Greenblatt, *Renaissance Self-Fashioning*, Chicago: University of Chicago Press, 1980.

[10] See Stein, *op.cit.*

> May all be bad; doubt wisely; in strange way
> To stand inquiring right is not to stray;
> To sleep, or run wrong is. On a huge hill,
> Cragged and steep, Truth stands, and he that will
> Reach her, about must, and about must go;
> And what the hill's suddenness resists, win so;
> Yet strive so, that before age, death's twilight,
> Thy soul rest, for none can work in that night.

(ll. 65-85)

These often quoted lines from the third *Satire*, written between 1603 and 1607, lack any reference to the senses; and the choice of imagery is as abstract as the truth that is being conveyed. Yet, in keeping with the shocks and about-turns of the rhythm, Donne's thought, as much as an abstract idea, indeed Truth itself, is nonetheless as concrete, physically, as the body or living matter. For Donne real thinking is in the first place a physical process:

> wee understood
> Her by her sight; her pure and eloquent blood
> Spoke in her cheekes, and so distinctly wrought,
> That one might also say, her body thought.

(Second Anniversarie, ll. 243-6)

Similarly, the union or separation of lovers, friends, is understood physically. In short, words are physical things. Pre-empting Bacon in his attack on "contentious learning" or on the "delicate learning" of the humanists (which leans "rather towards copie than weight" and is rather a study of words and not of matter), Donne's words are etymologically rooted and weighed-down paradigms of thought because thought, as experience, is no less weighed down by the specific gravity of human nature. Another example is the early *Progresse of the Soul* (1601), where, as Milgate has observed, the use of imagery, of the moon, like the commonplace bits of history or references to wearisomely familiar material (*Genesis*), are wrested out of the orthodox groove. If the gulf between human pretensions and practice is thus revealed, this is because words are plumbed for their sinister, ironic, or grotesque implications.[11]

---

[11] W. Milgate, ed., *The Satires, Epigrams and Verse Letters*, Oxford: Oxford University Press, 1967, 7. See also John R. Lauritsen, "Donne's *Satyres*: The Drama of Self-Discovery", *Studies in English Literature*, 16 (1976), 117-30; Arnold Stein, "Donne and the Satiric Spirit", *JELH*, 11 (1944), 266-82.

What counts for the unsettled quality of both Donne's rhythm and thought is also manifest in the unsettling connotations of words, in Donne's appreciation of them as paradigms of the criss-cross nature of the human individual in the midst of life. Donne says in a letter of 1613:

> Except demonstrations, that is, mathematical proofs, (and perchance there are very few of them) I find nothing without perplexities. I am grown more sensible of it by busying myself a little in the search of the eastern tongues, where a perplexity in the words cannot choose but cast a perplexity upon the things. Even the least of our actions taste thereof.[12]

It is here, I think, that Donne differs most from his contemporaries and imitators. In contrast to Spenser, Sidney, Jonson, Herbert, or Marvell, Donne reacts radically not only on the intuitive but also on the conceptual level. His intellectual cast of mind and passionate temperament, as well as his recusant Catholic background and scholastic training, would be part of this, in the same way that the accidents of temperament and circumstance affect the subject matter and style of any writer and of what he is capable. As others like Bredvold and Bald have noted, and as has been outlined above, here lies all the difference between Donne's "strong lines" and the smooth cadence of a pastoral poet such as Spenser, the mellifluousness of Sidney's verse in which classical mythology and allegory stand central or the obvious lack of pressure in a poem by Carew, Davenant, Cowley.[13] Donne does not present an idea, but the self's experience in the act of thinking. He shows how and where an idea, when thought and felt through experientially, does or does not qualify as sound thinking. It is the soundness or unsoundness of thought in an experience of it through all its circumstantially unsettling pressures, right down to an intuitive, more essentially rooted level, that is being conceptualized:

---

[12] Edmund Gosse, *Lives and Letters of John Donne*, *Volume 2*, London: W. Heinemann, 1899, 16.

[13] See also Morris W. Croll, "The Baroque Style in Prose", *Style, Rhetoric and Rhythm*, Princeton: Princeton University Press, 1966, 207ff, where he describes the characteristics of the baroque (the Anti-Ciceronian, "modern" or "new") style as "not peace but energy."

> And freely men confess that this world's spent,
> When in the planets and the firmament
> They seek so many new; they see that this
> Is crumbled out again to his atomies.
> 'Tis all in pieces, all coherence gone;
> All just supply, and all relation:
> Prince, subject, father, son, are things forgot,
> For every man alone thinks he hath got
> To be a phoenix, and that there can be
> None of that kind, of which he is, but he.
>
> (*First Anniversarie*, ll. 209-18)

Sectarian thinking informed by unbridled individualism is shown to be unsound in how the thought, and, paradigmatically, the thinker, appears to crumble into nothing of substance. The disintegration intones the difference between an experience of this world and static notions about it. The regular iambic rhythm is in-stressed with that irregular thinking too, in those trochaic inversions − "All just supply" and "None of that kind" − and in the stress-shifts in the middle of that penultimate line so that it is not even remotely iambic.

For Donne, the authenticity of an idea is determined by how it is gauged by the individual, criss-crossed, also circumstantially, with all his clarity and lack of it, down to the roots. But, as has been observed, it is not just this which informs the pressure peculiar to a Donne poem. In his conceptualization of the self's experience in the act of thinking, Donne's sense of his own person, with all its many often contradictory sides, is palpably involved. No other poetry in the period canvasses so acutely or variously not only the intimate joys and failures of love between men and women, or between God and the self, but also presents them with such inwardness and immediacy. In contrast to the other more individual and personal religious poets, Herbert, Vaughan, Crashaw, the personal note is always more aggressive, troubled and complex. Similarly, no poetry of the period evinces more closely the self in debate with itself. Next to those by others, Donne's poems are more invariably dialogues between the self and imagined positions within a relationship. And no poetry also uses so persistently both personal pronouns and a strongly personalized first person pronoun. Underlying the intensity and vividness of the imaginative apprehension of a situation − and the diversity of experiences is greater than in any other poetry of the period − is the poet's concern with emotional identity. The hyperbolic mode in Donne's hands shows this too.[14] Furthermore, any subject, however fantastic in Donne's treatment of it, is more than an exploration of the extent to which the perception of a situation is affected by an individual's position within it; often the situation is also presented as if it is being spoken about from first-hand experience.[15] This is certainly the case in the *Sermons* and the rest of the prose, as Donne indicates in his prefaces. *Biathanatos* (1608), the book on suicide, is the result of Donne's examination of his own inclination and that of his fellow Catholics to morbidity. *Pseudo-Martyr* (1610) argues for the taking of the oath of allegiance by Catholics. *St Ignatius his Conclave* (1611) subverts the logic of the Jesuits used by the Church of his own background and training. The *Essays in Divinity* (1614-15) were prepared in anticipation of ordination. The *Devotions* (1623) were written during a severe illness. The poet's exploration of an idea as it is rooted in the contingent, more or less perplexing forces making up experience is an exploration of the possibility of genuinely connected thinking. A radical connection between thought and how one stands in life is implicit. This is supported by the emphasis on practical theology in the casuistical writings.[16] His letters to his friends, documents of "my second religion, friendship", like his verse letters, which are more obviously directed towards seeking confirmation in patronage, are no exception:

> I would fain do something; but that I cannot tell what, is no wonder. For to chuse is to do: but to be no part of any body, is to be nothing.[17]

---

[14] See Brian Vickers, "The 'Songs and Sonnets' and the Rhetoric of Hyperbole", in *John Donne: Essays in Celebration* (ed. A.J. Smith), London: Harper & Row/Methuen, 1972, 132-74.

[15] See Judith Scherer Herz, "'An Excellent Exercise of Wit that Speaks So Well': Donne and the Poetics of Concealment", in *The Eagle and the Dove: Reassessing John Donne, Essays in Seventeenth-Century Literature*, 1, Columbia: University of Missouri Press, 1986, 3-14.

[16] See A.E. Malloch, "John Donne and the Casuists", *Studies in English Literature*, 2, 1962, 57-76; Dwight Cathcart, *Doubting Conscience*, Michigan: University of Michigan Press, 1975; Camille Wells Slights, *The Casuistical Tradition in Shakespeare, Donne, Herbert and Milton*, Princeton: Princeton University Press, 1981; Meg Lota Brown, *Donne and the Politics of Conscience in Early Modern England*, Leiden: Brill, 1995.

[17] Letter to John Hayward, *Letters to Severall Persons of Honour*, London, 1651,

In Donne then, the thoughts are deep and the cadence is rough because, for better or worse, "my riddling, perplexed, labyrinthical soule" has necessarily been involved too.[18] Thus we also encounter a man who, from time to time as poet, had to undergo the eruption of psychic self-will, which in the poetry and elsewhere manifests itself as a conceptual, philosophical, dialectical wilfulness.[19] Indeed, whether accurately accounted for or not, it is against this that Dryden and Johnson were reacting. The prose of the early and middle years is full of such straining in terms of both its ideas and rhythm, in the abstruseness of the logic and in the wrenched syntax. Similarly, in his treatment of a subject, Donne's tendency to subvert or to exhaust the genre or rhetoric traditional to it can turn into overkill. The first *Anniversarie* (1611), which was written in the difficult years before Donne's ordination, is, as Jonson observed, particularly marked by wilfulness in both its thought and rhythm. Yet, even at his most recollected, as in this passage from a sermon, we still have "ruggedness" and "dark truths", evincing how in Donne an idea of truth is conceptualized as one of circumstantially perplexed personal truthfulness: in a heart absolutely surrendered to God, vehement expostulation with God, and yet in full submission to God, and a quiet acquiescence in God; "a Storme of affections in nature, and yet a settled calme, and a fast anchorage in grace, a suspition, and a jealousie, and yet an assurance, and a confidence in God", may well consist together.[20]

Here, as in so many instances – when he notes his "hydroptic immoderate desire of human learning and languages"[21], "the queasy pain

---

51. For the emphasis on relationship in Donne's understanding of the nature of things evidenced in his understanding of human relationships, notwithstanding his own, see Patricia Thomson "Donne and the Poetry of Patronage", in A.J. Smith, *op.cit.*, 308-23; and Margaret Maurer "The Real Presence of Lucy Russell, Countess of Bedford, and the Terms of John Donne's "Honour is So Sublime Perfection"", *Journal of English Historical Studies*, 47 (1980), 205-34.

[18] *Sermons*, VIII, 332.

[19] See also Geoffrey Hill in "Keeping to the Middle Way: The 'Accurate Musicke' in Burton's Anatomizing of Worldly Corruptions", *TLS* (December 14, 1994), 6.

[20] *Sermons*, VII, 15.

[21] Letter to Sir H. Goodyer, in Gosse, *op.cit.*, 1, 191.

of being loved and loving", [22] Dr. John's twisting and turning about the "inordinatenesses" of the libertine Jack — there is an awareness of that very tendency towards wilfulness and its effects of dislocation. In the case of Donne, and more so than in the case of any of his contemporaries, they are *evidently* all of a piece with the pursuit of an integrated understanding of the nature of truth and truthfulness. And what of Donne's anticipation of his critics, his answer to Jonson that in the *Anniversarie* he was writing about an "Idea of woman, and not as she was", his ambivalence about the future of his poems,[23] his decision to leave off writing poetry? They reveal self-knowledge that is also based on an awareness of how an individual's perception of things is marked in sound and less sound ways by the accidents of temperament and circumstance making up the human personality. We can say this because any notion about integration or the reverse registers a desire for integration which, through Donne's conceptualizing of the criss-cross nature of the human psyche, shows itself not to be at odds with a feeling for particularity. Whatever may be the case, the "ruggedness" or the "lame measures", as much as the "dark truths" or the abstruseness of the thought that make up his "harsh verse", identified as such by so many of his critics and by Donne himself, apprehends a conception of self in which the *drama* of gauging the discontinuities within the continuity of things stands central.

For, although we may prefer a little less of the man in the poet, no other poet at the time had this singular capacity for fathoming the psychologically disruptive implications for an individual with both feet in the world of his day. And, if we are to believe Donne, it was a world shaken by vast changes.[24] This is what Coleridge saw in Donne, a pre-

---

[22] "The Calme", ll. 40-41.

[23] Cf. Donne in a letter to Sir Robert Ker in 1619 in Gosse, *op.cit.*, 2, 124: "But besides the poems, of which you took a promise, I send you another book [*Biathanatos*] .... Keep it, I pray, with the same jealousy; let any that your discretion admits to the sight of it know the date of it, and that it is a book written by Jack Donne, and not by Dr. Donne. Reserve it for me if I live, and if I die I only forbid it to the press and the fire; publish it not, yet burn it not, and between those do what you will with it."

[24] See Marjorie Nicolson, "The 'New Astronomy' and English Literary Imagination", *Studies in Philosophy*, 32/6 (1935), 428-62; and Charles Coffin, *John Donne and The New Philosophy*, Columbia: Columbia University Press, 1937, 111, 118. See also Hiram Haydn, *The Counter-Renaissance*, New York: Evergreen Books, 1950.

Romantic sensibility, which Dryden and Johnson from within their perspective and neo-classical concerns were less able to appreciate. Yet, they also saw that Donne was the first poet to give a hearing to the spiritual and metaphysical implications of a world in which man has been pushed to the periphery of an illimitable and apparently expanding universe as a result of the scientific and technological revolution which was then taking place. Either way they understood it was the man in the poet, that product of a particular make-up and circumstances in reaction to the turmoil of his time, which made the poetry.

Indeed, in the emphasis on individual consciousness, as a reaction to the experience of a world that was out of joint, Donne's person was more peculiarly involved than was the case with his fellow poets and imitators. Yet, if Donne's poetry and prose are forms of radical reaction, they are not merely solipsistic or self-reflexive responses to the new kind of sensibility that man, given the new kind of environment, was in the process of creating for himself. It was precisely because he understood the implications of that classical phenomenon, change, with its own pecularities at the time, that Donne neither rejected the old order, scholasticism or the Church of which he was a product, any more than that he affirmed the new. The early flamboyancy edged with self-assertion, like the tendency towards histrionics, is as much an indication of a young man pitched against the mediocrity of uniformity as of a talented man with a stroke of genius that seeks unity. The reaction to loss is radicalized through an understanding of what was and might yet be the experience of a whole and integrated relationship between man and nature, men and men, man and God. This is evident in his renowned advocacy of religious toleration, his scepticism towards both the advent of an empirical way of looking at the world and an unthinking acceptance of things, his eventual commitment to the Church of the *via media*. There is more than a theoretical or abstract knowledge of the dislocation inherent in integration and vice versa. The measure of Donne's soundness as an antenna for registering the impact of the changes which were setting in resides in his comprehensive understanding of how an individual's need to make sense of them involves his person as a product of history. Indeed, the truth-telling quality of Donne's prose and poetry lies in how his endeavours to make sound sense of his own moment are ratified by the backward reach of his personal engagement with the present. His arguments with himself and the world are as much against himself as they are with and not against history. So Donne recognizes the power of rhetoric and tradition to say what he had to say with the sort of urgency that was typical of himself and not of others. An example is his translation of that theme common at the time, the volatility of change and inconstancy. His tendency to use both a more familiar idiom and homely imagery, appropriate to the "modern" situations he creates, as well as a more highly personalized idiom and imagery, substantiates the more usual use of mythology or allegory and its trappings. When he makes the formal rhythms of the iambic line also carry the imprint of the rhythms of colloquial speech he attests this more than ever.

Although Donne's immersion in the social, theological, and religious problems besetting his age was deep, this was not unusual. Nor, as Eliot, Lewis, Evelyn Simpson and those after her have observed, was Donne a particularly "original" thinker. Yet, he conceptualized better than anyone else what an individual undergoes in his radical appreciation of a problem, when faced with having to make sense of the discontinuity of his own moment within continuity of history: "I am a reciprocall plague: passively and actively contagious"; "our selves are in the plot, and we are not only *passive*, but *active* too, to our own destruction." As Joan Webber has said about Donne's prose, "Augustine can make an idea exciting through sheer intellectual vigor, while Donne prefers to concentrate on its concrete, palpable application to his human situation." Deeply acquainted with his authors and the various traditions of thought that he taps, Donne "pulls together, with selective sensitivity but not always with logic, the thoughts of others."[25] His sometimes even perverse seeking-out of circumstantial evidence to probe the soundness of an idea illustrates this too. In a different way, to the same end but with better effect, there are the constant references to contemporary happenings, the wealth of everyday detail, and the tendency to side-track.[26] Even just these features, typical of both Donne's poetry and prose but not of the writings of others, reveal an uncommon sensitivity to the pressures encountered by the individual who must somehow make his life work privately, on his own, *and* in relation to others, also in the public sphere: "Wee are not sent into the world, to *Suffer*, but to *Doe*, and to performe the Offices of societie, required by our severall callings."[27] The emphasis is on the relationship between things, and on relationships that make sense. This is

---

[25] Joan Webber, *Contrary Music: The Prose Style of John Donne*, Ann Arbour: University Microfilms, 1977, 16.

[26] Milgate, *op.cit.*, xix.

[27] In A. Raspa, ed., *Pseudo-Martyr*, London: McGill University Press, 1993, 27.

attested by his listening with an inner ear to an experience of truth in which the physical, horizontal or two-dimensional aspects of knowledge are in constant interaction with its spiritual, vertical or three-dimensional aspects. Here, too, whatever his concerns, the modern questions of originality and individuality are synonymous with the question of authentic living.

For what Donne reacts to, in his style and in his thought, is the lack of relationship between things, the unsound practice of sacrificing the parts to the whole and vice-versa. As is particularly clear in the complementary works, *Biathanatos* and *Pseudo-Martyr*, he is not interested in either the particular or the universal on its own (as he is not interested in dualistic forms of thought, scholastic, Lullian, Ramist, Euphuistic, Jesuitistic, Casuistic or, for that matter, in any system of thought in itself, Aristotelian, Platonic, Augustinian, Thomist). Either way, these, on their own, are merely deterministic and superficial — horizontal, two-dimensional — forms of thinking, which for him characterize a deracinated sense of life. The eruptions of psychic self-will, the wilfulness here and there, are an integral part of Donne's reacting "radically" to tone-deaf thinking and feeling in order to reciprocate his experience of the more deeply rooted psychological truth-telling strains of the authentically lived life. In other words, ideas, thoughts, words and points of style, metre, an image or metaphor, any aspect which may be isolated for examination, can only be understood for what it is through how it is interpenetrated by Donne's sense of the deeper interconnectedness of things.[28] A fairly obvious example of this is his exegetical practices in the *Sermons*: a scriptural passage — the "shapeless and unsignificant rags of a word or two"[29] — is always interpreted within the gathering forces of the book from which it comes. Here too, as his invention of words with the prefix "inter" also reveals, the physical is recognized for what it is on its own *and* as it can be understood in its deeper, interpenetrated, symbolical sense.[30] Similarly, although there is no lack of fine descriptive passages throughout Donne's writing, his use of imagery is never only visual; the more it is visual the

---

[28] *Ibid.,* 111

[29] In Evelyn Simpson, ed., *Essays in Divinity,* Oxford: Clarendon Press, 1952, 39.

[30] Cf. Donne in *Ibid*, 40. On Donne's use of symbolism, see Dennis Quinn "Donne's Christian Eloquence", *Journal of English Literary History*, 27 (1960), 292.

more it draws in the spiritual.[31] "Seeing", or the visual imagination in all its physical flatness, as in the images of the individual and the world as a body or a map, or the celebrated image of the compass, stands in a parenthetical relationship with "hearing" in depth, that is, with the auditory imagination registering what can be "heard" spiritually. Thus individual time, the individual's own moment in all its specific gravity is rooted, as words are etymologically rooted, in history. It follows in Donne that just as thought in its rhythms intones how history is etymology and vice-versa in the most literal, physical, sense, so the individual's sense of his own moment intersects "parenthetically" the "original", "authentical", Word of God, which stands outside time:

> Before you sound that word, *present*, or that *Monosyllable*, *now*, the present, and the *Now* is past .... Tyme is a short *parenthesis* in a longe *period*; and Eternity had been the same, as it is, though time had never been.
>
> (*Devotions*, 79)

Of the poetry of this period, Donne's least approximates the condition of music; indeed, outside the hymns, it resists the contemporary classical understanding of harmonics (but more work in this area is necessary).[32] Certainly the fluctuations, often syncopated, of the human voice in dialogue are what we encounter. But, in comparison with Shakespeare or Jonson, who were also registering the human voice in dialogue in the blank verse of their plays, nowhere are those rhythms of the drama of the perplexed mind learning to "doubt wisely" *in medias res* as differentiated or fraught as in Donne.

Donne's originality lies in the stiff-necked individuality of his rhythm, where the "rough measures" are "dark thoughts" pressed back into authentic forms of living. For Donne this is the route back to the "middle" way. And, this is the specific achievement of the poetry and of the later prose, especially of the *Devotions* and the *Sermons*, when there was greater clarity in his life's direction. But as has been noted, that feeling for language, which is a feeling for ways of living that have

[31] See B.F. Nellist, "Donne's 'Storm' and 'Calme' and the Descriptive Tradition", *Modern Language Review* (1964).

[32] See Paul Gaston, "Britten's Donne and the Promise of Twentieth-Century Settings", in Summers and Pebworth, *op.cit.*, 201-13.

meant something, is everywhere. It is there in both the prose of the early and middle years, as in the poetry which, early, middle or late, religious or secular, is always both love poetry and poetry of accurate remembering. So too are those much debated *Anniversaries*, of which the first, with its appeal to Moses' Song in Deuteronomy (32) at its end, is just one more example of this poet's hard-won capacity for authentic thought:

> [God] spake
> To *Moses*, to deliuer vnto all,
> That song: because he knew they would let fall,
> The Law, the Prophets, and the History,
> But keep the song still in their memory.
> Verse hath a middle nature: heaven keeps soules,
> The graue keeps bodies, verse the fame enroules.

(ll. 462-74)

LANGUAGE AND CONTEXT:
JANE GARDAM'S *BILGEWATER*

MICK SHORT, JONATHAN CULPEPER AND ELENA SEMINO

Introduction

In this chapter we will use stylistic analysis to provide an account of the opening prologue of Jane Gardam's novel *Bilgewater* (1976), and, in the course of this account, discuss how different notions of context can help to explain the reader's understanding of that passage and its significance. *Bilgewater* is a novel which uses language to induce the reader to invoke contexts and then to re-contextualize, and so re-interpret, what has apparently already been understood. The focus of this chapter is particularly appropriate in a volume honouring Peter Verdonk, as his academic life has in large part centred on using careful stylistic analysis *in context* to elucidate literary texts. Indeed, the three volumes in his Routledge mini-series of stylistic analysis, which are devoted, in turn, to the analysis of each of the three main literary genres, all have the phrase "from text to context" as their subtitle.[1] Furthermore, in this chapter we will make reference to the work of three of Peter's colleagues at the University of Amsterdam, Mieke Bal, Teun van Dijk and Paul Werth, the latter two of whom especially have contributed to the explication of the notion of context in text processing and text analysis.

Below we present the entire prologue of the novel, which we will then analyse in some detail (though, for reasons of space, by no means exhaustively). We have numbered the sentences of the text for ease of

---

[1] Peter Verdonk, *Twentieth Century Poetry: From Text to Context*, London: Routledge, 1993; Peter Verdonk and Jean-Jacques Weber, eds, *Twentieth-Century Fiction: From Text to Context*, London: Routledge, 1995; Jonathan Culpeper, Mick Short and Peter Verdonk, *Exploring the Language of Drama: From Text to Context*, London: Routledge, 1998.

reference. We present the passage without any contextualization, as we would like the reader of this article to experience it in the way that a reader coming to the novel for the first time would. We will thus try to capture a first-reading understanding of the novel's prologue. After that analysis, which will constitute the major part of our chapter, we will then reconsider the passage from the perspective of a reader who has just finished reading the entire novel. As we go through our account of the passage, we will outline different ways in which different kinds of context interacts with the textual information to enable the reader to understand the prologue.

Prologue

(1) The interview seemed over.   (2) The Principal of the college sat looking at the candidate.   (3) The Principal's back was to the light and her stout, short outline was solid against the window, softened only by the fuzz of her ageing but rather pretty hair.   (4) Outside the bleak and brutal Cambridge afternoon — December and raining.

(5) The candidate sat opposite wondering what to do. (6) The chair had a soft seat but wooden arms.   (7) She crossed her legs first one way and then the other — then wondered about crossing her legs at all.   (8) She wondered whether to get up.   (9) There was a cigarette box beside her.   (10) She wondered whether she would be offered a cigarette.   (11) There was a decanter of sherry on the bookcase.   (12) It had a neglected air.

(13) This was the third interview of the day.   (14) The first had been as she had expected — carping, snappish, harsh, watchful — unfriendly even before you had your hand off the door handle.   (15) Seeing how much you could take.   (16) Typical Cambridge.   (17) A sign of the times.   (18) An hour later and then the second interview — five of them this time behind a table — four women, one man, all in old clothes. (19) That had been a long one.   (20) Polite though.   (21) Not so bad.

(22) "Is there anything that *you* would like to ask *us*?"

(23) ("Yes please, why I'm here.   (24) Whether I really want to come even if you invite me.   (25) What you're all

like. (26) Have you ever run mad for love? (27) Considered suicide? (28) Cried in the cinema? (29) Clung to somebody in bed?")

(30) "No thank you. (31) I think Miss Blenkinsop-Briggs has already answered my questions in the interview this morning." (32) They move their pens about, purse their lips, turn to one another from the waist, put together the tips of their fingers. (33) I look alert. (34) I sit up-right. (35) I survey them coolly but not without respect. (36) I might get in on this one. (37) But don't think it is a good sign when they're nice to you, said old Miss Bex.

(38) And now, here we are. (39) The third interview. (40) Meeting the Principal. (41) An interview with the Principal means I'm in for a Scholarship. (42) How ridiculous!

(43) I can't see her face against the light. (44) She's got a brooding shape. (45) She is a mass. (46) Beneath the fuzz a mass. (47) A massive intelligence clicking and ticking away − observing, assessing, sifting, pigeonholing. (48) Not a feeling, not an emotion, not a dizzy thought. (49) A formidable woman.

(50) She's getting up. (51) It has been delightful. (52) She hopes that we may meet again. (53) (Does that mean I'm in?) (54) What a long way I have to come for an interview. (55) The far far north. (56) She hopes that I was comfortable last night.

(57) We shake hands in quite a northern way. (58) Then she puts on a coat − very nice coat, too. (59) Fur. (60) Nice fur. (61) Something human then about her somewhere. (62) She walks with me to the door and down the stairs and we pause again on the college steps.

(63) There is a cold white mist swirling about, rising from the river. (64) The trees lean, swinging long, black ropes at the water. (65) A court-yard, frosty, of lovely proportions. (66) A fountain, a gateway. (67) In the windows round the courtyard the lights are coming on one by one. (68) But it is damp, old, cold, cold, cold. (69) Cold as home.

(70) Shall I come here?

(71) Would I like it after all?

This opening passage of *Bilgewater*[2] is clearly a representation of a potential female undergraduate being interviewed for a place at the University of Cambridge. At the end of the prologue the candidate wonders whether she will indeed become a student at Cambridge. Before reading on, it will be helpful if you, the reader, could now note your initial intuitive responses as to (a) whose perspective the majority of the passage is seen from, and (b) whether or not you think the candidate will take up the place she is apparently going to be offered.

Preliminary narratological observations and different notions of "context"

Even on a first reading of the opening of *Bilgewater*, it will probably become clear that there are actually three interviews described in the prologue, but that these are not given to the reader in chronological order. The first two paragraphs describe the end of the third and final interview. This is revealed in the first sentence of paragraph 3 (sentence 13), which then goes on to describe the first interview briefly and also begins the representation of the second one, which goes on until the end of paragraph 6 (sentence 37). We then return to the final interview in paragraph 7 (sentence 38). Paragraphs 7 and 8 describe what appears to be the beginning of that interview and then, at the beginning of paragraph 8 (sentence 50) we finally arrive at the point where we first entered the prologue, at the end of the final interview, from where we proceed to the end of the prologue in sentence 71, as the Principal and the candidate part company in the courtyard outside the building in which the interview has taken place.

In narratological terms, it would appear that the focalizer[3] of the prologue is the candidate. We would be very surprised if you, the reader, had come to any other conclusion in relation to question (a) above, and we will spell out in some detail why so much of this passage seems to concentrate on the candidate. We see most (but not all) of

---

[2] Jane Gardam, *Bilgewater*, London: Abacus, 1976.

[3] See chapter 7 in Mieke Bal, *Narratology: Introduction to the Theory of Narrative*, 2nd edition, Toronto: Toronto University Press, 1997.

what is described from the candidate's perspective, and we are given access to her thoughts and hers alone.

We will discuss the linguistic bases for these remarks below. But first let us focus on the sequence in which the three interviews are presented. As we mentioned earlier, the novel opens with the end of an interview, which turns out to be the third one for the candidate that day. Then there is a flashback to the first and second interviews (sentences 14-17 and 18-37 respectively). After the flashback we do not immediately return to the point at which the main narrative had been interrupted but to the *beginning* of the third interview. It is not until sentence 50 that the narrative returns to the point where the flashback started after sentence 12. Some of the possible effects of what could be described as the "chronological disorderliness" of this account of the three interviews are (1) that of reflecting the confusion of the candidate as she progresses through her whirlwind round of interviews, and (2) that of emphasizing the way in which memories and impressions of the first two interviews go through her mind as the third and final interview appears to move towards a close.

In pragmatic terms, the presentational sequencing of the three interviews can be seen as a flout of Grice's Maxim of Manner, which, among other things, contains the intimation "Be orderly". The reader is therefore prompted to find an explanation for the sequential disorderliness, or, more precisely, to draw an implicature from it. The effect we suggested at the end of the previous paragraph is an example of a possible implicature.[4] In Sperber and Wilson's Relevance theory, Grice's Maxims are replaced by the "Principle of Relevance", which alone accounts for the communicative and cognitive behaviour of

---

[4] H.P. Grice, "Logic and Conversation", in P. Cole and J. Morgan, eds, *Syntax and Semantics, III: Speech Acts*, New York: Academic Press, 1975, 41-58. Grice's theory of Conversational Implicature, albeit in a rather different way, clearly covers some of the same ground as the more general theory of foregrounding which lies at the heart of most stylistic analysis (see, for example Willie van Peer, *Stylistics and Psychology: Investigations of Foregrounding*. London: Croom Helm, 1986). In foregrounding theory, defeated expectations in a wide range of mainly, but not exclusively, linguistic phenomena lead to extra interpretative effort to explain deviations from language and text norms.

human beings.[5] Within this perspective, the (opening of the) novel is an instance of ostensive communication on the part of the writer, which comes with a presumption of its own optimal relevance. This means that the text carries an inbuilt guarantee that it is worth the addressee's/reader's while to process it, and that its linguistic make-up is the most relevant stimulus the author could have used to communicate the set of assumptions she intended to communicate. The (degree of) relevance of an utterance to an addressee depends on the balance between two factors: the processing effort required for the interpretation of the utterance and the contextual effects that it produces, i.e. the new set of assumptions which are derivable from it. The lack of chronological sequencing in the presentation of the three interviews can be seen as a source of extra processing effort (as compared with a chronological presentation). In the reader's search for optimal relevance, this additional processing effort needs to be offset by a suitable set of contextual effects: additional assumptions which could not have been derived from a chronological presentation of events. Once again, the communicating of assumptions to do with the candidate's confused state of mind can be seen as a possible contextual effect of the cognitively "expensive" way in which the interviews are introduced.

Crucial to this whole process of establishing relevance is the reader's active selection of a "context" within which the processing of each segment of a text leads to the greatest contextual effects with the smallest cognitive effort. Sperber and Wilson describe "context", in purely cognitive terms, as the subset of the reader's existing assumptions against which information is processed in order to arrive at new assumptions.[6] They stress that the context against which a text is processed is not fixed, but is a dynamic construct which evolves during processing, as new assumptions are incorporated, old assumptions are weakened or cancelled, and different sections of encyclopaedic knowledge are applied to the interpretation of new information. Sperber and Wilson's notion of context, in other words, is very broad in terms

---

[5] To be precise, in the second edition of Dan Sperber and Deirdre Wilson's book on Relevance Theory (*Relevance: Communication and Cognition*, Oxford: Basil Blackwell, 1995 [original 1986]), there are two versions of the Principle, applying, respectively, to communication and cognition.

[6] *Ibid.*, 132.

of the different types of assumptions it subsumes, including *(a)* assumptions derived from the processing of the preceding text or discourse, *(b)* assumptions derived from existing encyclopaedic or prior knowledge, and *(c)* assumptions derived from the extra-linguistic observable environment.[7]

We do not have the space here to provide a Relevance Theory account of how the sentence-by-sentence processing of the prologue to *Bilgewater* might proceed, and, indeed, Relevance theorists do not normally tackle texts with the kind of narratological and viewpoint complexities that our text presents. Nevertheless, it should be clear that, since we are dealing with a written fictional text, assumptions of type *(c)* do not, strictly speaking, apply to its processing, but types *(a)* and *(b)* do. In other words, readers can only make sense of the peculiarities of the text by constructing a context which contains relevant assumptions from encyclopaedic knowledge (e.g. that interviewers determine the structure and final outcome of interviews, that meandering thoughts can be a sign of a state of agitation, and so on), and assumptions derived incrementally from the processing of the sentences of the text (e.g. assumptions about the setting of the interview in paragraph 1, assumptions about the candidate's preconceptions of University of Cambridge in paragraph 3, and so on).

Other theories of cognition would see the different types of assumptions in Sperber and Wilson's broad notion of "context" as belonging to different types of "context". Generally speaking, it is possible to draw distinctions between at least four types of "context" relevant to text processing, which are outlined below. It needs to be stressed that we do not aim at a complete typology of different types of context, but rather seek to identify types of context which (1) are involved in making sense of a text, and (2) can add clarity and precision in textual analysis.

1. *The context that one segment of text provides for another.* This is frequently referred to as the *co-text*. The notion of co-text might be divided into two sub-types. The first relates to *surface form*. Foregrounding strategies may attract the reader's attention to the

---

[7] *Ibid.*, 140-1.

surface form.[8] An example from the prologue is the parallelism "cold, cold, cold", where the form "cold" unexpectedly acts as co-text to the same form. We will briefly return to this example later. The second aspect of the notion of co-text relates to *semantic structure*. This could include the semantic colouring one word lends another, a phenomenon that has been referred to as "semantic prosody".[9] We will discuss this below in relation to the prologue's words "cold" and "frosty". At a more macro level, the notion of semantic structure could also include the propositional structure of a text. Readers may infer relationships between explicit text propositions. Thus, in the sentence "The man shouted and Tom fled from him", it is likely that a bridging inference would be made that the pronoun *him* refers to the *man*, and that temporal relations between propositions would be inferred, such that the man shouted before Tom fled. Readers can have their attention drawn to this kind of co-text by texts which do not present information in a coherent and unambiguous manner.[10] This has already been illustrated in our discussion of the prologue, where information about the interviews is presented in a disorderly manner.

2. *The context that is projected by the text itself, or, in other words, the scenario that the reader constructs in processing the text.* This kind of "projected" context of situation has been referred to by a number of theorists, each from a rather different standpoint. Terms that have been used to refer to this kind of context include: "mental model", "situation model", "context of reference",

---

[8] R.A. Zwaan, "Toward a Model of Literary Comprehension", in B.K. Britton, and A.C. Graesser, eds, *Models of Understanding Text*, Mahwah: Lawrence Erlbaum, 1996, 241-55, 245-6.

[9] See W. Louw, "Irony in the Text or Sincerity in the Writer?: The Diagnostic Potential of Semantic Prosodies", in M. Baker, G. Francis and E. Tognini-Bonelli, eds, *Text and Technology: In Honour of John Sinclair*, Amsterdam: John Benjamins, 1993, 157-76.

[10] Zwaan, *op.cit.*, 247-8.

"text(ual) world", and "contextual frame".[11] In the case of the prologue to *Bilgewater*, this is the context projected by the text itself is that where a female candidate is going through a set of interviews for a place at the University of Cambridge. This kind of context is the rough equivalent *within the fictional world of the text* to our category (4) below, which relates to the extra-linguistic context in which the reader reads the novel, and therefore constitutes a kind of contextual embedding.

3. *The context of the reader's prior knowledge, i.e. the schemata, frames or scripts that the reader applies to the processing of the text.*[12] In our case, the reader needs to activate knowledge about (university) interviews, Cambridge, young people, and so on, in order to make sense of the text, and indeed be able to construct context (2) above in the fictional world of the novel. Different understandings of the text will result from differences in the amount of background knowledge the reader possesses about the places and experiences described in the novel. The prologue to *Bilgewater* relates to a very specific situation in a very specific culture: the procedure whereby places are allocated at the University of Cambridge in England. While it can be expected that any reader of the novel will have a schema for INTERVIEWS as gate-keeping encounters (with the JOB INTERVIEW probably being the most likely variant), only readers familiar with a university system like the British one will have a version of the schema where the aim of the interview is to verify the interviewee's suitability to

---

[11] These terms, respectively, from: P.N. Johnson-Laird, *Mental Models*, Cambridge: Cambridge University Press, 1983; T.A. van Dijk, and W. Kintsch, *Strategies of Discourse Comprehension*, London: Academic Press, 1993; Roger Fowler, *Linguistic Criticism*, Oxford: Oxford University Press, 1986; Robert de Beaugrande, *Text, Discourse, and Process: Towards a Multi-Disciplinary Science of Texts*, London: Longman, 1980, Elena Semino, *Language and World Creation in Poems and Other Texts*, London: Longman, 1997, Paul Werth, *Text Worlds: Representing Conceptual Space in Discourse*, London: Longman, 1999; and Catherine Emmott, *Narrative Comprehension: A Discourse Perspective*. Oxford: Oxford University Press, 1997.

[12] See M.W. Eysenck, and M.T. Keane, *Cognitive Psychology: A Student's Handbook*, Hove and London: Lawrence Erlbaum Associates, 1990, 270ff.

study towards a particular degree at a particular university. Even among this set of readers, only some will possess a variant of the UNIVERSITY INTERVIEW schema which relates to Cambridge University, where interviews may take place earlier than in other institutions (note the reference to "December" in sentence 4), and where candidates may go through a series of interviews (rather than just one), in order to determine which, if any, of the colleges to which they have applied might take them. For this better-informed set of readers, the context projected by the prologue is simply a particular fictional instantiation of a variant of a schema they already possess. The less informed the readers, the more they will have to rely on textual information to construct a situation which is partly new to them. Werth[13] uses the term "text-drivenness" to refer to the phenomenon whereby the same stretch of text may evoke existing prior knowledge in some readers and provide enough information for that knowledge to be inferred by readers who do not already possess it. He comments:

> Obviously writers do also assume things which cannot be inferred from textual structure, and someone who lacks crucial knowledge is unlikely to achieve the inferential detail of someone who possesses that knowledge. But the text-driven nature of the interpretation process ensures that even a fairly abysmal ignorance will not prevent a rather considerable proportion of the necessary information from getting through.[14]

4. *The extra-linguistic context in which communication takes place.* This can be variously approached as a physical, social or cognitive entity. Strictly speaking, this type of context is not highly relevant to the current analysis, since the writer and the reader do not share a physical environment in which communication takes place. Nevertheless, the particular context of reception in which the reader processes the text may well affect processing in significant

---

[13] Werth, *op.cit.*, 149-53.

[14] *Ibid.*, 153.

ways. For example, if you had encountered *Bilgewater* in the context of an examination and had you known that your tutor favoured particular interpretative strategies, you may well have read the text with a rather different set of goals and assumptions from those of someone simply reading the novel for pleasure.

Each of the contexts outlined above broadly corresponds to an aspect of van Dijk and Kintsch's model of text comprehension.[15] Major elements in their model include a surface representation and a textbase (or propositional) representation (our context (1)), a situation model (our context (2)) and prior knowledge (our context (3)). They also emphasize the extra-linguistic context in which communication takes place (our context (4)). Let us compare these four types of context with the different types of assumptions subsumed within Sperber and Wilson's scheme. Assumptions of type *(b)* in Sperber and Wilson's account seem to correspond with context (3). Assumptions of type *(c)* seem to correspond with context (4). Assumptions of type *(a)* seem to correspond with both contexts (1) and (2). Sperber and Wilson's account, however, is purely cognitive: there is no attempt to distinguish a linguistic context of the kind outlined in context (1).

The projected context of situation and point of view

In this and the next section, we will illustrate how the various types of context identified in the previous section are involved in an understanding and appreciation of *Bilgewater*. However, our main focus will be on the projected context of situation, and how textual features and prior knowledge are involved in its creation. Some justification for this focus can be found in van Dijk and Kintsch's view that creating what they call the situation model is the major goal in understanding the text: "If we are unable to imagine a situation in which certain individuals have the properties or relations indicated by

---

[15] Although devised some time ago, van Dijk and Kintsch's model has stayed the course of time. One might note, for example, its influence on many of the papers in Britton and Graesser, *op.cit.*

the text, we fail to understand the text itself."[16] In this section, we will pay particular attention to the creation of *perspective* or *point of view* in the situation model, and, then, we will pay particular attention to the creation of *character* in the situation model. Lastly, we will consider the epilogue of the novel and how this forces us to re-contextualize the initial context of situation of the prologue.

One aspect of the creation of a context of situation can be seen in the *in medias res* beginning of the novel. The definite reference of "the interview" in sentence 1 leads us to presuppose that we must be being given a perspective which assumes that the identity of the interview being referred to is already known. The use of the cognitive verb "seemed" also helps us to infer that the perspective involved is probably that of a character in the story, and particularly of a character who is not in control of when the interview ends, i.e. someone other than the interviewer. Sentence 2 is, however, indeterminate with respect to viewpoint. It is perhaps most likely to be seen as a statement by a 3rd-person narrator, external to both of the characters, but it could conceivably also be anchored within the perspective of either of the characters.

Sentence 3, however, is clearly anchored within the viewpoint of the candidate. We are presented with an outline of the Principal against the background of a window from a position in front of her, in which we would expect the candidate to be placed. To work this out, we have to invoke the context of the reader's prior knowledge. Given schematic assumptions which readers have about interviews and how they are normally conducted, we expect the interviewer and interviewee to be seated facing one another. It would be very unusual for an interviewer to sit with her back to the interviewee, and our schematic assumptions thus block this conceivable interpretation (whereby the viewing point is inside the room, and the Principal has her back both to the window and the candidate, who would thus have to be between the two). In other words, lexical items like "interview", "Principal" and "candidate" have led us to make reference to a pre-existing schema package which we have for interviews in general and interviews for university places

---

[16] *Ibid.*, 337. This view is also reflected in A. Garnham, and J. Oakhill "The Mental Models Theory of Language Comprehension", in Britton and Graesser, *op.cit.*, 313-39.

in particular. This schema triggering in turn helps us to establish the viewpoint from which most of the things presented are being described (the focalizer).[17]

So far, in beginning to establish the linguistic bases for the observation that the candidate is the focalizer for most of the prologue, we have used three different kinds of trigger, which Short has outlined in his checklist of viewpoint indicators: given vs. new information, cognition verbs and linguistic triggers for schema-activation.[18] These all help locate the candidate as the focalizer, and these mechanisms are used a number of times in the passage. There are, however, a large number of other ways in which the focalized viewpoint is established and maintained. In sentence 4, for example, the evaluative lexis in the phrase "bleak and brutal" can be seen as indicating the candidate's attitude to the weather, and "soft seat but wooden arms" in sentence 6 represents the candidate's contrasting tactile experience of the chair she is sitting in.

Another significant viewpoint indicator is the use of thought presentation[19] exclusively for the candidate, thus allowing us access to her mind, but no-one else's. In the second paragraph, she is subject of the verb "wondered" in sentences 5, 7, 8 and 10. These thought presentation verbs are part of either the Narrator's Representation of Thought Act (NRTA) or Indirect Thought (IT) presentational forms in these sentences. Then, as the passage unfolds, the thought presentation modes become more direct and vivid. In sentence 22, one of the

---

[17] It will be helpful to point out that the focalizer of narratological theory is a fairly large generalization. Even within passages where everything appears to be narrated with a particular character as focalizer there can still be, particularly in 3rd-person narrations, localized shifts from the perspective of the focalizer to that of another character or the narrator, and back again. For some discussion of this issue see Mick Short, "Graphological Deviation, Style Variation and Point of View in *Marabou Stork Nightmares* by Irvine Welsh", *Journal of Literary Studies* (forthcoming).

[18] Mick Short, *Exploring the Language of Poems, Plays and Prose*, London: Longman, 1996.

[19] *Ibid.*, 311-20; G.N. Leech, and M. H. Short, *Style in Fiction*, London: Longman, 1981, 336-48; and Monika Fludernik, *The Fictions of Language and the Languages of Fiction*, London: Routledge, 1993.

interviewers asks the question "Is there anything you would like to ask us?" which, according to our schema for interviews, suggests that the interview is drawing to a close. It would be legitimate to expect that the whole of paragraph 4, which is in inverted commas, would be in response to that question. However, what we actually get is the candidate's (Free) Direct Thought ((F)DT) in sentences 23-9. We can see that the mode is Direct because all the deictic and other "positional" features in these sentences are related to the candidate's position as speaker. There are a number of things which indicate that what occurs in these inverted commas is thought, not speech. Firstly, they are marked off rather unusually from the rest of the text by being placed inside brackets. Secondly a polite, and therefore socially cohesive, answer to the question is provided in Direct Speech form in sentences 30-1 at the beginning of the following paragraph: "No thank you. I think Miss Blenkinsop-Briggs has already answered my questions in the interview this morning." And thirdly, the content of sentences 23-9, in contrast to those of 30-1, is at odds with our schema for interviews: the sentences suggest that the candidate is unsure about her presence there, and include extremely personal questions (26-9) aimed at her interviewers, which would most likely cause offence if uttered aloud. The use of Direct Thought (DT) presentation for the candidate then becomes fairly prevalent in the rest of the passage. For example sentences 38-49 and the final two sentences of the passage are all arguably in this format, this time without the inverted commas, but with the deictic centre still clearly that of the candidate.

The viewpoint and thought presentation features we have seen so far are likely, other things being equal, to lead the reader to sympathize with the candidate. And given that most people will be familiar with the feelings of uncertainty and lack of power induced by being interviewed (e.g. for a university place or a job), that push towards sympathy appears to have no reason to be resisted. The Principal, on the other hand, appears more distant from us. It is not just that we do not see into her thoughts. When she speaks, in sentences 51-2 and 54-6, her speech is represented in the Free Indirect mode, thus distancing us from her.[20]

We have already seen that in terms of thought presentation Jane Gardam first represents the candidate's thoughts in indirect forms like NRTA and IT, and then moves us closer to the candidate by changing

---

[20] Leech and Short, *op.cit.*, 325-36.

the form of representation to DT. This effect of moving closer to the candidate as focalizer is also achieved in other ways. The first two paragraphs have only 3rd-person references to the characters and the narrative tense is past. This configuration of 3rd-person reference and past tense is that normally associated with a 3rd-person, heterodiegetic narrator. But by the time we get to sentence 33, in the middle of paragraph 6, we have been moved to a very different narratorial format, namely that of a 1st-person present-tense homodiegetic narrator. As it is the candidate who produces the narration, we have clearly been moved closer to her in viewpoint and sympathy terms.[21] These changes do not all take place at the same time however, and so the reader is moved gradually to the new narrator-viewpoint position. The first narration sentence in the present tense is sentence 32 in paragraph 6. But the previous two narratorial sentences (20-21) were elliptical and tenseless, and in any case are separated from sentence 32 by 56 words (10 sentences) of thought and speech presentation. The change from 3rd- to 1st-person narratorial format is finally achieved in sentence 33, but again the change does not appear to be sudden. Firstly, the last 3rd-person reference to the candidate is in sentence 14 (paragraph 3). Then, in the second half of that sentence, and the following one, the candidate is referred to through a generalizing version of the 2nd-person pronoun "you".[22] From then on, until

---

[21] One consequence of this is that some of the (F)DT sentences could actually be narration sentences (e.g. sentences 38-40), which leads to potential ambiguity.

[22] It could be argued that these sentences, with their use of a "you" which is ambiguous referentially between the generalized use associated with the pronoun and a specific reference to the candidate, constitute a shift into the increasingly fashionable 2nd-person narration (see Fludernik *op.cit.,* 85; and U. Margolin, "Narrative 'You' Revisited", *Language and Style,* 28 (1993), 1-21). This would be tempting, as one could then claim a neat shift from 3rd-person narration to 1st-person narration via 2nd-person narration. But like the concept of the focalizer, there is an issue of scope here. Critics and narratologists usually use the notions of 1st-, 2nd-, and 3rd-person narration to refer to relatively large chunks of text, and we would normally require more than a couple of short sentences to establish a new kind of narration. For example, even if the first couple of paragraphs of a 1st-person narration novel happened only to have 3rd-person reference because the narrator happened not refer to him/herself in person, we would be unlikely to want to claim that there had been a switch from 3rd- to 1st-person narration two paragraphs into the novel.

sentence 33, no narratorial reference is made to the candidate directly. This is achieved by the prevalence of grammatically elliptical sentences (see further below) which avoid specifying both tense and person-reference. The consequence of this strategy is that the form of the narration changes quite quickly but in a way that is unlikely to be noticed on first reading by many readers, thus achieving within a short stretch of text a subtle intensification in our feelings of closeness with the candidate.

We have already indicated how grammatical ellipsis is used to help move the narration from 3rd-person, past tense to 2nd-person, present tense. It is also worthy of note that a striking 38% of the sentences of this text are elliptical. This is reflected in the very short average sentence length of 7.85 words per sentence (measured using Microsoft Word, as are all the figures we will mention except that from Ellegård). By way of comparison, the Ellegård average sentence length for written texts in the Brown Corpus of 1964 is 17.8. Furthermore, Hoover,[23] in arguing for the simplicity of Golding's *The Inheritors*, points out that this novel has an average of only 13.8 words per sentence in a corpus of samples from 12 British novels, whose average runs from 12.5 to 19.0, and of which only one (*The Picture of Dorian Gray*) has a lower average than *The Inheritors*. He also reports that a representative sample from Raymond Chandler's *The Big Sleep*, which is widely regarded as having an extremely simple style, had an average of 10.8 words per sentence. Elliptical sentences have an "unanchored" feel because of the absence of tense and/or narrator reference, and so they often give the feeling of rapid, impressionistic perceptions and feelings. This is clearly appropriate to the representation of a young and somewhat confused reflector experiencing Cambridge and its interview system for the first time. In addition to this, there are a large number of simple sentences (e.g. sentences 6 and 9), and the sentences/clauses which do have verbs are predominantly stative or indicative of cognition or perception (e.g. sentences 43-5). There are very few dynamic clauses representing external actions, and those which do exist

---

[23] A. Ellegård, *The Syntactic Structure of English Texts: A Computer-based Study of Four Kinds of Text in the Brown University Corpus*, Gothenburg: Gothenburg Studies in English, 1978, 43; D.L. Hoover, *Language and Style in "The Inheritors"*, Lanham: University Press of America, 1999.

often represent small, insignificant movements (e.g. sentences 7 and 32). All this helps to achieve an effect whereby the reflector's actions are, by and large, seen to be unfocused and ineffectual.

The projected context of situation, characterization and suspense

Having spent some time establishing how the events are represented to us through the viewpoint of the candidate, let us now turn to the other question we asked near the beginning of this chapter: will the candidate accept the offer of a place? Just as the issue of perspective, discussed in the previous section, is pertinent to the construction of the context of situation, so is the attribution of intention to characters. It is clear from van Dijk and Kintsch that one's representation of "persons" is part of the context of situation. There is no reason to suppose that the representation of fictional persons, their characterization (their goals, motives, beliefs, traits and emotions) is any different in this respect. In fact, in the text-comprehension literature it is not only assumed that this is the case, but there is some supporting empirical evidence.[24]

Generally speaking, story beginnings are likely to raise questions, issues or doubts which will be answered later on. This is, after all, the most basic ploy to engage readers' attention and to keep them turning the pages. The prologue to *Bilgewater* is no exception in this respect. In fact, when we have discussed this extract with our students some of them have even been unsure as to whether the candidate was going to be offered a place. However, her inference that if she is meeting the Principal it must be because she is being considered for the financial support of a scholarship (sentences 41-2) suggests that she must be worthy of a place. Secondly, although it is not stated in an absolutely clear fashion, the fact that the Principal says that she hopes to meet the candidate again implicates that the scholarship interview has also gone well.

If the issue as to whether the candidate has been offered a place is to be solved by indirect methods, this is even more the case for the

---

[24] M.A. Gernsbacher, H.H. Goldsmith, and R. Robertson, "Do Readers Represent Characters' Emotional States?", *Cognition and Emotion,* 6 (1992), 89-111; A.C. Graesser, M. Singer and T. Trabasso, "Constructing Inferences during Narrative Text Comprehension", *Psychological Review,* 3 (1994), 371-95.

question of whether or not the candidate will accept the place. The fact that she asks the questions "Shall I come here?" and "Would I like it after all?" suggest that at the very least she must be unsure as to what to do, and there have been a number of sentences where her discomfort has been made clear in connotative terms. In addition to "the bleak and brutal Cambridge afternoon" of sentence 4, we also have the unpleasant characterization of the first interview in sentence 14 ("... carping, snappish, harsh, watchful − unfriendly even before you had your hand off the door handle"), the comment that this is "typical" of Cambridge in sentence 16, the depersonalized way in which the candidate refers to the Principal in sentences 45-9 ("She is a mass. Beneath the fuzz a mass. A massive intelligence clicking and ticking away − observing, assessing, sifting, pigeonholing. Not a feeling, not an emotion, not a dizzy thought. A formidable woman") and her feeling of damp and cold in the courtyard after the interview ("But it is damp, old, cold, cold, cold") (68).

But balanced against those negative evaluations there are more positive ones. The second interview was "Polite though. Not so bad" (20-21), the Principal has a "very nice coat, too. Fur. Nice fur. Something human then about her somewhere" 58-61) and the courtyard is "frosty, of lovely proportions" (65).

The positive characterization of the cold in the courtyard (sentence 65), as opposed to the negative one of sentence 68, relates to a type of context we have referred to as co-text. At the level of the word, co-text relates to the study of collocation, or, put simply, "the company words keep." The words "cold" and "frosty" gain their typical semantic associations from the lexical contexts in which they usually occur. A cursory look at examples from the British National Corpus reveals that "cold" is frequently coordinated with words like "lonely", "afraid", "dirty", "hungry", and "depressing". "Frosty", on the other hand, has fairly neutral connotations when it is used literally, but is frequently used metaphorically in contexts of social discomfort: "Britain and China's sometimes frosty relations", "has been given a frosty reception", "cool to the point of frosty formality", "frosty stare", "the atmosphere is decidedly frosty as Charles and Diana begin their tour of Korea." In our text, "cold" is (initially) part of the normal pattern in that it is grammatically adjacently paralleled with "damp" and "old". "Frosty", however, is adjacently paralleled by "of lovely proportions", a positive evaluation.

In addition to the opposing lexical characterizations above, we can point to a series of paralleled contrastive phrases, clauses and sentences using "but" which have the same effect:

> her ageing **but** rather pretty hair (3)
> a soft seat **but** wooden arms (5)
> I survey them coolly **but** not without respect (35)
> I might get in on this one. **But** don't think it is a good sign (36-7)
> lights are coming on one by one. **But** it is damp, old, cold (67-8)

In all of these examples, positive and negative characterizations of the same phenomenon are contrasted through adjacent syntactic parallelism. Not surprisingly, then, it appears that the candidate's decision as to whether to go to Cambridge or not is fairly finely balanced. This is also suggested by sentences 68-9, which occur very near the end of the prologue: "But it is damp, old, cold, cold, cold. Cold as home" (68-9). The repetition of "cold" three times in the context of "damp" and "cold" in 68 makes the negative evaluation seem very final, but then the following elliptical sentence appears to "latch on" to the syntax of 68 and adds a simile which involves the positive connotations of "home", a word which connects both with where she comes from ("the far far north" (55) so that cold is associated with home), and also with the Principal, who shakes her hand in "quite a northern way" (57). The fact that the positive co-textual associations come at the end and are linked back to the Principal lead us to infer that she probably will go to Cambridge after all, in spite of her reservations.

Finally, we would like to consider the way in which the characters are referred to. In spite of the fact that the focalized viewpoint we share is that of the candidate, we never know her name in this passage. Instead, lexical reference to her is through her social role: that of candidate. The same is true of the other major character in the scene, the Principal (who, unlike the candidate is consistently given an initial capital, presumably to indicate her status and help indicate the feeling of awe that the candidate has towards her). The only characters who are given names are more minor characters. In Gricean terms, the author's strategy of not naming the candidate and the Principal is a flouting of the Quantity and Manner maxims, but there is no obvious inference on the basis of the rest of the passage to explain the flout, except perhaps to maintain a vague sense of mystery as to the identity of the characters.

We will return to this in our consideration of the end of the novel below, but first let us notice some ways in which the prologue to the novel connects to, and provides a context for the main narration of the novel. The prologue is followed by a 1st-person narration on the part of a young woman called Marigold Green, describing the period from her sixth-form studies up to the point when she wins, and accepts, her scholarship to go to Cambridge. The title of the novel is her nickname, Bilgewater, given to her by the boys of the Boys' school where she lives because her father, Bill Green, is a teacher there. The name is derived by a kind of rhyming slang: Bill's daughter — Bilgewater. We are not explicitly told that Bilgewater is the candidate of the prologue, but we infer it through the Maxim of Relation or Principle of Relevance long before we get to the part in the narration which relates to her application to Cambridge. Why else would the prologue be there?

The projected context of situation and re-contextualization: the epilogue of the novel

The main narration ends at the point when Bilgewater/Marigold Green is about to go up to Cambridge, but the novel has a twist in its tale, an epilogue which effectively re-contextualizes the prologue, forcing us to reinterpret it. Indeed, many readers will feel the need to re-read the prologue and compare it carefully with the epilogue of the novel's last three pages. In this epilogue we apparently pick up more or less where the prologue ended, with the Principal walking out with the candidate after the interview. But now the candidate is referred to by the Principal as "Miss Terrapin" (not "Miss Green"). Miss Terrapin also comes from the north, and indeed went to the same school as the Principal, who apparently had known Miss Terrapin's parents in the past. Indeed, we know from the main narration that Bilgewater had a relationship with a boy called Terrapin before she fell in love with another young man called Boakes. All this effectively blocks the assumption that Bilgewater is the candidate in the epilogue. Indeed, the Principal is also referred to as Lady Boakes, and, as we know from the end of the main narration that she was in love with a young man called Boakes, who went "up" to Cambridge at the same time as her, we infer that they must have married and that they have both had very successful careers. Indeed, it transpires that Lady Boakes is the first woman principal of Caius college.

The effect of the parallels between the prologue and the epilogue, and the "blockings" referred to above, effectively make the identity of the two main characters in the prologue ambiguous, and thus provides an explanation of the author's avoidance of naming the candidate and Principal in the prologue. Effectively, the epilogue constitutes a recontextualization of the prologue, so that the candidate could be Bilgewater or Miss Terrapin and the Principal could be Lady Boakes (Bilgewater) or a previous incumbent. The chronological effect of the overall novel pushes us towards the assumption that the original candidate was probably Bilgewater, but the possible ambiguity leads to a vision of circularity and repetition, through the generations, of similar experiences.

Conclusion

In this chapter we hope to have laid bare some of the factors involved in Jane Gardam's skilful writing. She rapidly induces our sympathy for the prototypically young, vulnerable and confused prospective student, by invoking relevant schemas and moving us, via carefully orchestrated shifts in style of narration, tense, viewpoint markers and speech and thought presentation, from a relatively externalized, dispassionate perspective to one where we sympathize strongly with the candidate and look forward to her story in the rest of the novel. All this is achieved through Gardam's careful manipulation of language and her sensitivity to how readers respond to co-textual linguistic patterning, invoke stored schematic knowledge on the basis of textual stimulus and infer appropriate contexts in constructing the fictional world of the novel as they read. By these means she induces the reader to assume that the candidate of the prologue is the eponymous Bilgewater, whose ensuing tale takes up the majority of the novel. Then, at the end of the novel, as Bilgewater prepares finally to leave for her undergraduate career at Cambridge, the epilogue forces us to re-construe the identities of the characters presented in the prologue, by re-invoking the context projected by the prologue and re-contextualizing it in the light of new information. Thus Bilgewater is both candidate and Principal, interviewee and interviewer, and *Bilgewater* truly is a novel which exploits the interaction of language and contexts.

QUASI-TRANSCRIPTIONAL SPEECH:
A COMPENSATORY SPOKENNESS IN CONTEMPORARY ANGLO-IRISH LITERARY FICTION

MICHAEL TOOLAN

The interests of this essay are new tendencies in characters' rendered speech in recent English fiction: a pronounced preference for novels written in first-person dialectal English rather than "third-person" detached narration in Standard English, together with an increased inclusion, in the rendering of dialogues, of many of the ellipses and convolutions, repetitions and dysfluencies, that are a natural part of real conversation. In summary there are thus shifts in three respects: within narration, a move both to the first-person and to the dialectal; within direct speech dialogue, a move to reflect more closely the nature of actual speech.

These tendencies are not found throughout contemporary quality fiction. And in the written literary traditions of many cultures there have long been efforts to render, in the reporting of characters' speech, the illusion or effect of "living" speech; and this in turn is as often admired, by readers and critics, as "earthy", "direct", full of the flavour of dialect, the sound of real people speaking. But of late, rendering the spokenness of real speech has become a more prominent option in the fiction-writer's repertoire; and this, if true, causes one to wonder why. The kinds of novel I am thinking of here include the following: Graham Swift's *Waterland* and *Last Orders*, James Kelman's *How Late It Was, How Late*; Roddy Doyle's *Paddy Clarke Ha Ha Ha!*; Jeanette Winterson's *Sexing the Cherry*; Frank McCourt's *Angela's Ashes*; Ian McEwan's *Black Dogs*; Martin Amis's *Night Train*; and Kazuo Ishiguro's *The Remains of the Day*. It is possible that Amis's *Money* (1984, and now reissued as a Penguin Classic), was a British pioneer of this tendency (Amis has recently described it as a novel of "voice", by contrast with the novel of plot which is more traditional in fiction from England).[1] And it is possible also that the "spokenness" preference has been particularly exploited in recent years by writers rooted in the UK or Ireland (having been an established option with a longer heritage — back to Twain? — in North American fiction). But it is probably unhelpful to lean too heavily on geographically — or nationally-based categories, modern writers being such active travellers, passively resistant to external categorization.

By way of exemplification, consider Ishiguro's *The Remains of the Day*. The opening, like the entire novel, is fast becoming recognized as a contemporary classic. This is not least because it combines an abundant use of first-person references with incipient indications that, paradoxically, this speaker lacks a fully-developed Self. The opening runs:

> It seems increasingly likely that I really will undertake the expedition that has been preoccupying my imagination now for some days. An expedition, I should say, which I will undertake alone, in the comfort of Mr Farraday's Ford; an expedition which, as I foresee it, will take me through much of the finest countryside of England to the West Country, and may keep me away from Darlington Hall for as much as five or six days.[2]

This is not direct discourse, but, if this is something like an entry in Mr Stevens' diary, it is also noteworthy for being of that diary style which seems best suited to use in addressing a public meeting — that is, very much straddling the distinction between spoken and written, and between public and private. By comparison with third person narration, homodiegetic first-person narration — that is, a telling, by the protagonist him- or herself, of their own actions and discourse in the first person — is inherently more "spoken". Take Jeanette Winterson's *Sexing the Cherry*[3] which begins:

---

[1]   From an interview with Mark Lawson on BBC Radio 4 arts programme *Front Row*, 18.1.00.

[2]   Kazuo Ishiguro, *The Remains of the Day*, New York: Vintage, 1990.

[3]   Jeanette Winterson, *Sexing the Cherry*, New York: Vintage, 1991.

> My name is Jordan. This is the first thing I saw. It was night, about a quarter to twelve, the sky divided in halves, one cloudy, the other fair ...

When Jordan tells us it was night, and that the sky was divided in halves, and so on, we understand ourselves to be directly addressed, by a participant speaking to us, someone who has created an effect of presence, of immediacy before us, notwithstanding the absence enabled by the written medium. By contrast, for the novel to begin

> His name was Jordan. This was the first thing he saw ...

would create an entirely different and more distancing effect. *Whose* name was Jordan, we would then wonder; and − a question which cannot be asked of present-tense descriptions − did it at some point cease to be Jordan? Is he dead now? Where is this Jordan, and who, for that matter, is the person now *telling* us that a certain person's name was Jordan? Narration in the third person licenses such questions, and the sense of written distance that lies behind them, in a way that simply need not apply to narration in the first person. These are banal observations, perhaps, but they may be important to what lies behind the "quasi-autobiographical" turn, to first-person narration focalized by that speaker or thinker, and often proceeding in the form of extended monologue, that appears in a number of the major contemporary novels in English.

I now want to turn to the more specific second tendency in current novels, alluded to earlier: a particular enhanced "spokenness" which seems to be being contrived within the direct discourse parts of some recent novels. Good examples of this enhanced spokenness of character speech can be found in Don De Lillo's novels, particularly *Libra* and *Underworld*. The former treats of Lee Harvey Oswald and the Kennedy assassination. But it includes a compellingly detailed picture of Lee Oswald's mother, Marguerite, whose rambling conversational turns are a feature of the book. That Marguerite is prone to wandering monologue is something we are alerted to as early as page 6, when, from the viewpoint of Lee when a boy, we are told:

> Here it comes. She would forget he was here. She would talk
> for two hours in the high piping tone of someone reading to a
> child.[4]

The example I want to present is of one of Marguerite's monologues,
evidently delivered to someone else. With some effort, the reader can
deduce that Marguerite is speaking to a presiding officer at a truancy
hearing. She has evidently been summoned to this hearing as a result of
Lee's persistent absence from school. Marguerite is speaking in defence
of her son and their way of living:

> This is a boy who studies the lives of animals, the eating and
> sleeping habits of animals, animals in their burrows and caves.
> What is it called, lairs? He is advanced, your honor. I have
> said from early childhood he liked histories and maps. He
> knows uncanny things without the normal schooling. This boy
> slept in my bed out of lack of space until he was nearly eleven
> and we have lived the two of us in the meanest of small rooms
> when his brothers were in the orphans' home or the military
> academy or the Marines and Coast Guard. Most boys think
> their daddy hung the moon. But the poor man just crashed to
> the lawn and that was the end of the only happy part of my
> adult life. It is Marguerite and Lee ever since. We are a
> mother and son. It has never been a question of neglect. They
> say he is truanting is the way they state it. They state to me he
> stays home all day to watch TV. They are talking about a
> court clinic. They are talking about the Protestant Big Brothers
> for working with. He already has big brothers. What does he
> need more brothers for? There is the Salvation Army that is
> mentioned. They take the wrappers off the candy bars I bring
> my son. They turn my pocketbook all out. This treatment is
> downgrading .... How on God's earth, and I am a Christian,
> does a neglectful mother make such a decent home, which I
> am willing to show as evidence, with bright touches and not a
> thing out of place (10-11).

---

[4]   Don De Lillo, *Libra,* Harmondsworth: Penguin, 1991.

A little further on, she recalls, again defensively, how others have criticized her in the past:

> We ate red beans and rice on Mondays. Just because she let us stay a few weeks, I know what she says behind my back. They talk and make up stories, which I am not surprised. They have hidden reasons they aren't telling for how they feel. They say I fly off too quick on the handle. I just can't get along, so-called. They never say it could be they're the ones at fault. They're the ones you can't reason with. She says I take one little word and make a difference out of it, which stands between us until we see each other on the street when it's "Oh hello, how are you, come see us real soon" (36).

De Lillo's *Libra*, and the many renderings of Marguerite Oswald's speech in it, are the best exemplars I currently have of this quasi-transcriptional direct speech, which particularly interests me. But we might also consider James Kelman's much admired *How Late It Was, How Late* (1994), cast entirely in the Glaswegian vernacular used by Sammy, a desperate, even heroic, survivor. The opening is as follows:

> Ye wake in a corner and stay there hoping yer body will disappear, the thoughts smothering ye; these thoughts; but ye want to remember and face up to things, just something keeps ye from doing it, why can ye no do it; the words filling yer head: then the other words; there's something wrong; there's something far far wrong; ye're no a good man, ye're just no a good man. Edging back into awareness, of where ye are: here, slumped in this corner, with these thoughts filling ye. And oh christ his back was sore; stiff, and the head pounding. He shivered and hunched up his shoulders, shut his eyes, rubbed into the corners with his fingertips; seeing all kinds of spots and lights. Where in the name of fuck ...
>
> He was here, he was leaning against auld rusty palings, with pointed spikes, some missing or broke off. And he looked again and saw it was a wee bed of grassy weeds, that was what he was sitting on. His feet were back in view. He studied them; he was wearing an auld pair of trainer shoes for fuck

sake where had they come from he had never seen them afore
man auld fucking trainer shoes. The laces werenay even tied!
Where was his leathers? A new pair of leathers man he got
them a fortnight ago and now here they were fucking missing
man know what I'm saying, somebody must have blagged
them, miserable bastards, what chance ye got. And then left
him here with these. Some fucking deal.[5]

And so on. This is not in fact first-person narration, but third-person
narration with a quite extraordinary extent of free indirect and
vernacularized rendering of Sammy's thoughts. In fact the free — very
free, very character-based — indirect thought extends throughout the
novel; it is the means by which the entire narrative gets told. So while
the Kelman passage is of great interest, I would stress that Marguerite's
speech in *Libra* is the most exemplary of quasi-transcriptional
spokenness that may be emerging in fiction.

These trends seem quite established. They fit well with the way the
more memorable contemporary novels adopt first-person narration,
internal homodiegesis. While this does not guarantee greater use of
direct discourse, it facilitates it. In addition, arguably, the kinds of
individuals constructed as first-person narrators in recent novels from
Swift, Winterson, Rushdie, and so on, are typically more quirky and
less mainstream than those of earlier generations of English novels.
They point to the broad growth of first-person monologic fiction; but in
addition there is the particular interest of the transcript-like style in
which certain characters — not always first-person narrators — are
rendered. Parallel text can be found in the work of the other novelists
mentioned (Winterson, Amis, and so on). Such passages — often quite
extensive in contemporary fiction — are a genuine departure from
standard past practices. They display a degree of closeness to a
transcription of actual speech that goes beyond anything regularly
encountered previously.

Our narratological scrutiny of direct discourse, and in particular of
direct speech in fiction, is considerably more suspicious these days than

---

[5] James Kelman, *How Late It Was, How Late,* New York: Norton, 1994.

it once was. Particularly after Sternberg's important articles,[6] we are more guarded and even sceptical about any assertions to the effect that direct speeches in fictions are verbatim reports of speaker's actual words. We certainly need to recognize that all fiction involves authorial mediation and representation, and the suggestions of pure mimesis that arise if we refer to direct speech as a verbatim copy are, at best, deeply suspect. As Nash remarks, the rendering of characters' conversations (this "voicing", as he calls it) is one of the most powerful "illusions of resemblance" to be found in literature:

> The dominant illusion, cultivated with the help of a small repertoire of linguistic devices (personal pronouns, contractions, elisions, marked syntactic forms, familiar phrase-forms, etc.) is that writing can translate or "transpose" speaking. But if that were wholly true, it would be the death of literature ....
>
> All that an author can really achieve is "writing as speaking as writing", an illusion compounded of illusions: one, the illusion that writing imitates speech; but two, the further illusion that an abstract idea of speech may inform the conventions and devices of writing so effectively that readers will impute to a text a convincing power of *saying*, and will be satisfied that a beloved author is somehow "talking" to them [or, *mutatis mutandis*, that a fictional character is "talking"...][7]

Indeed, as an adherent to the principles of what is coming to be known as integrational linguistics, I would say that conceptualizing a direct speech report as a pure and identical copy of some prior communicational act is symptomatic of the orthodox linguistic mindset which integrational linguistics intends to contest, a mindset which we

---

[6] M. Sternberg, "Point of View and the Indirections of Direct Speech", *Language and Style*, 15/1 (1982), 67-117; and "Proteus in Quotation-Land: Mimesis and the Forms of Reported Discourse", *Poetics Today*, 3/2 (1982), 107-56.

[7] Walter Nash, *Language and Creative Illusion*, London: Longman, 1998, 41.

have characterized as segregationalist.[8] From an integrationalist point of view, asking "how faithful" or "how near to *verbatim* report" a direct speech report is is a misleading way to put matters, since by its nature a report *cannot* be faithful or *verbatim according to any stable or permanent set of criteria* (this latter principle is the crucial integrational one here). In different situations, different criteria for determining faithfulness will apply, and it is interactants and *their* criteria which determine these. They are not determined by the text: the criteria belong to situated interactants and not "the language" nor "the linguist" nor the text.

Fludernik[9] powerfully encapsulated how we should resist the easy idealizing assumption that direct speech is innocent and unproblematic, alluding to "the specious authenticity of direct speech." Literary direct speech, like all other forms of narrative quotation, is double-voiced, narratorially-mediated. Its status as direct speech, with or without typographical boundary-markers, does not render it autonomous of narratorial influence. And from Fludernik and others has come copious documentation of the ways[10] in which direct discourse is acknowledged by the narrator to be an invention, or an edited or schematic approximation, or a condensation, and so on. Just as much as is the case with such discourse types as Free Indirect Discourse, direct discourse can be shaped by tendencies to achieve a degree of typicality and schematism. And Fludernik adds:

> Constraints of the maxims of quality and quantity make it more important to present the "gist" of an utterance rather than its precise wording, which may be all but irrelevant to the

---

[8] Roy Harris, *The Language Myth*, London: Duckworth, 1981; N. Love, "The Locus of Languages in a Redefined Linguistics", in H. Davis and T. Taylor, eds, *Redefining Linguistics*, London & New York: Routledge, 1990, and *Signs, Language and Communication*, London: Routledge, 1996; and my *Total Speech: An Integrational Linguistic Approach to Language*, Durham, NC: Duke University Press, 1996.

[9] Monika Fludernik, *The Fictions of Language and the Languages of Fiction*, London: Routledge, 1993, particularly chapter 8.

[10] These are aspects of "anti-mimeticism", see *ibid.*, 414.

matter in hand: propositional and illocutionary content is much more important than precise phraseological reproduction even to the supposedly verbatim direct discourse representation.[11]

This in turn is so because what "drives" such representations are the intentions and motivations of literary narrators or authors, which are rarely those of the discourse linguist or conversation analyst, nor those of the lawyer, or journalist, or biographer. I would dissent from Nash's and Fludernik's theses only to the extent of suggesting that in some recent fiction an illusion of presenting to the reader something relatively close to a "precise phraseological reproduction" does seem to have become more important than hitherto. The product remains an effect of course, and one, which attends to phraseology to the neglect of other possible characteristics.

At this point it is important to acknowledge also certain much larger trends in English use and English language studies, which are perhaps not unrelated to my topic here. One such trend is the shift, in some kinds of linguistic studies, from an almost exclusive attention to written language and the grammar of relatively standard written English, to an unprecedentedly extensive interest in spoken English and its rather different grammatical patterns. Since 1970, but actually going back to work by Z. Harris and, in Britain, a pioneering article by T.F. Mitchell, there has been a greatly enlarged interest in Spoken English's differentness from written English, its abundant reliance on phrases and words which, by the lights of written English grammar, are hard even to assign to a particular word-class.[12] This interest reflects the

---

[11] *Ibid.*, 418.

[12] See, *inter alia*, the work of Cobuild grammarians (John Sinclair, *et al.,* eds, *Collins COBUILD English Grammar*, London: Collins, 1990), observations in Catherine Emmott, "Real Grammar in Fictional Contexts", *The Glasgow Review*, 4 (1996), 9-23 and *Narrative Comprehension: A Discourse Perspective*, Oxford: Oxford University Press, 1997, and the emerging findings of Ronald Carter and Michael McCarthy, "Grammar and the Spoken Language", *Applied Linguistics*, 16/2 (1995), 41-158 and "Discourse and Creativity: Bridging the Gap between Language and Literature", in G. Cook and B. Seidlhofer, eds, *Principles and Practice in Applied Linguistics,* Oxford: Oxford University Press, 1995, 303-23; P. Hopper, "Discourse and the Category 'Verb' in English", *Language and Communication*, 17/2 (1997), 93-102; J. Nattinger, and J. DeCarrico, *Lexical*

enormously enhanced current interest in a certain kind of "real English" — the English that native speakers actually routinely produce, kinds of English which are profoundly "customized" to fit the communicational situations in which speakers find themselves, kinds of English which are strikingly different from the conventional well-formed decontextualized sentence of traditional grammars and ELT textbooks. It is not just a matter of paying attention to the history and present-day functions, in spoken English, of discourse particles such as *well, like, stuff, after all,* and *just kidding,* although this is a part of it. Rather, it is part of the growth of interest in *discourse* analysis (meaning real discourse, and spoken at that).

A second large trend, evident in the ways and situations in which English (and, no doubt, other languages) has come to be used, concerns the spread of a colloquial and comparatively informal or conversational English into domains of use where, hitherto, a quite formal and even register-specific English was maintained. Part and parcel of this alleged vernacularization is the tendency of styles and genres increasingly to overlap, blend, and re-combine, often in subtle and calculated hybrids.[13] The language in which this new informality and hybridity is sometimes described, implying previous "standards" of formality, decorum, and pure, homogeneous genres and styles of distinct pedigree, is itself open to question, but I will not dwell on that here.

What are some of the more noticeable features of spoken English grammar, sometimes neglected in traditional accounts which are so geared to the written form? McCarthy discusses several, drawing on the Cambridge-Nottingham corpus of contemporary spoken English. Three of particular note are:

> i)   Information-staging by means of topicalizing, fronting, left- or right-dislocation, Subject-copying, participant-reiteration, or similar re-ordering and/or thematic role duplication:

> *He's alright, is that newsagent.*

Phrases and Language Teaching, Oxford: Oxford University Press, 1992, and many others.

[13] On hybridity of genres, see Norman Fairclough, *Discourse and Social Change,* Cambridge: Polity, 1992.

A friend of mine, she's got her railcard ... [14]

ii) Participant-and-process-assumption: this   is   called "situational ellipsis", by Carter and McCarthy, closely related to what generative linguists call "pro-drop":

> *Put the phone in as well for you, did they?*
> *Had lunch yet?* [15]

iii) A relatively low lexical density, by comparison with written language.   This   relates   directly   to   the   context-boundedness of much purposeful spoken language: McCarthy refers to "extremely context-bound types [of talk], such as language-in-action sequences, where language is generated by some task being undertaken at the time". [16] Such talk, he finds, is characterized by a low lexical density (well below the 40% lexical density average derived from a full range of spoken and written texts). [17] This notion of context-bounded talk may be   usefully   compared   with   Chafe's   distinction   between immediate and displaced experience. [18]

   When one contemplates speech representation in prose fiction (drama may often be a different case), where the speech accompanies the kind of activities that often accompany spoken language (meals, drinking, office work, watching TV, etc.) it is unlikely that such low lexical density will be tolerable or, conversely, that a high reliance on

---

[14] Michael McCarthy, *Spoken Languages and Applied Linguistics*, Cambridge: Cambridge University Press, 1998, 61.

[15] *Ibid.*, 64.

[16] *Ibid.*, 65.

[17] *Ibid.*, 40.

[18] Wallace Chafe, "Immediacy and Displacement in Consciousness and Language", in F. Coulmas and J. Mey, eds, *Cooperating with Written Texts: The Pragmatics and Comprehension of Written Texts,* Berlin: Mouton de Gruyter, 1992, 231-55, 251-2.

situation-aware disambiguation is reasonable or sensible. When two or more parties in a novel converse with each other, they do so at the behest of a narrator and for a reading third party. Their talk is designed (not by themselves but by their creator) to achieve several goals, one of which — perhaps the overriding one — is to make a variety of subtle impacts on the cognitive environment of the reader (here Relevance-theoretical terms are arguably helpful). Nothing remotely similar is involved if a friend and I set to work to bake a cake: our words and actions are not scripted in advance by some directorial instructor, nor are they performed for the benefit of a paying observer.

As indicated earlier, this is a relatively new area of interest for me, and everything I am suggesting is tentative and provisional. So, with that caveat lodged, here are some provisional general comments on the nature of this quasi-transcriptional direct discourse. Like the kind of actual spoken English being examined by Carter and McCarthy,[19] and like the spoken English to be found in the Cobuild corpus and elsewhere, this direct discourse often has some at least of the following properties:

1. It has incomplete grammatical constructions, and/or intra-sentential switch from one grammatical format to a different one. (Unless otherwise stated, examples below are from the *Libra*/Marguerite passages).

e.g. *They say he is truanting is the way they state it.*

Still, if Lucky Johnson here has a fancy. (Last Orders)

He was wearing an auld pair of trainer shoes for fuck sake where had they come from he had never seen them afore man auld fucking trainer shoes. (How Late ...)

2. It frequently ellipts pronominal clause subjects, very much as in spontaneous spoken English, when these are fairly predictable in the projected situation. In addition to pronominal subjects, the tensed auxiliary may also be dropped (e.g., *Heard the news?*; *Like your suit*; and so on). Borrowing the term used to describe default

---

[19] Carter and McCarthy, *op.cit.* and McCarthy, *op.cit.*

dropping of pronoun subjects in a language such as Italian, I shall call this feature "pro-drop"

3. It has seemingly unintentional divergences from written English standards in the use or production of idioms, multi-word constructions, and so on:

> *They say I fly off too quick on the handle.*

4. It has malapropisms and general infelicities of word-choice, no doubt in part a reflex of the pressure of composing utterances "in real time" without opportunity of review and revision as in writing:

> *They turn my pocketbook all out. This treatment is downgrading. It is not my fault if he dresses below the level.*

5. There is reiteration of sentence theme across strings of sentences (rather than, for example, coordination of multiple clauses within one sentential construction). This sacrifices thematic variety while facilitating compositional fluency and ease of processing:

> *They say he is truanting is the way they state it. They state to me he stays home all day to watch TV. They are talking about a court clinic. They are talking about the Protestant Big Brothers for working with.*

In fact, as the last two sentences indicate, the reiterated material may extend well beyond the grammatical theme or topic, well into the predicate: "*They are talking about a court clinic. They are talking about the Protestant Big Brothers ...*" In Halliday's systemic linguistic terms, the most relevant textual system to refer to here is that of Given vs New. Like unscripted naturally-occurring conversational English, the direct discourse under scrutiny here is often characterized by relatively enlarged or extended Given segments, and relatively brief New segments. This by definition tends to make speech easier to process, whether it is of the naturally-occurring or fictional and invented variety.[20]

6. But speech or direct discourse with briefer segments of New information does not in itself guarantee ease or transparency of processing. And in fact this quasi-transcriptional direct discourse is sometimes quite difficult to follow. Again, twentieth-century readers are by now quite used to the idea that certain kinds of character-based discourse will present us with sense-making difficulties, particularly interior monologue and stream of consciousness. But I would tentatively suggest that we are less used to expecting to encounter difficulties with direct speech. Or at least, the difficulties we are used to encountering have to do with renderings of dialect pronunciation and syntax, of dialect vocabulary, and so on. In the case of Marguerite Oswald and other characters rendered in this new quasi-transcriptional way, I would suggest the difficulties have little to do with dialect, her speech being not very noticeably dialectal at all. Whatever difficulties there are stem from her discourse being significantly closer to real spoken English, in all its non-written-ness, than we are used to seeing to fiction.

7. So we find stretches of theme-iteration and quasi-automatic utterance-construction.[21] But alongside these there are also abrupt shifts of topic from one sentence to the next, shifts that are unsignalled or under-signalled (e.g., via discourse markers):

---

[20] For discussions of repetition see, *inter alia*, D. Tannen, *Talking Voices: Repetition, Dialogue, and Imagery in Conversational Discourse*, Cambridge: Cambridge University Press, 1989; N. Norrick, "Functions of Repetition in Conversation", *Text*, 7/3 (1987), 245-64; and a narratological application in S. Ehrlich, "Narrative Iconicity and Repetition in Oral and Literary Narratives", in Jean-Jacques Weber and Peter Verdonk, eds, *Twentieth Century Fiction: From Text to Context,* London: Routledge, 1995, 78-95; see also my chapter on repetition, from a theoretical linguistic point of view, in Toolan, *op.cit.*.

[21] These are very much of the kind Tannen, *op.cit.*, has identified in spoken English and discussed as a kind of repetitive patterning.

He knows uncanny things without the normal schooling. This boy slept in my bed until he was nearly eleven ....

There is the Salvation Army that is mentioned. They take the wrappers off the candy bars I bring my son.

There is clearly a risk in some of this: abrupt and unexplained topic-shifts, from one sentence to the next, is often taken in lay and medical circles as an index of pathology or dysphasia, of one degree or another of incoherence and lack of attunement to addressee needs and expectations. Informally, there is a danger that the reader will stigmatize such characters as "rambling", dysfunctional, self-imprisoned, and so on. On the other hand, the kind of un-spelled-out topic shifting here — crucially, without the kind of disambiguating co-textual narrative commentary that might have been found in earlier kinds of fiction — often feels truer to the nature of the characters being disclosed than any more explicit and "spelled-out" version of the same discourse would be. And it is often a mark of a character's alert integratedness, within a situation, that such abridged direct discourse is adopted: it becomes a sign of smartness or sharpness rather than being an indicator of mental fogginess. This is very clear in the direct speech portions of Elmore Leonard's novels, for example.

8. Finally, what seems to me most centrally to characterize quasi-transcriptional direct discourse comes to the fore if we review again the nature of a verbatim transcript of actual conversation. By such a transcript I mean one that is silent on so many factors likely to be relevant to the occurrence of language within an integrated communicational situation, such as gaze, kinesics, proxemics, stress and intonation, and so on. Because in a somewhat similar way, in quasi-transcriptional direct speech, there is a strong sense of the text's incompleteness, and a strong sense of the need to supplement that which is explicitly given, on the page, with phrasings, tones of voice, attitudes, and gestures which are not directly stated but, if I may risk a tautology, which are palpably implicit. One reflex of this is that (it seems) you have to "voice" these texts as you read them (again, in a way that I think is *not* the case when we read dialectal direct speech in nineteenth-century

novels, or even earlier twentieth-century ones like Lawrence and Faulkner). Often you have to "intone" or "intonate" the text in order to grasp the sense-segmentation — just as you must with psycholinguistic test sentences such as the following:

> *Since Jay always jogs a mile seems like a short distance to him.*

In very broad terms, as has long been recognized, writing seems able to stand free of immediate context, conversational speech seems to require that we attend to its immediate nonverbal context. With that broad contrast in place, what kind of hybrid is speech represented in writing? That which it represents (speech) tends to require contextualization. That which we actually encounter — words on the page — clearly tries to be effective with a *limited* degree of such contextualization. And one way in which it has done so, traditionally, is by means of narratorial clarifications, in framing clauses, adjacent sentences, etc., of speaker's topics, motives, movements, etc. But I think the direct speech in novels such as *Libra,* or in any of Elmore Leonard's novels, is interesting because it stands with a sharply reduced supporting and disambiguating documentation, in the form of those co-textual commentaries. The literal or word-for-word record is fuller — by which I mean of course that it creates the illusion of being fuller; while the non-verbal contextualization is reduced. In following both these courses, similarities to natural speech are enhanced: as noted, in natural conversation we do repeat, repair, rephrase and ramble; and in natural conversation we are not independently told, by our co-conversationalists or anyone else that they are now speaking in a steely voice, nor are we told that as they are saying such-and-such they are wrinkling their nose or reaching for their glass of wine, and so on. *Libra*-like direct speech similarly tries to do without such running commentary too. In these various ways, quasi-transcriptional direct speech plays havoc with the kind of distinction powerfully articulated by Chafe in terms of immediate and displaced experience. Ordinarily, a participant in a conversation is involved in an immediate experience, while an addressee of a narrative, or a reader of fictional dialogue, might be said to be processing a displace experience; and in that spirit Chafe comments:

> Displaced experience is qualitatively different. First, whereas immediate experience is part of an uninterrupted flow, displaced experience has an island-like quality that motivates the provision of a setting, as well as the inclusion of proper introductions for important unshared referents. Second, whereas immediate experience has access to a wealth of fine-grained nonsalient detail, displaced experience does not.[22]

Part of the interest of *Libra*-like direct speech is that, *despite* its island-like quality, expectable settings and proper introductions are not provided: there is an out-of-the-ordinary projection of this displaced experience *as if* it were immediate experience.

Like metaphor-laden poetry, such discourse is in part a riddle or puzzle, for the reader to work at and figure out. And in this respect, at least, one aspect of the burden of characterization is passed on to the reader: the burden of fleshing-out these speaking entities as individuals, via inferencing. The characters do not merely speak on and on, in their rambling and protracted way; they also emerge as creatures shaped by complex combinations of affect. Clearly, this enlarged inferential-interpretive task is not merely a burden or responsibility, but also an opportunity and a pleasure.

My general thesis is that, as a part of a widespread contemporary understanding of "how to render characters" — thus, as part of the contemporary aesthetics of narrative fiction (in English, at least) — it has become accepted that it may be appropriate for "direct speech" in fiction to contain ungrammaticality, repetition, structurally-fractured sentences, "pro-drop", obscurely incomplete relative clauses, and so on, to an unprecedented extent. It is not the relative "closeness" of such writing to actual speech, by contrast with earlier styles, that is what is most interesting or worth celebrating. In the matter of "closeness" to authentic speech, written narratives will always be a distant second to what can be achieved in the audiovisual narrative mediums of film and television: on film, characters can speak entirely as naturally and authentically as they might in real life, with a kind of vanishing point of vraisemblance being reached when actors are filmed interacting, in their character roles, in spontaneous and unscripted dialogue. The kind of naturalness or "spokenness" of represented speech in written narratives

---

[22] Chafe, *op. cit.*, 251-2.

can never compete with the kind of actuality of speech achievable in film narratives. But then in the latter, speech appears simply to have been recorded and played back (as in an item in a TV news bulletin). By contrast the speech we seem to encounter in written narratives is of course not speech at all, but a transcript or representation. And since we know all along that these written passages are a contrivance rather than a neutral record, my interest is in why it is that writers are now going to such trouble to include in these representations such a plethora of features of naturally-occurring speech. To risk an analogy, the kind of shift I believe to be taking place is analogous to a judicial system rapidly and tacitly moving to a changed practice in the recording of proceedings. Imagine a situation in which a court's proceedings, hitherto recorded verbatim but without any indicators of speakers' intonation, abruptly began to be recorded in the official records with detailed markings of speakers' stress, pitch and volume.

But it is not *only* analogous to revised courtroom testimony recording, for in the latter "closeness" to the actual must in large measure remain a predominant goal, whereas "closeness" to actual speech, in fictional representations, is not at all a self-evident and unqualified goal. Alongside courtroom recording, by way of analogy, we should set something like the practice of rendering in modern art. Take Monet's multiple renderings of the east face of Rouen Cathedral. At least one of these can be found in the fine surroundings of the Rouen Musée des Beaux Arts. But at the expense of a short walk, one can situate oneself in front of the east face of Rouen Cathedral in actuality − and, if really punctilious, one can further wait for something like the time of day, the light, the fog, etc., that Monet rendered in one or other of his paintings of that prospect. This raises the broader question of why an artist would ever attempt to achieve "absolute fidelity or closeness" in the rendering of a straightforwardly observable physical object, particularly one that endures over time, such as a known cathedral, mountain, or field of olive trees. The question can probably answered in several divergent ways. One conclusion is that the exercise is absurd (in attempting something trivial and doomed to fall short), but still one would wonder why artists felt moved to paint easily observable and permanent objects, unless it were "for export only", as it were: paintings of the Taj Mahal for people who cannot get to the real thing. An alternative conclusion is that asking "Why aim for representational closeness?" reflects a false understanding of what the artistic representation of known objects attempts to do. The latter is surely the case. In Monet's interpretive rendering of Rouen Cathedral, as by extension in every kind of representational art, there is a "both-and" tension in play: there are respects in which Monet's painting can be assessed in its plausible rendering of the known cathedral, and there are respects in which plausibility (or, to use a more disciplinary term, "accuracy") is an irrelevant criterion, where, rather, unexpectedness and insight of interpretation, going "beyond" what the ordinary onlooker sees or the mechanical camera records, makes the criterion of accuracy erroneous and that of closeness alien.

If, as claimed here, there has been a slight general shift in contemporary fiction towards first person narration and more transcription-like direct speech, why might these trends have developed? Concerning the first, broad trend, away from third person narrative in favour of first-person fiction, typically from the voice and focalization of a predominant individual, it is possible that this is in part be due to a contemporary literary antipathy for anything that might imply omniscience or essentialist foundations. It is all a matter of effects, conventions, and illusions, of course: all narrators can be deemed omniscient, or non-omniscient, as one prefers. But if a writer wants to get furthest away from any implication that their narrative is all-knowing, that the characters are controlled by a covert higher power, then it is always appropriate to opt for the illusions of modesty, singulative bias, and human immediacy, that first-person projects.

As for the emergence of quasi-transcriptional direct speech, I suspect this may be related to the twentieth-century explosion of film and televisual narrative forms. It is surely incontestable that the contemporary range of contrasting means of making narratives has consequences concerning the particular effects sought in, and techniques developed by, each competing format within that range. Certain aspects of narrative which are hard if not impossible to convey in writing are almost incomparably easy to achieve in film. And vice versa: consider the difficulty of conveying, on film, the complex ironic proposition expressed by the opening sentence of Jane Austen's *Pride and Prejudice*. Short of recourse to a narratorial voice-over, or a superimposed written caption — both of which introduce kinds of artificiality or framing that may be acutely inappropriate — it is hard to see how one can swiftly and precisely communicate the proposition that "a single man in possession of a good fortune must be in want of a wife (everyone seems to know)." At any rate, despite its many seductive charms, it seems fair to say that one thing film narrative cannot easily resort to is the purveying of inspectable written transcripts of characters' speeches (notwithstanding the various functions and effects of captions in silent movies, foreign films, and as aids for the hearing-impaired). So this is one area for growth or elaboration, in written narratives, which film narratives cannot plausibly colonize. Films are incontestably wonderful at conveying characters' speech, in whatever dialectal distinctiveness it may have. Take Graham Swift's *Last Orders*, a sequence of interrelated accounts from a group of Cockney English speakers: no matter how well we feel Swift has represented their speech on the page, the written page self-evidently cannot deliver to us the sound of these Cockney speakers; but the film medium, in a decent production, quite straightforwardly can. (This is not to say, however, that when we watch a film we hear actual speech: an audiotape of Meryl Streep speaking Cockney is not quite the same thing as Meryl Streep speaking Cockney). In the matter of rendering Cockney speech — or, for that matter, Irish speech, or Glaswegian, or that of pre-war English butlers or of Faulkner's Southerners — between the novel and the film there is no contest. The written narrative does not have it in it to relay to us any sounds at all. What it can do, however, is provide us with a record, a blueprint, an analysis, a fascinated dwelling-upon and inspecting of that speech which it cannot relay (in so doing, it is grappling with speech in a postmodern spirit). It can announce in advance that the character's following words were said in a husky voice, for example — something that film cannot easily or satisfactorily do (in these and other ways it can stretch the foundational linguistic principle of cotemporality). So speech in the novel is an artifice that differs in kind from that involved in reproducing speech in film, and writers can strive to conceal or moderate the artificiality entailed by this tautology, "speech in the novel". Alternatively, they can elect to embrace and elaborate that artifice, through extensive, transcript-like representations. Novelists who do this seem to be intent on furthering a kind of "self-characterization" (that is, characters reveal themselves by a "more *vraisemblable*" record of how they speak). But at the same time those novelists are taking the risk of alienating the reader, on account of their texts' naturalistic conversational fumblings, repetitions, incoherencies, and ellipses.

JOYCEAN SONICITIES

PETER DE VOOGD

It is a commonplace that text can at best suggest, but never reproduce reality.[1] Some time ago I discussed this truism in an article about that most "realistic" of modernist authors, James Joyce.[2] In that article I coined the concept of "sonicity" (the audible counterpart of "iconicity"[3] and distinguished between three different kinds of sonicity, all of them quite typical of Joyce's work: (1) the quasi-realistic representation of a sound; (2) the deliberately unrealistic anthropomorphic rendering of one; and (3) formal poetic onomatopoeia.

The last category is, of course, one of the better known rhetorical tricks, and the one most happily pointed out by our students. Its standard example is "cuckoo", and I am happy to say that I will be able

---

[1] This article is based on a paper given at the Second International Conference on Iconicity and Literature, held in Amsterdam in 1999. Shortly after (but with no causal connection) the author was struck by a double heart attack. This contribution was written supine, with two fingers and some effort, and very limited access to notes and other material.

[2] Peter de Voogd, "Joycean Typeface", in A. Fischer, M. Heusser, and T. Hermann, eds, *Aspects of Modernism*, Tübingen: Gunter Narr Verlag, 1997, 203-18.

[3] "Iconicity" is most completely and authoritatively defined in the website of the International Conference on Iconicity and Literature: "Iconicity as a semiotic notion refers to a natural resemblance or analogy between the form of a sign ('the signifier', be it a letter or sound, a word, a structure of words, or even the absence of a sign) and the object or concept ('the signified') it refers to in the world or rather in our perception of the world. The similarity between sign and object may be due to common features inherent in both: by direct inspection of the iconic sign we may glean true information about its object. In this case we speak of 'imagic' iconicity (as in a portrait or in onomatopoeia, e.g. 'cuckoo') and the sign is called an 'iconic image'."

to conclude with an example that does, indeed, contain that most onomatopoeic bird known to man.

Examples of the first category − the quasi-realistic representation of a sound − abound in Joyce (and it would be amusing to have them all on one compact disc, much in the way in which there exist collections of Joycean songs). The best-known example is probably Bloom's nameless cat in "Calypso", who gets increasingly hungry as Bloom potters about in his kitchen. She first goes "Mkgnao!" (*Ulysses,* 4.163), and more insistently "Mrkgnao!" (*U*.4.25), and even "Mrkrgnao! the cat said loudly" (*U*.4.32), all of which makes perfect sense to readers with cats. Bloom, many lines of text later, speaks to his cat in human language, saying "Miaow!", which is our standard orthography, and Joyce makes it very clear that this is the wrong way of doing it. Joyce specialized in the non-verbal interjection ("thnthnthn", for instance, in *U*.11.100, giving sound to the boots' rude imitation of Miss Douce's rejoinder; "hnhn" for Mrs Breen's "pigeon kiss" in 15.492; Bloom's clacking his tongue in compassion "Dth! Dth!" in 8.287-88). And there are borderline cases where it is difficult to decide whether the sound is in category one or the next.

The second category, the unrealistic anthropomorphic rendering of sound, can be best illustrated by Stephen's ashplant. As readers we know that his walking stick does not really say "Steeeeeeeeeeeephen!" (*U*.1.629) but its mildly accusatory screech makes sense in the circumstances. At the very end of "Circe" a horse neighs meaningfully to Bloom "Hohohohohohoh! Hohohohome!" (*U*.15.4879).

The next example combines this, and the third category, the one in which the sound is suggested through purely poetic means. In "Sirens", the most musical episode in *Ulysses*, when Bloom sits listening to Simon Dedalus singing the aria "M'Appari" from Von Flotow's opera *Martha*, this is how Joyce mimics the effect on the listener of the final sustained long note:[4]

---

[4] All references are to the Gabler edition of *Ulysses* (H.W. Gabler, *Ulysses/James Joyce: A Critical and Synoptic Edition*, New York: Garland Publishing, 1984). All my citations will have to be limited to very short bits only, because of copyright restrictions.

Come ...!

It soared, a bird, it held its flight, a swift pure cry, soar silver orb it leaped serene, speeding, sustained, to come, don't spin it out too long, long breath he breath long life, soaring high, high resplendent, aflame, crowned, high in the effulgence symbolistic, high, of the etherial bosom, high, of the high vast irradiation everywhere all soaring all around about the all, the endlessnessnessness ....

To me! (*U*.11.744-51).

The principle at work here (and it is the one that gives *Finnegans Wake* its great poetic force) is that the text itself is made to do what standard orthography cannot. Nor, for that matter, standard English — which is why Joyce invented "Wakese". Moreover, although a good singer can hold that "come" for as long as it takes, the reader of the text cannot possibly read that text in one single breath — nonetheless, a simple experiment will show that it takes as long to speak that text as it takes the tenor to sustain the note (all it needs is one speaker and one tenor — or a CD rendering).

Considering the variant possibilities of Joycean sonicity, it makes sense that the same sonic "word" in the text often leads to different "meanings", depending on the fictitious character hearing it. In the all but last episode, Stephen and Bloom both hear, at the same time, the bells of St George's Church strike the hour. This makes Stephen think of the Prayers for the Dying, while they sound cheerful to Bloom. The text states that Stephen hears "*Liliata rutilantium*" whereas Bloom hears "heigho". The reader knows that those bells don't sound like the Prayer for the Dying ("*Liliata rutilantium*") even though they have that connotation for Stephen. Bloom's "hearing" is correct. The narrator is wrong as well, by the way. There is obvious onomatopoeia in the wonderful sentence in which the bells are mentioned: "The sound of the peal of the hour of the night by the chime of the bells in the church of Saint George" (*U*.17.1226-27).

There is a curious problem with those church bells — those dactylics may yield the impression of rhythmical sound, they are in fact (realistically) wrong. As the orthography makes quite clear, the bells of

St George's Church do not emit dactylics at all. I know that all my students, born as they are in the Post-Disneyan era, read that text wrong, and so will quite a few of you. Consider the first time they are heard (by Bloom), at the very beginning of the book, in the 4th episode:

> Heigho! Heigho!
> Heigho! Heigho!
> Heigho! Heigho!

It takes a modern reader some time, I'm sure, to realize that we should read, NOT the Seven Dwarves'

" - / - /"

but

"/ \ / \"

— the colonial sound of Big Ben, echoing throughout the British Empire, in 1904, the year of *Ulysses*. To understand this correctly, we must know about Big Ben, and realize that what we hear is the signal for "three quarters of the hour", at, presumably, a quarter to nine in the morning.

In this article I will focus on one specific episode, and select three concrete cases of Joycean sonicity. The episode selected is known as "Nausikaa", the 13th, but at the very centre of the book. The time is 8 o'clock in the evening, the scene Sandymount beach. The chapter divides itself between alternating points of view, first through the consciousness of romantic Gerty Macdowell, then through that of Bloom. The action is threefold: on the beach is Gerty Macdowell, with friends; in the Church nearby a prayer meeting takes place; behind the parapet stands Bloom, looking at Gerty — there are fireworks (time-honoured cinematic symbol) at half past eight, when it gets dark, during which Gerty exposes herself and Bloom masturbates (and Gerty, too, it seems, climaxes). The episode is rounded off by the clock on the mantlepiece in the rectory of the church. Here is the first and straightforward example:

and the choir began to sing the *Tantum ergo* and she just swung her foot in and out in time as the music rose and fell to the tantumer gosa cramen tum.

There is no way in which one could either hear the text that garbled, or swing one's foot without disrupting the rhythm of the music — the nonsensical "tantumer gosa cramen tum" (for, of course, *tantum ergo sacramentum*) can only mean that to Gerty the Latin is meaningless — again, as with the church bells, the text's seeming verisimilitude turns out to be utterly misleading.

Of a different category of sonicity altogether is the long fragment which concludes the fireworks, and which is worth looking at in some detail:

And Jacky Caffrey shouted to look, there was another and she leaned back and the garters were blue to match on account of the transparent and they all saw it and they all shouted to look, look, there it was and she leaned back ever so far to see the fireworks and something queer was flying through the air, a soft thing, to and fro, dark. And she saw a long Roman candle going up over the trees, up, up, and, in the tense hush, they were all breathless with excitement as it went higher and higher and she had to lean back more and more to look up after it, high, high, almost out of sight, and her face was suffused with a divine, an entrancing blush from straining back and he could see her other things too, nainsook knickers, the fabric that caresses the skin, better than those other pettiwidth, the green, four and eleven, on account of being white and she let him and she saw that he saw and then it went so high it went out of sight a moment and she was trembling in every limb from being bent so far back that he had a full view high up above her knee where no-one ever not even on the swing or wading and she wasn't ashamed and he wasn't either to look in that immodest way like that because he couldn't resist the sight of the wondrous revealment half offered like those skirt-dancers behaving so immodest before gentlemen looking and he kept on looking, looking.

She would fain have cried to him chokingly, held out her snowy slender arms to him to come, to feel his lips laid on her

white brow, the cry of a young girl's love, a little strangled
cry, wrung from her, that cry that has rung through the ages.
And then a rocket sprang and bang shot blind blank and O!
then the Roman candle burst and it was like a sigh of O! and
everyone cried O! O! in raptures and it gushed out of it a
stream of rain gold hair threads and they shed and ah! they
were all greeny dewy stars falling with golden, O so lovely,
O, soft, sweet, soft!

There are four sentences here, a short introductory one, a very long
central one, which contains a wonderful mix of idioms (advertising:
"the fabric that caresses the skin", the inappropriate fleeting thought of
the price "four and eleven"; the language of romantic fiction: "the
wondrous revealment"), a third penultimate one, in which Gerty gives
free reign to her favourite reading matter, and lastly the openly not so
very symbolic one that saw to it that the American censor banned the
book.

There is a high ambiguity from the start about the status of words in
this text: "shouted to look, there was another" combines indirect and
direct style, the "it" in "and they all saw it" is one thing for all and
another thing for Bloom, "up, up" and "high, high" does not only go
for that Roman candle. The last sentence need not be spelled out in this
learned discourse — but allow me to say that it seems to make it clear
that the very end of *Ulysses* ("yes I said yes I will yes") was intended
by Joyce to be comparable.

The "Nausikaa" episode ends at nine o'clock. As indicated by a
threefold:

> Cuckoo.
> Cuckoo.
> Cuckoo.

But the "correct" reading here is not a simple onomatopoeic one. It
is first suggested by Buck Mulligan in an earlier episode ("Cuckoo!
Cuckoo! Cuck Mulligan clucked lewdly. O word of fear!", *U.*, 175),
and reinforced in "Circe", when another timepiece goes "cuckoo" three
times, to be answered by the jingle of the bed quoits on which Molly
Bloom has enacted her adultery. Bloom is a cuckold, and the supposed

cuckoo clock does in fact not contain a cuckoo at all, but "a little canarybird" — so much then for onomatopoeia.

Derek Attridge has argued, in a very learned and theoretical article, that Joyce only seems to use onomapotoeia.[5] It seems to me that he overstates his case. Joyce is having his cake while eating it, as so often. In Ulysses he employs all styles, and all the tricks of the writerly trade, over a very broad spectrum indeed, at times mockingly, at times in all seriousness. Thus, Joyce gives and takes at the same time, just as he at one moment deliberately (and satirically) deflates emotive rhetorics (in "Aeolus", for instance) while openly using it for effect elsewhere (the last moment of "Circe"). He did not deny the potential of language to imitate sound, but also showed by example that sounds are as misleading as the printed word. A detailed analysis of all of Joyce's sonicities, obviously beyond the scope of a modest contribution to a Festschrift, would, I think, bring to light that Joyce both exulted in the onomatopoeic potential of language and demonstrated its limitations. When all is heard and done, Joyce's sonic experiments show that his sonicities' meanings only exist within the context created by his text.

---

[5] Derek Attridge, "Language as Imitation: Jakobson, Joyce, and the Art of Onomatopoeia", *MLN*, 99 (1984), 116-40.

EDUCATING THE READER:
NARRATIVE TECHNIQUE AND EVALUATION
IN CHARLOTTE PERKINS GILMAN'S *HERLAND*

JEAN JACQUES WEBER

Herland is an early feminist utopia written by Charlotte Perkins Gilman in 1915. Though it may seem dated in some of its late-Victorian attitudes, towards sex in particular, it is still full of stimulating ideas that can challenge even the modern reader. In fact, many recent critics have insisted on the book's power to shake the reader out of her, or mostly his, unquestioned, naturalized assumptions about women and men. For instance, Burton points out that feminist utopias such as *Herland* "forbid a passive reading, and demand, in their various ways, that the reader participate, think, work at her or his reading and understanding."[1] Ferns contrasts *Herland* with earlier utopias written by men and similarly claims that it "encourages what most utopian fictions prior to it seek to suppress: an active participation on the part of the reader".[2] Here is a final quote from another contemporary critic, again insisting on the active role demanded of the reader of *Herland*:

> The alert contemporary reader is already familiar with the information, which the women want to elicit from their male visitors and so has privileged access to the resisting text. The men themselves are the uncharted territory which gets mapped and plotted: in this novel the colonizers are colonized, the

---

[1] D. Burton, "Linguistic Innovation in Feminist Utopian Fiction, *Ilha do Desterro: A Journal of Language and Literature,* 14 (1985), 82-106, 93.

[2] C. Ferns, "Rewriting Male Myths: *Herland* and the Utopian Tradition", in V. Gough and J. Rudd, eds, *A Very Different Story: Studies on the Fiction of Charlotte Perkins Gilman*, Liverpool: Liverpool University Press, 1998, 24-37, 31.

explorers explored .... It is the ironic process of discovery and filling, the parodic moment of American colonial history, which the novel itself "fills in" for its readers, and the readers fill in for the novel. Part of the novel's didactic purpose then is to challenge the boundaries between what is given and what is withheld in order to allow the reader to be active in the construction of the women's texts, which remain of the novel, part of its range, but not *within* the novel, not part of its text.[3]

What I should like to investigate in this paper is exactly how Gilman succeeds in actively involving the reader. As Bennett points out, the exploration of Herland *by* three men turns into an exploration *of* the men and their attitudes towards women. This in turn becomes, at least by implication, an exploration of the reader's assumptions. And to close the circle of exploration, we can return to the text and analyse what it is about Gilman's narrative technique that allows her to challenge the reader in this way.

Herland is the story of three American men who hope to discover the "strange and terrible Woman Land."[4] The three are clearly differentiated in their attitudes towards life in general, and women in particular: Van, the narrator, is a sociologist with, he claims, a scientific approach to life; Terry is the experienced womanizer with a "practical" attitude towards life, ready to exploit and use women for his own purposes; and Jeff is the chivalrous, gentle and romantic Southerner who idealizes women. In a first encounter upon their arrival in Herland, they get to know three Herland women, Ellador, Alima and Celis, and eventually will fall in love with them and marry them. But

---

[3] B. Bennett, "Pockets of Resistance: Some Notes towards an Exploration of Gender and Genre Boundaries in *Herland*, in V. Gough and J. Rudd, *op.cit,* 38-53, 48.

[4] Quotations are from the 1997 Women's Press edition of *Herland* with an introduction by Anne J. Lane. All words in square brackets are mine, unless otherwise indicated: C.P. Gilman, *Herland*, London: The Women's Press, 1997 [1915], 2.

before this, they go through a number of adventures: they are taken "prisoner" and held in a kind of fortress, and after a futile attempt at escape, they are taught the language and history of Herland. They find out that Herlanders are indeed a new race of women who can reproduce through parthenogenesis (virgin birth capacity) and whose lives are centered around this experience of motherhood. They are amazed at how these mothers have constantly "striven for conscious improvement" (78) in every area of their lives: their religion is a religion of progress, and the sole aim of their system of education is to "allow the richest, freest growth" (102) for the children. During their discussions with the Herland women, the men gradually reveal — willy-nilly — the deficiencies of their (our) own world and become more and more aware of the positive achievements of Herland.

The triple wedding between the three American men and the three Herland women brings out their completely different views of sex and love. Indeed, for the last 2,000 years, these women have had no notion of sex, nor do they know anything about marriage and married life. In his utter frustration, Terry tries to rape his "wife" Alima, but he is overpowered and finally expelled. Ellador and Van leave with Terry, with Ellador due to report back to the Herlanders on the outside world, while Jeff and his by now pregnant Celis stay on in Herland.

A major theme of the book is defeated expectation. What the three men find in Herland goes against all their expectations:

> And we had been cocksure as to the inevitable limitations, the faults and vices, of a lot of women. We had expected them to be given over to what we called "feminine vanity" — "frills and furbelows", and we found they had evolved a costume more perfect than the Chinese dress, richly beautiful when so desired, always useful, of unfailing dignity and good taste.
>
> We had expected a dull submissive monotony, and found a daring social inventiveness far beyond our own, and a mechanical and scientific development fully equal to ours.
>
> We had expected pettiness, and found a social consciousness besides which our nations looked like quarreling children — feebleminded ones at that.
>
> We had expected jealousy, and found a broad sisterly affection, a fair-minded intelligence, to which we could produce no parallel.

> We had expected hysteria, and found a standard of health
> and vigor, a calmness of temper, to which the habit of
> profanity, for instance, was impossible to explain — we tried
> it.[5]

But the male characters' expectations are not the only ones to be
defeated in *Herland*. In this chapter I focus on how the reader's
expectations — both generic and "evaluative" — are defeated. As far as
generic expectations are concerned, the reader might well have
expected a feminist utopia to be told from a female point of view,
whereas in Gilman's text we actually have a male narrator, Van. What
makes *Herland* nonetheless a feminist utopia is the fact that the male
narrator's patriarchal assumptions are deconstructed, thus eroding his
traditional male narrative authority, until the power to name and
construct reality passes into the hands of the Herland women. This is
very different from Gilman's famous short story "The Yellow
Wallpaper" where, despite its female narrator, the power to construct
reality remains in the hands of her cold, sane and rational husband-
doctor, who by contrast defines his wife as irrational, mentally sick and
in need of a particular medical treatment — a diagnosis that the wife
explicitly accepts even while struggling against it. In *Herland*, on the
other hand, the relation between what is normal and what is abnormal
has been inverted by the end of the book. Even though we are in the
presence of a male narrator, he gradually learns to accept the
Herlanders' world as the norm, while seeing his/our world more and
more as a negative deviation from it:

> We had quite easily come to accept the Herland life as normal,
> because it was normal — none of us make any outcry over
> mere health and peace and happy industry. And the abnormal,
> to which we are all so sadly well acclimated, she [Ellador] had
> never seen.[6]

---

[5] Gilman, *op.cit.*, 81.

[6] *Ibid.*, 136.

Another expectation that many readers may have held, at least in the initial stages of their reading, is that, in the contrast between Herland and our world, the Herland women would be evaluated positively, whereas the men (especially Terry) and their world would be evaluated negatively. But again, our expectations are defeated at least to some extent. In the brief analysis below, we shall see that in fact the Herlanders as well as Terry are evaluated both positively and negatively. The evaluative devices that I have looked at are the following:

Main evaluative devices in *Herland*:

1. explicit evaluation
   a.   evaluative adverbs and adjectives
   b.   evaluative comments

2. implicit evaluation
   a.   metaphor
   b.   other lexical innovations

The main distinction is between explicit and implicit evaluative devices, the difference being that in the latter the evaluative element is not directly inscribed in the text, but has to be inferred and (re)constructed by the reader.[7] First I focus on evaluative adverbs and adjectives, of which Gilman makes frequent use in her descriptions of the characters' verbal, and other, behaviour. In order to keep the analysis manageable, I ignore Van and Jeff, and only concentrate on what we might expect to be the two extremes of Gilman's evaluative continuum in *Herland*, namely Terry at one end and the Herlanders at the other. As expected, Terry is indeed associated with a large number of negative dimensions of behaviour:[8]

---

[7]   For the distinction between explicit and implicit evaluation, see Clara Calvo and Jean-Jacques Weber, *The Literature Workbook*, London: Routledge, 1998, 130-4.

[8]   'ly' between brackets means that both adverb and adjective forms occur.

- *negative behaviour or attitude*: bitterly, drily, grim(ly), rudely, savagely, sourly, angry, critical, immensely disgusted, irritable, jealous, severe.
- *sense of superiority (often in connection with irony or sarcasm)*: grandly, incredulous(ly), mightily, triumphantly, that funny half-blustering air of his, contemptuous, defiant, masterful, patronizing, suave.
- *lack of restraint*: he quite desperately longed to see her, madly in love, who fretted sharply in his restraint, in desperate impatience.
- *lack of honesty or intention to deceive*: most winningly, his brilliant ingratiating smile.
- *lack of intelligence*: fondly imagining.

The Herlanders, on the other hand, tend to be associated with the positive end of these and other behavioural dimensions:

- *positive behaviour or gentleness*: apologetically, civilly, courteously, gently, kind(ly), polite(ly), sweet(ly).
- *good humour*: delightedly, gaily, laughingly, merrily, smiling(ly), contented, mischievous.
- *sense of restraint or emotional balance*: calm(ly), patient(ly), smoothly and evenly, the evenest tempers, restrained, serene.
- *sense of morality or honesty*: frank(ly), honestly, frank and innocent, sincere.
- *intelligence or desire for knowledge*: farsightedly, eager(ly), subtly, intelligent, deeply wise.
- *courage or strength*: daringly, decidedly, solidly, steadily, assured and determined, brave and noble, powerful, sturdy, wholly unafraid.
- *feelings or sensitivity*: wistfully, deeply, reverently tender, a deep, tender reverence.

So far, the distribution of explicit evaluative devices conforms to the reader's expectations, but this is by no means the whole story.

Interestingly, Terry is also attributed evaluative devices, which situate him on the positive side of many of the above dimensions:

- *positive behaviour*: [Terry] finished politely, made a polite speech.
- *good humour*: he added cheerfully, he pleasantly inquired, when specially mischievous.
- *restraint*: Terry patiently explained, he cried softly in restrained enthusiasm.
- *honesty*: he honestly believed.
- *intelligence*: said Terry sagely, he was considerably wiser.
- *courage or strength*: He was a man's man, very much so, generous and brave and clever.
- *feelings or sensitivity*: Terry was keenly mortified.

Moreover, the Herland women are also given negative evaluative devices stressing in particular their emotional coldness: grave, grim, severe(ly), stern, unsmiling. Sometimes, though, when a negatively evaluated adverb or adjective is used of the Herlanders, its effect is toned down by being combined with a more positively evaluated one:

> Zava, observing Terry with her *grave sweet* smile
> She explained to me, with *sweet seriousness*
> strength was of small avail against those *grim, quiet* women
> one or two more *strong grave* women followed
> Moadine, *grave and strong*, as sadly patient as a mother.

We can conclude that, just as with Terry, the evaluation of the Herland women is both positive and negative. Though presented in a basically positive way, the Herland world is perhaps a bit too serious, too bland. For Terry, it is like "perpetual Sunday school" (99), and Van calls the Herland view of love and sex "rather ... prosaic" (138). Even Ellador, a Herlander herself, is aware of this when she says: "I can see how monotonous our quiet life must seem to you, how much more stirring yours must be" (135).

This blandness and monotony of Herland life is further emphasized by an implicitly evaluative metaphor, which is repeated a couple of times in the text, in which Herlanders are compared to ants or bees:

"Go to the ant, thou sluggard − and learn something", he
[Jeff] said triumphantly. "Don't they cooperate pretty well?
You can't beat it. This place is just like an enormous anthill −
you know an anthill is nothing but a nursery. And how about
bees? Don't they manage to cooperate and love one another?"
(67)

"You're talking nonsense − masculine nonsense", the
peaceful Jeff replied. He was certainly a warm defender of
Herland. "Ants don't raise their myriads by a struggle, do
they? Or the bees?" (99)

Note, however, that in both contexts the metaphor is not wholly
negative, unlike in Huxley's anti-utopia *Brave New World*, where the
Brave New World citizens are also compared to ants, aphids and
maggots.[9] The Biblical quote in the first extract ("Go to the ant thou
sluggard") emphasizes the positive implications of the image.
Moreover, in each case the speaker is Jeff, who is in fact the staunchest
advocate and admirer of Herland among the three men, as the narrator
himself points out (in the second extract above: "He was certainly a
warm defender of Herland"). The evaluative implication of this
metaphor is therefore somewhat ambiguous: whereas it may have been
seen in a rather positive light by Gilman herself and many of her
contemporary readers, it will probably be interpreted in a more

---

[9] Aldous Huxley, *Brave New World,* Harmondsworth: Penguin, 1966 [1932]. In
Brave New World the contexts for the metaphor are wholly and consistently
negative, as in:

> The approaches to the monorail station were black with the ant-like
> pullulation of lower-caste activity (65)

or:

> Like maggots they had swarmed defilingly over the mystery of Linda's
> death. Maggots again, but larger, full grown, they now crawled across
> his grief and his repentance (165).

negative way by late twentieth-century (or early twenty-first century) readers — unless, perhaps, they are devout Christians.

Other evaluations of Herland characters are equally ambivalent. To give just one more example, discusses Ellador's reaction to Van's sexual advances in the following scene:

> She was impressed visibly. She trembled in my arms, as I held her close, kissing her hungrily. But there rose in her eyes that look I knew so well, that remote clear look as if she had gone far away even though I held her beautiful body so close, and was now on some snowy mountain regarding me from a distance. (138)

and comments on the ambivalence of Ellador's stance: "is she admirably detached and objective or cold and unemotional?"[10]

In the face of such ambivalent evaluations of Herland and its inhabitants, the reader is left free to make up her or his own mind. However, the reader who takes a more negative perspective is brought up short, because his perspective then comes close to Terry's views, which are more and more discredited and ridiculed within the novel. Even his best friends, Jeff and Van, gradually turn against Terry and reject his totally inadequate attitudes towards women. Here is a sample of Van's negatively evaluative comments about Terry:

> It was really unpleasant sometimes to see the notions he had. (9)
>
> I hated to admit to myself how much Terry had sunk in my esteem. (74)
>
> But when all that is said, it doesn't excuse him. I hadn't realized to the full Terry's character — I couldn't, being a man. (130)

But again, as we almost expect by now from Gilman, there is also a reverse side to the presentation of Terry. Van's negatively evaluative

---

[10] V. Gough, "'In the Twinkling of an Eye': Gilman's Utopian Imagination", in V. Gough and J. Rudd, eds, *A Very Different Story: Studies on the Fiction of Charlotte Perkins Gilman*, Liverpool: Liverpool University Press, 1998, 129-43, 139-40.

comments are balanced by positively evaluative comments such as the following:

> I always liked Terry. (9)
> Terry, at his worst, in a black fury for which, as a man, I must have some sympathy. (123)
> "After all, Alima was his wife, you know", I urged, feeling at the moment a sudden burst of sympathy for poor Terry. For a man of his temperament − and habits − it must have been an unbearable situation. (139)

Even Ellador, towards the end of the book, learns to empathize, at least to some extent, with Terry:

> "And I begin to see − a little − how Terry was so driven to crime". (139)

Thus even Terry is not evaluated wholly negatively, mostly because of the friendship between Van and Terry, which has only gradually been weakened. An open-minded evaluative stance similar to Van's would also seem to be the normal position to take up for the (male) reader of *Herland*; he might well adopt the perspective of Van who learns to appreciate more and more both Herland in general and Ellador in particular, as can be seen from the following comments, in each of which the key-word is *grow* or *growth*:

> There was *growing* in our minds, at least in Jeff's and mine, a keen appreciation of the advantages of this strange country and its management.(77)

> I think it was only as I *grew* to love Ellador more than I believed anyone could love anybody, as I *grew* faintly to appreciate her inner attitude and state of mind. (109)

> I can see clearly and speak calmly about this now, writing after a lapse of years, years full of *growth* and education. (121)

> So we *grew* together in friendship and happiness, Ellador and
> I. (130; author's italics)

Female readers might perhaps tend to identify more directly with the
Herland women's position, so that their process of reading the male
narrator's text becomes a process of reading between the lines, of
seeing through the language, of noticing and deconstructing the
androcentric assumptions, norms and values underlying what Van says.
But since Van himself is involved in a process of growing, since he
becomes more and more aware of the gaps in his own text and of the
untenability of his male-dominated world's assumptions, there is no
fundamental difference any longer. The text moves from initial
divergence of world-views to final convergence, which makes possible
the happy-end between Ellador and Van. Moreover, it is not just Van
who moves towards the Herlanders' position, but there is a similar
movement on Ellador's part towards Van's position, as we have seen
for instance in Ellador's expression of sympathy for Terry quoted
above. Thus both Ellador and Van are involved in a process of
ideological growth, and the reader, whether she or he identifies more
with the Herlanders or with Van, cannot help being involved in a
similar process of questioning and learning. As Gough puts it, "the
text enacts a mothering process upon its implied reader, who must
'grow' ideologically in the same way that Jeff, and particularly Van, as
narrator, 'grow'."[11]

In the final part of this chapter, I should like to consider briefly why
Gilman may have opted for this particular didactic technique. Her
ultimate aim would seem to be a reconceptualization of our cognitive
schemata or mental models, especially concerning the nature of love
and the roles of women and men. She wants us to change our notions of
what is essentially feminine and what is merely male-constructed, as
Van does in the following extracts:

> Here you have human beings, unquestionably, but what we
> were slow in understanding was how these ultra-women,

---

[11] V. Gough, "Lesbians and Virgins: The New Motherhood in *Herland*, in David
Seed, ed., *Anticipations: Essays in Early Science Fiction and its Precursors*,
Liverpool: Liverpool University Press, 1995, 195-215, 204.

inheriting only from women, had eliminated not only certain masculine characteristics, which of course we did not look for, but so much of what we had always thought essentially feminine. (57)

These women, whose essential distinction of motherhood was the dominant note of their whole culture, were strikingly deficient in what we call "femininity". This led me very promptly to the conviction that those "feminine charms" we are so fond of are not feminine at all, but mere reflected masculinity − developed to please us because they had to please us, and in no way essential to the real fulfilment of their great process. (58-9)

Gilman wants us to step out of fixed gender roles, as defined by our society, and to see femininity as well as masculinity as ideological constructs. She makes us aware of this by contrasting the Herland schemata of men and women with our own:

When we say *men, man, manly, manhood*, and all the other masculine derivatives, we have in the background of our minds a huge vague crowded picture of the world and all its activities. To grow up and "be a man", to "act like a man" − the meaning and connotation is wide indeed. That vast background is full of marching columns of men, of changing lines of men, of long processions of men; of men steering their ships into new seas, exploring unknown mountains, breaking horses, herding cattle, ploughing and sowing and reaping, toiling at the forge and furnace, digging in the mine, building roads and bridges and high cathedrals, managing great businesses, teaching in all the colleges, preaching in all the churches; of men everywhere, doing everything − "the world."

And when we say *women*, we think *female* − the sex.

But to these women, in the unbroken sweep of this two-thousand-year-old feminine civilization, the word *woman* called up all that big background, so far as they had gone in social development; and the word *man* meant to them only *male* — the sex. (137; author's italics)

One important way in which Gilman strengthens the effect upon her reader is through the use of lexical innovations, which frequently include an evaluative element.[12] You may already have spotted the expression "ultra-women" in one of the quotes above, but perhaps more interesting examples of lexical innovation from an ideological and evaluative point of view are "womanfully" and "loving up":

We were borne inside, struggling manfully, but held secure most womanfully, in spite of our best endeavors. (21)

These were women one had to love "up", very high up, instead of down. They were not pets. They were not servants. They were not timid, inexperienced, weak. (141)

While both coinages challenge the masculine preconception of women as weak and easily frightened, the latter also reminds us that even love includes a vertical dimension of power. Terry's view of love

---

[12] Deirdre Burton, *op.cit.*, has written a paper on "linguistic innovation in feminist utopian fiction" (including *Herland*), but disappointingly she only comments on Gilman's frequent use of inverted commas to "make strange" certain words and concepts. However, Gilman does introduce a large number of lexical innovations in *Herland*. These include: "struggling manfully, but held secure most *womanfully*" (23), "It's better than we'd have been likely to get in a *man-country*" (28), "these *ultra-women*, inheriting only from men" (57), "No *pentagonal bodyguard* now!"(74), "As I've said, I had never cared very much for women, nor they for me — not *Terry-fashion*" (90), "We have our *woman-ways* and they have their *man-ways* and their *both-ways*" (97), "We do things *from* our mothers — not for them" (112), "I will give two illustrations, one away *up*, the other away *down*" (123), "How could we be *aloner?*" (125), "we get tired of our *ultra-maleness* and turn gladly to the *ultra-femaleness*" (129), "she deliberately gave me a little too much of her society — always *de-feminized*, as it were" (130), "He professed great scorn of the penalty and the trial, as well as all the other characteristics of 'this miserable *half-country*'"(134), "as for Jeff, he was so thoroughly *Herlandized*" (135), and "These were women one had to love 'up', very high *up*, instead of *down*" (141).

is obviously "loving down", with the male in control, which can turn nasty as in his attempt to master and rape Alima. Their relationship founders on a conflict of attitudes, a mismatch of love schemata, whereas Elladour and Van manage to bridge these differences in their respective world-views, and thus achieve a more fulfilling, and positively evaluated, relationship of "loving up".

Our study of Charlotte Perkins Gilman's narrative technique in *Herland* has shown how the author skillfully defeats her reader's expectations. In particular, by presenting balanced views of both the male chauvinist individual and the utopian female community and by avoiding any kind of black and white stereotyping, she unsettles the reader's "evaluative" expectations. The resulting evaluative ambivalence of the text puts the reader in a position of potential ideological growth, similar to the male narrator's and his female partner's. In the process of constructing their own evaluations of Herland and the Herlanders, many readers, again like Van, are forced as it were into questioning or revising some of their deeply rooted views about the sexes and their relations. It is this highly effective narrative and evaluative technique which makes *Herland* an extremely rewarding reading experience and ensures its lasting appeal.

LANGUAGE, TEXT AND DISCOURSE:
ROBERT BROWNING'S "MEETING AT NIGHT" AND "PARTING AT MORNING"

GERARD STEEN

While working on the relationship between language, text and discourse in metaphor, I came across Peter Verdonk's well-known essay "Poems as Text and Discourse: The Poetics of Philip Larkin", which he wrote some fifteen years ago and which was republished in 1991 in a collection of academic papers entitled "Literary Pragmatics".[1] The essay gives an account of Verdonk's own contextual stylistics, and its style is so charming and persuasive that I have not been able to resist the temptation to parody the opening paragraph in full.

> The essay presents a general characterization and a particular demonstration of a pragmatic approach to poetic style. Such an approach does not stop at a consideration of the formal structures of language, but seeks to explain how these structures are actually used and experienced by the participants in an act of communication performed in a particular context ...[2]

Assumptions of this approach are then explicated and subsequently applied to an analysis of Philip Larkin's "Talking in Bed." The final statement of the essay sums up the author's achievement in characteristically modest terms:

---

[1] Peter Verdonk, *How Can We Know the Dancer from the Dance? Some Literary Stylistic Studies of English Poetry,* Amsterdam: Amsterdam University Press, 1988, and "Poems as Text and Discourse: The Poetics of Philip Larkin", in R.D. Sell, ed., *Literary Pragmatics*, London: Routledge, 1991, 94-109.

[2] Verdonk, 1991, *op.cit.*, 95.

I have ... tried to uncover some of the meanings of "Talking
in Bed" as a mode of discourse, and to link these with the
poem's "inwardly turned meaning" (Verdonk 1984), that is
the meaning generated by its structuring elements, in the firm
belief that here a verbal device has been constructed which
will reveal a deeply human experience every time this reader
goes to it.[3]

The predicament of the linguist working with literary texts, or of the
literary scholar who attempts to "go linguistic", could not have been
dramatized more forcefully than in the contrast between these two
quotations, separated by a mere thirteen pages of print. For the essay
sets out as an explanatory and general endeavour in behavioural
linguistics, but ends as an individually interested attempt at semantic
discovery in literary artifice. This predicament is genuine, as I know
only too well from personal experience, and the result of a tension
between the traditions of linguistic and literary studies. Verdonk's work
can be seen as a life-long attempt at resolving the predicament in one
particular fashion, which at the same time is characteristic of many
practitioners of a linguistic approach to literature. The approach often
combines a great knowledge of general principles of language and
language use, including register and style, with a profound literary-
critical interest in individual texts and their interpretation. The general
linguistic principles are used as arguments for specific literary-critical
readings, which turn out to be the major point of interest. And because
these are readings, the impression is conveyed that the general
principles of language and its use explain the particular aspect of this
language use by this individual reader, and that the goal of a pragmatics
of literature and its style has also been achieved.

However, there are basic methodological objections to this mode of
procedure if it is to be taken for scientific research. Explanations of
behaviour, including reading, require well-motivated general claims
that link one proposition to another in a causal connection. An example
would be the given-new contract: if a linguistic element occurs in

---

[3]   *Ibid.*, 108 (referring within the text to "Poetic Artifice and Literary Stylistics",
Dutch Quarterly Review of Anglo-American Letters, 3 (1984), 215-28).

clause-initial position, it will be taken as given; if it occurs towards the end of a clause, it will be taken as new.[4] Of claims of this type there is no shortage in linguistics. But solid explanations also require well-established and independent facts, which have a critical bearing on each of the propositions. To continue the previous example, we would need reliable observations about the positions and attributed information status of linguistic elements before we can proceed to test the general claim against the data and their relations, or before we can say that one part of the data is explained by the other part of the data, in conjunction with the general claim. And this requirement for an explanation, of course, does not fare very well in linguistic approaches to literature of the kind described above. For the linguist or literary scholar performs his or her data collection on the reading process by studying his or her own reading process, which may be prolonged and altered throughout the data collection process. And apart from this methodological objection, there is the issue of the object of study itself: the kind of reading which is studied in this approach may be one class of reading indeed, but it would require an ingenious argument to see it as representative for literary reading as a more wide-spread phenomenon. My conclusion is that not much is strictly explained about the actual usage and experience of structures in literary reading. Instead, what is achieved is a well-founded justification of a professional interpretation, which includes sophisticated moments of understanding and appreciation. Let there be no mistake, this is no small or invaluable feat. But it does represent only one kind of solution to the tension between the traditions of literary and linguistic research, and it is based not in explanation, but in argumentation.

In my own research, the temptation usually works in the other direction: personal reading interest often gives way to an attempt to formulate general explanations of language use that are amenable to empirical testing. The present contribution aims to illustrate this interest and its origins in personal reading. In this manner, my contribution provides a mirror image to Verdonk's essay, but discusses language, text, and discourse from an empirical rather than a hermeneutic

---

[4] H.H. Clark, and S.E. Haviland, "Comprehension and the Given-New Contract", in R.O. Freedle, ed., *Discourse Production and Comprehension*, Norwood, NJ: Ablex, 1977, 1-40.

perspective. In particular, my own mode of working includes a movement from my reception of a particular text to the formulation and testing of general claims. I do not have to attempt to understand a text and appreciate its value completely before I can proceed in inductive fashion to build causal connections between generalizations of particular observations. It is especially this disrespect for the unique text in the service of nomothetic research, which has troubled many scholars like Peter Verdonk, but their own idiographic research cannot do without it. Since somebody has to do the work on the general before the particular can be described and explained, let alone be understood and valued against that background, it is best to think of this situation as a sensible division of labour.

Another aspect of this cause of unease to the hermeneutic scholar is the fact that provisional hunches on the basis of one text may have to be partly adjusted by examining other texts first, in the interest of arriving at more generally valid claims than may be justified by one particular passage in an individual text. And finally, a third aspect of this work is the objective that the testing of the generalizations does have to be possible and eventually carried out, which places all kinds of restrictions on the kinds of terms and concepts that may be used. These are three rather alienating aspects of doing empirical research to the hermeneutic scholar, even though this is also research that "seeks to explain how these structures are actually used and experienced by the participants in an act of communication performed in a particular context". I hope that my usage of terms like "scientific", "research", "explanation", "empirical", "hermeneutic", and so on, is not too disturbing. They are meant as descriptions of aspects of two traditions of academic study from the vantage point of empirical science. I believe that linguistics is an empirical science, albeit with problematic areas, and that literary study can be one too, and may already be one in many quarters, in particular in literary history. But literary studies also includes literary criticism, and that has been such a strong paradigm for many academics in the Arts Faculties that it seems to have been forgotten that there may be other kinds of approaches, too. The present linguistic approach to poetry attempts to provide a case in point.

"Meeting at Night"

The anthology for my first-year introductory course to poetry back in the mid-seventies, nowadays fashionably restyled as "literary comprehension", contained the following poem by Robert Browning:[5]

Meeting at Night

> The gray sea and the long black land;
> And the yellow half-moon large and low;
> And the startled little waves that leap
> In fiery ringlets from their sleep,
> As I gain the cove with pushing prow,
> And quench its speed i' the slushy sand.
>
> Then a mile of warm sea-scented beach;
> Three fields to cross till a farm appears;
> A tap at the pane, the quick sharp scratch
> And blue spurt of a lighted match,
> And a voice less loud, through its joys and fears,
> Than the two hearts beating each to each!

This is a perfect poem for demonstrating all kinds of typically poetic usage of language, as well as form and content of text, and even of the poem as a discourse between a sender and an addressee. There is something for everybody on the linguistic plane. There is, for example, much iconicity. There is sound symbolism in "quench its speed i' the slushy sand", "a tap at the pane", "the quick sharp scratch and blue spurt". There is rhythm mirroring meaning, for instance in the steady movement of rowing in line 5 which is subdued in line 6, and in the beating of the hearts in the last four words of line 12.[6] There is syntax mirroring meaning in the series of metonymically connected sense impressions in the first stanza and the urgent sense of purpose in the first lines of the second stanza. On the semantic plane there is the

---

[5] Reprinted from Helen Gardner, ed., *The New Oxford Book of English Verse: 1250-1950*, Oxford: Oxford University Press, 1972.

[6] See W. Gierasch, "Browning's MEETING AT NIGHT", *The Explicator*, 1 (1942), 55.

marked deviation of the metaphorical use of "quench" in line 6, while the personification of the waves in line 3 is combined with a striking paradoxical quality of "fire" caused by the light of the moon. One evident pragmatic device of the poem is the use of the many definite determiners in the description of the environment in the first stanza, increasing the reader's involvement with the scene by presenting it as familiar and given. (Notice how this pattern is given up in the second stanza, where we see "a mile", which may be read as "one mile", but in particular "a farm", as if this is following an instruction for the first time).

Widening our attention from the linguistic code and its usage to the text as a complex conceptual structure which is conveyed by the code, we observe that the poem is headed by a phrase which is the caption of a little scenario which will be familiar to all of us, if only through the products of Hollywood. It is important to observe how this indication of the topic of the poem points to a more complex conceptual structure that has room for most if not all of the referential components of the poem.[7] It also affords the creation of an overall text type in the form of a narrative, which is to be closely aligned with the participants, actions, settings and props of the scenario.[8] From text type it is a short step to text form, which turns out to be divided into two sections. They present the landing on the beach and the arrival at the farm, the two most important sub-goals of the action plan of the main character who wants to meet his lover. The chronological form of the story supposedly creates suspense and then relief at the main character's achievement of the final goal.[9] What is striking about the content, in this connection, is that the poem does not contain any explicit descriptions of his emotions, but suggests his anticipation through a listing of his acute observations of the environment and the distance that still separates him from his lover. The only emotion words in the poem are attributed to the woman, who has "joys and fears". But it should not be forgotten that this is narrated by the "I", whose perspective has provided a highly

---

[7]   Teun A. van Dijk, and Walter Kintsch, *Strategies of Discourse Comprehension*, New York: Academic Press, 1983.

[8]   W.F. Brewer, and E.H. Lichtenstein, "Stories are to Entertain: A Structural-Affect Theory of Stories", *Journal of Pragmatics,* 6 (1982), 473-86.

[9]   *Ibid.*

selective and biased filter on the story throughout the poem, as may be analysed by paying close attention to the language. It should also be noticed how stereotypical his view of the situation is, even when he is able to distance himself from his perspective in the last line in order to speak of "two hearts beating each to each". He may be seen as watching himself perform as an actor in the scenario of the title.[10] This may also provide a clue to the use of the indefinite determiner "a" in "a farm", "a tap at the pane", "a lighted match", and "a voice" in stanza 2: they are not part of first-time instructions but of a list of expected and therefore general props and settings in a set-piece. A tinge of irony may be detected here, which may be able to salvage the poem from its dependence on stereotyping.

Irony naturally leads us on to consider the poem as a piece of discourse, or as a message with a communicative function between a sender and an addressee. However, before we can actually deal head-on with the question of irony, we need to make some preliminary observations. At a global level, this piece of discourse aims to divert the reader in a specific artistic fashion, by evoking a literary experience: its function is aimed at stimulating the emotions in the context of a culturally recognizable domain of discourse, namely literature. One way of phrasing what a literary experience is may be found in the last sentence of Verdonk's essay on Larkin. The means by which the divertive function is achieved is through the deliberate use of verbal artifice, as suggested in my description of the language of the poem, and through the original thematization of an important theme in human experience, love, as suggested in my description of the text of the poem. Additional features of such a literary act of communication are the fictional nature of the speaker and of what the speaker says, which allows for a large degree of playfulness and polyvalence in the discourse situation. For instance, there is a pleasant and intriguing quality to the question raised in the last paragraph, whether the poem is to be seen as conveying an ironic stance of self-awareness and perhaps even a "message". It would take some more sophisticated analysis to determine whether the balance will swing one way or the other, in favour of romantic love or dramatic irony, or whether this will have to

---

[10] See C. de L. Ryals, *Becoming Browning: The Poems and Plays of Robert Browning, 1833-1846*, Columbus: Ohio State University Press, 1983, 8.

remain an undecided or open question. Part of this analysis will be offered below, but that will only be the beginning. Of course, I never read the poem in this ironic fashion when I was a first-year student. What I did instead was read it as a highly romantic poem about the raptures of love. And according to the sources, this is how Browning himself intended the poem to be read. And if you miss what may be subtle clues for potential irony, the poem satisfactorily functions as such a discourse in the relation between poet and reader. But the point is: this would be individual reading. It is not the same as the fore-going technical analysis of language, text and discourse, either for its own sake or as an instrument to investigate reading behaviour. It may be called "introspective study", but that would only be the first, heuristic step in the empirical research process.[11]

Genuine empirical research begins with the reliable and valid analysis of language, text, and discourse, of which I have attempted to illustrate some aspects above, and proceeds from there. Such research may be theory-driven, in that one begins with a controversial issue in the theory of language and language use, like metaphor or irony and its understanding, and then formulates testable hypotheses and designs feasible studies to pronounce on the predictions. Texts and their analysis come in at a relatively late stage, either as stimulus texts or as part of a corpus. This is the kind of research process that is most alien to literary scholars of the more traditional kind. However, empirical research may also arise out of personal interests in texts, which offer suggestions for interesting theoretical insights that may be amenable to testing. In the present case, for instance, one might wish to see how long it takes for a reader to hit on the ironic clues of the poem, if it is granted that some parts of the text may be attributed such a potential function. There are important methodological problems about both the analysis of the text in this fashion as well as the operational definition of amount of time before an ironic interpretation is reached, but they can be solved and controlled. Other factors to be taken into this kind of consideration include the class of readers used for the test, the task set to the readers and the situation in which the readers are placed to perform their task. But the basic message is that it can be done. And the

---

[11] See R.D. Sell, "Literary Pragmatics: An Introduction", in *Literary Pragmatics*, London: Routledge, 1991, xi-xiii.

other basic message is that it should be done, and in this way, too, if we wish "to explain how [language] structures are actually used and experienced by the participants in an act of communication performed in a particular context."

"Parting at Morning"

The example of an ironic reading of "Meeting at Night" is not really spectacular, neither as an interpretation of the ironic poet Browning nor as an inspiration for general theory formation about irony. Interesting ideas about understanding metaphor and irony in literature have been around in the theoretical literature for a long time, and it does not take an individual text to hit on an idea for an empirical study along the lines sketched out above. In fact, the situation is quite the contrary. I was working on "Meeting at Night" because I was engaged in setting up a metaphor recognition study and was looking for suitable texts. When I had spotted "Meeting at Night" and had examined its suitability, I was in for a great surprise. To return to the framework of the tension between linguistic and literary research, the surprise was the very occasion of this essay and its theme of the movement from text to empirical work instead of the other way around.

On the next page of the anthology I was using for the purpose, namely, Helen Gardner's *The New Oxford Book of English Verse*, I found another poem, which was called "Parting at Morning". The title aroused my curiosity as to the connection with the poem on the previous page, and it turned out that it was very close indeed.

Parting at Morning

> Around the cape of a sudden came the sea,
> And the sun looked over the mountain's rim:
> And straight was a path of gold for him,
> And the need of a world of men for me.

I am neither a Browning scholar nor an expert in nineteenth-century English poetry, and I had never come across the companion poem before. As it turned out, the two poems are part of one complete poem, called "I. Night" and "II. Morning", which were published as one whole in 1845 in Browning's *Dramatic Romances and Lyrics*. In 1849, they were reprinted as two poems with the new, now familiar titles "Meeting at Night" and "Parting at Morning". And in 1863, when Browning performed a complete regrouping of his poetry, they appeared in the first volume of his *Poetic Works*, as part of the *Lyrics*. It has been observed by several commentators that they have since appeared separately on more than one occasion. I happen to have found that even as early as 1870, William Cullen Bryant acted as critical editor of a volume called *Library of World Poetry* which only included "Meeting at Night".[12]

The implications of this textual history for an empirical study of reading are truly fascinating. What I had read as one text, presenting one complete story with a potential ironic twist at the end, turned out to be part of a more encompassing story, which had a much clearer and greater ironic twist at its end. And it is not just the last line, which comes as a surprise, it is the complete companion poem which turns the first poem on its head. For what would one expect after a night of love, which has been initiated as romantically as it has been in "Meeting at Night"? What would the association with "Parting at Morning" be, except negative, one of loss, sadness, and regret? But this is not what we get. The sea coming round the cape may be read as a symbol for freedom after confinement, and the sun looking over the mountain's rim may have the same effect. It adds light, gold, and a straight path toward the open sea in the third line: all of these are positive elements, which do not indicate any loss, sadness, or regret. They are explained by the fourth line, which may be interpreted as offering freedom from confinement in the world of women by promising a world of men at sea, the word "need" being the tell-tale lexical sign of a problem, the solution of which we have to guess ourselves.

This is not regret at parting. But it is not satisfaction after the night before either, as has been suggested by Condee.[13] Satisfaction looks back and is pleased; by contrast, this looks forward and finds glory in looking forward — there is as much anticipation here as in the first poem, albeit of a diametrically opposed kind. The second poem sounds

---

[12] W.C. Bryant, ed., *Library of World Poetry*, New York: Avenel Books, 1970 [1870].

[13] R.W. Condee, "Browning's 'Meeting at Night' and 'Parting at Morning'", *The Explicator,* 12 (1953), 23.

more like the positive escape by a man from the clutches of a woman in her love nest. In this interpretation, you may feel a sense of relief of the tension ("of a sudden"), when the man has made it to the point where the cape will hide him from the woman's view whom you can imagine standing by her farm while waving him goodbye. By the same token, the second poem waves goodbye to all romance built up in the first part.

"Parting at Morning" does even more. It turns the superficially heterosexual world of the stereotypical scenario of "lover meets lover at night and departs in the morning" into a homosexual world where the path back to the ship full of sailors is lit by the sun and turned into gold. Moreover, the path is just as straight as the speaker's need of a world of men is straight (no pun intended). There might even be phallic symbolic value in the word "straight", which is the only adjective in the second poem, as opposed to no fewer than fourteen in the first. If there was a subtle hint of irony at the expense of the stereotypical scenario of "Meeting at Night" at the end of the first poem, the second poem is nothing less than an ironic blow to the romantically biased reader. And it was Browning's intention to be ironic about the whole affair, for he said about the last line that "it is his confession of how fleeting is the belief (implied in the first part) that such raptures are self-sufficient and enduring – as for the time they appear."[14] I do not know if Browning would accept my controversial, homo-erotic reading of this irony, though.

However, more to the point for the present essay than my private reading are the theoretical and empirical questions raised by this poem. My personal reading history has shown that there is a strong influence on the effect and experience of "Meeting at Night" of the absence or presence of the companion poem, "Parting at Morning". And this may of course be turned round just as easily: one may also consider the effect of the presence or absence of the first poem on the reading of the second poem. One phrasing of this relationship between the two poems has been proposed by Condee: "Read separately, 'Meeting at Night' loses much, and 'Parting at Morning' is almost destroyed. Read together, each sets off and enhances the total effect of the other."[15] I do

---

[14] Quoted by the editors in Gierasch, *op.cit.*, 6.

[15] Condee, *op.cit.*, 23.

not quite agree with Condee's reading of the poems, but some observations may be made without arousing too much controversy. The function of the dramatic irony of the last line of each of the two poems is one point, which is heavily affected by assuming one of the four above reading situations. For instance, the uncertainty about the last line in "Meeting at Night" may be completely dissolved in the knowledge of "Parting at Morning", whereas it may be left open and undecided in a pleasantly stimulating way if it is considered on its own.

The interpretation of the narrative text(s) is also different if one looks at either poem in isolation or if one considers each in combination with the other. To pursue the latter perspective for a moment, the question arises as to what has actually happened during the night itself. Was this a special event with a negative consequence, which is the specific cause of the feelings displayed in "Parting at Morning", or was it an ordinary "meeting at night" which results in this kind of "parting at morning", revealing more about the character than about the sequence of events? The reader's inference process about the causal structure of the story is heavily determined by the (lack of) preceding context.[16] Another aspect of the narrative(s) and its or their processing concerns the affective structure.[17] What is the relation between the two affect-boosting episodes? Does the second come as an anticlimax after the first, is it another story of suspense which has to be seen on the same level, or does it form the unexpected climax? And at the level of language, there are some conspicuous contrasts, which are indeed offset by examining the two poems in conjunction. For instance there is the level of detail by means of adjectives and verbal modifiers in the first poem as opposed to the simple and straightforward indication of entities and relations in the second poem. And a final linguistic aspect involves the tense switch from present to past between the two poems.

None of these observations could be made as easily if one had only one of the two poems at one's disposal. However, a more abstract formulation of the relationship between the two poems is the final and most interesting topic of this essay. What we see happening here is that one text can act as a context for the interpretation of another in a way

---

[16] A.C. Graesser, and R.J. Kreuz, "A Theory of Inference Generation During Text Comprehension", *Discourse Processes,* 16 (1993), 145-60.

[17] Brewer and Lichtenstein, *op.cit.*

that reminds us of the effect of intertextuality. However, the effect is much closer and stronger, in that the presence or absence of particular assumptions will guide the reader to one reading or another. This, in turn, points to the importance of studying the role of cognition and cognitive representations of context. Since the present instance of context is nothing less than the preceding text, which moreover turns out to be no more than a preceding section of the same text, we have landed squarely in a cognitive discourse approach to language, text, and discourse and their role in reading. This is a good demonstration of the assumption that context, whether it be seen as within one text or between several texts, is mentally represented context. Context has an effect on reading if it is part of the reader's mental model(s) of the text, and this also holds for the role of previous text. It will be hard to find a better justification for the experimental manipulation of texts and their parts in reading research.

When empirical researchers of literature try to uncover effects of particular text properties on reading, they often have to offer texts in different guises or versions to readers in order to study the consequences of such treatments. In the present case, one could entertain an empirical study of companion poems but also of single poems in which text parts are or are not present in different conditions, in order to establish their function in the process of meaning construction by the reader. The predictions of such a study would be heavily dependent on the point of interest, which may pertain to aspects of language, text, or discourse processing, as we have seen. This kind of exercise often looks like a lack of respect for the original text and its integrity. Robert Browning's poems offer a forceful denial to this accusation. Poets manipulate their texts just as much as empirical researchers. The dependence of one stretch of poetry on another is a given in literary criticism and in the poetics of individual poets. By the same token, it makes it possible for empirical researchers to analyse the mechanics of the textual dependencies in order to study and explain their contributions to the overall textual effects.

TRISTRAM SHANDY'S NARRATEES

GENE MOORE

In her classic study of *Fiction and the Reading Public*, Q.D. Leavis remarked that the technique of Laurence Sterne's *Tristram Shandy* depends on what she called "the establishment of a social tone."[1] Perhaps more than any other novel in the history of English literature, Sterne's work regularly and thoroughly reminds the reader that the act of reading is not only a solitary but also a *social* act, and that the discourse of fiction can merge solitary with social gestures in ways quite impossible in the "real" world.

The "social tone" of *Tristram Shandy* is established chiefly through the narrator's involvement with his numerous readers and addressees: you and me, Sir and Madam, various worships and reverences, critics and dedicatees, and specific interlocutors ranging from Tristram himself to David Garrick and the Goddess of the Moon. The figures addressed in various ways by the narrator can be described as his "narratees," to use the term first proposed by Roland Barthes as *le narrataire*.[2] Although

---

[1] Q.D. Leavis, *Fiction and the Reading Public*, London: Chatto & Windus, 1932, 220.

[2] R. Barthes, "*Introduction à l'analyse structurale des récits*", in *Communications*, 8 (1966), 7-33, 16. This was then translated, amplified, and developed by Gerald Prince ("Notes Toward a Categorization of Fictional 'Narratees'", *Genre*, 4/1 (1971), 100-6, "*Introduction à l'Etude du Narrataire*", *Poétique*, 14 (1973), 178-96, "The Narratee Revisited", *Style*, 19/3 (1985), 299-303, and *A Dictionary of Narratology*, Lincoln and London: University of Nebraska Press, 1987), and Gérard Genette (*Figures III*, Paris: Seuil, 1972, in English as *Narrative Discourse: An Essay in Method*, trans. J.E. Lewin, Ithaca: Cornell University Press, 1980, and *Nouveau Discours du Récit*, Paris: Seuil, 1983, in English as *Narrative Discourse*

both Genette and Prince cite *Tristram Shandy* as a work of particular
interest in connection with narratees,[3] the term has yet to be applied to
Sterne's text in any systematic or extended fashion. In general, it has
failed to gain common currency as a critical term to the degree one might
have expected. As Pascal Alain Ifri noted in the introduction to his study
of narratees in Proust's *Recherche*, "since the publication of
Piwowarczyk's article, the narratee, although figuring in a few isolated
studies, has more or less fallen back into oblivion, hidden behind the
reader, who has become one of the favorite objects of study of
contemporary critics."[4]

Why should this be the case? Ifri suggested that the lack of interest in
narratees can be attributed to the relatively minor and passive role they
play in most novels, so that critics tend to be more interested in
narrators;[5] but perhaps the lack of popularity of the narratee can also be
attributed, at least in part, to the rather narrow, anti-social, and isolating
manner in which the term has been defined.

From the beginning, Prince and others have stressed the importance
of distinguishing the narratee from the real reader, primarily on the basis
of analogies drawn from the position of the narrator. The narratee is
distinguished from the real reader by being situated or "inscribed" within
the text, at the same "level" of narration (intradiegetic or extradiegetic
with respect to a given story) as the corresponding narrator "Like the

---

Revisited, trans. J.E. Lewin, Ithaca: Cornell University Press, 1988), and Mary Ann
Piwowarczyk ("The Narratee and the Situation of Enunciation: A Reconsideration
of Prince's Theory", *Genre*, 9/2 (1976), 161-77. The term "narratee" is relatively
simple to define, as narratological terms go; yet although the basic idea of the term
has remained the same, Prince's own definitions have become increasingly specific
with the passage of time, passing from "the receiver of the narrator's message"
(1971, 100) via "*quelqu'un à qui le narrateur s'adresse*" (1973, 178) to "The one
who is narrated to, as inscribed in the text" (1987, 57).

[3] Genette, 1972, *op.cit.*, 262 and 265; and 1983, *op.cit.*, 91; and Prince, 1973,
op.cit., 178 and 186.

[4] P.A. Ifri, *Proust et son Narrataire dans "A la Recherche du Temps Perdu"*,
Genève: Librarie Droz, 1983, 9. Unless otherwise indicated, all translations are
my own.

[5] *Ibid.*, 57.

narrator, the narratee is one of the elements in the narrating situation, and he is necessarily located at the same diegetic level."[6] This equation of levels makes possible a symmetrical and hierarchical model of communication whereby, in the words of Mieke Bal, "Theoretically, each instance addresses itself to an addressee situated at the same level"[7] the real author speaks to the real reader, the implied author to the implied reader, the narrator to the narratee, and characters to one another.

For all its analytic clarity, this model is difficult to apply to actual texts, in which the boundaries between levels cannot be rigorously maintained, since characters become quasi-narrators whenever they speak, and narratees become quasi-characters whenever they are described or addressed. The very existence of the narratee as a distinct and necessary instance depends on the possibility of identifying the region it shares with the narrator, situated between the level(s) of the characters and that of real (or implied) readers; but the logic of maintaining a strict distinction between levels — the "*bonne logique*" so frequently and proudly invoked by French critics — has led, in some cases, to the absurd necessity of banishing the real reader and the real author from the text altogether. Thus Ifri, who distinguishes narratees from readers on the grounds that the former are intradiegetic and the latter always extradiegetic:

> the real reader is the extradiegetic addressee of the narrative text, while the fictive reader, the narratee, is the intradiegetic addressee inside the story. This explains why the "*cher lecteur*" of Stendhal, for example, being inscribed in the story, is addressed not to the real reader but to the narratee: in effect it is not Stendhal who is speaking here, but his narrator. Only Stendhal could speak to the real reader. The "*cher lecteur*" can therefore indicate the real reader only within a non-fictional work.[8]

---

[6] Genette, 1972, *op.cit.*, 265 or 1980, *op.cit.*, 259.

[7] Mieke Bal, *Narratologie*, Paris: Klincksieck, 1977, 33.

[8] Ifri, *op.cit.*, 27. Since Ifri seems to use *le vrai lecteur* and *le lecteur réel* interchangeably in this passage, I have translated both terms as "the real reader". The requirements of definition have led W. Bronzwaer to a similar absurdity in claiming that "the public reading situation does not bring the writer into direct contact with the real reader, since both are still wearing masks, the former that of

Such excesses are symptomatic of the difficulties attending a strict definition of narratees. Moreover, critical opinion continues to differ widely on a number of questions of primary importance, such as, what is the diegetic status of the narratee? Is it intradiegetic, or extradiegetic, or both? What is the nature of the difference between implicit narratees, who are never addressed directly but can be derived from certain signs in the discourse of the narrator (who, for example, takes certain things for granted but explains others), and narratees who are directly addressed, who become "characterized readers"?[9] How is an implicit narratee to be distinguished from an implied reader, and how is a "characterized reader" different from other characters and other readers? We shall examine these questions in the case of *Tristram Shandy*, where it is clear that the problems attending the notion of the narratee have to do with a general failure to appreciate the *social* nature of literary reception: while the discourse of a narrator is usually construed (at least for purposes of definition) as singular and specific to a particular level, the listening or reading audience can be very large indeed and involves all receiving instances "upward" in the narrative hierarchy, up to and including the real reader. Of course narrators can also be multi-voiced and multi-levelled (as in the case of *The Turn of the Screw*, where the governess's text exists simultaneously in at least three forms: as a handwritten written memoir, as the public reading of that memoir, and in a printed version including the later narrator-editor's frame); but the narrator invoked for the purpose of defining the narratee tends to be stripped of this complexity and presented as a monological instance, addressing the narratee as a counterpart at the same diegetic level. The heuristic distinctions between various diegetic levels, originally made for purposes of analysis, have all too often hardened into hermetic barriers defined so as to prevent the voice of the narrator from being heard by anyone other

---

the implied author, the latter of the implied reader" (in "Implied Author, Extradiegetic Narrator and Public Reader: Gérard Genette's narratological model and the reading version of *Great Expectations*", *Neophilologus*, 62/1 (1978), 1-18, 13). I would submit that if a public reading is not an occasion of direct contact, it is rather because a situation of reading is replaced with one of performance, so that the words of the text arrive through the ear and not through the eye.

[9] W. Daniel Wilson, "Readers in Texts", *PMLA*, 96/5 (1981), 848-63.

than the narratee. In the ardor of their rigorous logic, critics have often tended to forget that, as Genette reminds us, "there are always people *off to the side.*"[10]

The prison-house of the narratee
The birth of the narratee into modern criticism bears comparison with the difficulties attending the conception and delivery of Tristram Shandy. In an attempt to define the narratee as a structural position, an outline or framework to be filled in each specific case (not to mention the implicit homage to Barthes), Prince and Piwowarczyk began by positing a "degree zero narratee" (later equated by Prince with the "maximally covert" narratee)[11] as a means of establishing a standard by which all specific narratees could be measured in terms of their "deviance" from this minimal norm. This construct soon began to appear quite abnormal in its own right, however, since it required one to imagine the narratee not as a human reader or auditor but as an abstract and minimal addressee credited with the imaginary capacity, for example, to "understand" the denotations but not the connotations of the narrator's words. At "degree zero," the narratee is nothing more than a *tabula rasa* of receptive possibilities; strictly speaking, the "degree zero narratee" is not a narratee at all in terms of Prince's definitions, since no "real" narratee could ever be so utterly devoid of specification. The problems attending the "degree zero narratee" were discussed by William Ray,[12] and this particular construct now appears to have been laid to rest; although Prince has registered his belief that "it can be a useful *garde-fou*",[13] the "degree zero" narratee appears neither in his *Narratology* nor in the definition of "narratee" given in his *Dictionary of Narratology*.

But if Ray laid one terminological ghost to rest, he conjured up another in the form of the "meta-narratee" who emerges whenever the

---

[10] Genette, 1972, *op.cit.*, 267, or 1980, *op.cit.*, 262.

[11] Prince, 1985, *op.cit.*, 300.

[12] William Ray, "Recognizing Recognition: The Intra-textual and Extra-textual Critical Persona", *Diacritics,* 7/4 (1977), 20-33.

[13] Prince, 1985, *op.cit.*, 300.

narratee is addressed directly by the narrator and therefore becomes a characterized reader, or in Ray's words, whenever "from recipient of the message, the narratee becomes its content."[14] This content, according to Ray, implies a new recipient and hence requires the generation of a new "meta-narratee" behind the character's back; and the process can be repeated indefinitely. In Genette's terminology, the narratee as defined by Ray must always remain extradiegetic, outside the "world" constituted by the narrator's discourse. By mentioning the narratee, the narrator not only brings him (or her) into the story but makes him a part of the story, subjecting him to prerogatives analogous to those exercised by the narrator over all the other characters and depriving him of his autonomy; as Ray puts it, "his functionally self-positing movement is imprisoned in its own thematization."[15] Paradoxically, this requirement that the narratee be always both extradiegetic and non-thematized in effect re-establishes a kind of "degree zero" condition outside the story: the moment the narrator mentions a narratee, the narratee ceases to exist as such and is supplanted by a new meta-narratee who will survive only as long as he or she remains unspecified. Although this "ontic shift" maintains the theoretical autonomy of the narratee, one can imagine the impossibility of applying a term which shifts ontically the moment one tries to define it on the basis of textual evidence, because just like Rumplestiltskin, Ray's narratee vanishes the moment it is named.

Ray's insistence on the extradiegetic status of the narratee also runs counter to a more general tendency among critics (including Sherbo, Prince, Genette, and Ifri) to stress the intradiegetic qualities of the narratee as a means of distinguishing the narratee from the real reader: citing Genette, Ifri defines the narratee as "*le destinataire intradiégétique de tout récit.*"[16] In effect, if the narratee is not construed as autonomous

---

[14] Ray, *op.cit.*, 23.

[15] *Ibid.*

[16] Ifri, *op.cit.*, 21. Strictly speaking, A. Sherbo ("'Inside' and 'Outside' Readers in Fielding's Novels", in *Studies in the Eighteenth Century English Novel,* East Lansing: Michigan State University Press, 1969, 35-57, 35ff.) is concerned not with narratees, but with the distinction between "inside" and "outside" readers. But I agree with Ifri, who describes Sherbo's essay as "the first real study of the question of the narratee" (*op.cit.*, 48).

but as dependent on the narrator, and since narrators can be either intra-diegetic or extradiegetic (the problem of distinguishing inside from outside is one to which we shall return), then three terms are needed: with respect to the narrator, the real reader is always more than extradiegetic. As Bronzwaer has noted, "What Genette calls the extradiegetic narrator does not stand outside the narrative but is in fact a logically and linguistically defined element of the total narrative situation."[17] Hence, the extradiegetic narrator stands outside the diegesis but not outside the text. Narrators and their narratees may, in principle, be either intradiegetic or extradiegetic; but with respect to all four of these possibilities, the real reader is always (to coin a new term): *ultra*diegetic.

Tristram's impossible narrative

Every narratee requires a narrator, so we must begin the search for Tristram's narratees with an examination of the narrator of *The Life and Opinions of Tristram Shandy, Gentleman*. How can we describe his narrative situation? Is he extradiegetic or intradiegetic? Homodiegetic or heterodiegetic? And finally, to whom is he speaking or writing, and what can his narrative tell us about the nature and quality of his narratees? In Cervantes' *Don Quixote*, an indeterminate number of narrators or commentators stand between the authentic events of Don Quixote's life and the final edited version of Cide Hamete's translated manuscript. The narrative of Tristram Shandy seems refreshingly simple by contrast. Here there is only one narrator, Tristram himself, who tells his own story retrospectively in the first person. But as it happens, no story was ever more impossible to tell. And in lieu of a promised autobiography the reader is presented with a perpetual postponement, a deferral of the story proper in favor of the belated and repeated insertion of various kinds of prefatory material, including dedications, prefaces, new beginnings, and the like.

One of the most important elements of this strategy of deferral consists in Tristram's apostrophic appeals to a complex world of narratees. Tristram's dilemma as a narrator is that he needs to hold the attention of his audience, to keep open phatically the possibility of getting on with his story, while at the same time his digressive involvement with

---

[17] Genette, 1978, *op.cit.*, 2.

the narratees comes to constitute an alibi for not getting on with it. *Tristram Shandy* is the story of a failure to tell a story. His "life" as more than a homunculus barely begins in the course of the nine volumes, and (with the exception of Vol. VII) he scarcely exists as a character in his own story; while the "opinions" he records are chiefly those of his father or his Uncle Toby. Tristram is in the nightmarish predicament of an entertainer facing an audience and finding that he has nothing to say. The elements of rudeness or *Publikumsbeschimpfung* that have been noticed in Tristram's discourse[18] can be understood as signs of his own frustration with his impossible task. Since he cannot manage to narrate, he charges his readers with misreading, or dismisses them altogether.

How can Tristram's narrative be classified in terms of the rather cumbersome territorial distinctions developed by Genette to define the narrator's position with respect to his own story? Is he telling his own story, or that of someone else (i.e., is he a homodiegetic or heterodiegetic narrator)? And is he telling the story from within or from outside the world of his narrative (intradiegetically or extradiegetically)? His status as a first-person narrator would appear to make him homodiegetic by definition, but the degree to which his own story is deferred in favour of stories about others leaves room for argument. How can he be telling his own story if he has not yet been born? And by the same token, how can he be described as "inside" the world of his narrative when so much of his narrative describes events that happened elsewhere or before his birth, and records conversations he never actually heard? According to Prince, the narrator of a primary narrative is by definition always extradiegetic,[19] yet Volume VII, in which Tristram tells the story of his own tour through France, is arguably intradiegetic. Is Volume VII therefore not part of the primary narrative? These difficulties are reflected in differences of critical opinion: Genette himself has described the narrator of *Tristram Shandy* as "*un narrateur-homodiégetique-extradiégetique-auteur-fictif.*"[20] But if narratees are always intradiegetic, as Ifri argues, then narrators

---

[18] By Erwin Wolff, "*Der intendierte Leser: Überlegungen und Beispiele zur Einführung eines literaturwissenschaftlichen Begriffs*", *Poetica*, 4/2 (1971), 141-66.

[19] Prince, 1987, *op.cit.*, 29.

[20] Genette, 1983, *op.cit.*, 99.

must (according to the logic of equivalent levels) be intradiegetic whenever they address their narratees. Similarly, Rimmon-Kenan sees the ubiquitous "Madam" as an intradiegetic narratee, and equates the extradiegetic narratee with the implied reader.[21]

Where, then, is the diegesis to be located? Which is the "primary" narrative in *Tristram Shandy*? Here again, if we understand the primary narrative as the story Tristram *intends* to tell of his life and opinions, then except for Volume VII and a number of scattered observations, most of the text will be non-primary and therefore useless as a standard for defining the narrator's general diegetic status. The term "primary," as used by Genette, is purely heuristic: any narrative can be taken as "primary" with respect to the others; the point is simply to choose, in any given case, the narrative which gives one the greatest explanatory leverage.

Reading, writing, and public speaking

In the case of *Tristram Shandy*, at least three narrative situations are continuously superposed, each of which involves its own "story" and its own relationship with narratees. As narrator, Tristram is simultaneously a writer, a speaker, and a reader of his own text, and the nature of the diegesis and of its narratees will differ according to which of these aspects one chooses to examine. These three levels can be specified if we look at the famous passage where Tristram chides "Madam" for not paying proper attention to the preceding chapter:

> – How could you, Madam, be so inattentive in reading the last chapter? I told you in it, *That my mother was not a papist.* – Papist! You told me no such thing, Sir. Madam, I beg leave to repeat it over again, That I told you as plain, at least, as words, by direct inference, could tell you such a thing. – Then, Sir, I must have miss'd a page. – No, Madam, – you have not miss'd a word. – Then I was asleep, Sir. – My pride, Madam, cannot allow you that refuge. – Then, I declare, I know nothing at all about the matter. – That, Madam, is the very fault I lay to your

---

[21] Shlomith Rimmon-Kenan, *Narrative Fiction: Contemporary Poetics*, London and New York: Methuen, 1983, 104ff.

> charge; and as a punishment for it, I do insist upon it, that you
> immediately turn back, that is, as soon as you get to the next
> full stop, and read the whole chapter over again. (I.20, 56)[22]

Where (i.e. in which fictional "world", and at which diegetic level) does
this exchange take place, and in what sense can Madam be said to have
been (mis)reading?[23] How, given the privacy of the act of reading, can
the narrator *know* that she has failed to draw a particular inference? The
narrative is presented here simultaneously as something written or printed
(in any case, something to which one can return), as an ongoing oral
performance, which continues in Madam's absence, and as a text to be
(re)read. Madam is dismissed, sent as if out of the room, and ordered to
"turn back" to reread the previous chapter, which she apparently does
while Tristram continues to entertain everyone *else*. Where, exactly, is
Madam to be imagined as going, and by what means? She presumably
obeys, scrutinizing Chapter 19 (some seven pages long in the Work
edition) in the time it takes Tristram to progress by only a single
paragraph, which she indeed "misses". The language in which she is
welcomed on her return leaves no doubt that Tristram is addressing a
larger group of listeners; instead of quoting her directly, as in the first
exchange, he repeats her replies for the benefit of the rest of the
audience:

---

[22] References to *Tristram Shandy* will be given by volume, chapter, and by page in
the edition prepared by James Aiken Work (L. Sterne, *The Life and Opinions of
Tristram Shandy, Gentleman* [1759-67], ed., James Aiken Work, New York: The
Odyssey Press, 1940), which after sixty years remains one of the handiest one-
volume editions of the novel.

[23] The passage in which Tristram charges Madam with misreading has been cited
by, among others, Andrew Wright ("The Artifice of Failure in *Tristram Shandy*",
Novel, 2/3 (1969), 212-20, 213), Erwin Wolff (*op.cit.,* 152), W.C. Dowling
("Tristram Shandy's Phantom Audience", *Novel,* 13/3 (1980), 284-95, 287), W.
Daniel Wilson (*op.cit.,* 848), and H. Ostovich ("Reader as Hobby-Horse in
Tristram Shandy", *Philological Quarterly,* 68/3 (1989), 325-42, 336). Rimmon-
Kenan cites it as an illustration of unreliability on the part of the narratee (*op.cit.,*
105), but the first-time reader will surely fall into the same trap as Madam, and
feel charged with the same spurious "inattention". This exchange also illustrates
Tristram's own unreliability as a narrator who continuously violates the terms of
the implicit contract he has established with his narratees and readers.

– But here comes my fair Lady. Have you read over again the chapter, Madam, as I desired you? – You have: And did you not observe the passage, upon the second reading, which admits the inference? – Not a word like it! Then, Madam, be pleased to ponder well the last line but one of the chapter, where I take upon me to say, "It was *necessary* I should be born before I was christen'd." Had my mother, Madam, been a Papist, that consequence did not follow. (I.20, 57)

As Tristram says elsewhere, "Writing, when properly managed, (as you may be sure I think mine is) is but a different name for conversation" (II.11, 108), but the act of reading is just as firmly embedded in Tristram's text, because in glossing himself for Madam's benefit, Tristram is necessarily a reader of his own words, referring even to their position on the page, in "the last line but one". Eventually, the reader will likewise be sent back to reread previous chapters when Chapters 18 and 19 of Volume IX are first omitted, then interpolated into Chapter 25. This mixing of the frames or situations of writing, speaking, and reading also occasions a mixing of diegetic levels, since the narratee called Madam is presented as both an extradiegetic reader and an intradiegetic interlocutor, whose words become part of the narrator's text, while the narrator is himself both intradiegetic in his conversation with her and extradiegetic as author of the text she is ordered to reread.[24] Tristram, as narrator, plays all three roles of writer, speaker, and reader, while his narratees appear as readers, listeners, and occasional speakers, and as writers only at second hand, when their spoken words are recorded by the narrator. These roles are also sometimes doubled in the text, as when Corporal Trim as narrator reads Yorick's sermon on Conscience to his narratees, Mr. Shandy, Uncle Toby, and Dr. Slop, all of whom frequently interrupt him, while Tristram manages the narration of this

---

[24] Genette noted this mixing of diegetic levels in *Tristram Shandy*, but the example he cites – where "Tristram asks me to help him carry Mr. Shandy to his bed" (1983, *op.cit.*, 91, or 1988, *op.cit.*, 132) – is erroneous if it refers to the passage in Volume IV, Chapter 13, where Tristram asks for help in getting his father and Uncle Toby off the stairs and into bed not from the reader but from a "chairman" and a "*day-tall* critick" (285). The deictic terms ("do step into that bookseller's shop") suggest that this moment of the narrative situation takes place in the street.

scene for the benefit of other narratees. A second (metadiegetic) level "Sir" also serves as narratee for Walter Shandy, whose characteristic addle-pated misogyny is reflected in the fact that he never addresses himself to "Madam".

In general, these three aspects of writing, speech, and reading recur as distinct frames of reference invoked more or less regularly throughout Tristram's narrative. Tristram describes his own *Erzählsituation* as a writer in some detail: he mentions his table, his chair, his pen and ink, his books and furniture, his fireplace and clothing. Moreover, unlike the disjointed story he attempts to tell, the *Erzählzeit* or time of his writing is chronological and progressive. On four different occasions, the moment of writing is even dated, e.g. "this very day, in which I am now writing this book for the edification of the world, – which is *March 9, 1759,* – " (I.18, 44). Tristram is also painfully aware of the temporal paradoxes generated by the double time of his life and his writing, between the *erzählte Zeit* and the *Erzählzeit* of his narrative. In a famous passage he notes with dismay that since it has taken him a full year to write only one day of his life, "at this rate I should just live 364 times faster than I should write – It must follow, an' please your worships, that the more I write, the more I shall have to write – and consequently, the more your worships read, the more your worships will have to read" (IV.13, 286).[25] The narratees, here as fictive readers, have a full share in the temporal difficulties attending Tristram's narrative, which tends generally, as in the case of the misreading Madam, to minimize the necessary temporal gap between writing and reading. Thus his narratees apparently "read" him as they would hear him — instantaneously.

For whom does Tristram write? His audience as a writer is far more extensive than the audience or congregation gathered within the range of his voice (all the more, since he complains increasingly of a "vile cough"). The narratees invoked by Tristram extend ultimately to include "all mankind" (I.9, 15), excluding no one; yet his posture as a writer

---

[25] A similar temporal quandary attends the writing of Tristram's father's *Tristrapoedia*: "he was three years and something more, indefatigably at work, and at last, had scarce compleated, by his own reckoning, one half of his undertaking: the misfortune was, that I was all that time totally neglected and abandoned to my mother; and what was almost as bad, by the very delay, the first part of the work, upon which my father had spent the most of his pains, was rendered entirely useless, – every day a page or two became of no consequence" (V.16, 375).

seated at a table makes it difficult to imagine anyone in his immediate presence. As Dowling observes, "The audience at which Tristram gazes when he looks up from the page is more numerous than the room can accommodate, and he is in this respect something like an orator sitting at his desk imagining the large crowd he will address the next day."[26] But members of this imaginary audience often interrupt his writing, and soon establish their latent potential in this respect, creating an immediacy between narrator and narratee, which suggests that whatever Tristram writes is directly perceived as speech by narratees such as Sir and Madam (although once it has been "spoken," it becomes something to be reread). Madam, in particular, is imagined as seated quite close to the narrator: "– Pray reach me my fool's cap – I fear you sit upon it, Madam – 'tis under the cushion – I'll put it on –" (VII.26, 511). Other narratees who do not interrupt the narrative, such as the actor David Garrick (III.24, 208; IV.7: 278; VI.29: 455), can more easily be imagined as eventual readers of Tristram's words, while the "criticks" who are continually baited by Tristram are at one point teased with the possibility of gaining admittance to his presence, joining the party and becoming "guests" seated "at table" (II.2, 84; here Tristram's solitary writing-table doubles as a convivial dinner-table). In general, Tristram's narratees can be understood as an extended, indefinite mass of readers who can become auditors and even interlocutors, depending on their proximity to the narrator's table. The distance separating Tristram from his narratees is defined by social and linguistic conventions, relations of courtesy and discourse, which are used by the narrator to establish the "social tone" that defines his audience and thereby shapes the parameters of the real reader's response.

This "tone" is perhaps most evident in the verbal exchanges recorded between Tristram and his narratees, particularly with "Sir" and

---

[26] Dowling, *op.cit.*, 287. Although Dowling here speaks of Tristram as the narrator, he proceeds, on the basis of details such as Tristram's reference to his "two bad cassocks" (III.11: 179; cf. VII.17: 498), to advance the provocative thesis that the narrator of *Tristram Shandy* is not Tristram Shandy at all, but "an unnamed Yorkshire clergyman who uses [...] Tristram as a fictive voice" (290) – a clergyman who bears an uncanny resemblance to Laurence Sterne. Can textual evidence be used to prove that Tristram was *not* an Anglican clergyman? Given his abundant knowledge of scholastic argument and church politics, one may as well assume that perhaps he is indeed a clergyman, and that this information has been omitted in what Genette calls a "paralipse".

"Madam". It should be noted that while critics have tended to interpret these exchanges as though Sir and Madam were unique and singular *personae*, Tristram could use these generic terms to address *any* gentleman or lady narratee, and not necessarily the same one each time. One must not forget the "social" nature of the terms, which helps to explain why Sir and Madam suffer so little development in the course of the narrative. If they never seem to learn anything, perhaps that is because they are never the same, and are therefore impossible to characterize in other than generic, social terms. If Sir is a model of "bourgeois stolidity" and Madam the embodiment of "innocent incomprehension",[27] this is because any and all such gentlefolk reflect these social characteristics; it is not a matter of individual character or personality.[28] Tristram does distinguish between them on the basis of gender, inviting Madam to be scandalized by his sexual allusions while sharing with Sir a more worldly and "philosophical" basis for conversation: e.g., "There are a thousand resolutions, Sir, both in church and state, as well as in matters, Madam, or a more private concern;" (VI.16, 434). In their general interests and responses, Sir and Madam sometimes bear a surprising resemblance to Walter Shandy and the Widow Wadman, yet although they take part in numerous brief exchanges with the narrator, Sir and Madam possess no individuality as characters. As narratees their function is generic and social rather than specific and individual. Tristram seems to grow weary of them in the final volumes, where his appeals to his various narratees become increasingly frantic and irritable, "Now, for what the world thinks of that ejaculation – I would not give a groat" (IX.9, 611). He even renounces the apostrophical style explicitly in addressing the Widow Wadman: "Nothing can make this chapter go off with spirit but an apostrophe to thee – but my heart tells me, that in such a crisis an apostrophe is but an insult in disguise, and ere I would offer one to a woman in distress – let the chapter go to the devil; provided any damn'd critick *in keeping* will be but at the trouble to take it with him" (IX.26, 638).

---

[27] *Ibid.*, 287.

[28] It should be noted that not everyone agrees about Madam's personality. Wayne Booth, for example, described her as a "lecherous prude" ("The Self-Conscious Narrator in Comic Fiction before *Tristram Shandy*", *PMLA*, 67/2 (1952), 163-85, 182).

The narratees are addressed not only in writing and in speech, but also by a great many signs, which can only be understood in the context of reading, including not only the narrator's many self-conscious references to his own chapters, but also the wide variety of typographical and visual devices employed throughout the novel, including, black, marbled, and blank pages; squiggled story-lines and gestures, asterisks, dashes, brackets, pointing hands, and various type-faces. These devices require instruments of printing and design that go far beyond the local situation of Tristram sitting at his table with pen and ink, or even speaking before an audience: they serve as a reminder of the social nature of the book's production. Tristram's story proves impossible to tell, and it is fitting that the volumes in which it first appeared (1759-1767) were extremely difficult to print. In the first editions, every marbled page was unique and had to be printed separately by means of a special process. Whenever Tristram uses or calls attention to these visual devices, he addresses his narratees in the guise of fictive readers who are holding the printed book in their hands. There is no way in which a row of asterisks, let alone a page of mourning or marbling, could be easily "spoken": and "Madam" is presumably sent back to reread a printed copy of Tristram's text. Tristram's vivid and eccentric punctuation helps to break down the division between spoken and written language, and to dramatize his discourse in the relatively breathless and fragmented forms of conversation. But the stars and bars of his text can also serve as barriers to any perception of his words, when, for example, asterisks stand for censored passages or when dashes denote the privacy of Tristram's own reading (VII.35, 528).

A barrier of a different kind is established whenever the interpolated texts are presented in languages other than English. Tristram apparently assumes that his narratees are all capable of understanding French and Latin, but as one might expect, his conventions of quotation are inconsistent, since the text of the Sorbonne memoir on baptism is cited only in French (I.20, 58-62), while the English translation of Slawkenbergius' Tale is glossed with a "specimen" of the original Latin on the facing page (IV.244-251). Sometimes English words or phrases are glossed with untranslated references in French, Latin, or Greek. All these mock-scholastic techniques suggest that Tristram's text is something to be read and studied, rather than an oral performance to be heard. As usual, the oral and reading modes are mixed: Dr. Slop reads Ernulphus' curse of excommunication aloud in Latin, while the extradiegetic reader is

supplied with a facing English translation interspersed with the comments
of Slop and his auditors (III.11, 170-179). Given the playful and erratic
nature of Tristram's translations – where *Amicus Plato sed magis amica
veritas* can be rendered as "DINAH was my aunt ... but TRUTH is my
sister" (I.21, 68) – the reader is invited to read and compare both
versions of the translated texts.[29] Like the brackets used to signify two
statements made simultaneously, translations also disrupt the linear flow
of the narrator's discourse, making it momentarily double-voiced or
polyphonic, and impossible to read in linear fashion.

Tristram also provides a number of footnotes to his text, which as
"surjustifications"[30] could be helpful as an indication of the kinds of
knowledge he takes for granted on the part of his narratees. Yet
whenever Tristram's narrative employs a special jargon, whether of the
law, church doctrine, or the science of fortifications, these annotations
tend to be particularly sparse. This feature of the text is rather easy for
modern readers to overlook, since most editions of the novel now come
fully equipped with explanatory footnotes, and some include a glossary of
military terms.[31] But even Tristram's own notes are apparently beyond
the reach of Madam and Sir, and are directed instead at the narratee as a
reader of the printed text.

In summary, then, Tristram's narratees occupy at least three different
settings: they are called to witness his difficulties with pen and ink at his
writing desk; they provide an active audience for his spoken discourse (in
the context of which they are sometimes singled out as Madam or Sir);
and they constitute a readership addressed by the novel as a printed book.
It is only in this last role, as readers, that they can be doubled by the real

---

[29] Coincidentally, this proverb also appears in Don Quixote's letter to Sancho (in
Part Two, chapter 51).

[30] Prince, 1973, *op.cit.*, 185.

[31] The original notes are now conventionally marked with "[Sterne's note]" to
distinguish them from the annotations of modern editors. It is curious to note that
while critics (and narratologists in particular) are wary of equating the real author
with the narrator, editors continue to regard Tristram's text as having been annotated
by "Sterne". When the footnoter says "I" as in the first note to Slawkenbergius's
Tale, are we really to assume that here Sterne is speaking, and not Tristram? If so,
the original footnotes cannot be seen as a form of "surjustification" on the narrator's
part, and cannot be used as evidence in connection with narratees.

reader, in what Genette calls a case of "syncrisis".[32] But when Madam can be sent out of an oral situation to reread something she has just heard, or when Tristram conversationally "points" to printed features like the marbled page, it becomes exceedingly difficult to separate the various roles played by the narratees. As Béatrice Didier remarked of the narratees in Diderot's *Jacques le Fataliste*, "The question of the situation of the 'reader,' of his space and time, remains extremely fluid and unstable."[33]

This instability also makes it difficult to find a point of leverage at which to situate the primary narrative or diegesis. If we take the story of Tristram's life as the primary narrative, then all the narratees are apparently extradiegetic (with the exception of the metadiegetic "Sir" addressed by Walter Shandy (I.18, 47 and I.19, 50)). If we take the writing/telling of Tristram's story as the primary narrative, then the narratees inscribed in the text can be defined as intradiegetic. In either case, such a general application of the terms seems rather unproductive, and contributes little to an understanding of Tristram's specific relations with his listeners and readers.

Genette's second pair of terms, "homodiegetic" and "heterodiegetic," apply to narrators more readily than to their narratees. If the prefix is understood as applying to the narrator's "own" story, then the addressee of a homodiegetic narrator is not therefore necessarily also homodiegetic. (A homodiegetic narratee would be one who shares the world of the narrator's story, and who is in some sense addressed with his "own" story). Perhaps the best example of this in *Tristram Shandy* occurs when the (male) reader is addressed as "Sir" and invited to contribute his own illustration to the text (VI.38, 470f.). Tristram also serves occasionally as his own (necessarily homodiegetic) narratee (III.8, 166; III.28, 215; IV.32, 337).[34] But here again, the boundaries of the narrator's world are

---

[32] Genette, 1983, *op.cit.*, 91, or 1988, *op.cit.*, 132.

[33] B. Didier, "*Contribution à une Poétique du Leurre: "Lecteur" et Narrataires dans Jacques le Fataliste*", *Littérature*, 31 (1978), 3-21, 15.

[34] Another interesting example of a homodiegetic narratee occurs in the opening pages of Faulkner's *Flags in the Dust*, where Bayard Sartoris is (re)told events of his own youth by Old Man Falls, who was not present when they occurred.

impossible to determine with precision, given the fluid and shifting mixture of writing, speaking, and reading situations.

One might be tempted to equate these three aspects of the narrative with the basic narratological distinction between story, text, and narration, so that what Tristram writes or tries to write (the contents of his *fabula*) could be seen as the "story", his oral performances as the "narration," and the final printed product as his "text".[35] However, Prince and Genette have defined narratees always and only as the addressees of narrators, so that strictly speaking, the question of narratees involves only the aspect of "narration", and not that of the content of the story, or the words of the printed text. Tristram's addressees, on the other hand, are by no means limited only to the audience of his oral or written narration; they also hold the text in their hands, and are involved not only in the presentation of the narrative, but also in its content and its final form. Indeed, Tristram's strategy can be described as an attempt to exclude no one from the process of making a book, and the course of literary history has proven that prophecies like the following are more than mere figures of speech: "As my life and opinions are likely to make some noise in the world, and, if I conjecture right, will take in all ranks, professions, and denominations of men whatever, – be no less read than the *Pilgrim's Progress* itself – and, in the end, prove the very thing which Montaigne dreaded his essays should turn out, that is, a book for a parlour-window; I find it necessary to consult every one a little in his turn" (I.4, 7). This consultation of everyone by turns, at every turn, continues throughout the narrative and becomes far more than just a strategy of narration. The consultation of narratees soon constitutes a large part of the story, and the text as well.

In conclusion, we can see that the difficulty of applying the notion of narratees to a novel like *Tristram Shandy* stems from the radical difference between the expansive, all-inclusive spirit in which the novel was constructed and the narrowly restrictive constraints governing the definition of the term. While narratologists continue to insist that the boundaries separating the text from the world beyond must be

---

[35] This tripartite distinction is the foundation of Genette's narratology, but Rimmon-Kenan's (*op.cit.*, 3) terms are less prone to confusion than those used in Jane E. Lewin's English translations of Genette. "Story" (*histoire*) is common to both systems, but Lewin's equivalents for "text" and "narration" are "narrative" (*récit*) and "narrating" (*narration*), respectively.

reinforced[36] the audience addressed by Tristram Shandy continues to transgress these boundaries, refusing to limit itself to the confines of "the text itself". From the very beginning, the narratee was defined as a singular addressee confined to the diegetic level of a given narrator.[37] Moreover, the methods employed to chart the possible characteristics of narratees posits either an impossibly minimal "degree zero narratee"[38] or a "meta-narratee", whom the narrator is unable to mention.[39] In both cases, the construct is far too abstract and narrow to be of use in dealing with actual narrative situations.

The term "narratee" is useful, however, precisely because of its inclusiveness, since the narratee is the addressee of the narrator's discourse by all and any means, not only as a reader but also as a listener, eavesdropper, decoder, or in any other manner. And because the medium of the narrator's discourse is not specified or restricted, the term can also serve as an important reminder of the social dimension of the act of reading. Theorists of the narratee have often been quick to complain of the "confusion" introduced by critics who fail to make distinctions as fine as their own, and who confuse "readers" with "narratees",[40] or who fail to distinguish between authorial and narrative audiences.[41] But "confusion" can also result when the distinctions drawn between addressees at various levels inside and outside the text become hardened into cells of solitary confinement, so that the real reader is ultimately

---

[36] F. Schuerewegen, *"Réflexions sur le Narrataire: Quidam et Quilibet"*, *Poétique,* 70 (1987), 247-54, 248.

[37] Peter Rabinowitz's discussion of "audiences" ("Truth in Fiction: A Reexamination of Audiences", *Critical Inquiry,* 4/1 (1977), 121-41) offers an alternative approach, which emphasizes the plurality of narratees and readers. But his insistence on maintaining a strict distinction between four kinds of audiences (actual, authorial, narrative, and ideal) leads to similar difficulties in applying the terms, as is shown by his own inconclusive discussion of the audiences in Nabokov's *Pale Fire.*

[38] Prince, 1973, *op.cit.* and Piwowarczyk, *op.cit.*

[39] Ray, *op.cit.*

[40] Ifri, *op.cit.*, 41.

[41] Rabinowitz, *op.cit.*, 130.

excluded from the text altogether, and banned from a share in the society constituted by narrators and their narratees. The voice of the narrator can never be confined to a prison-house known as "the text itself". Whenever narrators interact with their narratees, the real reader is always being addressed as well. The narratee is not always a reader, but the real reader is always a co-narratee. In the history of critical theory, the idea of the "reader" as a collective entity or "readerhood" has proven far more useful in accounting for these social aspects of narration than the abstract and restricted notion of the narratee. The "social tone" of *Tristram Shandy* is a collective production involving the participation of real readers and fictional narratees, as much as real authors and fictional narrators. So perhaps the time has come to liberate the narratee from his narrow nook opposite the narrator, and to recognize that the voice of the narrator speaks to us all.

THE UNRECOVERABLE CONTEXT

H.G. WIDDOWSON

This is an essay in speculative stylistics about the relationship between text and context in Shakespeare. The topic is an appropriate one for a volume in honour of Peter Verdonk, since it touches on issues in literary analysis and interpretation that he himself has explored with such distinction over the years. He may not approve of the speculation. The paper is, I admit, something of an off-duty indulgence, rather informal and fanciful. It has a rather festive air to it, I think. But then, that too might be appropriate, given the nature of this publication.

First, a little preliminary tuning to key in the textual topic and set it in time.

> Webster was much possessed by death
> And saw the skull beneath the skin ...
> (T.S. Eliot: Whispers of Immortality)[1]

Webster was of course not the only one of his time so possessed. Mutability and mortality are prominent themes of his period. Shakespeare's sonnets are obsessive variations on the theme, of nature's changing course, and minutes hastening to their end. At the same time, of course, their very composition counteracts the process they talk about, and this too is a recurrent theme. Time itself is held in textual check. Shakespeare is here writing for posterity, and there is every reason to suppose that he took great pains to ensure that his texts survived in print, thus providing a recurrence of readings whereby he and his lover would, so to speak, be endlessly resurrected:

---

[1] T.S. Eliot, *Collected Poems, 1909-1962*, London: Faber and Faber, 1963, 55-6.

His beauty shall in these black lines be seen,
And they shall live, and he in them still green.[2]

So long as men can breathe and eyes can see,
So long lives this, and this gives life to thee.[3]

And gives life to the poet too.

But for Shakespeare the playwright, things were apparently quite different. All the evidence here points to textual neglect and an indifference to posterity. The texts were composed as scripts to be publicly performed, only becoming a reality when activated by speech, not essentially written texts as such at all, and so not designed to be permanent. The writing was a means not an end in itself. Only that odd fellow Ben Jonson thought quaintly of plays as literature, and published them as his "works".

Sonnets and plays were, then, texts of different kinds. One was a reading text, stable and designed for direct reception, with the assumption that its meaning, textually enclosed and complete, would survive intact over time. The other was a speaking text, unstable and indirect in the sense that it could only be apprehended by the mediation of performance, and not infrequently modified in the process. In this sense the plays depended on the immediate spatio-temporal context that the sonnets were written to transcend.

Part of this context can of course be replicated. Indeed this has been done in the recent reconstruction of the Globe Theatre on the south bank of the Thames. This is a replica of the Elizabethan stage. But it cannot replicate the conditions of staging. To use a distinction proposed by Dell Hymes,[4] it reproduces the *setting*, the physical circumstances of the context of performance. But it cannot reproduce the *scene*, the

---

[2]   Sonnet 63.

[3]   Sonnet 18.

[4]   D.H. Hymes, "The Ethnography of Speaking", in T.C. Gladwin and W.C. Sturtevant, eds, *Anthropology and Human Behaviour*, Washington: Anthropological Society of Washington, 1962. Reprinted in J. Fishman, ed., *The Sociology of Language*, The Hague: Mouton, 1968.

socio-psychological construction placed upon those circumstances so as to realize their significance as a cultural event, for this, obviously enough, depended on the customary ways in which the performance was originally apprehended. You can reproduce the Elizabethan stage, but not the Elizabethan audience.

One obvious feature of staging in the Elizabethan period was its dependence on language for framing the internal context of the play. The wooden O was open to the sky and there was little in the way of stage scenery, so whatever visual effects were called for had, for the most part, to be verbally created.

> Think, when we talk of horses, that you see them,
> Planting their proud hoofs i' th' receiving earth.
>
> (*Henry V*, I i, 25-26)

The hurly-burly of battle is sometimes, of course, off-stage, as with the one the witches refer to in *Macbeth*, and represented second hand by commentary. Where it is on-stage, it is commonly presented by token figures and symbolic action, relying on the "imaginary forces" of the audience to project them inwardly and give them wider significance. But there are other features of staging which call for a more imaginative piecing out of the imperfections of the unworthy scaffold. Without the special electrical effects so common a feature of modern productions, darkness had to be spoken into existence, conjured up somehow in the minds of an audience sitting in broad daylight. In general, then, the spatio-temporal dimensions of context had to be textually projected in ways that present day productions on stage and screen have made redundant. All the blood and thunder of battle, darkness and day, sunshine and moonlight can in modern productions be directly represented, particularly on screen, in an immediate direct appeal to the senses without verbal mediation. We do not *need* the language any more.

So it is that what for the Elizabethan audience would serve as the crucial function of locating where a particular scene takes place can these days become little more than verbal embellishment. To take one simple example. *Macbeth* again. At the beginning of Act 3, Scene 3, the men that are to murder Banquo make their appearance. On the Elizabethan stage, there would be no visual indication of what time of day it is, so this has to be provided verbally. One of the murderers obliges:

> The west still glimmers with some streaks of day ....

Right. So it is almost dark. The audience in a modern production would know this already and so the murderer's speech is redundant as contextual information: it simply adds a little poetic decoration. But we should notice that the murderer's words do not only serve to place the scene, and so are functionally equivalent to "It's getting dark." The very "poetic" elaboration serves to *create* the darkening evening, to invoke it, to call it into being. This becomes evident from the rest of the murderer's speech:

> The west still glimmers with some streaks of day.
> Now spurs the lated traveller apace
> To gain the timely inn, and near approaches
> The subject of our watch.
>
> *(Macbeth*, III iii, 4-8)

If the twilight is already visually provided, as it would be in a modern production, then of course the creative impact of these lines is, to some degree at least, bound to be diminished. And the greater the visual impact on the audience, then, obviously, the more likely it is to distract attention from the verbal representation.

The speech here, then, does not only indicate the time of day to the original audience but actually *represents* it as a perceptual experience; it gives it, one might say, not only a name but a local habitation. But the very fulfilment of this contextualizing function creates something of a problem. For the language that fulfils it has to be spoken by somebody in the play. And this particular speech we have been considering does not seem to be the kind of thing that a murderer would actually say. It is true that this one is never identified by name or status (he may be a courtier, for all we know), nevertheless, these lines sound somewhat incongruous in the mouth of a hired cut-throat. They do not seem to be in character.

The issue here is the possible incompatibility between the contextualizing and the characterizing functions of Shakespeare's dramatic language. Contextualization is verbally rather than visually represented, but this can only be done by characters in the play. How then we do know when they are being used by the playwright simply as a mouthpiece for setting, and indeed (as we have seen) creating the scene, and when they are speaking in character, in their own voice? In the case we have been considering, for example, are we to think of the murderer as a character with a penchant for poetic expression?

This problem of possible incompatibility is not, of course, confined to Shakespeare. It confronts every playwright. At the beginning of any play, even one which can draw on modern technology for its staging or screening, the audience needs to be provided with contexual information of one kind or another: who the characters are in relation to each other, what past events are presupposed and so on. All of this is known to the characters *in* the play as part of their fictional world, but not to the audience outside the play, looking on. On screen, much of this can now, of course, be presented directly by flashback sequences, but on stage, it has to be done indirectly as a function of dialogue, and this has to carry conviction as "normal" interaction. The contextual information has to be naturalized. Tom Stoppard[5] gives a comic illustration of what happens when it is not:

> MRS DRUDGE (*into phone*) Hello, the drawing-room of Lady Muldoon's country residence one morning in early spring? ... Hello! — the draw... Who? Who did you wish to speak to? I'm afraid there is no one of that name here, this is all very mysterious and I'm sure it's leading up to something, I hope nothing is amiss for we, that is Lady Muldoon and her houseguests, are here cut off from the world, including Magnus, the wheelchair-ridden half-brother of her ladyship's husband Lord Albert Muldoon who ten years ago went out for

---

[5] Tom Stoppard, *The Real Inspector Hound, and Other Entertainments*, London: Faber and Faber, 1993, 1.

a walk on the cliffs and was never seen again – and all alone, for they had no children.

(Stoppard: *The Real Inspector Hound*)

We can account for the absurdity of this by invoking Grice's co-operative principle.[6] Mrs Drudge, we may say, is violating the maxims of quantity and relevance in that she is off-loading more information than is required for, or is relevant to, the presumed purpose of the telephone call. But to say that is to assign her the role of character in a play, in which we would expect dialogue to have some resemblance to normal conversation. In this case, her flouting of the maxims results in implicatures which we interpret as indicative of her personality as a character - that she is garrulous, not very bright, insensitive to others, and so on. But if we take her to be the mouthpiece of the playwright, a contextualizing informant only, then what she says does conform to these maxims, to the extent that she is providing information, which is relevant to the play. She is being co-operative with the audience. But the problem is that this results in her being uncooperative within the enclosed world of the play itself.

One way round this difficulty of using characters as contextual informants and running the risk of triggering off unwanted implicatures is to take them out of the action of the play and have them directly address the audience as the chorus. This device, which shifts the mode of representation to narrative, is a device which Shakespeare, of course, quite often uses. He does so, as we have seen in *Henry V*, to overcome the narrow confines of the stage to represent events on a large scale. In *A Winter's Tale*, a chorus (figured as Time) conveniently fills the audience in on the 16 year gap between Act 3 and Act 4. In these and other cases the chorus bears independent witness, and provides a non-participant third person perspective on events. The chorus option seems not to be taken where the characters themselves are personally involved in the contextualization. *The Tempest* is an interesting case. The events preceding the action of the play could conceivably have been narrated in a prologue. Instead it is Prospero who recounts them to Miranda (Act 1, Scene 2), and he does so at

---

[6] H.P. Grice, "Logic and Conversation", in P. Cole and J.L. Morgan, eds, *Syntax and Semantics. Volume 3, Speech Acts*, New York: Academic Press, 1975.

considerable length (100 lines and more), only interrupting his monologue to make sure that she is paying attention. Miranda's turns at talk are entirely determined by Prospero, and after a few minimal, and dutiful contributions to the exchange, she eventually (and not surprisingly) falls asleep.

Prospero's contextualization here raises a number of interesting questions, and in considering them we come, I think, to a central issue about how the Elizabethan audience interpreted the use of language in dramatic representation. To begin with, we might ask how convincing is this one-sided interaction within the play itself. Certainly it is not very co-operative conversation. Prospero is verbose and provides more information, it seems, than Miranda can readily take in. But it may be that she does not *need* to take it in because it is not *relevant* for her. This would depend, of course, on whether she has heard it before. It is quite irrelevant if she has. But if she has not heard it before, one cannot but wonder why she apparently takes so little interest in it, why she does not react in some positive way. Instead of being rivetted by such momentous events, her attention wanders and she nods off. One would also expect that Prospero himself would pause occasionally and elicit some kind of response to what would, after all, be an extraordinary revelation, rather than simply check that the channel is still open for transmission. This would suggest that Miranda *has* heard it all before, and it is redundant and so irrelevant. In that case an implicature of a Gricean kind results in respect to Prospero's character: namely that he has a way of going on about past injustices, talking about them obsessively to the only other human being on the island. Alternatively, of course, if we are to suppose that everything that Prospero says *is* indeed news to Miranda, her lack of response would reflect on *her* character too. Here is a very dull and unresponsive creature indeed, quite insensitive to her father's suffering. But this does not square with Miranda of the "piteous heart", who feels for the "poor souls" in the shipwreck and appeals to her father for their lives.

Whether you assume that what Prospero says is relevant or not, the interaction between him and Miranda does not seem to carry conviction either way. The implicatures that arise about character (Prospero as paranoid or Miranda as moronic) do not seem satisfactory. So it would seem reasonable to abandon the idea (in this case at least) that contextualization and characterization can be complementary. If so, then the only alternative, it would seem, is to suspend the operation of the co-operative principle as it might apply to the dramatic dialogue, and edit out the unwanted implicatures. In other words, we simply take Prospero to be functioning here as a non-participant in the play proper, as in effect a chorus providing contextual information to set the scene, and relevant to the audience only.

But I would like to suggest that we can entertain conjecture of a different kind. We have been assuming so far that what the characters of a play have to say is to be interpreted in much the same way as we would interpret everyday speech off-stage. But a play is not the *replication* of everyday life, but a *representation* of an alternative reality. What is represented in dramatic speech, therefore, may not be what is normally associated with spoken interaction at all, in which case, it would then make no sense to expect conversational verisimilitude. I have already suggested (with particular reference to the murderer in *Macbeth*) that language was used in Shakespeare to represent the essential being of contextual features, and not just to indicate their outward appearances. I want now to suggest that the same point applies to the representation of character, that what we find in Shakespeare is language used by characters not only to engage in overt interaction, but to express their covert thoughts, feelings and perceptions, to represent the essential being of their inner selves. There is then, I suggest, a dual perspective at play, the inner and the outer, with characters constantly shifting from one to the other, and settling into neither. One might draw a pictorial parallel with portraits which show both full face and the profile of the subject simultaneously, thus integrating two perspectives in a perceptually impossible fusion. The Elizabethan audience, primed in these conventions of representation on stage, would not expect characters to be "realistic" by the criteria of "normal" speech behaviour. They would indeed be taken as *characters*, embodiments of character, persona, not persons.

And as characters, they are representations not of people as such, but as constituted of natural forces both inside and outside them, different permutations of interacting humours and elements, human beings as microcosmic embodiments of the macrocosm. Here is another fusion: of inner character and external reality. It was not only that the characters spoke a context into being, but that context could also be the external projection of their inner selves. Context and character then cease to be distinct. So it is that the conditions of Elizabethan staging themselves provide for a mode of fused representation which the modern audience can no longer appreciate.

Consider the case of *King Lear*. In modern productions, on stage and on screen, the storm itself is perceptually presented, with special effects, visual and aural, designed to make a direct impact on the senses. And the more sensational the presentation, the more, one might say, is emphasis given to the physical privations that Lear suffers. At the same time, the significance of Lear's actual words diminishes, because they are no longer needed to set the scene. But what is *represented* in the scene is also changed, and changed radically, from what would have been apprehended by the Elizabethan audience. For now, instead of having the one storm that Lear himself verbalizes, we have two: the aural/visual one of the staging, and the verbal one of the text. And they compete for attention, with the former, appealing immediately to the senses as it does, likely to prevail. There are indeed productions in which the staged storm is so dominant that the audience scarcely hears what Lear is actually saying and all they are left with is the gist and a general impression of passion. Note that, paradoxically enough, even if Lear's words *were* to be noticed, they would somehow have to be matched in ferocity with the staged storm to carry conviction in a modern production, with the consequence that the words would then fail in their creative effect.

Let us then speculate on how the scene might be understood by the Elizabethan audience as it is verbally represented on the bare stage. The first sign of the storm occurs in Act 2 Scene 4 as a stage direction *(Storm and tempest)*, and signalled not verbally but by noises off, presumably by some rudimentary device (a wind machine, rolling cannon balls). The timing of its occurrence would not be lost on the Elizabethan audience. It comes after Lear has appealed to the gods to keep him from ignoble tears. It comes as a kind of response.

Lear: If it be you that stirs these daughters' hearts
Against their father, fool me not so much
To bear it tamely; touch me with noble anger,

And let not women's weapons, water drops,
Stain my man's cheeks ....
You think I'll weep.
No, I'll not weep.
(Storm and tempest)
I have full cause of weeping, but this heart
Shall break into a hundred thousand flaws
Or ere I'll weep. O fool, I shall go mad!
(Exeunt, Lear, Fool, Kent, and Gloucester)
Cornwall: Let us withdraw; 'twill be a storm.
                                   (*King Lear,* II iv, 277-282)

For the Elizabethans, the external turbulence of the storm is not simply coincidental with the internal turbulence in Lear's mind but corresponds with it. And this correspondence would be taken not as a matter of symbolism but symbiosis: the disruption of natural order, or degree, in one place (as in the deposing, or disposing of a monarch) triggers off empathetic reactions of a cosmic kind. As Ulysses puts it in *Troilus and Cressida*:

Take but degree away, untune that string,
And hark what discord follows.
                                   (*Troilus and Cressida,* I iii, 109-10)

So what discord follows the rejection of Lear, as both king and father at the hands of the "unnatural hags" his daughters? Lear mentions impending madness, Cornwall an impending storm. In the next scene (III i) we are given a vivid description third person description of both:

Kent: Where's the king?
Gtlemn: Contending with the fretful elements;
         Bids the wind blow the earth into the sea,
         Or swell the curled waters 'bove the main,
         That things might change or cease; tears his white hair,
         Which the impetuous blasts, with eyeless rage,
         Catch in their fury and make nothing of;
         Strives in his little world of man to outscorn
         The to-and-fro conflicting wind and rain ...
                                   (*King Lear*, III i, 3-11)

Here the disturbances, the two manifestations of discord, in the weather and in Lear's mind, co-occur. At the beginning of the next scene, Lear himself makes an appearance:

> *Lear:* Blow winds, and crack your cheeks. Rage, blow.
> You cataracts and hurricanoes, spout
> Till you have drenched our steeples, drowned the cocks.
> You sulph'rous and thought-executing fires,
> Vaunt couriers of oak-cleaving thunderbolts,
> Singe my white head. And thou, all shaking thunder,
> Strike flat the thick rotundity o' th' world,
> Crack Nature's moulds, all germains spill at once,
> That makes ingrateful man.
>
> *(King Lear,* III ii, 1-8)

Now if, as in a modern production, a storm has been perceptually provided on stage or screen, then Lear's speech, for all its vocative address and exclamatory power is essentially (like that of the Gentleman in the previous scene) *descriptive*: his words relate to a world that has a separate contextual existence. But if there are no such visual and aural provision of context (apart perhaps from rudimentary noises off) then the only storm we have is the one that comes out of Lear's mouth. He verbally creates it. His speech brings it into being. In this case, the vocatives actually *invoke*: He does not call *to* the winds and cataracts and hurricanoes, he calls them *up* as Prospero calls up the tempest. And the obvious effect of this, for the Elizabethan audience, is that the disturbances in the outer weather and inner state of mind converge. Lear, in effect, *storms*: his words project the discord which is raging *inside* him. Context and character are no longer distinct.

I would suggest that with modern staging, this dramatic representation of experience tends to reduce to the theatrical reproduction of weather, and the function, and effect, of Lear's speech is radically altered. And this is not an isolated instance. There are innumerable occasions in Shakespeare when the staged presentation of context undermines the representation of the text. One thinks, for example, of the opening scene of *Macbeth*. Here again the provision of contextual effects outside those projected in the language of the witches shifts attention away from the reality, which the language represents. As with Lear, the elements have no separate existence outside the witches: the blasted heath, the thunder, lightning and rain are called up by their words. And if, distracted by theatrical staging, you do not attend to the words, then something of their dramatic effect is inevitably lost.

And this effect again has to do with the fusion of context and character. A modern audience, watching the play on stage or screen, generally fails to notice the significance of what Macbeth himself says on his first appearance. Up to that point he has figured in the play (Act 1 Scene 2) only in third person description as news of his exploits are recounted to Duncan, and these are in support of the natural order and sustain his degree. He is "valiant cousin", "worthy gentleman", a paragon of good. But he has already been mentioned by the witches in the very first scene of the play. They arrange to meet him after the battle, and disappear with words that express the very discord that they represent:

> Fair is foul, and foul is fair,
> Hover through the fog and filthy air.
>
> (*Macbeth*, I i, 11-12)

But the witches are agents of evil, unnatural disorder, so the more emphatically Macbeth is presented as an agent of good, of natural order, the more puzzling it becomes as to what they can possibly have to do with him. Act 1 Scene 3, and the witches appear again. The meeting is about to take place, and the puzzle resolved. Macbeth comes on stage with Banquo, and the Elizabethan audience would, I speculate, be particularly attentive to his first words as holding perhaps the clue to the mystery. Macbeth's first words are:

> So fair and foul a day I have not seen.
>
> (*Macbeth*, I iii, 38)

The very words of the witches. Is it too fanciful to imagine a gasp of horror from the groundlings? Macbeth is condemned out of his own mouth. For all his apparent virtue, he is already tainted by evil.

These are cases, I would argue, of unrecoverable context. It is not only that much of the contextualizing function of Shakespeare's language in the location of the setting has necessarily disappeared with changed conventions of staging, but the representation of the inner selves of characters achieved through the very verbalization of context has disappeared as well. And disappeared forever. We can, of course, learn about how the Elizabethans conceived of the interplay of microcosmic and macrocosmic forces in nature, their notions of degree and discord and so on, but we cannot directly experience them, we cannot feel them on the pulses. Nor can we recover their experience of language, their attentiveness to verbal nuance. The verbalizing of context was, in the absence of other staging facilities, a matter of necessity, but it also had the virtue of providing conditions for the integrated representation of context and character, and for creating dramatic effects of a particularly striking kind. But the appreciation of these effects depends not only on modes of thought but also on modes of listening which are remote from modern experience. The original effects are lost on us, and lost to us forever.

This is not to say that the contemporary staging and screening of Shakespeare provides only an impoverished experience of the plays, but that it is inevitably a different one: one which is, I think, less essentially and intrinsically a verbal experience. There is no point in deploring this, or pretending that things can be otherwise: no point in talking about the "real" Shakespeare, because the reality is in the eye, and ear, of the beholder. We can never see or hear the plays as the Elizabethans did. But what we can do is to try to understand how they would have seen and heard them, and this involves the close scrutiny of the language and its possible implications. This is the purpose of stylistics: to study the text and to speculate on its significance. We cannot thereby recover the unrecoverable context, but we can get an inkling of what it is that we have missed.

SATIRICAL HUMOUR AND CULTURAL CONTEXT: WITH A NOTE ON THE CURIOUS CASE OF FATHER TODD UNCTUOUS

PAUL SIMPSON

Introduction

This final chapter examines comic discourse from a contextualized-stylistic perspective. More specifically, it sketches a general model for the study of satirical humour before offering a short analysis of certain patterns of dialogue in a television situation-comedy. It is hoped that the analysis, which refers specifically to comic dialogue in an Irish context, will feed directly into larger issues to do with culturally-situated aspects of verbal humour. The paper also assesses the manner by which discoursal and generic properties of comic discourse resurface across time, and asks if it is feasible to talk of diachronic, culture-specific verbal humour. Another aim is to develop the notion of satirical discourse beyond that conventionally classified as "literary". To this end, the principal satirical material analysed will be taken from the television series *Father Ted*, a popular sitcom, which has been screened extensively in both Britain and Ireland.

Background to the present study

Although this short study is focused principally on localized features of dialogue in the context of Irish humour, it is underpinned theoretically by a broader-based analytic model. This model is currently being developed as part of an ongoing research project on satirical humour.[1] The present

---

[1] Paul Simpson, *The Discourse of Satire: A Stylistic Model of Satirical Humour* (in preparation).

study sets a certain type of comic discourse against the backdrop of possible types of comic discourse, and then extrapolates from this contrast to explore the notion of culturally-situated humour. To this extent, it needs therefore to be located within the larger theoretical model that frames it. In the following brief over-view of the broader model, some of the theoretical assumptions made, are, of necessity, defended elsewhere, while the categories that comprise it are, at this early stage, inchoate, partial and provisional.

The model, as it stands, operates from the premise that satirical discourse comprises at least four basic components. These components obviously do not constitute the full set of necessary and sufficient conditions for a definition of verbal and pictorial satire, though further refinements to the model will be carried out with this goal in mind. The four components are: *setting, method, uptake* and *target*. Figure 1, below, gathers together the principal constituents and their sub-components under the rather improbable acronym "SMUT". Into the four components have been factored some concepts and categories from the "General Theory of Verbal Humour" (GTVH), which is a contemporary model of humorous discourse drawn mainly from research in psychology and cognitive linguistics.[2] In particular, Figure 1 subsumes the GTVH's three key stages for the production of a comic text, which are: *setup, incongruity* (or *script opposition*) and *resolution*.[3] The additional criteria present in the SMUT model are there to highlight the special nature of satire when compared to humorous discourse generally.

---

[2]   See, for example, S. Attardo, "The Semantic Foundations of Cognitive Theories of Humor", *Humor*, 10/4 (1997), 395-420; V. Raskin, *Semantic Mechanisms of Humor*, Dordrecht: Reidel, 1985; and T. Veatch, "A Theory of Humor", *Humor*, 11/2 (1998), 161-215.

[3]   Attardo, *op.cit.*, 396.

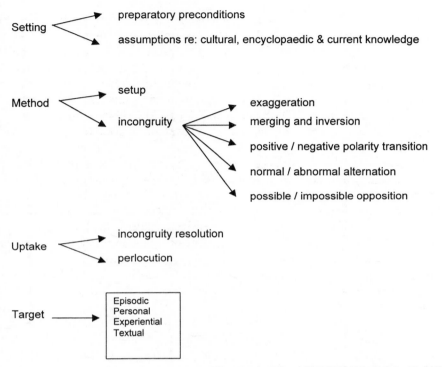

Figure 1: The 'SMUT' Model in Brief

The first of the four categories is *setting*. This is intended to tally with Nash's observation that any "act" of humour requires as its initial, principal reference a *genus*, which is "a derivation in culture, institutions, attitudes, beliefs."[4] In terms of the criteria offered here, the notion of setting follows in part the traditional argument in linguistic pragmatics about how utterance interpretation is shaped by and is heavily dependent

---

[4] W. Nash, *The Language of Humour,* London: Longman, 1985, 9-10.

on features of interactive context.[5] Setting therefore is essentially a non-linguistic component covering the preparatory preconditions necessary for the construction of satirical discourse. Such preconditions take as given the fact that satire is ultimately an ironic, non-literal reading of a text (and not a heavily cued reading as many other text types are) and in consequence is perpetually prone to failure or misfire. Thus, the preparation of a satirical text requires the satirist to calculate, *a priori*, the potential knowledge base of the reader, viewer or listener (or, to coin a term, the "satiree").

This translates into inferences not only about the satiree's cultural and encyclopaedic knowledge, but, in the case of contemporary political satire, about their knowledge of contemporary events and current affairs as well. For instance, when its source material is a topical news item, a satirical text works within a highly restricted cognitive backdrop, with preparatory preconditions requiring some assessment of how much recent news coverage can be assumed to be known to potential satirees. This is one index of the "shelf-life" of contemporary political satire: as its target fades from collective memory, the satirical text, in direct proportion, becomes progressively more opaque.

Method, the second of the SMUT model's four components, is a linguistic stage proper. This category corresponds to Nash's general observation that humour requires both "a locus in language" and a "characteristic design, presentation, or verbal packaging."[6] In keeping with the GTVH, this is a temporally ordered, two-stage process with the *setup* phase (normally) preceding the *incongruity* phase. The setup lays the groundwork by establishing an accessible, neutral context which is congruent with the experience of the receiver of the text.[7] Although not funny *per se*, the setup is a necessary preliminary to the incongruity. The concept of incongruity is based on the notion of "script opposition" but

---

[5]   J.L. Austin, *How to Do Things with Words,* Oxford: Clarendon Press, 1962, and J. Searle, *Speech Acts,* Cambridge: Cambridge University Press, 1969.

[6]   Nash, *op.cit.*, 9-10.

[7]   Attardo, *op.cit.*, 411.

has been expanded outwards by humorologists to account for a host of potential cognitive-psycholinguistic oppositions. Semino (whose work on text worlds in poetry complements that on the GTVH in several respects) notes the humorous potential of this device when she remarks that jokes commonly "achieve their effect by leading interpreters to activate a particular script and then forcing them to switch to another, often leading to absurdity."[8] This setup-to-incongruity transition is most apparent in formulaic jokes comprising a triad of scenarios in which the violation occurs on the third scenario (that is, of the "An Englishman, a Scotsman and an Irishman walked into a pub ..." variety). However, in satire, the set-up phase may be altogether more sophisticated, often because it is built around "garden path" reasoning. The following extract is the opening of a short piece that appeared recently in the British satirical magazine *Private Eye*:

OUTRAGE OVER SHOCK
CHANNEL 4 PROGRAMME

by Our Media Staff **Gay Search**

There was fury last night after
Channel 4 transmitted a two-
hour programme containing
no scenes of full frontal nudity,
under-age homosexual sex or
explicit bad language ...

The headline to this "spoof" report, which is either mimicking or reproducing verbatim a contemporary news report, marks the set-up phase. This was written in the context of major press "outcry" against a series of Channel 4 programmes that featured sex scenes of an allegedly explicit (by British terrestrial television standards) nature. Although the

---

[8] Elena Semino, *Language and World Creation in Poems and Other Texts,* Harlow: Longman, 1997, 137.

setup begins to crumble at the byline — "Gay Search" is actually the name of a real television personality, though known primarily for her gardening skills — the incongruity proper develops in the opening text. In common with much satire, this text pulls an anterior discourse event (the press outcry) into a kind of creative buffer zone, before relaunching it as a posterior, satirical text. Connections between the anterior and posterior discourses are often reinforced and embellished by puns and other forms of verbal word-play: notice, for example, how Gay Search's name acquires new significance in the posterior context.

The space between the set-up and incongruity phases varies in size in different satirical contexts. In pictorial satire, such as political cartoons, the space is narrow, while it is often expansive in the work of the canonical literary satirists. For instance, it is only after one thousand words of Swift's "Modest Proposal" that its mild-mannered speaker suggests, shockingly, that "a young healthy child well nursed is at a year old a most delicious, nourishing, and wholesome food, whether stewed, roasted, baked, or boiled."[9]

The incongruity phase itself may be created though a number of overlapping discourse strategies, yet most of these are consonant to some degree with the type of script opposition identified by Attardo, Semino and others. Figure 1 attempts to capture some of the possible discourse strategies available. These include: the creation of grotesques or caricatures through exaggeration of features associated with the object of attack; the merging and inversion of scripts and schemata; the transition between positive and negative polarities; the alternation between normal and abnormal scripts; and the opposition of possible and impossible discourse worlds. There is not the space here to offer detailed illustrations of all these types of satirical method, though it might be worth noting in passing how the two examples mentioned so far slot into the model. The opposition in the Swift text, which advocates the eating of infants as a solution to poverty and suffering, is principally a shift from a normal to an abnormal script. This type of opposition is the type of humorous device which Veatch classes as a violation of the "the emotional system of

---

[9] Jonathan Swift, "A Modest Proposal", in M.H. Abrams, ed., *The Norton Anthology of English Literature,* New York: Norton, (1986) [1729], 2174-2180.

opinions about the proper order of the social and natural world", though he also notes that this "subjective moral order" tends to destabilize across cultures and across time.[10] By contrast, the incongruity in the *Private Eye* text is activated, in the first instance, by the transition from positive to negative polarity, with the negative particle in the opening text ("containing *no* scenes ...") subverting the anterior discourse and arguably the prudish cultural *mores* it espouses.

The third of the SMUT model's four components is *uptake*. Like the setting stage, this category is drawn largely from concepts in linguistic pragmatics and is meant, particularly, to echo Austin's concept of "uptake". In Austin's framework, uptake encompasses the understanding of the illocutionary force and content of the utterance by its addressee, and the perlocutionary effects on the addressee brought about by means of uttering the sentence, such effects being special to the circumstances of the utterance.[11] The concept of perlocution in satirical discourse relies heavily on inferencing by the satiree; an inferencing which requires the resolution of the incongruity created in the method stage along with an identification of the satirical *target* (see below). Humorologists working within the GTVH model have suggested that satisfactory resolution of incongruity requires the deployment of a "local logic mechanism".[12] This mechanism functions by conserving in "working memory" the multiple scripts projected by the incongruity for the period of time necessary for the research of a cognitive rule capable of solving the incongruity.[13] Interestingly, Attardo also adds (409) that incongruities are least likely to be resolved definitively in "absurd humour", suggesting, in effect, that

---

[10] Veatch, *op.cit.*, 168.

[11] Austin, *op.cit.*, 116.

[12] S. Attardo, and V. Raskin, "Script Theory Revis(it)ed: Joke Similarity and a Joke Representation Model", *Humor,* 4 (1991), 293-347, 303; A. Ziv, *Personality and Sense of Humor,* New York: Springer-Verlag, 1984, 90.

[13] Attardo, *op.cit.*, 412.

absurdism is fundamentally the most open-ended of all forms of humorous discourse.

The emphasis here on satire as a perlocutionary, rather than illocutionary concept, throws up an interpretative paradox: satire is only satirical when understood as such. In other words, when satirical method remains undetected, a "monologic" reading, in Bakhtin's sense, is privileged over a potentially "polyphonic" reading of the discourse. The consequences of this are interesting. George records his experience of teaching "Modest Proposal" to beginning undergraduates. He notes that on a first reading of the text, "knee-jerk, naive responses" are often offered, in typical remarks like "This Swift guy is sick!"[14] Yet this is not to suggest that texts cannot work in their own terms when satirical processing is withheld. For example, children who have never heard of totalitarianism or of Stalin's Five Year Plan continue to enjoy Orwell's *Animal Farm* as a fairy tale about, not to put too fine a point on it, a spat between a gang of farmyard animals.

The last of the four categories is *target*. What arguably separates out parody from satire is the latter's perceived "object of attack". As Dane has remarked, "satire refers to things; parody to words. The target and referent of satire is a system of content .... that of parody is a system of expression."[15] This distinction between satire and parody is not straightforward, as Dane later observes, and in certain discourse contexts the two areas may fuse and overlap. The implications of this for the present model will be assessed shortly.

On Figure 1, a provisional list containing four types of satirical target has been drawn up. These four subtypes are best thought of as interlocking domains or zones rather than discrete units. The targets have been boxed in on the figure in order to capture this relationship of contiguity. The first of the four is *episodic* where the target is a particular action or a specific event that has taken place in the public sphere. The example from *Private*

---

[14] W. George, "Teaching Satire and Satirists", *English Journal,* 78/3 (1989), 38-43, 38.

[15] J. Dane, "Parody and Satire: A Theoretical Model", *Genre,* 13 (1980), 145-59, 145.

Eye discussed above would, for instance, be classified in the current model as episodic on the grounds that its stimulus is a specific event in the public domain (that is, an actual press and public outcry against an actual programming schedule). In satirical discourse whose target is *personal*, the object of attack is, unsurprisingly, a particular individual, though by imputation that individual's personality is often projected as some stereotypical or archetypical trait of human behaviour. A great deal of contemporary political satire (and much of that in *Private Eye* magazine) is focused on politicians, media personalities and others in the public eye, and as with episodic satire, the resolution of personal satire is heavily dependent upon a presumed expansive knowledge base on the part of the satiree (see above). *Experiential* satire targets more stable aspects of the human condition and experience as opposed to specific episodes and events. Swift's proposal, with its focus on starvation, poverty and human suffering, is a *prima facie* example of experiential satire. Finally, *textual* satire, which straddles most closely the interface between parody and satire, targets the linguistic code itself as its principal object of attack. In other words, this form of satire appears to turn discourse inwardly upon itself and to this extent is best considered as *meta-discourse*. Textually oriented satire does not necessarily parody specific texts that others have produced but can instead encompass both dialectal and diatypic varieties of language as well as any generalized aspect of everyday social interaction. Bex makes a similar point in connection with parodic texts when he says that "they do not take any particular anterior text as their model. Rather, they take characteristic ways of 'saying' that are associated with particular social functions."[16] It is this form of satire, which most typically characterizes the "absurd".[17] Furthermore, following the tenets of the

---

[16] Tony Bex, "Parody, Meaning and Literary Genre", *Journal of Literary Semantics,* 15/3 (1996), 225-244, 237.

[17] This is manifest in the plays of Eugene Ionesco, and particularly in his *The Bald Primadonna*, where the arid cultural *mores* of the bourgeoisie are mediated on the stage through utterly vacuous and meaningless conversation between the characters. Deirdre Burton's *Dialogue and Discourse,* London: Routledge and Kegan Paul, 1980, is still an excellent stylistic exploration of the ways in which Ionesco manipulates the formulaic and routine in everyday social interaction.

GTVH, this form of satire is also the most resistant to incongruity-resolution. This low "resolvability", coupled with the fact that its first point of reference is neither an episode, an experience or a person, but an aspect of discourse, makes textual satire the most oblique of all of the types assessed so far. It is worth noting that Dane, although working in a markedly different scholarly framework, coins the term "gentle satire" to cover the sorts of texts that parallel the category defined here. He suggests that "gentle satire" occupies one extreme of a continuum at the opposite pole of which sits "invective, polemic".[18]

By way of conclusion to this section, it is important to reinforce the point that a single satirical text may realize multiple targets. Thus, discussing a text in terms of its perceived target is largely a question of balance and emphasis; the principal impetus may be from one subtype but that can be expanded outwards to cover the other three. Furthermore, all categories of target can expanded upwards to critique the ideological practices of elite groups, dominant institutions or powerful individuals. Whereas, for instance, Alexander Pope's attack on Timon and his tasteless villa (in "Epistle to Burlington" [c.1735]) may start on the personal plane, it can easily be "upgraded", as it were, to cover the arrogance and folly of *nouveau riche* sections of Eighteenth century society. This is not to suggest that the satirist's own ideological standpoint is necessarily a radical or progressive one; in fact, according to Dunne, there is little evidence that satirists are motivated by any clearly articulated political principles, or by any consistent political ideology.[19] However, this point (and the other issues raised in this conclusion) are from an area of investigation that is beyond the scope of this chapter and so they must be dealt with elsewhere. The next task in the present study will be to look more closely at certain aspects of verbal humour in their cultural context.

---

[18] Dane, *op.cit.*, 152.

[19] G. Dunne, *Satire: A Critical Reintroduction,* Kentucky: University Press of Kentucky, 1994, 149-50.

Verbal humour and textual satire: *Father Ted*

Father Ted currently ranks as one of the most popular sitcoms in British television history. The principal characters featured in the series are three Irish priests, and their housekeeper, who inhabit a parochial house set on the fictitious Craggy Island. The original idea for the series was taken initially by its two writers, Arthur Linehan and Graham Mathews, to RTE (the Republic of Ireland's terrestrial TV station). RTE turned it down, allegedly on the grounds that the material it contained was too sensitive. It was then offered to Hatrick Productions who went on to produce all three series and a Christmas special for British TV's Channel Four. The first series very quickly achieved so-called "cult status", and having proved hugely popular in Britain, was then sold on to RTE whereupon it became, in 1997, the most watched television programme in the Republic of Ireland.[20] Aside from its less than prescient business acumen, RTE's nervousness about taking on the production initially was understandable. For a start, the launch of the series coincided with a period in Ireland when the institution of the Catholic Church was in turmoil, and when, for the first time in its history, it experienced a marked shortfall in new recruits to its seminaries.[21] Moreover, the three priests who inhabit Craggy Island are strident satirical caricatures indeed: Father Jack (played by actor Frank Kelly) is a decrepit, foul-mouthed alcoholic; Father Dougie (Ardal O'Hanlon) is a ludicrously asinine novice whose ignorance of matters spiritual beggars belief; and the eponymous Father Ted (the late Dermot Morgan) is an ambitious schemer whose mysterious financial past has brought about his exile to Craggy Island. Ardal O'Hanlon, who like Dermot Morgan began his career as a stand up comic, has remarked of this characterization that:

---

[20] Readers interested in finding out more about this programme, its history and the actors who have featured in its three series, might wish to consult *The Craggy Examiner*, the official *Father Ted* website, at:

< http://www.geocities.com/paris/2694/craggy.html >

It should be noted that all the *Father Ted* data used in this study has been collected from this official website.

[21] J. Ryan, "Brothers in Brown", *The Big Issue,* 83 (1997), 6.

there are only three types of people in the world. The old drunk
letch, the young naive innocent and the shifty cagey wannabe.
Father Ted discovered that and so did Shakespeare.[22]

And finally, Mrs Doyle (played by actress Pauline McLynn) is an
absurdly selfless and devoted housekeeper who possesses a frenzied sense
of loyalty to the trio of inept clerics.

    The world of *Father Ted* is indeed a bizarre one, as would any world
be if it were inhabited almost exclusively by objectionable clerics.
Furthermore, the actual location for "Craggy Island", where most of the
outdoor action is shot, is Ennistymon in County Clare which, with its
striking limestone scree slopes and cliffs, creates a spartan and often
alienating backdrop to the plot lines of various episodes. The dynamics of
this sitcom undeniably offer ample opportunity to pillory the Catholic
church relentlessly. Yet, while it is true that the image of the clergy does
not emerge positively from *Father Ted*, one would nonetheless be hard
pushed to call the production "hard-hitting" by any stretch of the
imagination. For one thing, the few secular denizens who also inhabit this
curious clerical world fare no better than the priests.[23] However, it is
arguably certain aspects of the discoursal construction of the programme
that are primarily responsible for its sometime oblique satirical thrust. A
more detailed explanation of this hypothesis will be presented later in the
discussion.

---

[22] Ardal O'Hanlon, "Divine Comedy: Interview with Ardal O'Hanlon", *New Woman*
(January 1998), 82-5, 83.

[23] The set of non-clerical characters regularly featured in the series includes a
viciously fractious couple who barely manage to disguise their domestic disharmony
from the priests. This couple, along with Father Jack, have contributed the word
"feck" to the English language. This word has all the venom of the four-letter word it
so obviously replaces, yet at the same time manages to circumvent potential TV
scheduling constraints attendant on the use of taboo language. T-shirts bearing the
logo "FECK!" over the whiskey sodden visage of Father Jack appeared on the streets
within weeks of the first few episodes of the series.

Before that, and to give a flavour of the discourse universe that is *Father Ted*, I propose to examine a short sequence of dialogue which featured in the one-off Christmas Special first screened in 1997. In this episode, Father Ted has just learned that he is about to receive the "priest of the year" award (a meaningless achievement by any stretch of the imagination, but one which means all to the ambitious Ted). The scene is the sitting room of Craggy Island parochial house, where much of the indoor action tends to be shot. After a knock at the door, a stranger is shown in by Mrs Doyle. Perhaps inevitably, the visitor turns out to be a priest. The new priest, played by the actor Gerard MacSorley, speaks with a marked Northern Irish accent which is somewhat in contrast to the Southern Irish English spoken by all the other characters present. The new priest appears to know Ted intimately: his embraces, slaps on back, pretend shadow boxing and remarks to the effect that Ted hasn't changed a bit after all these years are clearly the actions of someone who considers Ted an old and close friend. So intimate is the new priest's behaviour that Ted feels too embarrassed to ask him to identify himself. After a failed attempt to get the stranger to write his name in the parish visitors' book, and when Mrs Doyle has just asked to be introduced to the "new Father", Ted finds himself "interactively cornered", so to speak. It is this impasse which triggers the following quick-fire sequence of dialogue:

Mrs Doyle:	[To Ted] Father ... aren't ye goin' to introduce me to the new Father?
Ted:	[Squirming] Oh, right ... right. [7 second pause] Actually, I'll tell you what. See if you can guess!
Mrs Doyle:	[Puzzled] Guess?
Ted:	C'mon! Have a go!
Mrs Doyle:	God, Father, sure it could be anythin'.
Ted:	[Through gritted teeth] Still, though, give it a try.
Mrs Doyle:	[Resigned. 11 second pause while she thinks and then, confidently, proclaims] Fr Andy Riley?
New Priest:	No. [Laughs]
Mrs Doyle:	[More quickly] Fr Desmond Coyle?

New Priest: No.
Mrs Doyle: [More quickly again] Fr George Burke?
New Priest: No.
Mrs Doyle: Fr David Nicholson?
New Priest: No.
Mrs Doyle: Fr Declan Lynch?
New Priest: No. [Smiling] I'll give you a clue.
Mrs Doyle: [Suddenly vociferous, and wagging her finger] NO CLUES!
[With renewed vigour] Fr Ken Sweeney?
New Priest: Nope.
Mrs Doyle: Fr Neil Hannon?
New Priest: [Shakes head]
Mrs Doyle: Fr Keith Cullen?
New Priest: [Shakes head]
Mrs Doyle: Fr Kieran Donnelly?
New Priest: No.
Mrs Doyle: Fr Mick McEvoy?
New Priest: No.

[a slow dissolve out of shot into a black screen, then a fade in again to suggest the passage of time. Other characters present now appear to be falling asleep]

Mrs Doyle: [rapidly now] Fr Henry Bigbiggy?
New Priest: No.
Mrs Doyle: Fr Hank Tree?
New Priest: No.
Mrs Doyle: Fr Hiroshima Twinkie?
New Priest: No.
Mrs Doyle: Fr Stig Bubblecart?
New Priest: No.
Mrs Doyle: Fr Johnnie Hellsapoppin?
New Priest: No.
Mrs Doyle: Fr Luke Duke?

New Priest:	No.
Mrs Doyle:	Fr Biggy Furry?
New Priest:	No.
Mrs Doyle:	Fr Chewy Lewy?
New Priest:	No.
Mrs Doyle:	Fr Hairy Cakelineham?
New Priest:	No.
Mrs Doyle:	Fr Reboola Conundrum?
New Priest:	No.
Mrs Doyle:	Fr Peewee Stairmaster?
New Priest:	No.
Mrs Doyle:	Fr Jemima Rakhtoum?
New Priest:	No.
Mrs Doyle:	Fr Spodo Komodo?
New Priest:	No.
Mrs Doyle:	Fr Todd Unctuous?
New Priest:	[Suddenly elated] YES! WELL DONE!
	[12 seconds of Mrs Doyle beaming amid audience applause and laughter]
Ted:	[Incredulous] Is that it? Father Todd Unctuous?

We never know for sure if Todd Unctuous is the new priest's name. As it happens, his arrival on Craggy Island marks the first stage of his nefarious scheme to steal Ted's "priest of the year" trophy. Unctuous, it seems, is a priest unnaturally obsessed with awards; later in the episode, after he is unmasked as a thief, he attributes the origins of his covetous obsession to "backhanders" at Holy Communion and Christenings. Thereafter, he confesses, he became ever more fixated on the ultimate prize: the "priest of the year" award.

All this matters relatively little in the context of *Father Ted*. What does matter is the delight taken in stretching to their limit the structures and boundaries of social interaction. The axiom "dialogue for dialogue's sake" is apposite here, just as it is in much of *Father Ted*. In this episode, Mrs Doyle, after some initial reticence, is prompted to guess the name of a complete stranger. Assiduous in every respect, she attempts to guess *both* first name and last name, and decorously, always prefixes this pair of names with the title "Father". Mrs Doyle's task is nigh on impossible by any reasonable measurement, and the implications and ramifications of her extended name-search will be discussed a little later in this section. For the moment, it is necessary to say something about the discourse structure of this conversation in more rigorously linguistic terms.

Drawing on the categories and notation developed in Francis and Hunston's model of discourse structure, Mrs Doyle's name-search exhibits a symmetrical pattern of *eliciting* exchanges.[24] Subsequent to the organizational exchanges which prompt it, a regular discoursal structure is initiated with Mrs Doyle's first question to Unctuous. The contiguous exchanges which flow from this are all two-part structures exhibiting the elements of structure *Initiation* (I) and *Response* (R). The discourse moves which fill I and R are respectively, *eliciting moves* (from Mrs Doyle) and *informing moves* (from Unctuous). Each of the move elements is realized by a single discourse *act*. The eliciting moves all contain a *neutral proposal* which seeks polarity information, thereby requiring the addressee to make a decision between "yes" and "no".[25] In all but one of the informing move slots, a *reject* is offered. This is realized by "no" or its variants (notice Unctuous's shaking of the head in places) and its function is to reject the underlying presuppositions in a previous eliciting move.[26] The pattern, of course, breaks down in that last startling exchange where the eliciting move from Mrs Doyle receives an informing move containing a polarity-endorsing act known as a *confirm*.[27] To highlight the regularity of the whole pattern, while acknowledging there are brief interruptions when Unctuous offers a clue and at the fade-out sequence, here is a structural breakdown of last four exchanges of the transaction:

---

[24] G. Francis, and S. Hunston, "Analysing Everyday Conversation", in M. Coulthard, ed., *Advances in Spoken Discourse Analysis,* London: Routledge, 1992, 123-61, 126.

[25] *Ibid.*, 130.

[26] *Ibid.*, 132.

[27] *Ibid.*, 131.

DISCOURSE TRANSACTION:　MRS DOYLE'S NAME SEARCH

EXCHANGE	Eliciting Move	Act	Informing Move	Act
ELICIT	**Mrs D:** Fr Peewee Stairmaster?	*n.pr*		
			Unctuous: No.	*rej*
ELICIT	**Mrs D:** Fr Jemima Rakhtoum?	*n.pr*		
			Unctuous: No.	*rej*
ELICIT	**Mrs D:** Fr Spodo Komodo?	*n.pr*		
			Unctuous: No.	*rej*
ELICIT	**Mrs D:** Fr Todd Unctuous?	*n.pr*		
			Unctuous: YES! WELL DONE!	*conf*

As a footnote to the analytic part of this section, and for reasons that will become clear in the next section, I wish to render down further the structural units in this sequence of exchanges into a *schematic structure*.[28] Within systemic-functional linguistics, this form of idealization of data has proved a useful method for exploring the generic properties of certain discursive practices; as in, for example, Ventola's study of the generic proprieties of service encounters.[29] Although this type of abstraction is difficult in conversational interaction where there are looser constraints on

---

[28] S. Eggins, *An Introduction to Systemic Functional Linguistics* London: Pinter, 1994, 34.

[29] E. Ventola, *The Structure of Social Interaction: A Systemic Approach to the Semiotics of Service Encounters*, London: Pinter, 1987.

what units follow what,[30] it is still possible, in a highly rigid discourse pattern like Mrs Doyle's name-search, to filter out the raw elements of schematic structure. First of all, this two-part structure comprises an **A** element (realized by the eliciting moves) and a **B** element (the informing moves). Stage **A** obviously precedes stage **B** in a fixed order, thus: **A^B**.[31] Moreover, as the sequence as a whole is recursive, this will be signalled by a preposed, right-angled arrow in the following schematic structure formula:

$$\lrcorner\{A\char`^B\}$$

This schematic structure is intended to tease out only the most core of the structural features of this series of exchanges. There will be good reason to return to it shortly, but before that some comment needs to made about Mrs Doyle's search in terms of the SMUT model outlined earlier. First of all, it would fair to say that this type of exuberant play on the routines of social interaction is typical of much dialogue in *Father Ted*. Although the programme's satirical targets are multiple, much of its emphasis is *meta-discoursal*. This greater focus on textual (rather than personal, experiential or episodic) targets does not exactly let the clergy let off hook, but it does have a deflective function and, as Dane suggests, some forms of "gentle satire" (for which the present text is strong candidate) are actually "affirmative".[32] Standing in marked contrast to this, argues Dane, is the negative and subversive satirical subgenre "invective", in which "the individual's behaviour is stressed over his societal role and the ideals of that role." It is true that the actions of the priests in *Father Ted* are highly questionable, but their impact is often parried by the focus on the comic excesses of the dialogue. To put it another way, were the focus of attack personal in the first instance, then greatly increased would be the discoursal proximity of the programme as a whole to vitriol or invective. This brings us to the question of satirical method. As mentioned earlier,

---

[30] Though, again, see *ibid.*

[31] Eggins, *op.cit.*, 40.

[32] Dane, *op.cit.*, 152.

Mrs Doyle's bizarre interactive routine is activated by the opposition between possible and impossible. What is more, she sets about her task with gusto. The fact that the names offered after the fade out sequence are markedly outlandish, while those of the preceding half would not have passed muster in any Irish telephone directory, suggest that she has trolled deep and wide for her suggestions. And the *coup de grâce* to all this is, of course, that she succeeds!

In terms of some of the issues developed in the previous section, the type of incongruity that this impossible-possible opposition engenders makes it difficult to reach a resolution; and the lower the degree of "resolvability", the greater the degree of absurdism. In fact, the interactive world of *Father Ted* in general seems to tread a fine line between, on the one hand, full-blown absurdism, and on the other, a slightly out-of-kilter surrealism. I have suggested elsewhere that an index of "classic" absurdism is the way characters in a represented world are never surprised by the improbable or unexpected.[33] A formula for this might be that characters in an unbelievable world act believably, so to speak, whereas in the context of the surreal, characters in a believable world act unbelievably. One of the enigmas of *Father Ted* is that it seems to straddle the two domains: characters may question initially the oddity of certain situations, but they quickly acquiesce and comply. For instance, Mrs Doyle is puzzled at first but follows Ted's lead anyway, while Ted's incredulity at the end of the name-search gives way to his acceptance that Unctuous is indeed the new priest's name.

Linguistic humour: culturally situated?

This short concluding section attempts to situate the analysis of *Father Ted* within a wider discourse context before discussing some of the theoretical issues attendant on the contextualized-stylistic study of verbal humour. As a first step towards this, I propose to consider briefly a further sequence of dialogue which is taken from Irish comic writer Flann O'Brien's novel

---

[33] See my "Odd Talk: Studying Discourses of Incongruity", in J. Culpeper, M. Short and P. Verdonk, eds, *Exploring the Language of Drama: From Text to Context*, London: Routledge, 1998, 34-53.

The Third Policeman (1967). The centrality of comic dialogue in O'Brien's work as a whole has been well documented, and its place in this particular novel often singled out for particular attention.[34] In this passage, the unnamed first person narrator is quizzed by a grotesque and intimidating police sergeant. In spite of having been told quite clearly that his interlocutor has no name, the sergeant initiates the following series of exchanges:

> Then he [the Sergeant] spoke.
> "Are you completely doubtless that you are nameless?", he asked.
> "Positively certain."
> "Would it be Mick Barry?
> "No."
> "Charlemagne O'Keeffe?"
> "No."
> "Sir Justin Spens?"
> "Not that."
> "Kimberly?"
> "No."
> "Bernard Fann?"
> "No."
> "Joseph Poe or Nolan?"
> "No."
> "One of the Garvins or the Moynihans?"
> "Not them."
> "Rosencranz O'Dowd?"
> "No."
> "Would it be O'Benson?"
> "Not O'Benson."
> "The Quigleys, the Mulrooneys or the Hounimen?"[35]

---

[34] A. Clissmann, *Flann O'Brien: A Critical Introduction to His Writings,* Dublin: Gill and Macmillan, 1975, 163.

[35] Flann O'Brien, *The Third Policeman*, London: Picador, 1974, 87-8.

Readers may have already registered the discoursal connections between this segment of dialogue, which continues in this manner for a further 32 lines before the sergeant gives up, and Mrs Doyle's name search. I have noted in a earlier stylistic commentary on *The Third Policeman* (predating the *Father Ted* series) that much of the dialogue of the novel is comprised of recursive strings of exchanges which are often triggered in the opening phase of interaction and which have no obvious end-points.[36] Looking again at this dialogue in the light of the schematic structure potential proposed for the *Father Ted* sequence, the ⌐{A^B} formula is very much in evidence here also. This formula represents coding at the broadest and most abstract level, so there will of course be obvious differences between the two texts in terms of characterization, period and genre. Moreover, the outcome of the two name searches is not the same: Mrs Doyle is successful, the Sergeant is not. These differences apart, these two sequences nonetheless exhibit remarkably strong convergence in terms of their underlying schematic structure. As to whether Linehan and Mathews consciously drew upon the O'Brien material or whether they unconsciously replicated the formula, we will never know. The point at issue is that the same form of metatextual verbal humour resurfaces and is indeed congruent with a new discourse context created some thirty years later; the discoursal formula is therefore both resurgent within a culture and across time. It is interesting to note that much of what is said about Flann O'Brien's brand of verbal humour can readily be applied to Linehan and Mathews' sitcom. For example, critics have said of the former that it borders on the edge of nonsense and is tinged with the grotesque, and that it displays enough playfulness to keep it from crossing over into absurdity and enough inconsistency to prevent it

---

[36] See my "The Interactive World of *The Third Policeman*", in A. Clune and T. Hurson, eds, *Conjuring Complexities: Essays on Flann O'Brien,* Belfast: Institute of Irish Studies, 1997, 73-81.

from becoming fantasy.[37] All of these points are as apposite to *Father Ted* as they are to O'Brien's work.

It may even be possible to look further back for diachronic evidence that the verbal pattern discussed here has an even longer tradition in Irish humour. The *Ulster Saga* is a collection of Celtic tales that were originally written in the eighth century and which have survived through extant manuscripts compiled in the twelfth century. While the absence of direct speech representation in the tales themselves makes parallels with the present data difficult to draw, there is nonetheless a clear emphasis in the tales and in the scholarly literature surrounding them of the comic potential of verbal "flyting". These linguistic duels often occur in the initial stages of interaction and involve lengthy interrogation by a speaker about the other interlocutor's identity and capacities. For example, Mandel notes that the trickster Bricriu, a particularly mischievous figure in the Irish tales, employs "verbal battle" instead of "real battles, which he avoids like the plague."[38] Mandel's conclusions suggest that elements of metatextual satire were developing in this early period of Irish literary history:

> The verbal exchanges within early [Irish Gaelic] myths and tales, the flytings with warlike and magical power that were in the arsenal of the trickster, became transformed into satire.[39]

Another major tale in the Saga, the *Táin Bó Cúailgne* (The Cattle Raid of Cooley) suggests additional parallels with the *Father Ted* passage examined here. One feature of Mrs Doyle's questions is that they comprise names which gradually progress from the commonplace to the

---

[37] See W. Tigges, *An Anatomy of Literary Nonsense,* Amsterdam: Rodopi, 1988, 205-16; and D.F. Nilsen, *Humor in Irish Literature: A Reference Guide,* Westport, CT: Greenwood, 1996, 188-9.

[38] S. Mandel, "The Laughter of Nordic and Celtic-Irish Tricksters", *Fabula*, 23, 1/2 (1982), 35-47, 44.

[39] *Ibid.*, 47.

abstruse. Kelleher[40] has noted that a common stylistic element in the *Táin* is the use of a litany, which develops from the mundane to the almost farcical. For instance, Cú Chulainn's daily activities begin with leaps and rope-walking — unremarkable preparation for a warrior prince. However, this litany develops into what Kelleher calls a "spoof list" which culminates in the seemingly impossible feat (translated here from Old Irish) of "climbing a javelin with the stretching of the body on its point, with the demeanour of a noble warrior."[41]

The evidence presented on the connections between discoursal patterns in the Celtic myths and in the more recent data is admittedly thin, and is at this stage more general observation than rigorous inquiry. More proof will be needed to sustain a convincing argument in favour of a diachronic model of culture-intrinsic verbal humour. This opens up another issue which concerns the possibilities of humorous forms occurring outside the culture under scrutiny. There are, for instance, obvious connections that can be made between the Irish material and *Monty Python* comedy — that very Anglo-Saxon of humorous genres. In one of the many Python sketches built around public services encounters that go badly wrong, a customer enters a "National Cheese Emporium" with the intention of buying two ounces of Caerphilly cheese. On being told that Caerphilly is out of stock, and after a tortuous search through most of the world's other known varieties of cheese, the customer discovers that he is in a cheese shop which doesn't have any cheese to sell. The point is that the set of exchanges which take place between the two interlocutors in the Python sketch has a similar structural profile to the dialogue examined in the present study. It may simply be, then, that cultural connections to certain forms of textually-based satire are largely a question of degree and proportion; that in the Irish context there is a *tendency* towards metalinguistic humour in preference to, say, visual slapstick. This might be what Nilsen has in mind with his comment that Irish humour is "not about an ambassador in a tuxedo and top hat slipping on a banana skin as

---

[40] J.V. Kelleher, "Humor in the Ulster Saga", in H. Levin, ed., *Veins of Humor*, Harvard English Studies 3, Massachusetts: Harvard University Press, 1972, 35-56.

[41] *Ibid.*, 53.

he walks down the embassy steps. It is Oscar Wilde's 'Work is the curse of the drinking classes'."[42] Another question which needs to be addressed is how the formal properties of textually-oriented satire can be accommodated within functional models of genre.[43] This study has been operating on the assumption that satire is *not* a genre of discourse; but a discursive practice that does things *to* genres of discourse. That is to say, satire has the capacity to consume, assimilate or recontextualize other discourse genres. In an observation that tallies with the diachronic perspective taken in this section, Threadgold remarks that generic repetition over time brings about "a recontextualizing and resemanticizing which produces 'degenerescence' and generic change."[44] The notion of "degenerescence" and its relationship to satirical discourse is one of a number of topics that undoubtedly merit further study. Clearly, much more work will need to be done if this embryonic model of satirical discourse is to acquire anything like a sufficient degree of explanatory power.

---

[42] D.F. Nilsen, "The Religion of Humor in Irish Literature", *Humor*, 10/4 (1997), 377-94, 377-84.

[43] Such as that of Eggins, *op.cit.*

[44] T. Threadgold, "Talking about Genre: Ideologies and Incompatible Discourses", *Cultural Studies*, 3/1 (1989), 101-27, 114.

AFTERWORD

RONALD CARTER

This volume is an appropriate testimony to Peter Verdonk. Its range of problem-solving analytical practices, descriptive frameworks and innovative theorizations serves as a tribute to a scholar who has never ceased to face the awkward problems of his field. Throughout his distinguished career Peter has never lost faith in his recognition that literature is made from, indeed is fundamentally constituted by language and that, complex though this articulatory medium is, its exploration can do much to illuminate and make accessible some of the main ways in which literature works as a human artefact.

"Making accessible" is something to which Peter Verdonk has always been committed and we owe him a debt for a number of illuminating analyses of texts which serve as inspiration to our students as they search for ways in to texts. It is no wonder that examples of his work, both in the form of individual essays and analyses and in the form of edited collections, figure regularly on reading lists for students and teachers of literary stylistics, including the stylistics of prose, poetry and drama. But, as his many friends and all the contributors to this volume will know, Peter is not one for resting on the laurels of his lucid pedagogic practice, however exemplary it is.

Peter Verdonk has also worried away at the boundaries of his territory. Over a number of years and particularly through the last decade of the last century Peter has sought to explore and better define the relationship between language and context, between the words on the page and the social, historical, and cultural determinants which produce those words and which are in turn simultaneously produced by them. Unlike a good many literary linguists of his generation he has also sought to produce a better understanding of context by attempting to account for it as a cognitive as well as a socio-cultural phenomenon. The term "contextualized stylistics" has entered the lexicon of literature and language studies largely as a result of the stimulus and inspiration generated by Peter's work.

The friends, collaborators and fellow football-supporters and graffitti writers (we all know Professor Nash doesn't just *write* about them) gathered in this volume, as well as many well-wishers and supporters, all wish unanimously to congratulate Peter Verdonk on his achievements. But they will all wish simultaneously to hope that Peter's retirement and the publication of this Festschrift will not somehow conspire to suggest that his work has come to a conclusion. Long may he continue to explore, to provide those exemplary analyses, to support the work of others, and to inspire by his example.

NOTES ON CONTRIBUTORS

TONY BEX is a Senior Lecturer at the University of Kent. He is a contributing editor to *Standard English: The Widening Debate* (Routledge: 1999), author of *Variety in Written English: Texts in Society: Societies in Text* (Routledge: 1996) and has published with Rodopi's collections *New Essays in Deixis* and *Poetics, Linguistics, History: The New Interdisciplinarity*. He is also currently the Chair of the international Poetics and Linguistics Association (PALA) and the Treasurer of the International Association for Literary Semantics (IALS).

MICHAEL BURKE has lectured in translation studies and second language acquisition at the University of Utrecht and University College Utrecht. He is has also lectured in stylistics at the University of Nottingham and at the University of Amsterdam. He is currently working towards the completion of his PhD thesis at the latter of these institutions under the supervision of Peter Verdonk. His book, *Echoes from a Shallow Bay*, on the cognitive and emotive processing of literary discourse, is forthcoming (with Amsterdam University Press).

RONALD CARTER is Professor at the University of Nottingham. He was a founder member of PALA and has published extensively. Among his many publications are: *Language and Literature: A Reader in Stylistics* (Allen and Unwin, 1982); *Seeing Through Language*, with Walter Nash (Blackwell, 1990); *Language, Discourse and Literature*, edited with Paul Simpson (Unwin Hyman, 1989); *Exploring Spoken English*, with Michael McCarthy (Cambridge University Press, 1997); *Working with Texts* (Routledge, 1997); *Investigating English Discourse* (Routledge, 1997). He is currently working on *Standard Spoken English: Common Language, Creative Discourse* (Routledge) and *The Cambridge Grammar of English* (with Michael McCarthy) based on an eight-year research project into spoken and written grammars.

JONATHAN CULPEPER is a Lecturer in the Department of Linguistics at Lancaster University. Much of his research focuses on "spoken" interaction as it appears in writing. He is currently building (with Merja Kyto, University of Uppsala) a million-word corpus of speech-related Early Modern English texts. He has published numerous articles, written an introductory book on the history of English, co-edited a book on the stylistics of drama (with Peter Verdonk and Mick Short), and is currently completing a monograph on language and characterization.

OLGA FISCHER is Professor of Germanic Languages at the University of Amsterdam. She has published extensively in international journals in the area of English historical linguistics. Some of her publications include *The Syntax of Early English,* with Ans van Kemenade, Willem Koopman and Wim van der Wurff (Cambridge University Press, 2000); and the "Syntax" chapter in the Middle English volume (Vol. II, 1066-1476) of the Cambridge History of the English Language, edited by Norman Blake (Cambridge University Press, 1992). She is also a member of the editorial board of English Language and Linguistics for Cambridge University Press.

KEITH GREEN is Senior Lecturer in Linguistics and English Studies at Sheffield Hallam University. He is the co-author, with Jill LeBihan, of *Critical Theory and Practice* (Routledge, 1996) and editor of *New Essays in Deixis* (Rodopi, 1995). He has published widely in linguistics, critical theory and stylistics and has recently completed *Spectres and Scimitars: Bertrand Russell, Language and Linguistic Theory*, the first full-length study of the philosopher's work on language.

E.M. KNOTTENBELT lectures at the University of Amsterdam. She is the author of *Passionate Intelligence: The Poetry of Geoffrey Hill* (1990) and has written on a number of other modern and contemporary writers and on religion and politics in the Renaissance. She is currently completing a book on C.H. Sisson.

GENE M. MOORE lectures in English and American literature at the University of Amsterdam. He is the author of *Proust and Musil: The Novel as Research Instrument* (Garland, 1985), the co-author of the *Oxford Reader's Companion to Conrad* (Oxford University Press, 2000), and the editor of *Conrad's Cities* (Rodopi, 1992) and *Conrad on Film* (Cambridge University Press, 1997). He is a contributing editor to *The Conradian* and currently the Treasurer of the "Netherlands American Studies Association" (NASA).

WALTER NASH is Emeritus Professor of Modern English Language at the University of Nottingham. He has published extensively. His most famous works include *Rhetoric: The Wit of Persuasion* (Blackwell, 1989); *Seeing Through Language: A Guide to Styles of English Writing*, together with Ronald Carter (Blackwell, 1990); *Language in Popular Fiction* (Routledge, 1990); *The Language of Humour* (Routledge, 1990) and *Language and Creative Illusion* (Longman, 1998).

WILLIE VAN PEER is Professor of Intercultural Hermeneutics at the University of Munich. He is the author of *Stylistics and Psychology* and *Investigations of Foregrounding* (Croom Helm, 1986). He is also the editor of *The Taming of the Text* (Routledge, 1988) and, together with Seymour Chatman, *New Perspectives on Narrative Perspective* (SUNY, in press). He is currently editing *Interdisciplinary Studies in Thematics*, together with Max Louwerse, and is writing *Standards of Interpretation*, from which his contribution in the current volume is taken.

BOUWE POSTMUS is a Lecturer at the University of Amsterdam. He is the author of numerous articles on Gissing and the following books: *George Gissing's American Notebook* (Edwin Mellen, 1993); *The Poetry of George Gissing* (Edwin Mellen, 1995); *George Gissing's Memorandum Book* (1996) and *An Exile's Cunning: Some Private Papers of George Gissing* (Stichting Uitgeverij Noord-Holland, 1999). He is one of the editors of the *Gissing Journal* and acted as convener of the first "International George Gissing Conference" in Amsterdam in 1999.

ELENA SEMINO is a Lecturer at Lancaster University. She is interested in stylistics, corpus linguistics and cognitive linguistics. Her work on topics such as text worlds, deixis, discourse representation, and metaphor has appeared in *Language and Literature, Poetics, Style, Narrative* and *Discourse and Society*. Her book *Language and World Creation in Poems and Other Texts* was published by Longman in 1997. She is currently involved in a corpus-based study of discourse presentation in narratives, and in a range of projects to do with metaphor analysis. She is currently co-editor (with Mick Short) of the Longman series Textual Explorations.

MICK SHORT is Professor of English Language and Literature at Lancaster University. He has written *Exploring the Language of Poems, Plays and Prose* (Longman, 1996) and, with Geoffrey Leech, *Style in Fiction* (Longman, 1981). He has edited *Reading, Analysing and Teaching Literature* (Longman, 1989), and co-edited *Using Corpora for Language Research* (Longman, 1996, with Jenny Thomas) and *Exploring the Language of Drama: From Text to Context* (Routledge, 1998, with Jonathan Culpeper and Peter Verdonk). He is also co-editor, of two series of books for Longman, *Learning About Language* (with Geoffrey Leech), and *Textual Explorations* (with Elena Semino). He founded PALA in 1979 and was the founding editor (1992-6) of *Language and Literature*, the official international journal of PALA.

PAUL SIMPSON is a Reader in English at Queen's University, Belfast, where he teaches a variety of undergraduate and postgraduate courses on language and linguistics. Most of his published work is in stylistics, critical linguistics and related fields of study. His books include *Language, Ideology and Point of View* (1993) and *Language through Literature* (1997), both published by Routledge. His current research interests include a project on humorous discourse.

GERARD STEEN is Lecturer in English at the Free University Amsterdam and Lecturer in Discourse Studies at the University of Tilburg. He has published on metaphor, the empirical study of literature, and discourse studies. He is the author of *Understanding Metaphor in Literature: An Empirical Approach* (Longman, 1994) and has co-edited

Empirical Studies of Literature with Elrud Ibsch and Dick Schram (Rodopi, 1991) and *Metaphor in Cognitive Linguistics* with Raymond Gibbs (Benjamins, 1999). He is currently a guest editor for the *Journal of Pragmatics*, *Metaphor & Symbol*, and *Language and Literature*, preparing special issues on metaphor in linguistics, psycholinguistics, and stylistics, respectively. He is the co-coordinator of an international Special Interest Group in Metaphor including linguistic, literary, and psychological participants.

PETER STOCKWELL is a Lecturer at the University of Nottingham. He has published in the areas of literary linguistics, science fiction and surrealism. His recent books include *The Poetics of Science Fiction* (Pearson, 2000), *Investigating English Language*, with Howard Jackson (Stanley Thornes, 1996), *Impossibility Fiction*, with Derek Littlewood (Rodopi, 1996), and *Subjectivity and Literature*, with Philip Shaw (Pinter, 1992). He is currently preparing work on Sociolinguistics, Cognitive Poetics, and Surrealist Poetry.

MICHAEL TOOLAN is Professor of Applied English Linguistics at the University of Birmingham, where he coordinates the MA programme in Literary Linguistics. His research interests include stylistics, narrative, discourse analysis and processing, and legal language. Recent books include *Total Speech: An Integrational Linguistic Approach to Language* (Duke University Press, 1996) and *Language in Literature: An Introduction to Stylistics* (Hodder, 1998).

PETER DE VOOGD is Professor of English Literature at the University of Utrecht, and the founding editor of *The Shandean*, an annual volume devoted to Laurence Sterne.

KATIE WALES is Professor of Modern English Language at the University of Leeds and Dean-elect for Learning and Teaching in the Faculty of Arts and Humanities. She is also currently a Visiting Research Fellow at Lucy Cavendish College, Cambridge. She was formerly Professor and Head of the Department at Royal Holloway, University of London, and Chair of PALA. She is currently editor of its journal

Language and Literature. Her many publications include the *Dictionary of Stylistics* (Longman, 1989), a new edition of which will be published shortly; and *Personal Pronouns in Present-day English* (Cambridge University Press).

JEAN-JACQUES WEBER is Professor of English at University Centre Luxembourg. His publications include *Critical Analysis of Fiction* (Rodopi, 1992); *Twentieth-Century Fiction* with Peter Verdonk (Routledge, 1995); *The Stylistics Reader* (Arnold, 1996) and *The Literature Workbook* with Clara Calvo (Routledge, 1998). He is currently preparing a book on the contemporary novel. He is also Vice-President of the Belgian-Luxembourg American Studies Association (BLASA).

H.G. WIDDOWSON is Professor of English Language and Applied Linguistics at the University of Vienna. His most well known publications include *Stylistics and the Teaching of Literature* (Longman, 1975); *Aspects of Language Teaching* (Oxford University Press, 1990) and *Practical Stylistics: An Approach to Poetry* (Oxford University Press, 1992). He is currently the English Language series editor for Oxford University Press.

INDEX

THEME PARKS, RAINFORESTS AND SPROUTING WASTELANDS
European essays on theory and performance
in contemporary British fiction

Ed. by Richard Todd

Amsterdam/Atlanta, GA 2000. 236 pp.
(Costerus NS 123)
ISBN: 90-420-0502-5   Hfl. 80,-/US-$ 44.-

This lively and fascinating new collection of European essays
on contemporary Anglophone fiction has arisen out of the
ESSE/3 Conference, which was held in Glasgow in September
1995. The contributors live and work in University English
Departments in Bulgaria, Croatia, France, Germany, Hungary,
Italy, The Netherlands, Portugal and Spain, as well as in the
United Kingdom itself.

Essays on general theoretical aspects of the subject head and
conclude the collection, and there are also essays on individual
writers or groups of writers, such as John Fowles, A.S. Byatt,
Charles Palliser, Peter Ackroyd, William Golding, Doris
Lessing, Daphne du Maurier, Angela Carter and Christina
Stead. The performative aspect of the subject-matter of these
essays is balanced by a locational aspect, including utopian and
dystopian writing in authors as diverse as Michael Crichton,
Jenny Diski and Salman Rushdie, and the travel literature of
Bruce Chatwin.

These essays show theoretical alertness, but no single
theoretical position is privileged. The aim of the collection is
to provide an indication of the range of work being carried out
throughout European academe on Anglophone (mainly British)
writing today.

-------------------------------- *Editions Rodopi B.V.*

USA/Canada: 2015 South Park Place, Atlanta, GA 30339, Tel. (770)
933-0027, *Call toll-free* (U.S.only) 1-800-225-3998, Fax (770) 933-9644

All Other Countries: Tijnmuiden 7, 1046 AK Amsterdam, The Netherlands.
Tel. + + 31 (0)20 6114821, Fax + + 31 (0)20 4472979
orders-queries@rodopi.nl — http://www.rodopi.nl

INSTRUMENT ZITAT
Über den literarhistorischen und institutionellen Nutzen
von Zitaten und Zitieren

Hrsg. von Klaus Beekman und Ralf Grüttemeier

Amsterdam/Atlanta, GA 2000. 445 pp.
(Avant-Garde Critical Studies 13)
ISBN: 90-420-0759-1 Bound + access to Internet version for
the subscribers

Hfl. 220,-/US-$ 121.-
ISBN: 90-420-0749-4   Paper Hfl. 75,-/US-$ 41.50

Die Entwicklung des künstlerischen Feldes war im
20.Jahrhundert radikalen Veränderungen unterworfen und hat
sowohl für Künstler wie für Kritiker ein breites Spektrum an
Strategien und Kunstgriffen zur Profilierung verfügbar
gemacht. Eine zentrale Rolle dabei spielt das Zitat, wie der
vorliegende Band belegt. *Instrument Zitat* soll das Spezifische
im Umgang mit Zitaten und Zitieren bei Kritikern und
avantgardistischen, modernistischen und postmodernistischen
Künstlern zeigen, als Vorarbeit zu einer Geschichte des Zitats
und des Zitierens.

\-   *Editions Rodopi B.V.*

USA/Canada: 2015 South Park Place, Atlanta, GA 30339, Tel. (770)
933-0027, *Call toll-free* (U.S.only) 1-800-225-3998, Fax (770) 933-9644

All Other Countries: Tijnmuiden 7, 1046 AK Amsterdam, The Netherlands.
Tel. + + 31 (0)20 6114821, Fax + + 31 (0)20 4472979
orders-queries@rodopi.nl —— http://www.rodopi.nl

CULTURAL VISIONS: ESSAYS IN THE HISTORY OF CULTURE

Ed. by Penny Schine Gold and Benjamin C. Sax

Amsterdam/Atlanta, GA 2000. VII,308 pp. (Internationale Forschungen zur Allgemeinen und Vergleichenden Literaturwissenschaft 41)
ISBN: 90-420-0490-8   Hfl. 120,-/US-$ 66.50

This collection opens with an inquiry into the assumptions and methods of the historical study of culture, comparing the "new cultural history" with the "old." Thirteen essays follow, each defining a problem within a particular culture. In the first section, "Biography and Autobiography," three scholars explore historically changing types of self-conception, each reflecting larger cultural meanings; essays included examine Italian Renaissance biographers and the autobiographies of Benjamin Franklin and Mohandas Gandhi. A second group of contributors explore problems raised by the writing of history itself, especially as it relates to a notion of culture. Here examples are drawn from the writings of Thucydides, Jacob Burckhardt, and the art historians Alois Riegl and Josef Strzygowski. In the third section, "Politics, Nationalism, and Culture," the essays explore relationships between cultural creativity and national identity, with case studies focusing on the Holy Roman Emperor Maximilian I, the place of Castile within the national history of Spain, and the impact of World War I on work of Thomas Mann. The final section, "Cultural Translation," raises the complex questions of cultural influence and the transmission of traditions over time through studies of Philo of Alexandria's interpretation of the Hebrew Bible, Erasmus' use of Socrates, Jean Bodin's conception of Roman law, and adaptations of the Hebrew Bible for American children.

\-   *Editions Rodopi B.V.*

USA/Canada: 2015 South Park Place, Atlanta, GA 30339, Tel. (770) 933-0027, *Call toll-free* (U.S.only) 1-800-225-3998, Fax (770) 933-9644

All Other Countries: Tijnmuiden 7, 1046 AK Amsterdam, The Netherlands. Tel. + + 31 (0)20 6114821, Fax + + 31 (0)20 4472979
          orders-queries@rodopi.nl —— http://www.rodopi.nl

DISRUPTED PATTERNS
On Chaos and Order in the Enlightenment

Ed. by Theodore E.D. Braun and John A. McCarthy

Amsterdam/Atlanta, GA 2000. XIII,221 pp. (Internationale Forschungen zur Allgemeinen und Vergleichenden Literaturwissenschaft 43)
ISBN: 90-420-0550-5   Hfl. 85,-/US-$ 47.-

This collection of essays explores the significance of modern chaos theory as a new paradigm in literary studies and argues for the usefulness of borrowings from one discipline to another. Its thesis is that external reality is real and is not merely a social construct. On the other hand, this volume reflects the belief that literature, as a social and cultural construct, is not unrelated to that external reality. The authors represented here furthermore believe that learning to ·communicate across disciplinary divides is worth the risk of looking silly to purists and dogmatists. In applying a contemporary scientific grid to a by-gone era, the authors play out Steven Weinberg's exhortation to mind the clues to the past that cannot be obtained in any other way. It is of course necessary to get the science right, yet the essays in this collection do not seek to do science, but rather to suggest that science and literature often share common assumptions and realities. Thus there is no attempt to legitimize literary study through the adoption of a scientific approach. Interaction between the disciplines requires mutual respect and a willingness to investigate the broader implications of scientific research. Consequently, this volume will be of interest to students and scholars of the long eighteenth century whether the focus is on England (Locke, Milton, Radcliffe, Lewis), France (Crébillion, Diderot, Marivaux, Montesquieu) or Germany (Kant, Moritz, Goethe, Fr. Schlegel). Moreover, given its multiple thrust in employing mythological, philosophical, and scientific notions of chaos, this volume will appeal to historians and philosophers of the European Enlightenment as well as to literary historians. The volume ultimately aspires to promote communication across centuries and across disciplines.

------------------------------   *Editions Rodopi B.V.*

USA/Canada: 2015 South Park Place, Atlanta, GA 30339, Tel. (770) 933-0027, *Call toll-free* (U.S.only) 1-800-225-3998, Fax (770) 933-9644

All Other Countries: Tijnmuiden 7, 1046 AK Amsterdam, The Netherlands. Tel. + + 31 (0)20 6114821, Fax + + 31 (0)20 4472979
orders-queries@rodopi.nl —— http://www.rodopi.nl

GENRES AS REPOSITORIES OF CULTURAL MEMORY

Ed. by Hendrik van Gorp and Ulla Musarra-Schroeder

Volume 5 of the Proceedings of the XVth Congress of the International Comparative Literature Association *"Literature as Cultural Memory"*, Leiden 16-22 August 1997. Amsterdam/Atlanta, GA 2000. 568 pp. (Textxet 29)
ISBN: 90-420-0440-1   Hfl. 225,-/US-$ 121,50

This volume deals with the inherent relation between literary genres and cultural memory. Indeed, generic repertoires may be regarded as bodies of shared knowledge (a sort of 'encyclopaedia' or 'museum' of stocked culture) and have played and still play an important role in absorbing and activating that memory.
The contributors have focused on some specific memory-linked genres that prove especially relevant in remembering and transforming past experiences, i.e. the (post)modern historical novel and various forms of (post)modern autobiographical writing. They deal with such renowned authors as Carlos Fuentes, Vargas Llosa, Umberto Eco, Antonio Tabucchi, John Barth, Julian Barnes, Michel Butor, Nathalie Sarraute, Alain Robbe-Grillet, Claude Simon, Georges Perec and Marguerite Yourcenar. The volume, thus, constitutes an attractive and representative sample of (post)modern forms of rewriting and problematizing individual and collective pasts.

-------------------------------   *Editions Rodopi B.V.*

USA/Canada: 6075 Roswell Rd., Ste. 219, Atlanta, GA 30328, Tel. (404) 843-4314, *Call toll-free* (U.S.only) 1-800-225-3998, Fax (404) 843-4315

All Other Countries: Tijnmuiden 7, 1046 AK Amsterdam, The Netherlands. Tel. + + 31 (0)20 6114821, Fax + + 31 (0)20 4472979
orders-queries@rodopi.nl —— http://www.rodopi.nl

GENDERED MEMORIES

Ed. by John Neubauer and Helga Geyer-Ryan

Volume 4 of the Proceedings of the XVth Congress of the International Comparative Literature Association "*Literature as Cultural Memory*", Leiden 16-22 August 1997.

Amsterdam/Atlanta, GA 2000. 150 pp. (Textxet 28)
ISBN: 90-420-0430-4   Hfl. 60,-/US-$ 33,-

How does gender shape memory? What role does literature play in cultural remembering? These are two of the questions to which the present volume is addressed. Even if we agree that remembering is not biologically determined, we can assume that memory is influenced by the particular social, cultural and historical conditions in which individuals find themselves. And since men and women generally assume different social and cultural roles, their way of remembering should also differ. So, do women and men remember different events, narrate different stories, and narrate or read them in different ways? *Gendered Memories*, then, not only looks at memory gendered by literature, but also wants to know how gender shapes the memory of literature.

-------------------------------   *Editions Rodopi B.V.*

USA/Canada: 6075 Roswell Rd., Ste. 219, Atlanta, GA 30328, Tel. (404) 843-4314, *Call toll-free* (U.S.only) 1-800-225-3998, Fax (404) 843-4315

All Other Countries: Tijnmuiden 7, 1046 AK Amsterdam, The Netherlands. Tel. + + 31 (0)20 6114821, Fax + + 31 (0)20 4472979
            orders-queries@rodopi.nl —— http://www.rodopi.nl

SUBJECT MATTERS
Subject and Self in French Literature
from Descartes to the present

Ed. by Paul Gifford and Johnnie Gratton. Amsterdam/Atlanta,
GA 2000. 243 pp. (Faux Titre 184)
ISBN: 90-420-0630-7   Hfl. 80,-/US-$ 44.-

Contents: Johnnie GRATTON: Introduction: The Return of the
Subject. C.E.J. CALDICOTT: Disguises of the Narrating Voice
in *Discours de la Méthode*. Michael O'DEA: Rousseau's
Confessions: Modes of Engagement with the Other. Carole
DORNIER: Writing the Inner Citadel: The Therapeutics of the
Soul in Rousseau's *Revêries d'un promeneur solitaire.*
Gabrielle CHAMARAT: Identity and Identification in the
Preface to Nerval's *Les Filles du feu.* Ian HIGGINS: Who am
I Dying? Adrien Bertrand's *L'Appel du sol.* Myriam
BOUCHARENC: Plural Authorship in Automatic Writing.
Joseph LONG: A Company of Shades: Subject and Authorship
in Samuel Beckett's Prose. David GASCOIGNE: Dreaming the
Self, Writing the Dream: The Subject in the Dream-Narratives
of Georges Perec. Anne CHEVALIER: The Book and the
Tree: Writing the Self in Marguerite Duras's *La Pluie d'été.*
Lorna MILNE: From *Créolité* to *Diversalité*: The Postcolonial
Subject in Patrick Chamoiseau's *Texaco.* Stephen
SCHWARTZ: The Exceptional Subject of Michel Foucault.
Paul GIFFORD: The Resonance of Ricoeur: *Soi-même comme
un autre.* Paul GIFFORD: Conclusion: Subject and Self.
Bibliography. Index.

-------------------------------   *Editions Rodopi B.V.*
USA/Canada: 2015 South Park Place, Atlanta, GA 30339, Tel. (770)
933-0027, *Call toll-free* (U.S.only) 1-800-225-3998, Fax (770) 933-9644

All Other Countries: Tijnmuiden 7, 1046 AK Amsterdam, The Netherlands.
Tel. + + 31 (0)20 6114821, Fax + + 31 (0)20 4472979
        orders-queries@rodopi.nl —— http://www.rodopi.nl

THE CONSCIENCE OF HUMANKIND:
Literature and Traumatic Experiences

Ed. by Elrud Ibsch in cooperation with Douwe Fokkema and Joachim von der Thüsen

Volume 3 of the Proceedings of the XVth Congress of the International Comparative Literature Association "*Literature as Cultural Memory*", Leiden 16-22 August 1997
Amsterdam/Atlanta, GA 2000. 423 pp.
(Textxet 27)
ISBN: 90-420-0420-7   Hfl. 170,-/US-$ 94,-

The traumatic experiences of persecution and genocide have changed traditional views of literature. The discussion of historical truth versus aesthetic autonomy takes an unexpected turn when confronted with the experiences of the victims of the Holocaust, the Gulag Archipelago, the Cultural Revolution, Apartheid and other crimes against humanity. The question is whether - and, if so, to what extent - literary imagination may depart from historical truth.
In general, the first reactions to traumatic historical experiences are autobiographical statements, written by witnesses of the events. However, the second and third generations, the sons and daughters of the victims as well as of the victimizers, tend to free themselves from this generic restriction and claim their own way of remembering the
hsitory of their parents and grandparents. They explore their own limits of representation, and feel free to use a variety of genres, and realist or postmodernist, ironic or grotesque modes of writing.
With respect to the literature discussed in this volume the truth claim is not suspended. It is, however, not the truth of factual details or the logic of chronology and causality that is at stake here, but the truth of the victims.

-------------------------------   *Editions Rodopi B.V.*

USA/Canada: 6075 Roswell Rd., Ste. 219, Atlanta, GA 30328, Tel. (404) 843-4314, *Call toll-free* (U.S.only) 1-800-225-3998, Fax (404) 843-4315

All Other Countries: Tijnmuiden 7, 1046 AK Amsterdam, The Netherlands. Tel. ++ 31 (0)20 6114821, Fax ++ 31 (0)20 4472979
orders-queries@rodopi.nl —— http://www.rodopi.nl

COLONIZER AND COLONIZED

Ed. by Theo D'haen and Patricia Krüs

Volume 2 of the Proceedings of the XVth Congress of the International Comparative Literature Association *"Literature as Cultural Memory"*, Leiden 16-22 August 1997
Amsterdam/Atlanta, GA 2000. 643 pp.
(Textxet 26)
ISBN: 90-420-0410-X   Hfl. 260,-/US-$ 144.-

Over the last two decades, the experiences of colonization and decolonization, once safely relegated to the margins of what occupied students of history and literature, have shifted into the latter's center of attention, in the West as elsewhere. This attention does not restrict itself to the historical dimension of colonization and decolonization, but also focuses upon their impact upon the present, for both colonizers and colonized.
The nearly fifty essays here gathered examine how literature, now and in the past, keeps and has kept alive the experiences - both individual and collective - of colonization and decolonization. The contributors to this volume hail from the four corners of the earth, East *and* West, North *and* South. The authors discussed range from international luminaries past and present such as Aphra Behn, Racine, Blaise Cendrars, Salman Rushdie, Graham Greene, Derek Walcott, Guimarães Rosa, J.M. Coetzee, André Brink, and Assia Djebar, to less known but certainly not lesser authors like Gioconda Belli, René Depestre, Amadou Koné, Elisa Chimenti, Sapho, Arthur Nortje, Es'kia Mphahlele, Mark Behr, Viktor Paskov, Evelyn Wilwert, and Leïla Houari. Issues addressed include the role of travel writing in forging images of foreign lands for domestic consumption, the reception and translation of Western classics in the East, the impact of contemporary Chinese cinema upon both native and Western audiences, and the use of Western generic novel conventions in modern Egyptian literature.

------------------------------   *Editions Rodopi B.V.*
USA/Canada: 6075 Roswell Rd., Ste. 219, Atlanta, GA 30328, Tel. (404) 843-4314, *Call toll-free* (U.S.only) 1-800-225-3998, Fax (404) 843-4315

All Other Countries: Tijnmuiden 7, 1046 AK Amsterdam, The Netherlands. Tel. ++ 31 (0)20 6114821, Fax ++ 31 (0)20 4472979
orders-queries@rodopi.nl — http://www.rodopi.nl

POETRY AND OTHER PROSE/ POÉSIES ET AUTRES PROSES

Edited by/edité par Matthijs Engelberts,
Marius Buning, Sjef Houppermans

Amsterdam/Atlanta, GA 2000. 222 pp.
(Samuel Beckett Today/Aujourd'hui 8)
ISBN: 90-420-0700-1   Bound Hfl. 160,-/US-$ 88.50
ISBN: 90-420-0690-0   Paper Hfl. 40,-/US-$ 22.-

------------------------------   *Editions Rodopi B.V.*

USA/Canada: 2015 South Park Place, Atlanta, GA 30339, Tel. (770)
933-0027, *Call toll-free* (U.S.only) 1-800-225-3998, Fax (770) 933-9644

All Other Countries: Tijnmuiden 7, 1046 AK Amsterdam, The Netherlands.
Tel. ++ 31 (0)20 6114821, Fax ++ 31 (0)20 4472979
orders-queries@rodopi.nl —— http://www.rodopi.nl

Architecture and the
Principle of Harmony

In memory of my Father

Architecture
and the principle of
harmony

Peter F. Smith

RIBA Publications Limited

Published by RIBA Publications Limited
Finsbury Mission, Moreland Street, London EC1V 8VB

ISBN 0 947877 76 2

Printed and bound in Great Britain by
Billing and Sons Limited, Worcester

Drawings and photographs by the author unless stated otherwise.

Contents

Foreword

*Started Thurs –
21 – 1 – 88 –*

Peter Smith's books command attention for their analytical power,
their keen perception and their fascinating combination of rich
detail and forceful generalisation. Their author's voice is a very
special voice that should be heard everywhere.

Architecture and the Principle of Harmony, like *The Dynamics of
Urbanism*, the first of his books that I read and the first that he
wrote, is immensely stimulating. It covers a huge range of time and
space and draws effectively on several disciplines. At the same
time it is strikingly original.

As the author implies in his brief introduction, the standard of
debate on architecture in this country is not high. It is obvious to me
as a non-architect that it must be far higher if we are properly to
appreciate the old buildings which we are lucky to inherit and to
create new buildings of real interest. Dr Smith gets rid of the
primitive contrasts and the jejune judgements which stand in the
way of real understanding.

It is not written for architects or for aestheticians but for everyone
prepared to bring mind and spirit to the study. The pictures, it need
hardly be said, are an integral part of the whole. It is assuring to
deduce from them what Dr Smith actually sees as well as what he
has to say.

Asa Briggs

Worcester College
Oxford
March 1987

Preface

There is no special language with which to describe the aesthetic qualities of architecture. It seems that princes and commoners alike have to resort to simile and metaphor.

This book attempts to define a structure for analysing the appearance of buildings and the relationship between them. It offers a considered and individualistic vocabulary of concepts rather than haphazard and specious additions to the current proliferation of architectural buzz words.

I hope it will appeal to a wider readership than students and practitioners of architecture, and provide a framework within which serious and informed public debate can take place, free from angry invective and emotive metaphor.

Peter F. Smith
May 1987

Introduction

Architecture conveys messages; it is a medium of expression which, like language, relies upon an agreed code.

A building is a sign, expressing its purpose through its form – thus a house can be distinguished from a church. In some buildings, such as a garage or a storage shed, expressive quality is exhausted at this level. But a house may also be a home, giving it a deeper, symbolic level of meaning. (A symbol is an object or sound or smell with emotional overtones and no finite boundaries. It is usually unaffected by the passage of time.)

A house may symbolise the love and affection of a close-knit family. The nineteenth century terraced houses demolished as 'slums' were saturated with symbolism, representing community care in the face of hardship. When whole communities were dispersed into planners' and architects' 'dream' estates of order and high rise, it was as if a limb of memory had been amputated. Even the most mundane and unmemorable architecture can resonate with symbolism; the architecture of towns and cities represents an elaborate lattice of symbolic meanings charged with emotional energy. Demolishing a single building may break the circuit and earth the emotional current.

Buildings also possess expressive potential at the level of aesthetic performance. In Britain, we tend to feel uneasy about the term 'aesthetic', but the formal expressive quality of buildings which are part of the daily landscape is a matter of considerable importance. This book elaborates on this topic, and investigates the nature of harmony and dissonance in architecture.

In the past, the subject of aesthetics has tended to be confined to the detached contemplation of formal relationships: colour, tone, shape, and texture. My view of the subject is wider. I suggest that aesthetic potential resides in complex informational interactions, and is heavily influenced by myth and symbolism. Furthermore, the mind requires aesthetic nourishment just as the body needs food and drink.

I believe that the present time is uniquely appropriate for such an enquiry. This is the first time this century that the prevailing cultural ethos has been reasonably respectful towards the past, as evidenced by the powerful conservation movement which has gathered pace in Europe and the USA. It is true that previous periods have idealised particular cultural phases: the Renaissance looked back to Greece and Rome for authority, whereas for early nineteenth century apologists the early Middle Ages was the golden age. But today we have no all-embracing philosophy to distort our view of the past and vision of the future – the blinkers of the Modern Movement have fallen away. No longer do we believe that whatever we create will be an improvement on the past.

Thus it seems that the intellectual climate in which this investigation is being conducted is reasonably free of cultural bias. Perhaps the communication explosion has brought this about, or perhaps a loss of confidence in our own age has generated a nostalgia for the past. Whatever the reason, it is in the distant past, long before recorded history, that our investigation begins.

Chapter 1   **Beauty and the Beast**

There has been substantial research into aesthetic perception, and the assumption is sometimes made that conclusions obtained from investigations using abstract figures and isolated colours can be transposed to architecture and urbanism. The trouble is that architectural data are 'impure', adulterated by intervening variables such as symbolism and cognitive meaning. My view is that in discussing harmony in architecture, such variables *must* be taken into account.

Symbolism and semiotics are still greatly underexplored. I believe that Jung was on the right track when he suggested that a limited number of archetypal themes generates a collective response. This applies to certain forms and arrangements of light and dark which are attributed with common symbolic meaning. It may be the result of inherited 'fuzzy' brain programs, reinforced by acculturation. (The universality of architectural and urban symbols suggests a degree of 'hard wiring' at birth.)

But whatever the cause, the fact is that people experience emotional reward from certain urban configurations. Why else do hordes of tourists converge each summer on historic cities where this fundamental resonance is strongest?

This capacity to respond to symbols merges into the other major source of emotional reward in cities – aesthetic pleasure. Since Aristotle, and probably before, aesthetic reward has been associated with the clash between complexity and order, 'similarity within dissimilars'. Only since Baumgarten has the term 'aesthetic' been employed, usually to describe the 'detached contemplation' of the abstract relationship between colour, tone and texture, or tone and timbre in music.

Cognitive and symbolic meaning are said to interfere with pure aesthetic experience. I have challenged this view for some time, on the grounds that the human brain is an interactive system, parts of which cannot be shut off. Thus cognitive and symbolic meaning cannot be isolated from aesthetic judgment; on the contrary, they make a powerful contribution to it. At the same time, the scope of the term 'aesthetic' needs to be widened, since it implies a pattern of psychological events which occurs in situations often far removed from the rarified milieu commonly associated with aesthetics.

To a biologist, the fact that something evokes pleasure is usually a sign that it represents adaptive success, that is, it improves survival prospects. So how does this relate to the pleasure we derive from an encounter with harmony? The answer lies in the probable origin of aesthetic perception.

There is wide agreement that aesthetic pleasure is linked to the classification ability of the brain. The survival prospects of higher animals depend upon this ability. For example, inability to classify a red traffic signal correctly will substantially reduce chances of survival. But this is not simply a stimulus-and-response situation; the classification capacity is closely linked to the exploratory drive.

All higher animals are inwardly driven to extend the boundaries of knowledge, progressively enlarging their mental model of the world and thus reducing the gross weight of uncertainty. (This has the obvious advantage of narrowing the odds against their being taken by surprise.) The process of marrying-up each new set of experiences with the existing model or schema of reality involves the reorganisation of existing knowledge structures. Everything is altered; reclassification takes place right down the line. As Lumsden and Wilson observed in *Genes, Mind and Culture* (1982)[1]: 'The operations of the human mind incorporate (1) the production of concepts and (2) the continuously shifting reclassification of the world'. This is the essence of adaptation, the adjusting of the environmental model so as to achieve a better and better fit between expectation and reality.

Drives are generated by positive and negative incentives, emotional rewards and penalties. Two kinds of reward attach to the exploratory drive. The first involves the pleasure gained from confronting novelty and surprise, and is connected with arousal and its physiological consequences. After this preliminary excitement, the new information is grafted on to the corpus of knowledge. At this point, a second kind of pleasure is experienced – the reward for successfully assimilating the new information and thereby improving survival prospects. This second reward is connected with the *lowering* of arousal and the suppression of its psychological effects. Another adaptive benefit derives from this behaviour cycle – an improvement in the capacity to process novelty (in psychological terms, the ability to process a higher rate of complexity). This sequence of curiosity leading to exploration, leading in turn to a higher state of orderliness, is said by Donald

Berlyne in *Aesthetics and Psychobiology* (1971)[2] and others to be at the root of aesthetic experience. Man long ago learned to create objects which offered this double-edged satisfaction. Through artefacts he encapsulated the tension between complexity and order, at times achieving the ideal ratio between them.

Summary of the main themes considered

Architects are frequently purveyors of surprise, even shock. Compared with other forms of art, architecture is massive and unavoidable. The public appetite for new architectural *experience* seems to be insatiable, but not necessarily for new *buildings* (with the exception of the Pompidou Centre, which is still overwhelmed by visitors). What seems to give most pleasure is more or less familiar architecture in new combinations. We might, for example, recognise the style as Dutch, and the period as medieval, but within these parameters we delight in perceiving novel relationships, especially where there is a symbolic dimension. This is the appeal of historic cities: the ratio of novelty to familiarity falls within acceptable limits. Curiosity is satisfied, but there are sufficient anchorage points to past experience to avoid overload.

To impose order on the mass of incoming sense impressions, the mind measures this information against existing mental models and classifies it accordingly. Where there is novelty, the existing knowledge structure is modified. But if the rate of novelty is excessive, that is, if it threatens the fundamental structure of information, the novelty is rejected. This is the kind of situation described by Alvin Toffler in *Future Shock*[3].

The next stage in the ordering process is to consider the *formal* properties of the information and detect any further levels of coherence and pattern. Classification is normally associated with relating sensory input to mental models, with achieving consistency between internal and external worlds. Where novelty is involved, there is the added benefit of achieving a higher level of orderliness. The information principles of complexity and orderliness or 'redundancy' (the element of repetition or pattern) can be transposed to other kinds of informational clash besides novelty versus familiarity. The basic classification routine can be adapted to judging the *quality* of the relationship between phenomena. This is where we cross the threshold into aesthetics.

After the classification stage, the mind searches for further levels of orderliness based on formal relationships. The first level results from the discovery of discrete, autonomous wholes in which the impression of unity and integration outweighs the individuality of the parts. This triumph of wholeness over partness is a primary condition for aesthetic success in architecture and much urban development. The most successful buildings are often those containing a wealth of clearly stated elements which combine as a totality much greater than the sum of the parts. Aesthetic success is conditional upon the victory of order, but there has to be sufficient complexity to make the victory worthwhile.

The same principle can be applied in a linear context. In Amsterdam, for example, the contrast between complexity and order is sustained at a fairly even pace throughout the older parts of the city. Its magical quality derives partly from the fact that although pattern outweighs variety, the tension between them remains acute; the overall wholeness of the city outweighs its diversity.

The second level of orderliness concerns the way information is deployed *within* the coherent whole, be it a building or an urban scene, the way information systems which belong to the same superordinate pattern can engage in creative clash. It is here, in the relative weighting of elements within a binary set, that harmony comes into its own.

Chapter 2   Novelty Tempered with Familiarity

Perhaps the link between the classification demand and art lies in the artificially-generated tension between familiarity and novelty. We operate successfully in the environment because of the existence of mental models, schemas or prototypes against which we judge incoming information. The whole elaborate edifice of aesthetic perception is founded on the urge to explore so as to enlarge our mental representation of the world. Familiarity and novelty are the original representatives of the basic information categories of orderliness and complexity; they are the progenitors of harmony. Perhaps there is even harmonic potential in the clash between new experience and memory.

Architecture has always been in the vanguard of the cultural thrust towards new sensory experiences; indeed, the principal aim of any artist is to exert outward pressure along the boundary of human experience. It is architecture which expresses most publicly the clash between innovation and tradition. In this context, the datum of harmony may be realised as novelty tempered with familiarity.

Psychologists insist that continual exposure to novelty and surprise is essential if mental performance, as measured by tolerance to complexity, is not to decline. (They would describe this outcome as a 'fall-off in optimum perceptual rate'. See *The Dynamics of Urbanism*[4].)

Because it derives from adaptive logic, information whose novelty content approaches the limit of tolerance is likely to be the most aesthetically rewarding. If it exceeds that limit, the result will be rejection and an indignant refusal to adjust to what I would term its related 'mnemotype'. (By mnemotype, I mean the accumulated experience within a subject category – churches, houses etc – from which the mind derives a fuzzy, prototypical image.)

The criterion of rhyme between the unfamiliar object and the mnemotype is at the heart of aesthetic performance on this plane of evaluation, performance determined by the relative strengths of novelty and familiarity. The optimum ratio varies between individuals, but the range of variation seems to be relatively narrow in the majority of people, which we shall ultimately see as supporting the view that there is a high measure of agreement about the nature of harmony.

Let us explore further this question of how the interaction between novelty and familiarity comes to possess aesthetic possibilities. Beauty is concerned with specific relationships and ratios, so how can fuzzy concepts like order and complexity be resolved into an aesthetic equation? The solution lies in the fact that the mind quantifies information, as it were ascribing the property of weight to a coherent matrix of information. Novelty and familiarity are fundamental classes of information: one representing maximum complexity, the other total redundancy or patterning. When analysing a scene, the mind first picks out features which relate to memory schemas – that is, classifiable features. It finally balances the 'weight' of the accumulated familiar features against the 'weight' of novelty. Emotional reward comes first from relating the sensory experience to a mnemotype and, second, from adjusting the memory model to accommodate the new information. Rhyme is a kind of proto-aesthetic experience, midway between primitive exploratory reward and higher aesthetic perception.

The problem with illustrating abstract theories in relation to specific buildings is that the subjective element is bound to intrude. I have tried to minimise this by taking several exemplars of each principle. However, if any example is judged to be inappropriate, I hope this will not be allowed to prejudice the principle. First, some buildings which seem to strike a fairly comfortable balance between novelty and familiarity.

The Schneider store in Freiburg [Fig 2.1] occupies a sensitive site opposite the Cathedral. Its design generated violent controversy at drawing-board stage, but it is now accepted as a legitimate component of the Münsterplatz. This is because various elements respond to the neighbouring buildings, especially the steep, red-tiled pitched roof whose outline is broken-up by protruding glass structures, and a number of miniature trees which add a dash of the exotic. It is unmistakably a contemporary building, yet it strikes an agreeable note of rhyme with its neighbours.

Another imaginative piece of rhyme between old and new can be seen in the new chemist's shop and doctor's surgery in the Stuttgart suburb of Bad Canstatt [Fig 2.2], an attractive little town in its own right with a pleasing central square, within which the new building occupies a critical site opposite the parish church. The architect, Werner Luz, has maintained the profile of the high-gabled traditional houses and has even echoed the slight overhang

Fig 2.1
Schneider store, Freiburg

Fig 2.2
Bad Canstatt

at each floor level. The real element of rhyme occurs in the facade on to the square, where the exposed, board-shuttered concrete frame has been sensitively designed to mimic the timber framing of medieval buildings. The interstices between the frame are either fully glazed or solid, creating a pattern of pleasing irregularity. This building shows that it is possible to respect our obligations to the past without abdicating from the present.

A variation on this theme can be seen in Stuttgart itself, where midway along the Königstrasse there is a gabled building [Fig 2.3] which follows the general shape of its medieval neighbours, including projections at each storey level. It is clad in vertically-ribbed sheeting which again echoes medieval timbers, while a U-shaped oriel window rising through three storeys firmly anchors the building to the present day.

Fig 2.3
Königstrasse, Stuttgart

This facade is part of a comprehensive development which has taken place behind the Königstrasse. Running parallel with this main street is a glass barrel-vaulted arcade, evocative of a tight-knit medieval street, packed with colourful boutiques and their eye-catching hanging signs [Fig 2.4]. It is a remarkable example of counterpoint between two streets which are different in scale, but which nevertheless reveal a degree of rhyme.

The relevant point about this enterprise is that it respects the existing fabric of the city. There is no sudden dislocation in the type and rate of information; new and old establish a creative partnership whereby both are enhanced.

Fig 2.4
Arcade off the
Königstrasse

The modest infill of flats and shops into the traditional market square of Lemgo near Bielefeld [Fig 2.5] shows how unpretentious architecture can achieve excellence by striking just the right ratio of 'modernity' to familiarity. The architect, von Lom, has linked the new-style buildings to the traditional-style ones, which provide containment for them. He has altered the ridge level four times to give variety and to relate to the terminal buildings, achieving a sense of climax at the centre. On the left side, the eaves gradually descend to meet the gable termination of the end building. There is rhyme also in the style of the dormer windows. A touch of modernity is cleverly added to the dormers by continuing the glazing down the slope of the roof and then straightening its descent to form bay windows.

Fig 2.5
Lemgo, Bielefeld

The scheme has consistency; the new stands out just enough to establish harmony. It sustains the overall 'grain' of the market-place in terms of its shapes and the density and variety of visual incident, but at the same time proclaims the 1980s in the style of the windows and dormers and the character of the shopping arcade. This kind of design brings Trystan Edwards' concept of 'good manners in architecture' right up to date.

Skill in retaining a foothold in tradition whilst creating fully contemporary architecture is exhibited by Joachim Schumann and his team in the Great St Martin's development in Köln [Fig 2.6]. The six-storey apartments plainly echo the traditional high-gabled German town house, but into this basic theme the architects have introduced a high level of complexity, which is made up of visual intricacy and a breaking of convention.

Fig 2.6
Great St Martin's
development, Köln

The apartments form three sides of a square, the fourth consisting of the massive Romanesque flank of Great St Martin's church, now fully restored. The requirement to create apartments which would complement the church was a challenge for Schumann's team. However, they seem to have struck the right balance and, aided by the space of the piazza, have established a harmony between opposites. There is just the right amount of space in the overall arrangement to ensure that the integrity of the constituent buildings is not compromised; individual 'energy fields' have room to dissipate. The square itself has been carefully designed with liberal amounts of planting, including semi-mature trees. The impression is of a space with a strong identity due to the robust harmony which stems from contest between contrasting visual forces.

The square itself is not an isolated phenomenon, but rather the major partner in a network of squares. The architecture varies in style and quality, but the overall result is a significant achievement in urban design. Planting, lighting, and floorscape have all received careful attention, whilst a sensitively-designed pattern of paving sets gives a lift to the experience of walking.

Fig 2.7
Housing development,
Kensington
(Photo: Martin Charles)

Good rhyme-makers are not confined to Germany, however. An imaginative development which captures the flavour of late Victorian terraced housing has been designed by Jeremy Dixon in north Kensington, London [Fig 2.7]. The houses are set at a challenging angle to the facades, and Dixon has responded with elevations powerfully modelled in a rich mixture of colours and materials. The development is perfectly in tune with the mood of the wider Victorian environment and is an outstanding example of rhyme in the relatively low key of surburban housing.

The university town of Louvain-la-Neuve is an example of a whole new city built on the principle of rhyme. The new town was built to relocate the French-speaking university from Leuven to linguistically-compatible southern Belgium. The most remarkable thing is that it has succeeded in being a viable town throughout its development over several years. Despite its 'sawn-off' appearance in a number of places, it is an agreeable town to inhabit. It 'works' as a functional and aesthetic entity.

Fig 2.8
Louvain-la-Neuve

The planning team, formed in the late 1960s, decided on a high-density low-rise concept to minimise circulation distances and achieve maximum pedestrian use. So that the new town would echo the medieval urbanism in which the unversity was formerly located, they designed its centre with tight-knit streets flanked by medium-height buildings, while towards its periphery they allowed more space between buildings and introduced natural landscaping. Vehicle parking in the town centre is confined to two- and three-storey underground parks directly beneath the shops and apartments flanking the principal pedestrian routes. Also in the centre is the terminus for the rail link with Brussels, which is only thirty minutes away.

The new city of Louvain-la-Neuve is coherent [Fig 2.8]. Transcending the variety of architecture is a unity which stems from near-uniformity of materials and architectural character. Considering that over fifty architects were involved in realising the project, there is remarkable homogeneity. Few buildings were designed to be apprehended as isolated works of art; the individuality of each architect has been subordinated to the need to express a total, living organism. Buildings and spaces intermingle in a way that produces a refreshing variety. Sometimes the medieval image is overtly stated, as in the overhangs of the houses of the Hocaille area. Elsewhere, the medieval flavour is evoked by metaphor.

Although still unfinished, the town is already pleasing to explore. It has the unpredictability of a historic town – a remarkable achievement in the contemporary milieu. Unlike Port Grimaud in southern France, for example, its architecture is not traditional in the revivalist sense; it represents an *extension* of tradition which satisfies our need for continuity whilst meeting a complex functional agenda.

Over the top

There are, of course, buildings which approach the limit of novelty. They are usually the subject of extreme controversy, not only because of their intrinsic novelty, but also because of their position within the hierarchy of urban settings. The Pompidou Centre in Paris generated tumultuous hostility because, as well as breaking all the rules of architecture, it did so in a prestigious city centre location.

The architecture of Lucien Kroll for the Catholic University of Louvain in Brussels (see Chapter 3, Fig 3.12) is much stranger and more heretical than the Pompidou Centre, but few have heard of it, so it remains a relatively unimportant idiosyncratic diversion from the mainstream. The Pompidou Centre on the other hand, because of its size and location, has left an indelible mark on architecture, to the extent that Richard Rogers has been able to build an anglicised version for Lloyds of London. The latter is clearly an exciting building, but the Pompidou Centre robbed it of much of its power to surprise. In a previous book (*The Dynamics of Urbanism*[4]) I argued in favour of occasional buildings whose high measure of innovation both advances the art and shakes us out of our complacency. I used the adjective 'pacer' to describe them. The Pompidou Centre is still the ultimate example of a pacer building; even after a decade it still has power to shock.

At first sight, pacer buildings seem to have nothing to do with harmony, but as their strangeness subsides with time they can be judged on their formal or intrinsic merits. Some may achieve a position somewhere within the outer limits of harmony, whilst others never make the transition. It will be interesting to compare how St John's and Keble Colleges respectively wear with time (see Chapter 9), but it is difficult to imagine how Lucien Kroll's creations for Louvain University will ever slide into the mainstream of architecture.

An interesting indication of things to come is the Schlumberger building in Cambridge designed by Michael Hopkins [Fig 2.9]. Its main superstructure is a Teflon-coated glass-fibre fabric tent supported by cables held by raking stanchions. (At night, it gives off a kind of extra-terrestrial glow.) It is a dramatic and evocative building which redefines architecture – a tribute to an enlightened client, as well as to the architect-engineer collaboration which inspired it.

Fig 2.9
Schlumberger Building,
Cambridge

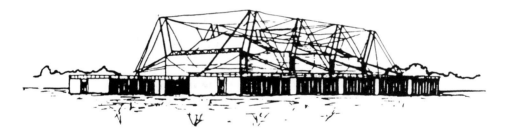

To sum up, in this contest between novelty and familiarity we are entering the territory of aesthetics, and therefore harmony. (Later in the book I shall elaborate on the theme that harmony is the outcome of the tension between complexity and order.) In the buildings discussed in this chapter, complexity has comprised the degree of novelty, and order the extent of the contacts with memory prototypes. Harmony results when order exceeds complexity by a margin sufficient to dispel uncertainty. The optimum acceptable 'pitch' or 'amplitude' of the contest varies with each individual, but the principle remains constant.

For this reason alone, opinions about particular buildings will vary. But this is not incompatible with the idea that underlying individual inheritance, learning and experience is a fundamental set of criteria (akin to Chomsky's 'deep structure'). For we all share the same brain system conditioned by a broadly similar channel capacity or rate at which we can digest information.

Chapter 3 First Level Orderliness: Unity out of Particularity

The tension between familiarity and novelty in art and architecture derives directly from the primordial tactics of survival. It is the progenitor of the clash between orderliness and complexity which, in art, is transposed to the purely formal or phenomenological level – the interaction between shape, colour, tone and texture. Our apprehension of harmony or discord depends upon the nature of that interaction. For harmony to exist, the constituent parts must form a logical whole; unity must perceptibly dominate fragmentation.

An advanced organism demonstrates the principle of harmony. Its individual organs have a clear identity and purpose and can be analysed in isolation, but they have no value outside the *gestalt* of the whole organism. Independence is subordinate to interdependence. The fine balance between partness and wholeness is at the heart of harmony in nature.

There is no doubt that most human beings are attracted to the challenge of extracting order from complexity, and a prime condition for aesthetic success in architecture is that this is allowed to happen. If our efforts to discover order are fruitless, the result is aversion.

There is some aesthetic satisfaction in simply achieving schema classification, and some are content to leave it at that. But the real aesthetic riches lie on the level of the interaction between architectural features – the clash between the autonomy of finite elements and the coherence of the whole. Aesthetic sucess depends upon the extent to which unifying factors outweigh fragmentation and disunity. Notre Dame in Paris [Fig 3.1] is a notable example.

The symmetrical towers are Notre Dame's most prominent feature. The essence of 'tower-ness' is carried through the facade by the four powerful buttresses, a strong vertical component which gives the towers a significant degree of autonomy. The basilica element is expressed by the gable end, the rose window, and the great west door. Integration with the towers is achieved by several prominent horizontal features. At ground level, subordinate doorways beneath the towers rhyme with the main door and provide lateral continuity. Above the portals, a band of sculptured figures establishes a strong rhythm across the elevation, with slight projections to acknowledge the buttresses. On the next level, the

Fig 3.1
Notre Dame, Paris

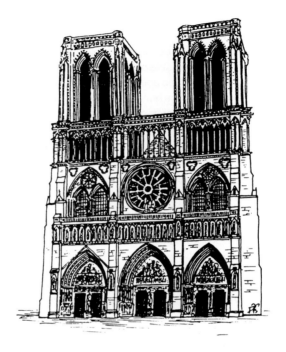

Fig 3.2
Lincoln Cathedral

rose window is complemented by twin-light windows in the tower element. The unifying process is completed by a delicate open arcade which becomes double across the space between the towers. The gable of the nave shows through the arcade, which changes tempo and steps forward, becoming 'blind' where it encounters the buttresses. Two balustraded galleries give the final thrust to the horizontal emphasis.

This west front is a marvellous example of the balancing of 'forces' and the unification of contrasting elements; there is vigorous tension between unity and variety. As we have already noted, aesthetic success depends on the victory of unity, but only if it is achieved at a price.

It is interesting to compare Notre Dame with Lincoln Cathedral [Fig 3.2]. Lincoln's chequered history is evident, especially in the west front, which is a prime example of disunity. The thirteenth century screen superimposed over the Romanesque structure to form an enormous facade effectively severs the towers from their base. The screen offers no acknowledgement to the towers and barely refers to the basilica element. Clearly juxtaposition is no guarantee of unity. Fortunately, the many other virtues of Lincoln Cathedral more than compensate for this outrageous piece of 'design'.

The Gothic cathedral was conceived as a giant projection of the eternal conflict between order and chaos. It symbolises the victory of the ordering will of God, but significantly such orderliness has to be unravelled from the complexity of buttresses, finials and string courses and frequent 'illogicalities' of form. Because it is born of struggle, the orderliness that finally prevails is the more significant. The Gothic cathedral has the quality of a parable.

In exemplifying in architecture the archetypal oppositions of order and chaos, the exquisite achievements of the Byzantine architects must figure prominently, especially the Greek architects Anthemius of Tralles and Isidore of Miletus. It is almost impossible to do justice to the Patriarchal Cathedral of Hagia Sophia [Fig 3.3]. No other urban disorder has had such a happy outcome as the Nike Riots of 532 A.D. Less than a month after peace was restored, Justinian's massive work force began its reconstruction, completing the task in five years.

Fig 3.3
Metropolitan Cathedral of
Hagia Sophia, Istanbul

Inside the cathedral [Fig 3.4], the sense of complexity marshalled into orderliness is overwhelming. Like the later Gothic cathedrals, matter almost dematerialises into light and space. The contemporary historian Procopius marvelled at the lightness of the great dome, which seemed to be 'suspended by a chain from heaven'. The logic of the internal space is expressed externally in the organisation of semi-domes and arches, which testify with equal force the ultimate victory of unity. To appreciate the scale of the aesthetic as well as technical achievement, one needs to erase the great buttresses and the minarets added after the fall of Constantinople to the Turks in 1453. However, the Byzantine heritage was continued under the Sultans, who adopted Hagia Sophia as the prototype for their mosques. The architect Sinan designed the Süleymaniye Mosque [Fig 3.5] in 1557, and it still monopolises the Istanbul skyline. The Byzantine civilisation never really recovered from the ravages of the Crusaders in the thirteenth century, so perhaps we are in debt to the Turks for revitalising a city which was rapidly losing its life force.

Fig 3.4
Metropolitan Cathedral of
Hagia Sophia, Istanbul

Sir Christopher Wren exploited fully the aesthetic potential in the contest between wholeness and partness. Absorbing influences from Italy, Holland and France, he evolved a unique style of architecture which was expressed most prolifically in his London churches. Commissioned to design the fifty-two churches destroyed in the Great Fire, Wren had to adopt an architectural system capable of numerous permutations. Dutch church architecture, which he first encountered as a refugee from the Plague, was his inspiration; the great churches of Amsterdam towered above the gabled city, their classical spires built up from variations on the Roman temple theme. Wren adopted the same tactic, maximising their inherent aesthetic potential.

Fig 3.5
Süleymaniye Mosque,
Istanbul

Sadly, many of his churches were burnt down in a later holocaust. However, his style became the norm for colonial buildings in the USA, one of the most elegant examples being Old Bennington Church, Vermont [Fig 3.6]. Built in timber and of economical design, it exemplifies a Renaissance version of the aesthetic of wholeness transcending partness. It consists of two elements, church and tower, which are excellently balanced in terms of informational weight. The tower dominates, but only sufficiently to avoid uncertainty as to which is the major partner.

In the front elevation, there are five clearly distinguishable systems of information. There is the entrance porch or narthex with a full pediment and a 'Palladian' window. Behind this the body of the church echoes the temple theme, though its pediment 'dies' into the base of the tower. (True to *gestalt* principles, the mind completes the picture of the temple front.)

The tower rises in three stages above the entrance pediment. However, the entrance projection contains elements of both tower and basilica and thus achieves visual integration of the two basic systems. Above the tower base sit two octagonal tempiettos, the lower comprising an open arcade, the upper a more solid cupola relieved by well-proportioned decorative oval motifs.

Each element of the composition has an independent integrity and is excellently proportioned and detailed. Yet the church is much more than a collection of autonomous elements; it succeeds as a coherent whole. Particularity is vigorously asserted, but finally succumbs to the greater weight of wholeness. A key factor in the success of unity over variety is the white-painted weather-boarding.

Fig 3.6
Old Bennington Church,
Vermont

One of London's familiar landmarks, St Martin-in-the-Fields
[Fig 3.7], exemplifies an uneasy marriage between spire and
Classical portico. As in the case of Lincoln Cathedral, elements
seem to collide, with the tower punching through the portico. Gibb's
earlier church, St Mary-le-Strand [Fig 3.8], is more successful as
an integrated composition and bears witness to his apprenticeship
to the Roman baroque architect, Carlo Fontana. The eighteenth
century architects of Rome were masters in creating unity out of
complexity, as we shall see later.

Fig 3.7
St Martin-in-the-Fields

Fig 3.8
St Mary-le-Strand

Looking back to the Middle Ages, it was customary in secular as well as sacred architecture to maximise the tension between unity and particularity. In certain great houses, the pattern formed by the exposed timber structure is the unifying agent. Bramhall Hall in Cheshire [see Fig 11.4] is one of the finest examples of enriched structure imposing pattern upon variegated shapes.

The same contest is played out in an entirely different style in numerous French chateaux. One of the most interesting (and least visited) is the chateau of Jumilhac in the Limousin region south of Limoges [Fig 3.9]. The main medieval section looks as if a number of separate elements have been pressed together into a single building. Each element has its own steeply pitched roof as if to emphasise its independence, yet they all combine to form a composition of rich multiplexity in which unity prevails. There is rhyme in the pitch and style of the roofs, which are punctuated by dormer windows with elaborately carved heads; the machicolation threads across all the major elements, binding them together. Windows are fairly evenly distributed across the facade, and are similar in proportion and style; pattern is stronger than variety. Finally, materials weld the whole composition together – rich golden buff stone and blue slate.

It could be argued that Le Corbusier was the first of the twentieth century pioneers to adapt the principles of the Modern Movement to the wider spectrum of aesthetic expression. Whereas in the true

Fig 3.9
Chateau Jumilhac,
Limousin

Fig 3.10
La Tourette Monastery

spirit of the Modern Movement the identity of elements was suppressed in favour of a clean geometric statement, Le Corbusier gave robust individuality to the component parts of a building. And the quality of the 'dialectic' between the parts was determined by aesthetic considerations. The monastery at La Tourette is a good example [Fig 3.10].

The two major elements of the building, the chapel and the residential parts, are expressed in stark contrast yet combine to form a unified whole. The use of a single material is undoubtedly a unifying factor, but the overriding integrator is the fact that the total composition forms a well-proportioned whole which takes precedence over the autonomy of constituent parts.

The functionalist aspect of Modern Movement philosophy inspired architects to express the purpose of the component parts of a building, in contradiction to the austere precepts of the Movement's purists. As buildings have become more complex in function, so the tension between overall unity and the fragmenting effect of expressing the diverse elements has become extreme. Sometimes the disorderliness is reinforced by stylistic excesses, as in the case of the Swiss church of St Klemenz in Bettlach [see Fig 3.16], which I discuss later.

An American architect who helped to establish this trend was Paul Rudolf with his Art and Architecture building at Yale in 1958 [Fig 3.11]. The main components of the design are pulled out and given a clear identity. Stair and lift towers are robust vertical features against the sheer glass walls, and the solid elements are bonded to the glass walls by pronounced horizontal bands of concrete, in the manner of traditional string coursing. Despite their vigorous expression, the parts never undermine the whole, and so in this respect Rudolf's building rhymes with a Gothic cathedral or Byzantine church. At the same time it is a successful piece of urban

design which turns a corner with elegance, echoing John Nash and
his various 'hinges' on the route from Carlton House to Regent's
Park.

Perhaps Lucien Kroll carried the 'debate' between variety and
unity to the limit. The design of the residences for medical students
of the University of Louvain [Fig 3.12] is said to have evolved as a
result of the extensive participation of future occupants. Almost
every contemporary style is represented, with even an occasional
gesture towards entropy. It is a visual representation of anarchy

and perhaps because of this it has generated a following amongst young architects. But in spite of its manifest contempt for discipline, it achieves some measure of aesthetic quality simply because the feverish rate of visual incident is fairly consistent across the whole complex. Pattern (of a sort) pushes through the chaos – a conclusion which I hope will not offend Mr Kroll.

Unity under threat

A discussion about harmony is only complete if it includes the *failures* as well as the successes in the complexity versus order contest.

Relatively few architects are commissioned to design 'prestige' buildings, so let us consider a small suburban building which strives to be appropriate civic architecture – a branch library in south Yorkshire [Fig 3.13]. On one side the wall element dominates, emphasised by a narrow full-height window; the other side, which contains the entrance, is totally glazed. The result is a visual dichotomy. There is hardly any sense of connectedness, the only perceptible patterning being the line of the entrance canopy which corresponds to the intermediate panel in the vertical window. This tenuous connection is assisted by the placing of the building's designation, whilst at parapet level there is some element of lining-through. These vestigial links are insufficient to establish the

Fig 3.13
Bentley Library,
Doncaster

minimum correspondence or pattern which is essential if the mind is to perceive opposites as part of an overriding whole. On the contrary, the two halves seem to split apart.

They also fail to harmonise in terms of psychological weight. The masonry half is visually heavier than the glazed half. The glazed section has a much higher rate of visual intricacy to compensate for its intrinsic 'lightness'; it comes near the weight of its neighbour but not quite, adding to the overall uncertainty and visual instability. The parts do not add up to a superordinate whole.

Maybe this is a case of the architect being misled by the drawing-board. It is easy to imagine a quite different end product from an elevational drawing.

The vertical rhythm of the concrete panels carries through, with a slight change of pace, to the aluminium glazing bars. On a drawing board, the line between the concrete panels may be more emphatic than in the finished article, so one may be deluded into believing that a pattern of rhythm will be established across the whole facade. The same applies to the horizontal joint. Similarly, at parapet level an elevational drawing can cause the discontinuous effect of a change of plane to be overlooked.

Even the most celebrated architects can sometimes fail this primary test of creating a unified building. Take, for instance, the

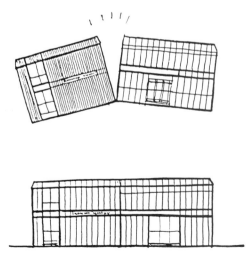

Fig 3.14
Danish Embassy,
London

Royal Danish Embassy in London [Fig 3.14]. Here two distinct styles of contemporary architecture are pressed together with hardly any connecting links. The forward block contains embassy offices, whilst the rear unit accommodates the Ambassador. The crisp Mies-like unit is the main architectural component, with the yellow window/wall modules planted on its front without rhyme or reason. There is no justification for this in terms of context, since the whole building strongly asserts its individuality with no deference to its surroundings. In the *Architectural Review* of May 1978[5], Alan Tye made this remarkable observation: 'It is . . . arguable that an architect of Jacobsen's stature should be allowed to create a building of our age and that conservative rules of fitting-in, being-in-keeping-with or preservation should be reserved for the lesser of us.' (Perhaps great men should also be granted immunity from Building Regulations?) Others might consider that conservative rules of fitting-in are at the root of good interstitial architecture, and that the creation of a masterpiece *within* these constraints is a true sign of greatness.

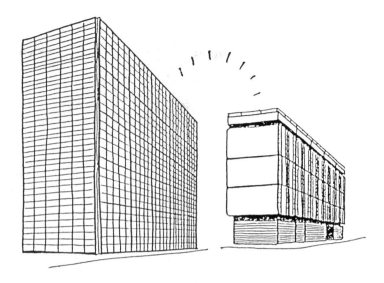

In effect, Jacobsen has designed two sophisticated buildings and failed to arrange a marriage between them. There is no rhyming contact, no coordinating principle. Here are two distinct visual entities with approximately equivalent weight, but which is the dominant element? The high curtain wall is dominant in size, but is visually austere. The lower forward element is smaller, but has a higher rate of complexity in terms of form and colour, resulting in contradiction and uncertainty. The marriage was doomed from the start.

In their search for contrasting juxtapositions, architects have sometimes been brazenly dissonant. The *Architectural Review* applied the term 'schizo' to a building which appeared in Rome in 1965, the Casa per Uffici ed Abatazioni situated on the Via Romana [Fig 3.15]. The Passarelli brothers designed this building, which comprises an underground car park, offices, and flats. The offices are directly in the Miesian tradition of sleek steel and glass curtain-walling. On the three office levels the building follows the layout of the surrounding streets until it suddenly erupts into an extravaganza of concrete columns and balconies draped with plants. There is no logical connection; contrasting species of architecture seem to have been juxtaposed by some gigantic upheaval of nature. Not only is there no sense of interconnection but neither building personality relates to its neighbours. This is the ultimate in architectural disorder and dissonance.

Fig 3.15
Casa per Uffici ed
Abatazioni, Rome

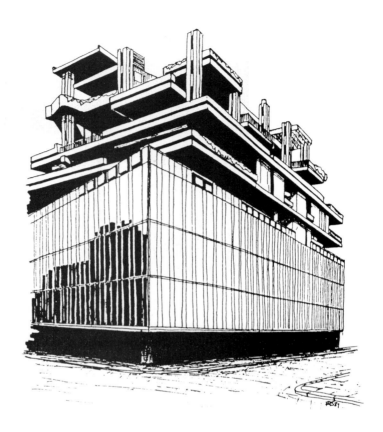

Fig 3.16
St Klemenz, Bettlach

Fig 3.17
L'église Héremence

St Klemenz in Bettlach [Fig 3.16] is an aggressively incoherent building, a *tour de force* of disjointedness. Its frenzied angularity denies the eye any rest, whilst the interior achieves an almost unrivalled pitch of dissonance. I say 'almost', because St Klemenz has a close relative in the village 'cathedral' at Héremence [Fig 3.17], where the interior is so bizarre that (in my case at least) it inflicts physical pain.

Fig 3.18
Market hall and car park,
Huddersfield

In designing buildings there is always the temptation to be *à la mode*. The result can be banal, as in the case of the market hall and car park in Huddersfield [Fig 3.18]. Every cliché is present: random-stone ground floor, giant sculptured panels hung from the stone facings laid in vertical beds and, to crown it all, fake mushroom-type projecting roofs which resemble the keyboard of some monstrous musical instrument.

Chapter 4   **The Parts versus the Whole in Urbanism**

Our attempts so far to clarify the concept of harmony have concentrated on individual buildings, amounting to a rehearsal for the wider application of the principle of unity transcending variety within the built environment. A building cannot properly be assessed in isolation; it is affected by whatever surrounds it, and distortion due to contiguity can be startling. These principles therefore only come into their own in the context of the wider built environment. And the concept of harmony must take into account the affective nature of buildings.

There is one fundamental difference between urbanism and the isolated building. In a single building, the informational contest is played out within a clear boundary – there is no problem of selection – whereas within the continuous flow of townscape, abstraction is important. A particular visual composition has to be isolated from its surroundings and treated as figure against ground.

In certain situations this is made easy by arches which bisect streets and provide a ready-made boundary, as in the case of the Gros Horloge in Rouen [see Fig 11.8]. From one aspect it frames the west front of the cathedral, and from the other focusses attention on the market place, recently enlivened by new architecture. (See *The Syntax of Cities*[6].)

But what is it that causes certain architectural combinations to spring out of their context as islands of harmony amidst a sea of complexity? Most historic towns offer this kind of visual reward. At intervals our attention is arrested by a combination of buildings and spaces which possesses internal coherence and balance. There are critical points in our progress along a street or through a square when, to quote Arnheim, '. . . everything has come to a standstill . . . no change seems possible, and the whole assumes the character of necessity in all its parts'. (*Art and Visual Perception*, 1954[7]. This, of course, is a paraphrase of Vitruvius' definition of beauty.) By critical point, I mean that the integrity of the composition can be undermined by altering the viewpoint by only a few metres. We could call it the 'critical fix'.

A somewhat undistinguished village in southern France will serve to illustrate the principle of the tension between unity and fragmentation. It is a typical composition, with the church tower rising above the houses. Despite the visual and symbolic contrast between church and housing, there are strong links deriving from consistency of age, materials and shapes. The two elements clearly belong to the same superordinate pattern; the scene qualifies as 'picturesque'.

Fig 4.1 is a view of the scene taken by a 55mm camera lens, but dramatic things happen when the same scene is taken by a wide-angle 28mm lens [Fig 4.2]. New information is added: crane, concrete slab with exposed reinforcing bars, and a recent smooth-rendered apartment block. These new elements violate the original pattern of shapes and materials; the sense of wholeness is vitiated and the scene becomes forgettable.

Fig 4.1
View of a French village
(*using a 55m lens*)

The extent to which visual information seems to combine into a holistic composition is of course ultimately a matter of subjective response. Yet there is a high degree of consistency in urban scenes which possess the quality of internal balance and harmony, suggesting that we use an intuitive code when ascribing perceptual weight and force to the constituent elements of a scene. This again suggests that aesthetic perception is part of the repertoire of inherited brain programs.

A major factor in establishing the position of the critical fix concerns the physiology of vision. In a strictly optical sense, a scene is surveyable when it comes within the visual field, which is

Fig 4.2
View of a French village
(*using a 28mm lens*)

approximately 180 degrees. Each eye overlaps the field of its neighbour, covering an arc of about 145 degrees. This produces an overlap of 110 degrees, which is the field that enjoys binocular vision, with the consequent benefits of being able to compute distance.

However, the arc which is in sharp focus at any given moment is as small as one degree. Therefore considerable eye and head movement is necessary for any kind of comprehensive perception, and it is important to understand their different implications for aesthetic perception. It has been suggested that if a scene is to retain its visual integrity, it must be perceivable *without* head movement, because such movement causes the visual field to change as relationships within it change, and this displacement may interfere with the coherent identity of the image. Eye movement, on the other hand, does not cause relationships to change.

As long ago as 1884, Maertens suggested that the optimum field of vision for the 'detached contemplation' of a scene or a picture is 27 degrees, an empirical conclusion which has subsequently been reinforced. Within this arc, a scene can be apprehended with normal eye movement alone. In the vertical plane, the field of vision is about 110 degrees, with approximately 45 degrees above eye level and 65 degrees below. With regard to eye and head movement, the same rules apply as for the horizontal field.

Unity can be imposed upon heterogeneity by a powerful polarising object, particularly in the urban context. The campanile of the Palazzo Pubblico in Siena [Fig 4.3] brings the whole city to order like some benevolent despot. There is also a gravitational analogy. We can all think of cities where there is one omnipresent building; it appears at the end of street vistas and over rooftops, its presence can always be felt. The dome of the cathedral in Florence, built by Brunelleschi against a tidal wave of disbelief, is an instance of this. Everything else, even Giotto's beautiful campanile and the fine Palazzo Vecchio, are subject to this massive and elegant tyrant, just as a sun might hold a variety of planets within its circle of influence. The gravitational field of the great dome extends over the whole city, establishing a vibrant equilibrium.

Fig 4.3
Palazzo Pubblico, Siena
and Duomo, Florence

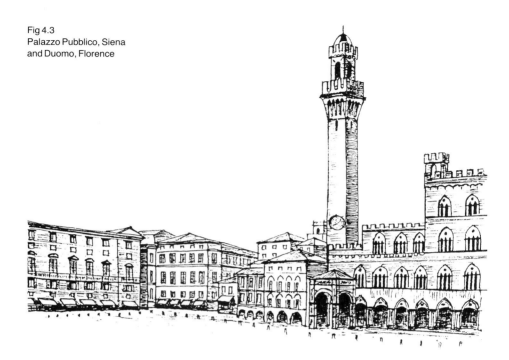

Fig 4.4
Rouen

A very different city in which the same principle applies is Rouen [Fig 4.4]. In the last century the cathedral took a further lunge towards the heavens with the construction of an iron lattice flèche reminiscent of the Eiffel Tower. It is like a huge maypole around which the whole city treads a continual dance.

Sometimes these buildings give a city a clear centre of gravity; at other times it is implied by the arrangement of buildings and spaces. A centripetal force field may be created by virtue of perspective, road pattern, or a powerful visual boundary; as a result, a metaphoric centre of gravity is generated.

However, this is not necessarily a guarantee of aesthetic value. In some of the earlier housing estates at Milton Keynes there are

Fig 4.5
The Strait, Lincoln

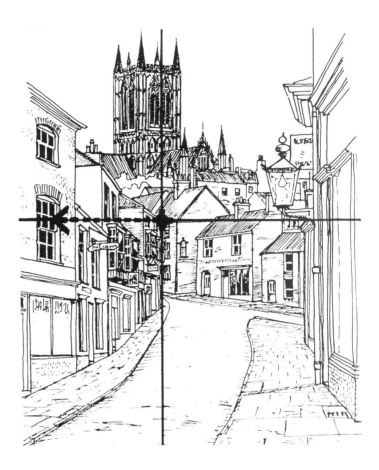

endless vistas of terraces inevitably producing centres of gravity but devoid of aesthetic value. There must be a sufficient rate of complexity for the contest between convergence and fragmentation to achieve aesthetic significance. The centre of gravity is only worth perceiving if it emerges from a vigorous interaction of vectors and force fields.

A few years ago I conducted an experiment with architectural and arts students. They were presented with a view along The Strait in Lincoln and asked whether it suggested a centre of gravity [Fig 4.5]. They all considered that there was a strongly implied centre of gravity, and the positions suggested for it were nearly all in a tight cluster which happened to average out at the vertical and horizontal coordinates of the golden section. Whether this was a case of people intuitively recognising the golden section proportions is a question which is currently being converted into an experimental research programme.

One of the most imaginative ideas in terms of the appreciation of townscape was the 'town trail', conceived by the Town and Country Planning Association. Such trails should be devised in all towns and cities, so that the greatest possible number of critical fixes could be plotted on trail maps. In this way it would be possible to 'read' the aesthetics of urbanism and at the same time learn the language of cities.

Perhaps architects, planners and urban designers should begin to design *for* the critical fix, plotting aesthetic climaxes into the fabric of the city not in any obviously contrived way, as happened with Renaissance architecture, but in a manner which combines subtlety with serendipity.

Chapter 5   **Just Short of Anarchy**

We have seen that the primary condition for good architecture is that it constitutes a coherent whole either independently or in concert with other buildings. Wholeness should prevail, but only at a price.

The same principle applies to extended linear townscape, except that *pattern* is substituted for wholeness. Numerous kinds of interaction can occur in buildings and cities with potential to establish harmony within a perceptual boundary, but the contest between complexity and order may also be enacted over extended territory where there are no frontiers. The clash is linear, like counterpoint in music, except that this is a contrapuntal arrangement of variety against pattern.

From earliest times, designers of buildings have exploited the aesthetic potential in counterpoising an overall theme against variety of shape, colour, and texture. This is also exemplified by paintings.

'Abstract' art aroused indignation because it departed from what many believed to be the primary purpose of art – to convey a cognitive message. But abstract painters had a much more profound purpose. They were depicting the archetypal contest between order and chaos in the raw, without interference from literal meaning. Theirs was a language 'too deep for words'. In psychological terms, they engaged exclusively the right cerebral hemisphere, and for many observers this required a radical perceptual adjustment. (Indeed it often still does, over half a century later!)

One of the earliest examples of the genre was Picasso's *Violin and Grapes*, completed in 1912 [Fig 5.1]. One's first impression is of disorder, but gradually a number of patterning factors assert themselves. In the first place, there is a limited range of colour applied with predominantly horizontal brush strokes. On the level of formal features, there is a strong pattern of vertical and horizontal lines sloping to the right and to the left and a rich contrasting pattern of curves. When each of these features is abstracted from the painting [Fig 5.2], the point becomes obvious. There does not need to be complete regularity in the direction, weight, or length of sloping lines or size of curve for the effect of pattern to overcome randomness; the mind will reduce the variation to a fuzzy 'resultant' or average in the interests of arriving

Fig 5.1
Picasso: Violin and
Grapes
Painted in 1912.
New York, Museum of
Modern Art

at a measure of orderliness. The same process occurs in the perception of architecture.

Harmony is normally associated with two or more entities which have certain common properties and yet a significant level of difference – that is, they rhyme. Harmony can also take shape out of the extended counterplay between the two ends of the information spectrum, variety and pattern. The dialectic is not contained with a precise boundary, but is apprehended as one moves through a street or town where these two informational extremes are simultaneously present, like counterpoint between two themes in music.

The city is the ideal scenario for this extended contrapuntal contest, a giant canvas on which the archetypal struggle between order and chaos can be depicted, not as a set piece but through the character of the streets and piazzas. The places which stand out are those where the contest is raised to a heroic scale, with the honours finally being awarded to the forces of order and pattern.

Amsterdam is surely such a city. When confronted with a particular view, our first taxonomic priority is to place information in space. Even if the precise view in Fig 5.2 cannot be identified, there are enough clues to place it firmly in Holland, while the detailed design of the houses points to Amsterdam. Many of the houses are clearly medieval, so this must be the old quarter of the city. Achieving this level of classification generates some satisfaction, but this kind of reward scarcely touches the fringe of aesthetic significance. There is much more to Amsterdam; its real aesthetic importance derives from the nature and disposition of visual information in an extended context.

First impressions are of a rather chaotic scene – a kind of amiable anarchy. But then the classification routine begins; the mind searches for connecting links on the level of features, shapes, and materials. Dutch architecture is characterised by the style of its gables, the 'trade mark' of the Hanseatic League (the medieval equivalent of the multinational corporation). There is significant variety in design, but there are also sufficient common factors to establish a pattern of 'gable-ness'.

Fig 5.2
Amsterdam

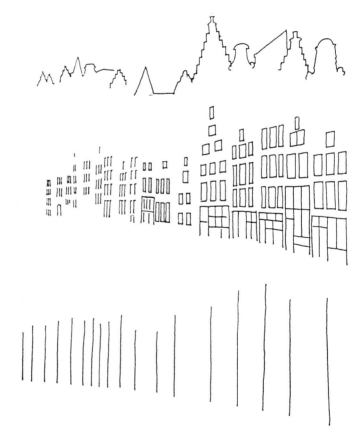

The windows also vary in size and position, but they share similar proportions in terms of height to width and usually occur in groups of three. Most of them have the reticular pattern of white astragals with white surrounds. They occur fairly consistently, so that the overall ratio of window to wall asserts pattern more strongly than randomness.

The same applies to unit size. All the plots vary in width, but the variation is contained within limits which suggest *rhythm* more strongly than haphazard demarcation. Altogether there are numerous levels at which this scene yields to pattern and order and aids classification. This is not pattern based on repetition, like a fabric or a wallpaper, but on the principle of *rhyme*.

Amsterdam is pleasing because it achieves a satisfactory ratio between elements which can be separately identified and elements which are stylistically or formally related. There is a vigorous interaction between the forces of complexity and orderliness.

The picturesque Greek island of Mykonos is an example drawn from the other end of Europe. All the buildings, rendered and painted brilliant white, conform in scale and character, resembling the adobe architecture of the American Indians [Fig 5.3]. Streets are narrow and serpentine, contracting at times to less than two metres. The woodwork of doors, windows and balustrades is often painted a bright mid-green or red ochre. Cafés abound, spilling into the minute streets. The town is punctuated by exquisite miniature Byzantine churches and an occasional windmill. The glowing white of the buildings contrasts with the kaleidoscope of colour provided by the boats in the harbour.

This is a rich aesthetic mixture full of gentle surprises. There is variety in abundance, but within firm constraints. Perhaps part of the appeal of Mykonos lies in the image it presents of a harmonious, close-knit society typical of fishing villages.

The principle of raising the pitch of the contest between pattern and complexity has been high on the agenda in urban design since the collapse of the Modern Movement. Let us look in more detail at the Great St Martin's development in Köln [see Fig 2.6].

Fig 5.3
Mykonos

These apartments display a high rate of visual intricacy, reinforced
by abundant planting on the balconies. Dark and light tones give
the design visual amplitude. Despite the high rate of complexity
and occasional asymmetry, there is pronounced rhythm. Standard
width window and bay panels provide an overall module which
establishes the pattern, together with light and dark tones
distributed fairly evenly across the elevations. Variety and
orderliness are both vigorously represented, with the honours
going ultimately to the latter.

The aesthetic relevance of rhythm

Rhythm is where aesthetics and biology intersect. Perhaps the first achievement of objective reasoning when 'homo' rose to the status of 'sapiens' was to realise that life is bounded on all sides by rhythm. Some of the most remarkable manifestations of early civilisation are concerned with systematising days and seasons into a calendar, and even predicting the behaviour of heavenly bodies. In this respect, Stonehenge seems to embody a sophistication which belies its primitive architectonics. Man echoed the rhythms of nature first in dance and incantation and then in more developed art forms such as music and architecture.

At its most obvious level, rhythm is a form of ordering which achieves a high level of patterning – for example, poetry is much easier to remember than prose because of its predictability; the number of word options is greatly reduced by metrical constraints. The mind intuitively seeks out rhythms, and tends to organise random data into metrical patterns. Telephone numbers are an obvious example. Now that worldwide direct dialling is possible, it is often necessary to hold a daunting sequence of numbers in short-term memory, so we automatically arrange these numbers into metrical groups and stress whatever element of pattern they contain.

Fig 5.4
Royal Naval Hospital,
Greenwich

Rhythm also has symbolic force. It is life-affirming, particularly when the beat is strong and at high frequency. Similarly, a rapid rhythm of columns in a building induces a strong compulsion towards movement. This can be experienced in Bernini's hemispheres encircling the Piazza of St Peter's in Rome. Double columns in two ranks exert a powerful thrust towards the entrance of the Basilica.

Straight colonnades have the same effect in Wren's Royal Naval Hospital at Greenwich [Fig 5.4], a marvellous piece of urban design. And the whole city of Bologna [Fig 5.5] is bound together by the rhythm of elegant, beautifully-vaulted arcades set off by patterned pavements and enlivened by predominating round arches. This is rhythm with a spring in its step.

I have suggested elsewhere[6] that rhythm offers primitive satisfaction and that our appetite for it is rooted in the parts of the brain which represent an earlier stage in human evolution – a kind of proto-aesthetic value system. This primitive mental processing seems to be responsible for the way we are awestruck by the gigantic. So rhythm *plus* massiveness results in a double reward.

Fig 5.5
Bologna

Rhyme and rhythm

Rhythm is one way in which redundancy can manifest itself –
obviously where the rhythm is strictly metrical, less obviously
where it is disjointed. (Some would say that it then ceases to be
rhythm.) But where there is an *approximation* to rhythm, the mind
tends to blur the discrepancies in favour of the regularities so that
'rhythm-ness' prevails over randomness. At the same time,
disjointed rhythm has appeal because it contains a measure of
complexity which has to be resolved. Richly diverse cities like
Amsterdam have great aesthetic appeal because the *essence* of
rhythm prevails.

Fig 5.6
Tübingen

Rhythm occurs at different rates. It may be found in the pervasive stonework of Assisi, for example, as well as in the giant tread of the ancient aqueduct in Segovia. As noted earlier, the rhythm of historic towns has much to do with the relative regularity of plot widths, imposing on cities such as Amsterdam or Tübingen [Fig 5.6] a measure of orderliness from the outset. Restrictions on plot width also condition building height and fenestration.

At first sight, the townscape of Brixham in Devon [Fig 5.7] seems haphazard. But closer inspection reveals a significant amount of pattern because house sizes are roughly consistent and, in particular, their windows are similar in shape and size.

Pattern behind the scenes

In all the examples considered it has been possible to identify the pattern-making features fairly easily. However, some places achieve aesthetic richness in a more discreet manner. In the case of Bridge Street in Chester [Fig 5.8], the first impression is of pure anarchy; there is a profusion of architectural styles and an almost total lack of continuity between one building and the next.

Fig 5.7
Brixham, Devon

Fig 5.8
Bridge Street, Chester

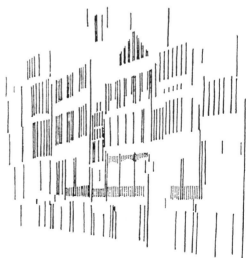

Yet out of this apparent confusion several interlocking patterns emerge. On a number of levels there is feature correspondence: most of the buildings terminate in steep gables facing the street; bay windows abound; half-timber patterning on facades is common. Furthermore, the pedestrian route at first floor level, known as The Rows, acts as a continuous thread binding together all the buildings in the centre of the city. But are these features enough to outweigh the abundant variety within this architectural sequence? If we consider that the scene is aesthetically rewarding, it must be because we have identified pattern beneath the surface of normal recognition.

When the mind analyses a scene to extract the rate of redundancy, it takes into account not only cognitive objects like gables and windows, but also abstract features such as edges, lines, and shadows. If we isolate most of the vertical features from this scene, it becomes immediately clear that a powerful pattern extends across the sequence beneath the level of the cognitive awareness. It is not strict rhythm, but a pattern in which the essence of rhythm prevails. When this is added to the feature patterns previously described, we have a formidable amount of orderliness, sufficient to outweigh the multiplexity.

Bridge Street is undoubtedly a rich aesthetic milieu; it raises to almost epic heights the contest between multiplexity and pattern. Orderliness only prevails after a fierce struggle.

It seems therefore that there is a fundamental condition for aesthetically rewarding townscape – that there must be a vigorous contest between disorder and pattern. If there is no real weight in either contender, or if pattern wins too easily, aesthetic potential evaporates. This is where a city such as Houston in Texas fails. There is size certainly, but little else; there is hardly any rhyme, likeness is tempered only with likeness (cat doesn't rhyme with cat). Nor does Houston rhyme with Dallas or even a satellite town such as Croydon, near London. In some respects the 'international style' has become the international lowest common denominator.

The Houston 'aesthetic' fails because there is no contest with complexity and no identity, but there are other places which frustrate all efforts to establish perceptual order and clarity, often because of excessive multiplexity and variety. This is common in North America: for example, one of the main streets in

Fig 5.9
Charlottesville, Virginia

Charlottesville, Virginia [Fig 5.9] is now a cacophony of commercial signs, wires, posts and parking lots, with only an occasional echo of colonial elegance. It is a display of uncoordinated items of information which defy any attempt to discover a prevailing pattern. The same problem can be encountered in large urban spaces.

When London celebrates, it usually does so in Trafalgar Square. Yet as a focal urban space appropriate to a great metropolis, it is a disappointment. There is a reasonable consensus in terms of scale, but its integrity is undermined by the profusion of streets opening from it. This means that the encompassing architecture largely consists of corner buildings which owe their main allegiance to the flanking streets. Thus the architecture of the square is fragmented, with the exception of the National Gallery. Even here there are design problems in that the size of the dome is insufficient to match the weight of the portico. The corner adjacent to the Gallery is occupied by the church of St Martin-in-the-Fields, a building whose design problems we noted in Chapter 3. Add to this the horrendous continual gyration of traffic around the square and it is clear why the giant Nelson's Column fails to bring the diverse elements to order. Perhaps this is why the assessors for the Grand Central Buildings competition chose a facsimile of the original – they could not countenance further complexity. It may also explain why there was such royal indignation at the competition-winning design for the extension to the National Gallery.

The only hope for Trafalgar Square is for some of its 'leaks' to be sealed and additional buildings inserted to establish coherence and a sense of containment. And this should coincide with the exclusion of all traffic from the square. If the Italians, who deify the motor car, can do it in the Piazza del Campo in Siena, why can't it be done in London?

The Piazza del Campo [see Fig 4.3] does not have a geometrically-derived plan. Nevertheless, it is a clear and positive spatial statement which can be apprehended in one sweep. There is a marvellous unity about the enclosing buildings which all defer to the glories of the Palazzo Pubblico, thanks to thirteenth century development control. The visual and symbolic weight of the Palazzo is sufficent to establish it as the dominant feature of the piazza without overwhelming the encircling buildings.

The urban aesthetic inventory is rarely confined to a single mode. In most historic towns several aesthetic systems overlap, and in the best instances, orchestrate into a grand affirmation of the principle of harmony. Plato laid the foundations of the principle of harmony when he said 'it is a characteristic of human reason to seek unity in multiplexity' (*Phaedrus 249b*), but it was Aristotle who first perceived that this mental contest held the key to beauty.

Chapter 6   The Ground of Harmony

Why does harmony exist, and why is it a source of pleasure? We have considered one aspect of the archetypal root of harmony, namely the urge to confront complexity so as to arrive at a higher level of orderliness. But schema expansion has to be incremental rather than catastrophic; maybe there is another element in the evolution of the harmonic sense.

In all higher animals, survival prospects are firmly linked with correct mating, and pair bonding must take place within the prescribed group, whether sub-species, tribe or clan. The chosen mate must possess adequate genetic variation within the parameters of the whole genus, to which the parts are subordinate. The ideal match was summed up by Gerard Manley Hopkins as 'likeness tempered with difference'. The concept of harmony may have its strongest roots in social behaviour, and in the survival advantages of a 'harmonious' marriage. Man rhymes with woman.

There is a considerable jump, however, from primitive survival techniques to the heights of aesthetic perception. The link may lie in the fact that at a given stage in human evolution man began to get ahead of the environment in the race for survival. As the environment became more bountiful and territory more secure, the drive to seek out and overcome challenges was more powerful than the actual needs of existence. But because these drives were programmed, their strength was not affected by external events, and as a result there was spare capacity. Such extra capacity is not confined to man; in many higher animals it is directed into rehearsals of real-life challenges such as play and elaborate sex rituals. Complexity is often deliberately created in order to achieve reward when it gives way to orderliness. It can be seen in victory in aggressive play or consummation following the sex ritual. In man, this spare energy found numerous outlets such as ritual contests, religious rites and his natural inclination to wage war. Few wars have started because of genuine fears for survival.

Perhaps the first signs of civilisation can be seen in the channelling of this emotional energy into cultural pursuits such as science, art, music and the adornment of buildings. In *Aesthetics and Psychobiology* (1972)[2], Berlyne reckons that art evolved as a way of *creating* complexity so as to present the challenge of discovering the underlying order. The same double-edged emotional reward results whether the complexity:order experience is related to primary or secondary needs. Primary needs relate directly to survival; secondary needs and rewards have an indirect effect on survival and operate wholly on the mental level. They may extrapolate into any stimulus pattern which can accommodate the contest between complexity and orderliness. This explains how the urge to experience complexity stimulated the growth of scientific enquiry, political and religious development and, of course, the arts.

The process of attaining 'civilisation' came about through the diversification of the basic drive to convert complexity to order into an ever-expanding range of activities. Today it may involve climbing a mountain, going to a football match, playing chess, reading a detective novel, listening to a Mozart quartet or contemplating a painting. All these activities share the fundamental characteristic of involving a build-up of complexity in order to provide the reward of ultimate orderliness. Art and architecture are, to use a theological analogy, eschatological: they point beyond themselves to an ultimate orderliness which implies a state of absolute security.

The wide agreement about what constitutes harmony and, conversely, dissonance, suggests that there is a degree of lawfulness which justifies the formulation of a comprehensive theory of harmony. There are two reasons for this. First, the brain mechanism remains the same regardless of taste and fashion. Secondly, the degree to which human beings can process complexity is limited by the channel capacity of the brain, which means that variation in terms of peak load or 'optimum perceptual rate' falls within a band width narrow enough for psychologists to talk of a '*consensus* optimum perceptual rate'. It is this that conditions aesthetic perception, and the band width which accounts for individual taste.

The concept of harmony derives from music. There is common agreement about which combinations of tone constitute simple harmony; no-one would describe a C-major chord as dissonant. Individual variation increases as the ratio of complexity to orderliness increases. In this context it is fair to assume that consistent intuitive reactions indicate lawfulness. If this is so with music, why not with architecture? We freely use terms like 'harmonious' or 'discordant' when describing buildings. In doing so, we refer to an *intuitive* code. In making value judgements about architecture we need to graduate from instinct to reason.

If we seem to be struggling to define harmony, it is probably because the term tends to be used inaccurately, especially by architects and planners. Harmony is too often equated with conformity: the lining-through of eaves or windows, consistency of materials, and so on. With this connotation, harmony is associated with the elimination of clash and tension.

Take the case of sound. There is general agreement that we perceive harmony where two tones are close enough to be considered a binary unit, such as a minor third. Between the tones there is good synchronisation of wave profiles but at the same time a significant level of discrepancy. Likeness is modified by difference. Music also demonstrates the principle of harmony in the structure of sound sequences, much of it in terms of theme and variation. It is the degree of divergence from the theme which decides the position on the orderliness:complexity scale. Similarly the *inversion* of a theme or phrase is another form of rhyme with harmonic potential.

The degree of difference between various themes locked together in a single whole is critical. Painters intuitively balance subjects between dominant and subordinate, or between figure and ground. 'Masterpieces' are those which strike a harmonic balance on the level of informational weight, which I discuss in the next chapter.

Chapter 7

Harmony and the Second Level of Orderliness

First level orderliness concerns the harmonic potential which lies behind the clash between wholeness and partness, or the forces of unity and complexity. But this is a long way from the limit of harmonic possibility; harmonic 'dialogues' can take place at several levels within that whole.

When considering harmony in architecture, we first think in terms of mathematical proportions, in particular the golden section (*phi*) and the related Fibonacci series. *Phi* has proved the most durable proportion across time and space, defining the limits of the front of the Parthenon, the Taj Mahal and (less obviously) the interior of the Cathedral of Chartres. Le Corbusier used it as the basis of his Modulor.

Psychologists account for the persistence of *phi* by suggesting that the ratio of 1.0:1.618 represents the ideal displacement between two identifiable but related bits of information – the point at which there is least uncertainty about the information being conveyed. For example, in the case of the *phi* rectangle [Fig 7.1], there is a clear dominant in the binary relationship of the two axes, but the subordinate axis retains its significance. In terms of simple geometry, the square is a clear pattern. As one coordinate is progressively increased, uncertainty follows a U-curve, returning to zero and minimum uncertainty around the *phi* rectangle. Another U-curve commences as the vertical coordinate continues to increase, creating ambiguity between a rectangle and a capital letter 'I'.

Fig 7.1
Classical proportions

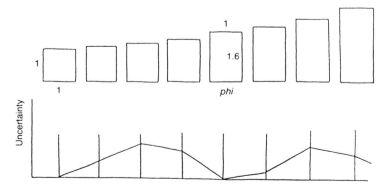

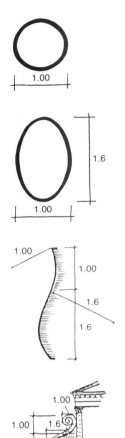

Fig 7.2

The same rules apply to the circle and its derivations [Fig 7.2]. When a circle is attenuated into an oval, the distortion must be sufficient to distinguish it clearly from a circle. By the time we reach *phi*, the ambiguity is eliminated.

The double curve of the Classical vase is also proportionally sensitive. In profile it comprises two related but coherent networks of information, namely the contrary curves; lower curve rhymes with upper curve. The complementary ideal occurs when the lower curve is the major element in a ratio to the minor, which approximates to *phi*. But if the situation is reversed to make the upper curve dominant, aesthetic success is undermined by the obvious instability which results. In such matters, empathy or *einfuhling* ('feeling into' objects) plays an important part. This is translated to architecture in the scroll which frequently decorates the gables of Hanseatic-style houses.

Some suggest that the golden section should be regarded as an immutable yardstick of perfection regardless of time and context. But the attainment of beauty is more often the consequence of *breaking* rules than adhering to them. The proportions of the golden section represent a harmonic ideal *in vacuo*, without the effect of propinquity. Thus it may work for an isolated building like the Parthenon, but it is not a valid yardstick in the majority of cases. Relationship affects perception, so that an attenuated architectural form may be harmonious in one context but unstable and dissonant in another.

Then there is the effect of shifting cultural norms. The cultural pendulum constantly edges towards complexity. When it exceeds the consensus limit of complexity tolerance, it swings sharply back towards a new simplicity – a reinterpretation of the Classical ethos.

Beyond numerical harmony

Most would agree that the seminal building in Western architecture is the Parthenon in Athens [Fig 7.3]. Some consider that its visual perfection derives from the fact that its front is contained within a golden section rectangle. Head-on, the Parthenon is certainly visually satisfying, but it is only possible to appreciate the quality of its overall proportion when it is presented as an elevational drawing; the view on the Acropolis is usually distorted by

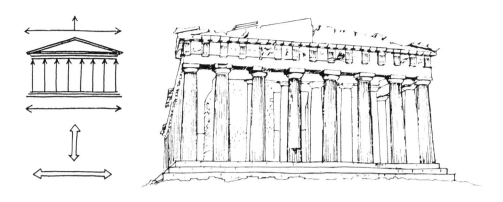

Fig 7.3
The Parthenon, Athens

perspective or angle. However, we can look at the facade in a way that accommodates distortion.

This building clearly encompasses a contest between the forces of horizontality and verticality; the columns represent repetitive vertical forces counterbalanced by the strong horizontality of the base or crepidoma, the entablature above and the pediment, in which the horizontal component is much stronger than the vertical.

Here then is a contest between two opposite but related classes of information taking place within a system which reads as a single major unit. Apart from oddities like the Erechtheion, the Greek temple is a clear geometrical concept, a unified composition where the contradynamics of information are an integral part, an arena in which the contest between complexity and order may be enacted and measured against the yardstick of harmony. If we add to traditional ideas about harmony and proportion the much broader concept of informational clash with a given *gestalt*, the potential for harmony seems unlimited. Wherever there is a juxtaposition or clash of two information networks, the mind seeks to establish an orderly relationship. When it succeeds there is a basis for harmony, but when it fails there is dissonance. Thus the concept of harmony can be extended to include any success in extracting orderliness from complexity.

The need to experience harmony within the environment compels the mind to try to reduce complexity by organising data into binary sets. In *Genes, Mind and Culture*[1], Lumsden and Wilson suggest that: 'In many instances the possible routes to a solution are legion, but the mind reduces the options to a binary choice . . .'.

They go on to point out that the mind tends to 'chunk information into binary alternatives'. We shall see the architectural implications of this in due course. The organisation of information starts with crude pairs of related opposites such as sacred:profane, child:adult, ingroup:outgroup, and proceeds along a path of increasing discrimination and subtlety.

The mind's tendency to favour stimuli which readily yield to binary classification has actually influenced the design process in architecture and urban planning. Painters and architects frequently compose in a binary fashion. The next step is to discover how a measure of orderliness occurs *within* the binary combination.

Binary relationship is the simplest form of system or pattern, and is a significant step towards orderliness. However, an urban scene or a building may consist of a hierarchy or progression of binary patterns which generates considerable complexity. Much architecture and urbanism can be broken down into related pairs of features. For a binary system to be valid in aesthetic terms, there has to be both likeness and difference. There has to be clear differentiation between, say, horizontal and vertical or sacred and secular, but at the same time there must be an overriding pattern which makes the binary relationship logical. Wholeness must prevail; it must represent a logical *gestalt*.

In order to achieve binary systemisation, the mind tends to emphasise patterns of correspondence and suppress differences in the interests of arriving at a clear, irreducible 'dialogue'. Aesthetic possibilities emerge when the binary clash results in a clear equation such as symmetry or harmony, a proposition which I develop in subsequent chapters.

Therefore binary organisation reduces complexity in two ways. First, it establishes a single overall unit where previously there were two, representing a significant reduction in perceptual load. Secondly, within this binary system there may be a further reduction in complexity if the respective informational weights approximate to a clear system such as balance or harmony.

We are concerned now with related but perceptibly different entities which interact to generate aesthetic potential. In certain architectural or artistic situations, the bipolarity is the most obvious thing about them as, for example, the bright light and deep shadow of a Rembrandt 'Nativity', or the brilliant red against more subdued colours of a Mondrian. In these works the creative clash is the dominant theme, and the aesthetic 'amplitude' is measured by the extent of the leap from one element to another, as in a metaphor in poetry. (At this point, a semantic problem arises, because there is no word to describe the clash of contrary elements in visual terms. We could adopt the term 'contramorphic' to suggest interaction between contrasting but related forms, akin to counterpoint in music.)

Mathematics apart, there are two ways in which the principle of harmony may be realised in architecture. The first concerns the clash between contrary but integrated systems of information which exist in parallel like contrapuntal themes in music, and which I term the *integral* binary condition (like the contraposed verticality and horizontality of the Greek temple).

The second binary condition is expressed where there are two semi-autonomous modules of information which belong to the same overall whole. They comprise readily identifiable 'chunks' which can be weighed against each other, like the tower and basilica elements of a church. I term this the *discrete* binary condition, and this is the subject of the next chapter.

The mind has a highly developed capacity to attribute the property of weight to visual phenomena. We commonly describe features of buildings or paintings as 'heavy' or 'light', 'strong' or 'weak'. We speak of 'weighing-up' the pros and cons of an argument.

When we look at the Parthenon, we intuitively identify logical binary couples like verticality and horizontality, and then aggregate them. Aesthetic quality is present if the aggregated weights counterbalance to produce balance or harmony. In this axial contest in the Parthenon the horizontal principle is victorious, due to the combined weight of entablature and crepidoma. Dominant prevails over subordinate within harmonic margins.

There are many other binary transactions within the Greek temple, such as between the round and the rectangular, the plain and the sculpted, the solid and the void. Perhaps the contest which most characterises it is between its 'inside-ness' and its boundary. The perimeter columns are a *soft* boundary, allowing space to pass in both directions. Because of their spacing and robustness, they ensure that the boundary effect is dominant, but again within the limits which prescribe harmony. This indicates that there can be harmonic interactions in architecture which lie outside formal, dimensional, harmonic proportions and which concern the dynamics of clusters or chunks of information.

What the Greeks did with restraint, medieval architects developed with gusto. In the west facades of the great Gothic cathedrals of the Île de France, the archetypal contest between the fundamental axes of existence takes place on an epic scale. Nowhere is this better illustrated than in the west front of Rheims Cathedral [Fig 7.4], which seems to reach triumphantly to the hem of God. But it was Roman baroque architects who intensified this contest to fever-pitch in churches such as S Agnese in the Piazza Navona [Fig 7.4] designed by Borromini. Perhaps we should see the outcome as a draw, consistent with the philosophy of the Renaissance. After all, man was thought to be at the centre of the universe.

This mental routine of bilateralising forces can also relate to a Renaissance dome. A hemisphere represents progression from vertical to horizontal dominance. In a Classical dome [Fig 7.4], the hemisphere is perfectly proportioned to balance these axes. However, other factors like the colonnade and the cupola supplement the vertical thrust so that verticality wins by a clear margin, suggesting truly Classical harmony.

Fig 7.4

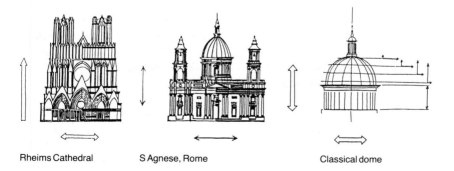

Rheims Cathedral   S Agnese, Rome   Classical dome

Fig 7.5

We can extend this principle of harmonic bipolarity to the various components of a building. An obvious example is the organisation of windows in an elevation which, in Renaissance architecture, was given considerable attention. Windows and walls are contrasting systems of information which can be dispositioned to create relative weighting which comprises symmetry or harmony.

It may be that the most harmonious balance in the Classical sense occurs in a facade where the wall accounts for sixty percent of the visual weight and the windows forty percent, or roughly the golden mean. This is a matter of perceptual weight rather than dimension and therefore involves subjective judgement. The relative weight can depend on many factors; for instance, a heavily rusticated wall has greater weight pro rata than if it were plain ashlar or rendered, so that the accumulated weight of window will need to be that much greater to strike a harmonic balance. This might be achieved by window size or placement or by the weight of surrounding decoration. A rhythm of columns can also change the balance by adding weight to the wall, especially if they are half-round projections [Fig 7.5].

Late medieval Dutch domestic architecture achieved striking results in the opposite direction with massive multi-storey windows heavily outweighing walls. One of the finest transitional window-wall houses in England is Hardwick Hall ('more glass than wall') in Derbyshire. The full-blooded Elizabethan lady 'Bess of Hardwick' selected a style for the reconstruction of the Hall which amalgamated Dutch, English, and Italian influences – and created a masterpiece.

The relationship between window and wall is one of the fundamental aesthetic systems in architecture. The window may have begun its existence as a purely functional device, but soon became charged with aesthetic significance as an internal and external feature.

One architect who brought the window-wall relationship into line with the twentieth century was Aalvar Aalto. His buildings, confined mostly to his native Finland, exploited modern technology to create a new relationship between windows and brickwork. Strip windows separated wall from roof, and fenestration carved its way into solid walls to establish an exciting new 'aesthetic'.

Frank Lloyd Wright conceived another radical approach to the window-wall relationship in the Johnson Wax headquarters [see Fig 8.6]. Uninhibited by cost restraints, Wright achieved a smooth skin elevation by using glass tubes bonded together to form a strongly horizontal translucent window. The interior is light and fresh but, characteristically, Wright allows no distracting views of the outside world. (To discourage typists from dozing off, he provided them with three-legged stools. If there was any deviaton from a normal upright posture, they fell off!).

Le Corbusier introduced the carefully-contrived 'random' window arrangement in a rendered and sloping wall at the Chapel of Notre Dame du Haut. Externally there is pleasing abstract patterning, which offers brilliantly-coloured relief to the cave-like interior – the numinous in twentieth century form. It was inevitably followed by a spate of random windows in walls, generally inferior to the prototype.

A recent building which adopts a playful attitude to the window-wall relationship is Robinson College, Cambridge [Fig 7.6]. Bay, oriel, conservatory, patio, and 'religious' windows all contribute to an animated exchange between these two fundamental components of architecture.

Fig 7.6
Robinson College,
Cambridge

In Cambridge, the integral binary aesthetic reaches great sophistication in Cripps Court at Queens' College [Fig 7.7]. The crisply-modelled concrete frame of round columns and rectangular bases, intended to reduce their apparent weight, creates a formal screen in front of a seemingly 'free' arrangement of windows and bronze panels. The Classical purity of the well-proportioned glistening white frame is the dominant theme, so that the subtleties of the panelling behind the frame only gradually emerge, like contrapuntal melodies. Opposites are harmonised in a way that transposes the Renaissance theme of windows between columns and architraves into a contemporary key.

Fig 7.7
Cripps Court, Queens'
College, Cambridge

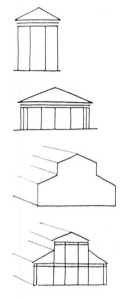

In this building there are at least two levels of harmonic expression. The first concerns the dimensional ratio of column to beam, which comes very close to the golden section. The second relates to the interaction between complementary systems of information, namely the orderly frame and variegated panelling. The outcome is surely harmonic balance, with the frame achieving dominance in line with the 'laws' of structural aesthetics.

To end this chapter on a historical note, a building with abundant harmonic counterpoint is S Giorgio Maggiore in Venice [Figs 7.8 and 8.1]. Palladio solved a problem which had confounded architects throughout the Renaissance – how to place a Classical temple front against the termination of a basilica, with its high nave and lower aisles. His solution was to integrate two temple fronts, both distorted in proportion. One was high and narrow, the other low and broad. One is clearly dominant, but the overall composition strikes a marvellous note of harmony.

Besides the west front, the building is rich in harmonic rhyme. The temple theme is echoed in the campanile, even to the miniature temple of Vesta beneath the conical spire. The whole superb composition seems to hover only inches above the waters of the lagoon, suggesting the eternal tension between nature and the works of man. Occasionally nature turns spiteful, doubtless to warn man of his hubris.

Fig 7.8
S Giorgio Maggiore,
Venice

Chapter 8   Discrete Interaction

Still on the second level of orderliness, the other major class of binary informational relationship concerns the interaction between related but semi-independent architectural elements. The difference between integral and discrete interactions is that, in the case of the latter, the architectural features retain their identity and integrity when considered in isolation yet remain subservient to the whole. Their autonomy is secondary to their allegiance to the principle of unity and coherence.

When a circular campanile was placed next to Justinian's great basilican church of S Apollinare in Classe in Ravenna [Fig 8.1], an enduring architectural partnership was established. Two distinct sub-wholes are clearly identified as belonging to the same superordinate whole by virtue of shared materials and architectural forms, and they also fall within the same symbolic boundary. Thus the condition for first level orderliness has been met: the whole is much more than an accidental collision of parts.

Fig 8.1
Binary balance

S Apollinare in Classe,
Ravenna

S Giorgio Maggiore,
Venice

The next task is to determine whether there is a second level of
orderliness in the relationship between the campanile and basilica.
Do their respective weights establish an aesthetically significant
relationship such as balance or harmony? The tower is a universal
religious symbol, packing a much greater symbolic punch than the
basilica unit. But although the campanile is much smaller than the
basilica, it seems able to balance it. The reason for this resides in
the imprecise subject of symbolism.

Students of aesthetics tend to confine their subject to the *detached*
contemplation of abstract relationships. In so doing they base their
rationale upon a fallacy, because in a situation which calls for value
judgements 'detached contemplation' is impossible; a value
judgement is the resultant of a 'force system' of emotions. There
will always be intervening variables, such as symbolism.

The campanile has a powerful archetypal resonance associated
with images of the sacred centre and the point of intersection
between the 'cosmic zones' of earth, heaven and the underworld.
Jung was the first to popularise the idea that archetypal images
reside in the collective unconscious. Today we would say that they
are part of our inherited predisposition to respond to certain
triggers associated with the fundamental problems of survival. Tall
towers, cathedrals on hilltops, architecture pitching itself against
nature, all evoke an emotional rather than a rational response
because they suggest answers to archetypal problems. The brain
responds to ancient myths as positively today as in the time of
Cro-Magnon Man.

As a result of all this, the Ravenna campanile has a much higher
saturation of symbolism than the basilica. It is more highly charged
with emotional energy, which is why, in terms of gross
informational weight, it is able to balance the visually larger
basilica. The aesthetic excellence of this combination derives from
the fact that first, it comprises a perfect case of unity transcending
diversity and, secondly, the contrasting systems of information
achieve orderliness in terms of balance. As discussed in the
previous chapter, this partnership was developed to perfection by
Palladio in S Giorgio Maggiore in Venice – the ultimate balance of
opposites: tower versus basilica, architecture versus nature. The
strength of the unified image of tower and basilica lies in the fact
that it reconciles and harmonises the opposed axes of the spiritual
and the wordly. Perhaps this is why its popularity has persisted

Fig 8.2
Proposed church and
housing,
Wesley,Methodist
Church, Cambridge

through numerous radical changes of architectural style, even figuring in my own designs [Fig 8.2].

But medieval cathedrals usually have multiple towers. What happens to binary ordering in such instances? The answer lies in the principle of redundancy and the mental tactic of 'chunking'.

In the matter of information, it is possible for one-plus-one to add up to, say, one-point-five. This is because redundancy or repetition intervenes in the process of mental quantification. Redundancy can play an important part in determining the way we bipolarise matrices of information in order to make aesthetic judgements. To understand what this means in basic terms, consider a Gothic cathedral west front.

In most respects the Gothic cathedral represents a logical development of the fourth century basilicas established under the Emperor Constantine. At first the profile of the west front followed the section of the nave and aisles [see Fig 7.8]; the medieval contribution was to place twin towers in front of the aisle terminations. As we have noted at Notre Dame [see Fig 3.1], the result is a composition with two themes – nave ending or basilica, and towers, which conform to the rule of rhyme in that they exhibit both likeness and difference. There are also coordinating factors deriving from style and materials.

Fig 8.3
A typical west front

At first we might perceive a typical west front [Fig 8.3] as comprising three architectural elements. But if the towers are identical, they constitute *one* information system because of redundancy or overlap. In terms of visual mass, the towers heavily outweigh the nave ending. But visual mass is not the same as perceptual weight; the redundancy factor reduces the psychological weight of the towers. Even so, the towers achieve dominance partly due to symbolic reinforcement, thus $A_1 + A_2 > B$.

In Chapter 7 we considered the question of harmony through mathematical ratios like the golden section. It is tempting to speculate whether it might be possible for ratios such as *phi* to register *outside* mathematics. It is certainly not unreasonable to suggest that a twin-towered west front would seem harmonically ideal if the towers outweighed the basilica in terms of attributed weight at a ratio of 1.62 to 1.00 – the attributed weight being a compound of visual intricacy, mass and symbolism. Perhaps one day we will find a way of quantifying the symbolic component.

The west front of York Minster [Fig 8.4] achieves exactly this kind of harmonic excellence. It reads as an integrated whole because of the unity of materials and style, and the fact that many features cross the boundary between towers and nave ending. The nave

Fig 8.4
York Minster (*west front*)

element asserts itself with a beautiful curvilinear window. Although the towers have a separate identity, this is subordinate to the whole scheme of the west front. The city gatehouse theme (first stated clearly in St Denis in Paris) is subtly inferred by the crenellations which cross the entire west front at the base of the towers. The towers depict the evolution of Gothic architecture from the geometric style of the thirteenth century at ground level, through fourteenth century curvilinear at the next stage, to fifteenth century perpendicular in the belfries, contributing to their independent character. Powerful buttresses reinforce the divisions between

Fig 8.5
Lincoln Cathedral

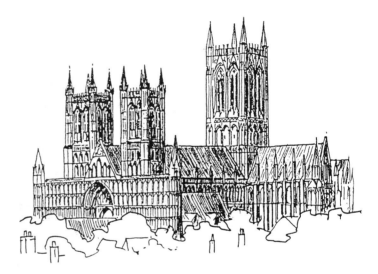

York Minster

them. Altogether there is a profusion of both likeness and difference, but the sum total is a profound sense of harmonic stability. This design system was employed with equal success at Canterbury Cathedral and Beverley Minster.

Despite the problem of its west front, overall Lincoln Cathedral [Fig 8.5] achieves harmonic excellence, its three mighty towers opposing the great bulk of basilica with its double transepts. The towers win the contest just sufficiently to dispel uncertainty. At the next level of analysis, there is dialogue beween the west towers and the central tower; redundancy allows the central tower to win by the same kind of margin. Canterbury Cathedral is equally rewarding in these respects, but at York Minster the central tower just fails to reach the right stature and rate of complexity to achieve supremacy. The result is uncertainty, and this undermines the aesthetic excellence of an otherwise marvellous building.

The archetypal contest between the vertical and horizontal principles is not confined to the religious sphere. In Wright's Johnson Wax building, referred to earlier [Fig 8.6], low streamlined

Fig 8.6
Johnston Wax Building,
Racine

Fig 8.7
Holkham Hall, Norfolk

horizontal masses are pitched against the elegant laboratory tower block bound into a unity by the warm brown bricks and buff copings together with the skin-tight tubular glass windows. It makes an interesting comparison with Dudok's earlier city hall at Hilversum, a symphony of interlocking cuboids crowned by an elegant tower (see *Architecture and the Human Dimension*[8]).

Holkham Hall in Norfolk [Fig 8.7] is a taut and refined example of successful hierarchical binary interaction. This Renaissance building, designed by William Kent in association with Lord Burlington for Thomas Coke, Earl of Leicester (also a dedicated Palladian), helped to establish English Palladianism. The design demonstrates a clear hierarchy of consonant relationships. First, there is tension between the autonomy of elements and the integrity of the whole. The flanking buildings are self-contained, yet they echo the main centre element, establishing just the right ratio of likeness to difference. The central portico has its own identity, which reverberates through the whole composition. This is a building full of rhyme, a superb orchestration of harmonic relationships.

We now progress from the general to the particular, and consider certain constituent elements of architecture.

Wall and roof

The most sophisticated visual binary interactions often stem from basic functional needs. As the design initiative spread from the Mediterranean countries to northern Europe in the Middle Ages, the significance of the roof as a powerful design element was widely exploited. It is often said that steeply pitched roofs are the natural outcome of a severe winter climate (even though Swiss vernacular architecture contradicts this assertion). I suspect that both aesthetic and climatic factors influenced the dramatic development of the roofscape in northern Europe.

The Hanseatic merchants set the tone in secular architecture, the steeply pitched roofs of their houses terminating in an elaborately modelled gable, the interface between wall and roof. It is the variety of gable designs which provides the aesthetic flourish to cities like Amsterdam and Lübeck, or the less well-known Bavarian town of Landshut.

However, credit must go to the French for raising roof design to a high artistic level. Even a fairly modest chateau like Jumilhac [see Fig 3.9] presents a pleasing clash between wall and roof. The wall element is dominant, but only enough to be within harmonic limits.

Few would argue that the opposite is the case in the royal chateau of Chambord [Fig 8.8]. Wall elevations are well-ordered and restrained, but above parapet level restraint is abandoned in favour of extravagantly sculpted dormers, pinnacles, chimneys and cupolas. Here is a marriage between order and reason in the wall architecture, and unbridled passion in the roofscape – the opposites of the human psyche amalgamated into a strident harmonious whole. Who would have thought that Francis the First could have sponsored a building so symbolic of the human condition!

But it is sad to reflect that when a major architectural element such as the roof starts to return to favour, there will always be those ready to trivialise it. This is what has happened to the concept of the pitched roof in apartments in Normandy [Fig 8.9]. The design is aesthetically unsatisfactory not only because it is not clear whether the elements which seem to mimic roofs are really wall, but also because of the frenzied complexity of shapes and planes.

Fig. 8.8
Royal Chateau of
Chambord

Fig 8.9
Apartment buildings,
Normandy

A by-product of the development of the roof in northern Europe
was the concept of the spire – at its most basic, a campanile with a
pitched roof. However, architects quickly developed the concept to
present a partnership between tower and spire which sometimes
reached a summit of grace and elegance. Where the tower
element is the major theme, harmony combines with stability.

Fig 8.10
Ledbury Parish Church,
Herefordshire

Harmony, together with a soaring of the spirit, is the message conveyed by such masterpieces as Newark and Louth parish churches in Lincolnshire, or the spire which presides over the beautiful medieval backlands of Ledbury in Herefordshire [Fig 8.10].

The aesthetic possibilities in the dialogue between wall and roof are now being rediscovered following disenchantment with the flat roofs of the Modern Movement which, to demonstrate complete mastery over the elements, required crisp white walls to confront the sky, their cubist integrity undefiled by a visible roof. Eventually architects conceded that their confidence in materials and technology was misplaced, and innumerable performance failures led to a return to pitched roofs. Reaction can sometimes be swift. No sooner had the pitched roof regained a hint of respectability than Robert Matthew Johnson-Marshall designed Hillingdon Town Hall [Fig 8.11], an uninhibited and entertaining riot of roofs.

But roofs rise and fall according to the dictates of fashion. In the Georgian age, the roof became entirely subordinate to the wall; it was often hidden behind a parapet. Occasionally, Tudor buildings such as Kentwell Hall in Suffolk, were re-roofed in the eighteenth century to make the ridge line less prominent.

Fig 8.11
Hillingdon Town Hall

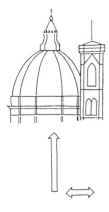

Fig 8.12
Duomo, Florence

Straight against curved, round against rectangular

Throughout the ages, architects have taken pleasure in juxtaposing rounded and rectangular forms. Once again it is the great cathedral which raises this dialectic of opposites to epic heights, and nowhere more so than in the marble-faced cathedral in Florence [Fig 8.12]. Giotto began the process with his exquisitely proportioned campanile, to be complemented later by the incredible dome constructed by the young Brunelleschi in the face of massive scepticism. It is a perfect marriage of opposites; the dome is dominant but never over-assertive. Palladio translated the tower and dome combination into the language of the Renaissance with the serenely balanced composition of S Giorgio Maggiore [see Fig 7.8], exploiting to the full the magical effect of distance.

The clash between the rounded and the rectangular clearly interested two of the mandarins of modern architecture, Frank Lloyd Wright and Le Corbusier. The Guggenheim Museum in New York [see Fig 10.7] and the government buildings at Chandigarh are cases in point.

The commonplace and the heroic

Discrete binary contrast can occur when a single building incorporates elements loaded with opposing symbolism. One of Palladio's enduring innovations was to mark the entrance to a house with a full Classical portico, as it were grafting the temple on to the home. Two fundamentally different types of architecture combine to result in harmony, as in the anglicised version of Prior Park, Bath [Fig 8.13]. Despite the contrast, unity is dominant.

In evaluating Prior Park, the mind 'weighs up' the primary clash which is between portico and house. Though clearly part of one coherent whole, these elements are isolated and weighed against each other to see if there is an orderly outcome. Symbolism again helps to tip the scales in favour of the portico. Though this feature is smaller in size, it outweighs the house element because of its high incidence of visual intricacy combined with the symbolism of antiquity and authority, and the contrast between light and shade. Overall, the portico is dominant, but within the limits of harmonic balance. This is not the case at Woburn Abbey [Fig 8.13], where the centre portico is weak in relation to the bulk of the house with its heavy projecting wings. Whereas the Prior Park portico exerts sufficient gravitational pull to hold the composition together, Woburn is pulled apart by the over-assertive wings.

Prior Park illustrates a further reason for the success of Georgian architecture: the well-judged ratio of window to wall. Not only are the windows well-proportioned, but there is harmonic balance in the aggregate of window to wall. Georgian architecture is wall-dominant by that critical margin.

Fig 8.13
Prior Park, Bath

Woburn Abbey,
Bedfordshire

Harmony and imagery

By placing a Greek temple in the centre of a house facade, Palladio was resorting to imagery analogous to the city-gate theme of the Gothic cathedral west front. Perhaps this is where architecture and poetry intersect on the common ground of simile and metaphor. The aesthetic component lies in the rhyme between past and present, between blurred image and sharp reality. As the imagery penetrates to archetypal levels in the Jungian sense, so the emotional impact increases. More and more contemporary buildings are pointing to images rooted deep in history.

One of the first post-war buildings which unashamedly set about evoking a host of images was the county administration building in Bensberg, ten kilometres east of Köln [Fig 8.14]. Some regard this as Gottfried Böhm's attempt to rekindle the expressionism of the 1920s and '30s; others see it as a thinly disguised fortress rising from the foundations of ancient fortifications. There is even the hint of a medieval city surmounted by a cathedral spire*.

Fig 8.14
County administration
building, Bensberg

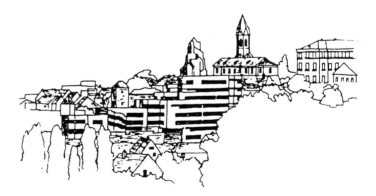

In England, the nearest thing to Bensberg is the Hillingdon Civic Centre [see Fig 8.11], conceived as a compressed medieval town with its complex shapes and tightly-packed pitched roofs. Architects have tended to disparage this building, but it was very well rated in a recent opinion poll. People clearly respond to its symbolism, which is just sufficiently understated to make the apprehension of the image rewarding.

* Gottfried Böhm was awarded the 1986 Pritzker Prize for Architecture for the Bensberg building.

Fig 8.15
The Sainsbury Building,
Worcester College,
Oxford

This medieval city theme has even found a place in a university setting. Robinson College, Cambridge [see Fig 7.6] has a city gate, watchtower and more than a hint of a moat. In Oxford, an addition to Worcester College, the Sainsbury building [Fig 8.15], recalls the most ancient architectural form, the Ziggurat. There is something oriental about its shapes and counterpoised single-pitched roofs; set amidst mature trees and still water, it suggests an eastern temple. Everything about the building is pleasing – the attention to detail and design of internal spaces as well as the overall composition.

These are contemporary buildings which rhyme with historic prototypes. The best examples of this genre have a metaphorical quality which reinterprets the connection between poetry and architecture, proving that it is still possible for an enlightened client to find an imaginative architect.

Figure and ground

In architecture as well as painting, a common binary transaction is between figure and ground. *Gestalt* psychologists illustrated in a variety of ways how one pattern of information achieves prominence when it is perceived as figure against the subordinate pattern, which becomes background. On the other hand, uncertainty can be generated where the relative informational weight is too evenly balanced.

The seventeenth century baroque architects of Rome exploited the interplay between figure and ground, inserting exotic church fronts into the lower key ground of domestic architecture. The medieval cathedral is figure to the ground of an entire city. In the eighteenth century, the dialogue shifted to the interplay between architecture and nature. This was the age of the great landscaped gardens which reached its climax in England in places like Blenheim Palace and Chatsworth, where nature was carefully modified to create an idyllic landscape. Artists such as Claude Lorrain and Poussin romanticised the interplay of architecture and nature, which doubtless generated feedback into real projects. In the United States of America, Thomas Jefferson brought the pastoral idyll to the University of Virginia, and to his own house at Monticello completed in 1775 and remodelled between 1796 and 1808.

Frank Lloyd Wright was a pacemaker in harmonising architecture with landscape in this century. His classic design is Falling Water at Bear Run, Pennsylvania [Fig 8.16]. The client, Edgar Kaufmann, asked for a house near a stream. Instead, he got a waterfall. Never one for half measures, Wright's response to the brief was: 'I want you to live with the waterfall, not just look at it, but for it to become an integral part of your lives'. From Taliesin to Bear Run, and then the later houses such as the Wingspread Residence or the Johnson Residence, Wright exhibited a unique sensitivity to the inherent beauty in the dialogue between architecture and nature.

There are many other ways of achieving harmonic contrast between the ingredients of architecture. For example, there is a poetic leap between the sober architecture of the outside of a baroque church and the riotous extravagance of the interior. Recently buildings have been designed to take on two personalities in a different way – by a dramatic change of character

Fig 8.16
Falling Water, Bear Run,
Pennsylvania

from day to night. An excellent example of such a building is the Willis Faber Dumas building in Ipswich. By day it is a wavy wall of smoked glass, but at night it pulsates with light. When time is the controlling factor, we could call the resulting harmony 'diachronic'.

So far we have been considering single binary transactions within a firm conceptual boundary, but these can also occur in a linear context. An excellent example is the Sir Thomas White building at St John's College, Oxford, designed by Arup Associates, which occupies two sides of an irregular quadrangle and greatly enhances this part of the College [Fig 8.17]. It is a fairly extensive building in which the architects have exploited the staircase character of college accommodation to generate tension between partness and wholeness. The design comprises a series of four-storey pavilions containing undergraduate and staff rooms; between each pavilion is a staircase tower. Both these basic elements are expressed as independent entities, and this means that the relationship between them can be adjusted vertically and horizontally to suit the requirements of the site.

The result is a strong rhythm of heavy stone-faced towers between delicate concrete-framed pavilions. The rhythm itself is aesthetically pleasing, but the real aesthetic impact lies in the perfect harmonic relationship between the expression of the parts and the unity of the whole. Even though the parts have substantial autonomy, the sense of unity prevails to a degree that leaves no room for doubt. On some of the pavilions there are solid stone panels which echo the towers, reinforcing the weight of pattern.

So, within this building there are two well-defined patterns of information, the towers and the pavilions, which embody contrasting architectural philosophies. The former are solid and apparently load-bearing in a traditional manner, while the pavilions are wholly contemporary in concept – an interpretation of the transparent wall characteristic of Arup designs of this era. The towers which abut the pavilions add strength to the almost filigree lightness of the concrete frame – a case of successful structural aesthetics. In this a-b, a-b rhythm, the pavilions achieve dominance due to their size and visual intricacy, but this dominance is harmonic. Rhythmically it represents an accented second figure, a-b, a-b.

The pavilions in themselves demonstrate successful binary interaction between frame and window-wall, each once again having a degree of independence. The frame is free-standing in

Fig 8.17
Sir Thomas White building, St John's College, Oxford

front of the smoked dark-framed storey-height glazing, while the central structural element of each pavilion consists of slender bush-hammered H-frame units stacked vertically. Cantilever beams, L-shaped on plan, carry the frame round the corners, widening at the junction with columns. There is a weathering chamfer at the vertical connection between columns. Each element of the frame is expressed as a separate entity with each H-frame distanced from the corner unit. Columns are as slender as the Building Regulations will allow. Thus even in the expression of the frame itself the aesthetics of partness and wholeness are fully exploited, illustrating how aesthetic integrity can carry through to the fine detailing.

Two rules have emerged from this chapter. The first is that second level orderliness in terms of single or multiple binary interactions cannot register if the building or architectural group fails to bond into a unified whole. Secondly, in the transactions between distinct but related features we should perceive a clear relationship, either symmetrical balance or an unambiguous statement of dominant to subordinate. And in the case of multiple binary interactions, the order of priority should be clear, especially at city scale.

Chapter 9   Discrete Interplay in Cities

The ordering of information into binary sets is a basic perceptual strategy even within the complexity of the city. Complementary opposites are identified, such as sacred and secular, light and shade, 'hereness and thereness', to quote Cullen[9]. The first pair of contrasts, sacred versus secular, is a fundamental binary pattern which has dominated towns and cities since the foundation of the first Jericho.

The city represents the point of intersection of these two axes of reality, and this is usually clearly expressed by the architecture. This urban formula can be adapted to the scale of a great city like London when it was dominated by the dome of St Paul's Cathedral, or a hamlet like La Garenne, Vale, on the island of Guernsey [Fig 9.1], where an informal group of simple houses and cottages clusters round the church, their differences subordinated to present a united front. Its greater symbolic saturation ensures that the church prevails, but the contest has a harmonic outcome, proving that beauty can reside in the commonplace.

Fig 9.1
La Garenne, Vale,
Guernsey

In the Herefordshire village of Ledbury [see Fig 8.10] the same architectural dialogue is expressed in well-preserved medieval buildings. Few other places in England so completely catch the flavour of the Middle Ages. On a slightly larger scale, the Altstadt in Landshut in Bavaria [Fig 9.2] demonstrates the same aesthetic arrangement. What at first appears to be a simple composition comprises at least four overlapping harmonic relations, the most obvious being the two basic architectural elements, houses and cathedral.

Fig 9.2
Altstadt, Landshut,
Bavaria

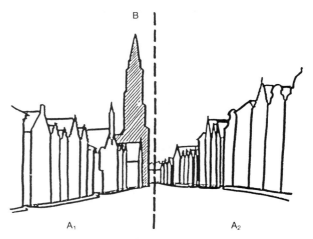

To achieve a clear binary relationship, the mind will suppress the differences in the houses A_1 and A_2, 'chunking' them so that their combined weight can be set against the spectacular tower and spire. Although tower B cannot compete in purely visual terms, it has powerful symbolic weight, and its sheer size generates an emotional response, a primitive reaction to gigantism. The scene may be judged aesthetically rewarding because the exceptional height of the tower combined with its symbolism makes it the harmonically dominant feature.

Like La Garenne and Ledbury, Landshut embodies a reconciliation between the fundamental axes of life – the horizontal, earthly axis and the vertical, heaven-bound thrust. Just as a Gothic cathedral integrates these two axes into a harmonious whole, so towns like Landshut or hamlets like Vale unify the polarities of life. This is the underlying orderliness, the ultimate orderliness; harmonic unity between the sacred and profane.

Altogether, the Altstadt is aesthetically satisfying because it accommodates harmonic relationships on several levels. In addition to the 'macro-aesthetics' of the scene, there are subordinate harmonic themes like the rich rhymes between the variegated buildings and the ordered colour in the facades. Thus what at first appears to be a simple view down a main street turns out to be an aesthetically rich orchestration of themes; rhyme, pattern, and binary clashes collaborate to produce harmony as complex as baroque music.

Aesthetic 'amplitude' is further increased by contours. At Lincoln, the sacred centre is also the 'high place', the primordial meeting place with deity. The dialectic between the sacred and the profane is raised to epic heights in the view along The Strait towards the magnificent central tower of the cathedral. Symbolic enhancement gives the cathedral the edge in the counterbalancing of informational weight to produce one of Europe's outstanding examples of urban harmony [Fig 9.3].

Fig 9.3
View along The Strait,
Lincoln

Fig 9.4
View of the Cathedral at
Quimper, Brittany

Closed vistas are among the most 'picturesque' urban situations
which suggest an aesthetic clash of opposites, as exemplified by
the tranquil Breton city of Quimper. There is a beautiful medieval
view towards the cathedral [Fig 9.4] unimpaired by the fact that the
elegant twin spires are a nineteenth century addition. At city scale,
the same aesthetic formula applies in places as different as Rouen
and Florence where great cathedrals dominate the secular
buildings, asserting the supremacy of the Faith.

But, as we have seen already, harmonic dialogue can be
encountered in ordinary situations when, for instance, we turn a
corner and are presented with a pleasing clash of friendly

Fig 9.5
Chateau, Josselin,
Brittany

opposites. This happens in Josselin, a small Breton town
dominated by an excellently preserved chateau. Round a corner
on the approach to the river, the towers of the chateau come into
view [Fig 9.5], establishing an immediate contrast with the town
architecture.

The chateau derives its perceptual weight from visual intricacy and
symbolic association. On both counts it is 'heavier' than the simple
vernacular buildings, but individuals will respond to it differently
becase of the symbolic content. Whereas there may be a broad
consensus about the relative weights of multiplexity, attribution of
symbolic weight varies according to personal experience and

Fig 9.6
Bootham Bar, York

attitude. The same scene viewed in 1795 by a member of the French Revolutionary Council would have had a very different aesthetic impact because of the aristocratic associations of the chateau, making it an unacceptable symbol of tyranny. For the average town hunter today, it is simply 'picturesque'.

Although there is contrast in form and symbolism, there is also a large measure of affinity. Local materials have a strong unifying influence; there is rhyme between roofs and chimneys, and a consistency in the rate of visual incident across the scene. Above all, there is a clear 'Frenchness' about the architecture; style reduces uncertainty. Thus contrasting principal elements are bound together within an overall pattern.

So far, the situations discussed have been relatively straightforward. But what happens in the case of a popular view of York Minster over Bootham Bar [Fig 9.6]? There are four main classes of information: statue, gate, houses and Minster, and the mind intuitively starts to prioritise. The main binary opposition is the sacred versus the secular, so the secular elements are chunked to create an aesthetic equation. The Minster prevails because of its mass, height and symbolic overtones. Further down the hierarchy there are other pairings with harmonic potential, such as the dialectic between 'hereness' and 'thereness'. (This aesthetic dimension will be considered more fully later.) Then there is the statue and its nodal strength within the square. Bootham Bar has evolved; other places are the result of acts of will, such as the Capitol in Rome.

When Michelangelo was commissioned in 1538 to reorganise the administrative centre of Rome, the Capitoline Hill was an arbitrary collection of medieval buildings. Two existing palaces, the Palazzo del Senatore and the Palazzo dei Conservatori, set the constraints for the plan. Under Michelangelo's direction the assymetrical Palazzo del Senatore was completely refashioned into a Renaissance building, its off-centre tower replaced by a similar design on the central axis. The Palazzo dei Conservatori was retained, even though its axis was at 82 degrees to the principal axis generated by the Palazzo del Senatore. Michelangelo clothed this building also in classical form and, to complete the composition, sited a symmetrically disposed palazzo opposite to the Palazzo dei Conservatori. By maintaining the same angle of inclination to the main axis in the new Capitoline Museum, he created one of the most powerful and aesthetically exciting ensembles of the Italian Renaissance [Fig 9.7]. The Capitoline

Fig 9.7
Campidoglio, Rome

Museum was completed by Rainaldi to Michelangelo's design. The statue of Marcus Aurelius was placed at the intersection of the axes, intensifying the sense of centripetal space.

The scene 'works' aesthetically because there is just the right displacement of weight between the dominant and the subordinate. The Palazzo dei Senatori has a dominant central position, and its scale and importance are underscored by the tower and ceremonial flight of steps. The two flanking palazzi have identical elevations to the piazza, and so their visual complexity is reduced by redundancy. (The towers of Lincoln Cathedral are an aesthetic parallel.) The three buildings are bound together by giant Corinthian pilasters which articulate and unite the space with their powerful rhythm. Other classical motifs reinforce the rule of pattern. Though not completed until 1655, the Campidoglio testifies to the genius of a man who was not only a great painter, sculptor, and architect, but also a supreme urban designer.

Between the historic and the contemporary

Binary clash is most obvious when new architecture is placed alongside familiar buildings. We tend instinctively to deplore the new because of the demands it makes on our ability to reduce complexity to orderliness – our 'orienting reflex'.

When Sir Christopher Wren added an extensive wing to Hampton Court Palace he made no stylistic concessions to Tudor building. Nevertheless, it is a harmonious addition because his design had certain fundamental links with the existing. It was earth-bound, wall architecture, constructed of the same materials in roughly the same ratios, bringing it within the limits of 'likeness tempered with difference'. Nowadays the architect has at his disposal a much wider vocabulary of form due to the development of modern materials, which allow buildings to be conceived of such visual lightness that they seem transient and ethereal.

Two contemporary additions to historic buildings which conveniently occur in adjacent Oxford colleges illustrate the constrast between traditional and high-tech 'slippery' architecture. One is the addition to St John's College (referred to in Chapter 8 in the context of binary harmony), which is wholly contemporary and yet maintains continuity with history. The Sir Thomas White building is devoid of historical references but nevertheless relates to existing college buildings in its earth-bound emphasis and stability, which suggest permanence.

A mark of quality in a building is its ability to relate successfully to different environments. From one aspect, the Sir Thomas White building interacts agreeably with the older buildings of the College. Viewed from St John's gardens [see Fig 8.17], the effect of perspective breaks up the regularity of the rhythm and heightens the dialogue between architecture and nature. This degree of harmony between nature and artefact compares well with anything produced in eighteenth century England. Finally, the building can be seen in relation to the Oxford townscape. Whilst it can be glimpsed from St Giles, it forms a major element of the streetscape of Museum Road [Fig 9.8]. In each case it enriches the city.

Fig 9.8
St John's College, Oxford
(Museum Road)

This is architecture of the highest quality, striking a harmonious relationship on numerous levels – dominant element to subordinate, solid to void, frame to glazing, independence of the parts to integrity of the whole, new building to old, architecture to nature. At the same time its geometric proportions are exactly right and it has all been executed with careful attention to detail. This building will age with dignity and elegance.

It is interesting that the St John's building shares Museum Road with some recent additions to Keble College by Ahrends Burton & Koralek [Fig 9.9]. The architects were faced with the challenge of providing accommodation for fellows, graduates and undergraduates within a constricted site. A reasonable solution was to build rooms along the boundary wall to Blackhall Road. Whereas Arup Associates maintained the same architectural expression whether the context was college or city, ABK have achieved the maximum possible contrast between the external elevation to Blackhall Road and the College aspect. The former is a massive turretted brick wall evocative of Carcassonne. Slit windows, just wide enough for a bowman, provide the only visual outlet to the street. This stern defensive wall represents the antithesis of the polychromatic playfulness of Butterfield's architecture in the main College buildings. At the same time it suggests that the College wishes to have no intercourse with the City.

Fig 9.9
Keble College, Oxford

Fig 9.10
C & A Store, High Street,
Exeter

Internally the architecture changes abruptly from brick rampart to a serpentine glass wall. At ground floor level, the glass wall billows out in a sensuous curve to provide a common-room, bar, kitchen, TV room, toilets, and launderette. Perhaps it was the intention of the architects to create restrained, reflective architecture which would not detract from the Butterfield buildings, but the result is an uncompromising essay in 'modern' architecture which shares no common ground with the existing buildings. It is the ultimate in bipolarity, which needs sufficient intermediate space if it is to work. Some might argue that critical distancing has been achieved here; others that there is architectural discord. It is certainly on the borderline.

How to fail in trying to marry new and old is illustrated by two examples of juxtaposed modern and historic architecture. The first is in the High Street, Exeter [Fig 9.10], where the C & A store has been extended to take the building round a corner. The original C & A store is a flamboyant Tudor-style timber frame building, a powerful visual accent in the High Street. Because presumably they did not want to compete with this Elizabethan-style *tour de force*, the architects decided to make the extension as neutral as possible. What they failed to realise is that blank walls generate visual weight. The result is that two powerful but incompatible systems of information are forced into an unnatural marriage. The result is severe dissonance; the likeness tempered with difference rule has been violated.

In the United States of America, the Conservation lobby has to contend with commercial priorities, which tend to overrule all other considerations. Philadelphia, like Boston, has still managed to conserve a bit of history where it does not get in the way of 'progress'. Where it does interfere with 'realty maximisation' we get the kind of solution of which, no doubt, the Penn Mutual Company is proud [Fig 9.11]. Its tower lunges over the remains of a Georgian facade as though triumphant over a slain victim!

Fig 9.11
Penn Mutual Tower,
Philadelphia

Sometimes calamitous juxtapositions seem to occur by accident. When inserting a building close to a historic edifice of character and quality, extra sensitivity is required – a point illustrated by default in a recent addition to Dale Street, Liverpool. The centrepiece of this part of the city is undoubtedly the elegant eighteenth century town hall, most of which was designed by John Wood [Fig 9.12]. Directly opposite, a vigorously modelled glass-walled building collides with the portico of the town hall when viewed from the south. The zig-zag motif is inherently aggressive, and wholly alien to the classical serenity of Wood's masterpiece. Perhaps this clash of uncoordinated systems was not predicted as it passed through the development control filter. It should be a lesson to advocates of *laissez-faire* planning.

Fig 9.12
Dale Street, Liverpool

We noted in Chapter 2 how successfully certain West German
buildings of the 1970s have responded to their ancient neighbours.
The present decade has also generated some excellent examples
of concord between old and new. Two instances can be seen in
Frankfurt, where villas flanking the river Main have been
transformed into exhibition galleries. The first is the Fine Arts
Gallery by Meier, which encompasses the villa without
undermining its architectural completeness. It is a masterpiece of
sensitivity which creates enough tension to be strident yet
harmonious. The same is true of the Architecture Exhibition
Gallery by Ungers farther along the river.

Chapter 10   The Charging of Space

Space is a significant contributor to the aesthetic equation, at times seeming to be highly charged with energy. This was proved by Michelangelo on the ceiling of the Sistine Chapel when he distanced the finger of God from the hand of Adam. Across this space leaps the spark of creation. It is an arcing of energy between the divine and the profane, locking them together in eternal partnership. In the case of cities, it is the space within them which gives life to architecture.

To think of space as something positive, as real and variable as solid objects, may require a shift of mental stance. Normally we perceive space as something negative into which objects are placed – a kind of Newtonian space in which dimensions and angles are the sum of its significance. However, space only becomes a reality when there are visible yardsticks to give it definition; therefore the identity of such perceived space will relate to the encompassing or defining objects.

Rudolf Arnheim proposes[10] that the space between buildings is charged with energy which varies according to the nature and proximity of the facades of buildings which surround it, that space has an infinitely variable 'density'. (The analogy of architecture as a generator of a force field across space has also been suggested by Portoghesi in *Le inibizioni dell'architettura moderna*, 1974[11].)

Space dimensions will obviously influence the character of an urban area such as a city square. The space:architecture relationship will determine whether it has a sense of security or of wilderness, whether it encourages or inhibits human transactions. (This question is discussed fully in *The Syntax of Cities*[6].) Scale, architectural expression, and spatial separation each create different intensities of spatial energy, or different space densities [Fig 10.1]. At the same time the perceived density of interspace B will depend upon whether it has been approached from space A or C. These three spaces may be said to possess different and

Fig 10.1
The 'density' of space

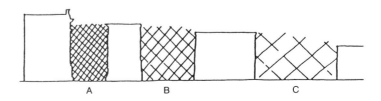

A   B   C

variable levels of energy, depending on separating distance, visual complexity and the nature of adjacent spaces. The potency of such space is better understood when we remember Einstein's conclusion[10]: 'We speak of "matter" when the concentration of energy is high, and of "fields" when the concentration is weaker. But in that case the difference between matter and field appears to be quantitative rather than qualitative.'

If the mind is able to energise objects, it will be equally adept at investing space with energy, and the difference between buildings and the spaces around and between them is one of degree rather than kind.

Space can also have a critical effect on the relationship between buildings. In an earlier book[8], and in Chapter 2 here, I argued that human beings need frequent exposure to surprise and even shock if they are to hold their ground in terms of mental performance, and that architecture plays an important role in this respect. Every town and city needs its quota of 'pacer' buildings which challenge established norms and shake up our whole architecture schema.

This psychological objective is not incompatible with harmonic values. Where there is maximum amplitude between contrary systems, space is a prime factor in deciding aesthetic success. Creative coexistence between opposites seems to depend upon the distance separating them, as though there has to be space sufficient to allow the 'energy field' of each building or feature to dissipate, whilst maintaining its visual association. If the distance is inadequate, the energy waves of the protagonists clash and conflict to produce high complexity or dissonance. Space has to be introduced to moderate the complexity to an aesthetically acceptable level.

Through the ages, architects have intuitively recognised the reconciling potential of space, especially in the later Renaissance. Palladio's S Giorgio Maggiore [see Fig 7.8] is a masterpiece in this respect, its campanile perfectly distanced from the body of the church. And some twentieth century architects have been equally aware of the need to optimise space to alleviate the stress of conflict between opposites.

Le Corbusier pioneered many ways of exploiting critical distance, including the practice of raising architecture above ground on pilotti. The rational argument was that it freed the space at ground level; the aesthetic reason was that it established a critical void between the crisp white cuboid architecture of the Modern Movement and the contrasting 'unruly' element of the ground, with all its underlying symbolism. Who could possibly conceive of the Villa Savoye at Poissy resting directly on mother earth? The same applies to the Unité d'Habitacion at Marseilles; architecture and nature must be separated by a critical space. On the other hand, the pilgrimage chapel at Ronchamp is perfectly married to the ground; the effect of mass and solidity is conveyed by visually thick battered walls and small windows (see *Architecture and the Human Dimension*[8]).

Space can become an almost tangible element of architecture. No building illustrates this better than the Taj Mahal at Agra [Fig 10.2]. The mausoleum would be naked without the four minarets which complete the composition; the space which they encompass is almost palpable. The same phenomenon commonly occurs between the towers and spires of a medieval cathedral; the space between them seems trapped and charged with particles of the architecture.

Fig 10.2
Taj Mahal

Critical distance in the wider environment

In music, silence can be as important as sound. The space between musical phrases is critical in establishing the proper relationship between them so that they are appreciated for their individual quality yet simultaneously perceived as essential parts of a whole. The same happens in painting. Two patterns of complexity need to be distanced on the canvas so that each can express its meaning and yet can enter into a dialectical relationship with the other. Between them is silence in paint.

The question of critical distance is a part of everyday experience. We encounter it in the placing of ornaments on a shelf or pictures on a wall. We make conscious judgements about the optimum proximity of objects. In emotional terms, the most significant aspect of critical distance concerns people. We are said to inhabit a bubble of 'personal space' which a stranger may not enter. There is an agreed critical distance to be maintained in social intercourse.

Buildings too have a kind of 'personal' space which relates to their scale and status, and is indicated by their decoration. This has implications for the critical size of a piazza as determined by the scale and richness of its encompassing buildings. The Piazza del Campo in Siena is an example of a perfect marriage between architecture and space [see Fig 4.3]. Most of the encircling buildings are high enough to give a sense of enclosure without being oppressive; their facades are dignified and elegant but sufficiently low key not to detract from the great Palazzo Pubblico. This splendid building needs generous space in which to discharge its energy, but also sufficient weight of surrounding buildings to strike a harmonic balance in terms of relative complexity. At Siena the balance has been perfectly judged. In a smaller piazza the palazzo and campanile would have been overwhelming, even sinister. In a larger space, the majesty of the building would have evaporated.

Bernini also judged perfectly the scale and shape of the piazza in front of Maderna's magnificent facade to St Peter's in Rome. If buildings had been allowed to crowd in closer to the basilica, its personal space would have been clearly violated. And Michelangelo precisely captured the correct ratio of building to space in the Capitol. The Museum and Palazzo dei Conservatori exhibit just the right mixture of mass and complexity in relation to the piazza and the focal Palazzo del Senatore [see Fig 9.7].

In a different key and style, the Hauptmarkt in Trier [Fig 10.3] is an example of optimised space; the enclosing buildings are the right size for the area of the square. Presiding over it is the typically Germanic tower of the Church of St Gangolf, the combination of its bulk, visual complexity and symbolic weight establishing a critical amount of dominance in an aesthetic contest with secular buildings. The dimensions of the square are sufficient to absorb the force fields of the church and secular buildings, while the tower itself is prominent enough to be a strong point of focus for the whole

Fig 10.3
Trier
The Hauptmarkt,
Simeonstrasse, viewed
from Portanigraplatz

of the Simeonstrasse. Seen from the Portanigraplatz it provides an appropriate termination to the space initiated by the great Roman Gate. Thus it performs a crucial role in relation to the nuclear space of the Hauptmarkt and the linear space of the Simeonstrasse. It is also a fine instance of urban binary clash.

The energy field of a space can change significantly with the insertion of a new building. This is demonstrated by The Moor in Sheffield, a typical post-war shopping street which was rebuilt soon after the Blitz when architectural imagination was thinly spread and planning control resembled an iron fist. At the end of The Moor there was no visual stop; the sense of city-ness evaporated. But recently a vigorously-modelled multi-storey government office block was completed which closes the vista; space is contained and The Moor has achieved a new coherence as a linear piazza [Fig 10.4]. The whole street has come to life as a pedestrian precinct complete with bandstand, market stalls, and the occasional repentance man. The Manpower Services

Fig 10.4
The Moor, Sheffield

Commission building designed by the Property Services Agency is clad in a warm red brick. Clearly a building belonging to the 1970s, with allusions to the ziggurat, it contrasts with the buildings of The Moor but not so as to be dissonant. The 'impossible' has happened: The Moor has become aesthetically rewarding!

Perhaps Italian Renaissance architecture can teach us the most about the pragmatic optimisation of space. We have referred to the Campidoglio, and the ordering by Bernini of the Piazza of St Peter's in Rome. There are also the marvellously extravagant Spanish Steps which transform the approach to S Trinità del Monte, and the Piazza del Popolo which enhances a principal entrance to the city. In Florence, the extraordinary space created by the Palazzo Uffizi links the Piazza della Signoria with the banks of the Arno.

The Uffizi, sited between two cliffs of agitated architecture, is an example of a deliberate violation of the 'law' of proximity. The rapid rhythms and assertive modelling of the facades call for much greater distancing to allow their force fields to discharge, and this constraint results in the tensile nature of the space. Designed as an office block to house the Medici bureaucracy, this highly mannered building seems deliberately to provoke stress, more so than any other built during the Renaissance. It generates thrust in either direction.

Fig 10.5
Piazza S Marco, Venice
(*The basilica as it is* **not**.)

Proximity becomes more critical the greater the contrast. The campanile in the Piazza of S Marco [Fig 10.5] would be totally absurd if it were an integral part of the basilica facade. It works aesthetically because it has been distanced from the basilica – a rhyme with S Giorgio Maggiore.

Architecture can itself succeed as an analogy of space. Denys Lasdun related his adventurous concept for the Royal College of Physicians to a classical Nash building in Regents Park across a gap of dark-tinted glass curtain-walling so devoid of features that it functions as space. Indeed it almost intensifies the idea of space – a kind of enriched negativity. Effectively, critical distancing has been achieved, allowing a classical building to retain its aesthetic integrity alongside what is still a pacer building, and creating a dialogue between architectural opposites.

The effect of space can be enhanced by symbolism. One of the most successful examples of the cohabitation of opposites is at Queens' College, Cambridge, where Powell & Moya have sited an elegant, almost classically-disciplined complex of buildings on the opposite side of the river Cam to the mainly medieval College buildings [Fig 10.6]. Water creates a psychological divide more profound than the actual distance implies; the act of crossing a river resonates with archetypal references. It is the psychological distance which counts when making aesthetic judgements.

Fig 10.6
Queens' College,
Cambridge

Though the architectural styles are at first sight incompatible, the augmented distance between them is sufficient to bring about a constructive dialogue through the creative clash of opposites, not only because each retains its territorial integrity but also because there is compatibility of scale.

What is it then that determines the appropriate distance between objects? Arnheim suggests[10] that architectural structures control each other's outreach the way countries stabilize their boundaries on the political map by power exerted from both sides. He offers the analogy of free-floating magnets whose interacting force fields produce equilibrium and thus correct distancing. Pursuing this analogy, the question of correct distance seems to be a matter of establishing equilibrium in the visual field. 'Proxemics' as defined by Arnheim concerns the 'proper distance prescribed by the nature of a thing', although the question as to *how* the nature of a thing actually determines the proper distance is left unanswered. It has something to do with establishing the correct balance between remoteness and connectedness. The interspace should be sufficient to enable proper perception of the respective buildings yet not so extensive as to undermine the links between them. In other words, there has to be enough space to allow a building maximum autonomy consistent with its being an integral part of the larger urban milieu. It must be possible to apprehend both partness and wholeness, and thus it is a matter of fundamental aesthetic importance.

What determines the appropriate space surrounding a building is a matter of size, shape and rate of visual complexity. The featureless megaliths of a street in Houston Texas, for example, can crowd together without a sense of encroachment because they have little individuality and a low rate of visual complexity. On the other hand, an idiosyncratic building such as Wright's Guggenheim Museum [Fig 10.7] needs to distance itself from the bland apartment blocks of Fifth Avenue. It requires generous space in which to discharge its energy. Not far away, on the waterfront of Manhattan, an ensemble of colonial building fights for breath at the feet of the giants of curtain-walled commerce [Fig 10.8].

The subject of appropriate distancing concerns some of the most subtle aspects of aesthetic perception – for example, the ratio between likeness and difference. It is affected by the 'density' of intervening space which in turn is determined by the complexity of

Fig 10.7
Guggenheim Museum,
New York

Fig 10.8
Waterfront, Manhattan

the buildings along its boundary. This is a matter of symbolic as
well as visual complexity. Cathedrals require more space than
banks, city halls more than insurance offices. In this respect, the
city fathers of Boston have to be congratulated for allocating
appropriate space to the boldly modelled City Hall. So does the
French Minister of Culture for providing space for fire-eaters and
the like alongside the Pompidou Centre.

Critical distance is also relevant in the positioning of the major elements within a building, for example, the traditional siting of twin western towers in a great church. The cathedral at Montreal is not a success in this respect: the towers are so far apart and slender that it is not clear whether they are large corner turrets to a defensive wall or elements of a single cohesive composition. The problem is compounded by the fact that the combined visual weight of the towers does not add up to an adequate counterbalance to the basilica unit; they are perceived as 'weak'.

In contrast, the western towers of Köln Cathedral appear to be crushing the basilica element out of existence. Their gargantuan scale and extraordinary proximity result in an uncomfortable composition. A substantially greater distance between them would have allowed the basilica component to assert itself more strongly. But York Minster presents one of the most serene western elevations; its towers are correctly distanced, and outweigh the basilica termination by the optimum harmonic margin [Fig 10.9].

Fig 10.9
Cathedrals compared

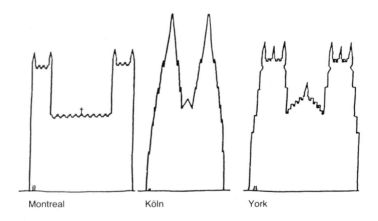

Montreal   Köln   York

Architecture, space and time

Much of the appeal of historic towns lies in the fact that they both inspire and reward exploration. An important element in the aesthetic inventory of towns is the accumulation of aesthetic experiences over time. As in music or literaure, the various sub-clashes are held in medium-term memory in the hope that they will form an aesthetic whole considerably greater than the sum of the parts.

A space like the Piazza del Campo in Siena [see Fig 4.3] has enormous intrinsic appeal. But even so, after a time one becomes increasingly drawn to the glistening white campanile and dome of the Cathedral high up in the distance. The Cathedral square dominated by the exuberant facade of the Duomo is quite different in scale and character from the Piazza del Campo. Together these piazzas mark the climax of the city. But the total aesthetic impact of Siena is also intensified by the cavernous streets shaded by heavy cornices and the variety of minor piazzas which punctuate one's progress. Siena is a monumental work of art comprising buildings, space and time. Perhaps this was the golden age of the art of creating cities; linear themes and majestic spaces orchestrate into a unity of epic proportions. In such places mortals may fancy that they rub shoulders with the gods.

Chapter 11   **Philosophies of Decoration**

The main course of the argument has now been mapped out, so it may be worthwhile to consider some of its tributaries, for example the often contentious matter of decoration, where architecture and morality traditionally clash.

Despite the re-evaluation of the Modern Movement, it is still normal to rate the importance of a building according to the amount of decoration enriching it. On the whole, the inhabitants of towns and cities have refused to be intimidated by the kind of architecture which is more medicinal than entertaining. Yet the architecture of asceticism was not invented by the pioneers of modern architecture.

Puritans have always been suspicious of decoration. An earlier great 'modernist', St Bernard of Clairvaux, condemned the excesses of Romanesque sculptors which, he feared, would deflect the brothers from the contemplation of divine truth: 'There appears on all sides so rich and amazing a variety of forms that it is more delightful to read the marble than the manuscripts and to spend the whole day in admiring these things, piece by piece, rather than in meditation on the divine law.'

So it seems that architecture must supply 'firmness' and 'commodity', but not 'delight'. In the case of the Middle Ages however, we should remember that Bernard's philosophy, combined with the rationalism of Peter Abelard, provided the inspiration for the amazing aesthetic achievement of the Île de France in the early twelfth century. Perhaps we need puritans to get us back on the rails.

In any case, we derive pleasure from decoration. We may admire the dexterity and patience of the artist, or simply enjoy being mesmerised by the complexity. But apart from this self-indulgent aspect, there is evidence that decoration has a definite role in architecture, serving both aesthetic and symbolic requirements.

Symbolism and decoration

The use of decoration is a way of signalling status. In human terms, rank is denoted by the 'weight' of decoration applied to symbolic dress. In buildings, the special importance of, say, the town hall is clearly communicated by its decoration (nowadays in the sublimated form of expensive materials or idiosyncratic shapes, such as Hillingdon Civic Centre [see Fig 8.11]. But the town hall must not eclipse the cathedral, so even the mighty Palazzo Pubblico in Siena yields to the marble splendour of the cathedral. The hierarchical profile of the historic town can be gauged not only from the size of the buildings in relation to the centre, but also by the rate of decoration on their facades.

In most cases, the symbolic and aesthetic aspects of decoration overlap and intertwine. The Greeks perfected a method of using the decorative potential of mouldings to sharpen the form of a building and convey the importance of special elevations such as the main portico. Decoration on buildings confers status on people – for example, the main entrance to a stately home proclaims by its embellishment that it is intended only for use by equals and betters. Others use the tradesmen's entrance, a simple opening with a plain door. Today the high-tech office block has a prestigious entrance complex with a guard to ensure that access is only allowed to those who appear to be of appropriate standing. (This frequently causes problems for architectural students when trying to see buildings; the sartorial signals of students are traditionally calculated to confuse.)

This is not the only symbolic function of decoration. In the Middle Ages, the laws of sacred geometry were drawn in space by shafts, ribs and string courses. Theological truth as well as political and commercial advertisement were communicated through carving and the exquisite art of the glazier. Chartres above all embodies the generative principles of sacred geometry and divine luminosity – light enriched by innumerable panels of coloured glass [Fig 11.1].

The rolled steel joist may seem to be light years away from the delicate carving of the medieval craftsman, yet this too can be a form of symbolic decoration. When Mies van der Rohe was compelled by fire regulations to encase steel in concrete, he used bare steel simply as a symbol of structure. The Seagram Building in New York has now become an archetype of symbolic functionalism – a somewhat deceitful symbolism, since uncased steel is structurally unacceptable in most instances. It is also arguable that the peripteral columns round a Greek temple were only partially functional; for example, in the Parthenon the weight of the roof was largely supported on the inner walls of the naos.

Fig 11.1
Cathedral of Notre Dame,
Chartres

The colonnade created an interspace between the sacred temple
and the secular world. It also gave the building a robust aesthetic
dimension in terms of metrical rhythm, marking out its proportional
module.

There are many other ways in which decoration can be used to point to something beyond itself. Not only can it signify importance, power and probity, it can also convey political and social realities. It was through decoration that Michelangelo expressed his revolt against the norms of the time. Today, revolt and cynicism are expressed more robustly, as in the university of Louvain buildings by Lucien Kroll, or Domenig's bank in Vienna. Humour too has traditionally been transmitted through decoration, particularly the figurative sculpture of the Middle Ages. Medieval carvers settled many an old score with the chisel.

We should remember that decoration is enjoyed for its own sake, whether it occurs in the complexities of a Gothic west front, a tightly-packed medieval street, or even the scintillating nocturnal lightscape of Las Vegas. A saturation of complexity stimulates primitive pleasure – which may or may not have anything to do with aesthetics – but when we search for order in these mêlées of visual incident we are seeking evidence which will convert the experience into one which is undoubtedly aesthetic.

Maybe this appetite for intensive visual complexity is related to the primitive pleasure we derive from the exotic. It symbolises life conducted at a fast pace, a massive accumulation of energy, but at the same time an extension of human expertise and dexterity. Saturation decoration usually testifies to a gigantic corporate human effort as, for instance, in the west front of Rheims Cathedral [see Fig 7.4]. Beneath our veneer of sophistication, we are all attracted to decoration, even though we may have been trained to call it 'vulgar'.

I have often argued that there is a place for exotic complexity in our sanitised city centres. At least open markets are now being admitted to architecturally ordered space, but stalls must not break ranks, and canopies must conform to a uniform pattern of tasteful colours. In the excellently rejuvenated Covent Garden galleria everything is in 'good taste' – even the buskers have to pass an audition!

To take the subject further, we may relate decoration to the main tenets of our argument, dealing with it first as an agent of harmony.

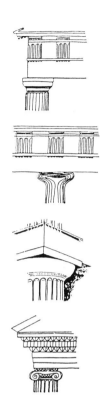

Fig 11.2

Decoration as a harmonising agent

Decoration can play a crucial role in establishing the ascendancy of unity over particularity. The great leap forward in this regard was achieved by the Greeks in the sixth century BC. The Greek temple of this time was a supreme achievement in reconciling the identity of the parts and the overriding integrity of the whole. Decoration and detailing were employed with great finesse to ease the transition from one plane to another, from side to front, roundness to squareness, and so on.

The junction between the column and the robust entablature which it supported represents one of the highest achievements in the aesthetics of reconciliation. The Doric capital can be viewed in several ways [Fig 11.2]. The most obvious is that it represents a swelling of the column under pressure, taking the strain, so to speak, of the weight of the entablature. The triple rings or annulets reinforce this impression of stress at the critical point. The profile of the capital, the echinus, varied from temple to temple, but in every case it prescribed a delicate and subtle curve, 'offering' the column to the entablature.

The fluting to the Doric column served to reduce the perceived weight of the column as well as to pronounce the basic building module. At the same time it emphasised its roundness; a rhythm of fluting enhances perception of the form of the column. But maybe there was a further aesthetic purpose. The cylindrical form of the column was inconsistent with the strong lineality of the remainder of the temple architecture, from the crepidoma base to the entablature above the columns, so lines were drawn on the columns to establish a common denominator with the predominant lineality; likeness modifying difference.

In the natural course of artistic evolution, the classical economy of the Doric architects was gradually undermined by a preference for decoration for its own sake. In the Corinthian capital, which developed in parallel with the Doric, the transition from vertical to horizontal no longer glides through the sensuous curve of the echinus but becomes blurred in a profusion of acanthus leaves. However, there is sophistication in the entablature of the Corinthian (and Ionic) orders. Whereas the architrave in Doric temples was plain, the Ionic and Corinthian orders showed a stepped section. This meant that the apparent weight of this massive stone element was greatly reduced by two lines emphasised by shadow.

Another Greek design innovation which has endured is the pediment. It is such a logical and inevitable way of tying a gable end to the sides of a building that now we take it for granted. But it was a brilliant invention which took the cornice round the profile of the gable, thus creating a triangle which could be filled with sculpture as well as achieving unity between side and front. In the pediment, the Greek architects created the single most enduring feature in the history of architecture, and in the tympanum of the pediment, Greek sculptors like Pheidias achieved the perfect marriage between architecture and decoration. These artists gave real architectural meaning to decoration, proving that it is not only relevant to architecture but is part of its fundamental rationale. This conflicts with Roger Scruton's view[13] that 'ornament is nothing more than detail which can be enjoyed and appreciated independently of any dominant aesthetic whole'. Certainly ornament can be this, but to say that it is nothing more is to do injustice to the Greeks, as well as their medieval and Renaissance successors.

There is a fine distinction between decoration and detail. Many contemporary architects get away with decoration under the guise of 'detailing'. Both are frequently involved in easing the transition between contrasting elements, such as window and wall.

Fig 11.3

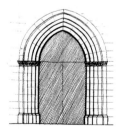

In Greek architecture an opening is often emphasised by shallow stepped mouldings, as in the architrave of the pediment, in preparation for a change in the condition of the wall. Romanesque and Gothic architects stepped the wall inwards, first by pronounced stages and later by delicately carved multiple mouldings [Fig 11.3]. The shape of the opening was thus declared several times in the solid wall before the situation changed to a void; the transition from solid to void was 'softened' by several rehearsals. Similarly, the decorative treatment of entrances is not merely symbolic, it also eases the transition from outside to inside. The blurring of spatial boundaries was one of the aesthetic preoccupations of the strand of the Modern Movement led by Frank Lloyd Wright and since replicated in countless office atria.

Perhaps the ultimate transition is between building and sky, of particular importance to medieval architects. Gothic cathedrals dissolved into space in a flurry of spires, pinnacles and crockets. The openwork spires of cathedrals such as Strasbourg, Freiburg and Regensburg were a marvellous way of achieving symbolic reconciliation between the material and spiritual, the unity of the earth with the cosmos. The decorated gables of the Hanseatic architecture of Holland and Germany and their playful mutations at Landshut celebrate the union of earth and sky with bravura. But as we have seen, it was the French who achieved supremacy in energising the roofscape in the chateaux of the Loire Valley.

Nowadays we are used to seeing clean-cut buildings which slice the sky with surgical precision. Yet this aspect of the modern style is gradually being eroded, for example by Powell & Moya. The roofscape of the Cripps building at St John's, Cambridge seems to disintegrate into the sky – perhaps a sublimated form of decoration. In Cripps Court at Queens' College nearby [see Fig 10.6] the same architects have punctuated the roofline with transparent structures of various shapes which dissolve the solidity of the building and reconcile the crisp 'classical' architecture with the ever-changing skyscape filtered through glass. At the same time there is rhyme with the variegated roofscape of Cambridge as a whole.

In the service of two masters

In the continual war between order and confusion, decoration can serve on either side; it can add to the coherence of a building and ease the transition between contrary elements or it can conceal orderliness in the interests of heightening complexity.

Strip the Colosseum in Rome of its applied half-columns and entablatures and you have an amorphous and overwhelming hulk. As it is, the scale is broken down by the rhythms of columns and arches horizontally, and entablatures acting like ring beams vertically. Decoration has enhanced its form and given it elegance. Perhaps it is this modulation of surfaces that enables the mind to comprehend its form and establish its scale – in other words, to perceive overriding orderliness.

Fig 11.4
Bramhall Hall, Stockport,
Cheshire

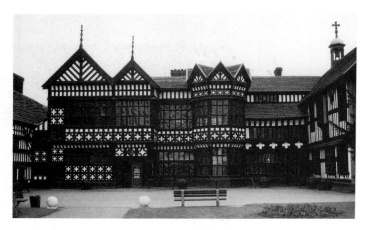

In the Renaissance, the same device of punctuating facades with applied columns or pilasters was commonplace. Corners were sometimes accentuated with double columns – a device used by Palladio as a kind of full-stop to an elevation. The unifying power of decoration was also evident in the late Middle Ages in Tudor architecture. At Bramhall Hall, Stockport [Fig 11.4], a vigorous pattern of mullions, transomes and quartrefoils integrates variegated shapes. This is aesthetic clash of a high order.

In the case of Amsterdam we have seen how a limited inventory of decorative motifs can give a powerful injection of orderliness. Colour too can contribute to the impression of order or diversity. If the colours are fairly consistent in terms of saturation and lightness, there is harmony (as evidenced by Tübingen or Landshut Figs 5.6, 9.2).

Towards confusion

Decoration may also be used to blur the clarity of form so as to heighten the challenge of discovering order behind the complexity. This is best seen in the interior of certain buildings.

It may seem perverse to link King's College, Cambridge [Fig 11.5] with the famous baroque pilgrimage church of Vierzehnheiligen in Franconia [Fig 11.6], yet they share the same philosophy of decoration. King's is widely regarded as the climax of that uniquely English phase of Gothic development, the Perpendicular style.

Whereas in the high Gothic of the thirteenth century, architectural elements are clearly defined and space mathematically transparent, Perpendicular architecture buries the anatomy of the building beneath a rapid rhythm of vertical shafts rising unhindered from floor to vault. There is no distinction between window and wall; the march of the mullions is relentless, giving the impression of *total* space. The climax occurs naturally in the vault, where ribs spread out into perfectly proportioned fans. Decoration triumphs over the logic of structure. This emphasis on creating a sense of total dynamic environment echoes the spirit of the baroque. There is a vibrant unity about this space, an electrifying harmony quite different from the serenity, repose and classical integrity of Chartres. Thus the link between King's College and the baroque-rococo Vierzehnheiligen is not too speculative.

Fig 11.6
Vierzehnheiligen,
Franconia
(*Pilgrimage Church of
the Fourteen Saints*)

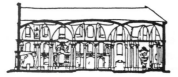
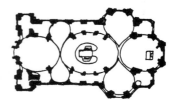

Nikolaus Pevsner's book *An Outline of European Architecture*[12] is an admirable and scholarly introduction to the subject of baroque architecture, and includes a chapter about this Church of the Fourteen Saints. Externally, Vierzehnheiligen appears a normal cruciform church, but on entering it any such expectations are immediately confounded – the whole spatial organisation is unconventional. The dominant feature is not the usual high altar but a nave altar of pure confectionery commemorating the fourteen saints. The white and gold rococo decoration conceals an architectural concept of great sophistication, a kind of fugue on the oval and circle. Three ovals mark out its length, the largest encompassing the fourteen saints. These are bisected by circles forming the main transepts, and vestigial western transepts which house additional altars. Whereas in traditional church design the crossing is the climax of the internal space, here it is marked by the junction of two ovals which are delicately curved in section. Consequently this conjunction of ovals marked by powerful double-curved ribs represents the lowest point in the longitudinal section of the church. The ribs prescribe a marvellous ogee curve, an aerial 'line of beauty'.

This supreme example of the art of Balthasar Neumann generates epic tension between the multiplexity of decoration and the logic of architectural form. The spatial system is subtle and has to be extracted from the exotic decoration. Some will only see it as a normal baroque church in which decoration is paramount, but those who are able to pierce the decoration and discover the orderliness that transcends the complexity are rewarded by a much higher form of aesthetic experience.

Integral binary harmony and decoration

The most obvious continuous dialogue which occurs in architecture is between window and wall, as discussed in Chapter 7. The permutations are innumerable, but the basic aesthetic condition remains the same – that it should be clear whether the wall or window element is dominant. The relative weight of one to the other can be significantly affected by decoration.

Fig 11.7

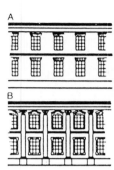

In elevation A of Fig 11.7, plain windows pierce a plain wall. If windows of the same size are embellished with surrounds and pediments and pilasters are placed between them, the change is remarkable (elevation B). The windows appear significantly larger in comparison with the wall. Why is this? Perhaps because the territory of the window has been made more important not only by the surrounds but also by the Corinthian pilasters, which create a 'bay' for the windows, extending their territory still further. So whilst the actual openings remain the same, the weight of the window element has been increased. Thus decoration can both significantly alter the perceptual weight of a feature and distort the perceived size.

A simplified version of this tactic has long been practised in vernacular architecture. The transformation it can effect on plain domestic architecture was demonstrated by David Harding when he was Town Artist to the Glenrothes Development Corporation, near Edinburgh. On his advice, coloured surrounds were added to the houses, and the visual quality of the place was dramatically enhanced. Decoration can do the same at roof level. Parapets, cornices, battlements and machicolation all add to the informational value of roof-ness – a fact now being vigorously exploited by the post-Modernists.

Decoration and the discrete binary aesthetic

Within this category, decoration may be used to create a concentration of interest within a lower key milieu. On the city scale, monuments, fountains and obelisks provide strategic accents which help to articulate the whole city. This is why Pope Sixtus V placed Egyptian obelisks at key points along pilgrimage processional routes.

The Great Clock in the rue Gros Horloge in Rouen [Fig 11.8] monopolises attention in either direction and brings the whole street to order. Even larger clocks adorn the stylish medieval gateways in Bern, Switzerland [Fig 11.9] in splendid contrast to the rather sombre buildings of the city centre. In Germany, the town hall is often the decorative climax of a community, and none more so than in Tübingen [see Fig 5.6].

Fig 11.8
Gros Horloge, Rouen

The deployment of materials

The way materials are used in a building can significantly alter the aesthetic balance. Historically, changes in materials have usually been a matter of necessity which subsequently developed into a decorative virtue. Today there is a multiplicity of materials available to the architect, and the temptation to use them cosmetically is strong. There is nothing inherently wrong with this, provided certain aesthetic parameters are recognised.

Fig 11.9
A gateway in Bern

The style associated with Sir Christopher Wren often consists of a
mixture of brick and stone. Perhaps economic constraints obliged
him to employ brick as his main building material and to confine
stone to porticos and dressings, but he transformed necessity into
the rich aesthetic vocabulary which is now associated with his
name. Buildings like the south and east elevations of Hampton
Court Palace and the Royal Hospital, Chelsea, excel partly
because of their inherent proportions and also because of the way
Wren deployed materials. In the first place he generally chose a
brick which would achieve maximum contrast in tone, colour and
texture with the dressed stone. Usually it was a glowing red
'rubbed' brick.

Secondly, he used stone for two purposes. It was obviously the appropriate material for prestigious elements in porticos, cupolas and niches, but it was also logical to use stone in more vulnerable parts of the building, such as corners and the surrounds to openings. Stone was much more durable than soft brick for exposed situations. What we perceive today as decoration was often conceived for practical reasons, and this in itself imposed a discipline upon the architect. The stone dressing of a Wren building seems totally appropriate, perhaps because we intuitively perceive the functional necessity underlying the change of materials.

The third characteristic of Wren's use of materials involves the aesthetics of informational weight. Wren invariably struck a harmonic ratio between the respective weights of the two principal materials which he employed. The stone of the quoins, window surrounds, cornice, balustrade and entablature would sometimes be the dominant material, especially since it was the vehicle for decoration. Its visual weight was supplemented by symbolic factors. In a building like the Royal Hospital at Chelsea, an elegant cupola crowns the portico, giving emphasis to the central focal feature and adding sufficient weight to proclaim dominance without tyranny.

In three respects therefore, Wren was expert in his use of materials. First, he sought maximum contrast so as to avoid ambiguity, confining himself to two principal materials. Secondly, the change to stone was frequently dictated by structural or symbolic necessity. Thirdly, the relative weighting between stone and brick achieved harmonic stability.

It is interesting to compare the Wren 'aesthetic' with the Cripps building at Selwyn College [Fig 11.10], which aspires to being included in the same genre. The principal materials are red brick and white stone or concrete with a quantity of exposed pebble aggregate. In a number of ways this building violates the rules which Wren tacitly established. In the first place, the stone dressings are used cosmetically and without any structural *raison d'être*. The design conforms to the box-and-panel style which was popular in the 1950s and early '60s. This is accentuated by the use of stone, which also serves to highlight the staircases and forms a boundary to a strip of white-rendered wall which erupts into an

Fig 11.10
Cripps Building, Selwyn
College, Cambridge

astonishing cantilevered penthouse. Perhaps the intention was to break up the roofline, but the result is calamitous top-heaviness, compounded by the structural illogicality of this feature.

The concrete panels add a further aesthetic complication. They are used to clad the sides of the 'box' in a way which is consonant with a framed building, whereas the brickwork on the face has the traditional load-bearing connotation. At the end of one elevation, the concrete cladding encroaches on to the facade in complete contradiction to the prevailing pattern. At ground level, the same concrete panels are used as infill to the colonnade where rooms replace the arcade. So this one material is used in three different situations, all of which are simultaneously visible. The same insensitivity towards the relationship between form and materials is evident in the college refectory, in which lack of coherence in shape is reinforced by a heavy-handed and irrational use of materials. The architect has used materials as if they were wallpaper.

Lucien Kroll, on the other hand, deliberately uses materials in an illogical manner. At the Brussels medical school he inserts random patches of brickwork into the concrete walls of the residential blocks [Fig 11.11]. Kroll seems to have difficulty in disciplining his sense of humour, with the result that he sometimes shocks, since normal aesthetic goals are replaced by symbolic statements often humorously expressed. There is more than just a coincidental link between Kroll and the marvellous inventions of Site Incorporated of New York. Both cause us to reshape our aesthetic criteria and enlarge our spectrum of aesthetic possibilities.

We have already noted how the rich variation in shape on the scale of a whole town can be unified by the homogenising effect of materials. The pink and buff stone of Assisi unifies the variegated shapes of the buildings to produce harmony between the works of man and nature. Texture and jointing can also have a decisive influence upon the aesthetic rating of buildings. The rate of visual complexity of a highly textured surface can change according to the angle of the sun. To a lesser extent, this occurs where there are deeply recessed joints. The colour and size of brick or stone jointing can have a decisive influence upon aesthetic performance. If jointing is too prominent, it can undermine the geometry of a building; pattern tends to usurp form. In using a variety of materials in a single building, the deciding aesthetic factor is the need for an unambiguous hierarchy of relationships. This is where Selwyn College fails and St John's College succeeds.

Fig 11.11
Medical school
residences, Brussels

A single wall material can impose unity upon a complex building, as proved by Gottfried Böhm in his Bensburg building [see Fig 8.13]. Board-shuttered concrete confers consistency of colour and texture upon a wild variety of shapes. The dramatic clash between wall and window is heightened by the virtual elimination of window frames. There is maximum amplitude between solid and void, strength and delicacy.

Currently there is a tempting array of materials available, but this creates the danger that too prodigal a use may undermine perception of wholeness. Materials should be so disposed as to establish a hierarchy of binary relationships to minimise aesthetic uncertainty and, at the same time, changes in materials may be most acceptable aesthetically when they have a logic based on structure and performance. This is not disguised nostalgia for the Modern Movement mandate that form must follow function; it simply acknowledges our intuitive sense of the appropriate and the inevitability of certain relationships.

Yet in some circumstances it might be entirely acceptable for an architect to violate expectations and erode the 'rightness' of things. This is the only way to break out of the tyranny of existing constraints and discover the promised land of a new rightness. Without prophets and iconoclasts, we would soon succumb to mental atrophy.

Chapter 12   Concerning 'Scale'

Another question which is at a tangent to the main argument concerns the meaning of perhaps the most commonly used word in architectural criticism – 'scale'. It is a fuzzy concept, broadly relating to achieving consistency between the various ingredients of a town milieu. Architects and planners tend to use 'scale' as a chameleon word which can change colour to suit the occasion. Its connotation often derives from instinct rather than reason. It might be possible to achieve a firmer definition if we analyse its aesthetic implications. After all, scale is to do with coherence; when architectural elements are said to be 'in scale' it usually means that they conform to the constraints of a superordinate pattern. So scale must be relevant to the concept of harmony.

The term scale is commonly used in two ways. The first equates it with human dimensions. Domestic architecture is where it is considered most desirable; the various elements should relate to human size. This means that although features may be larger than life, the excess must be within perceptually manageable limits so that the connection with human size is not severed. We reject megaliths of habitation such as Parkhill in Sheffield or the tower blocks in Glasgow because they violate the man-related scale which we now consider to be mandatory for housing. It was far easier for people to relate to the slums than to the monsters which replaced them.

But the concept of scale can also be applied where there is no fixed objective yardstick. New York City, for instance, has a scale which is immeasurably larger than life. In this context scale may refer to an overall consensus of information within a particular frame of reference – a street, a square, or a whole city. Scale represents the aggregate of the interplay between features which establish pattern and features which reinforce multiplexity and randomness; it stands for the norm which arises out of the contest between the opposite poles of information. This interpretation of scale is particularly relevant to the aesthetics of townscape. Each place has its own scale; it is an essential part of its *genius loci* and the consequence of the unique way it achieves overall unity. However, coherence and pattern are not the only ingredients of scale. It also implies the existence of rhyme.

After the second world war, planners and architects made the mistake of equating scale with uniformity, associating it with simile rather than metaphor. The result was dull characterless architecture in which windows and eaves all lined-through and materials conformed. There was a total absence of scale, because scale presupposes a significant rate of complexity. A sense of scale emerges when the vigorous dialectic between multiplexity and orderliness is ultimately resolved in favour of orderliness. We have demonstrated that coherence can emerge from a scene which at first sight seems disorderly. The Altstadt in Landshut has been cited as an example where likeness convincingly outstrips difference in the race for perceptual prominence. The sense of rhythm is stronger than randomness in matters like plot size, height, window size and placement, and so on. Despite their rich variety of shapes, the gables conform to the same overriding principle, and all these factors confer upon the Altstadt the quality of scale. In this sense, scale is compatible with many of the elements which make up the contramorphic aesthetic (see Chapter 7).

'Scale' is one of the most misused words in the architectural vocabulary. In the rue Matignon in Paris there is an individualistic insertion at number 22 [Fig 12.1]. The *Architectural Review*[14] endorsed Jacques Chirac's view that it 'respects the scale and rhythm of (existing) facades, the quality of the street in layout and profile . . .'. In fact, the only way it respects the scale of the existing

Fig 12.1
22 rue Matignon, Paris
*(Photos: The
Architectural Press Ltd)*

facades is in its height; in every other way it violates scale and rhythm. It represents a total break with everything in its vicinity, and this is what makes it a thoroughly entertaining building. An ordinary street has been transformed by this snippet of sophisticated humour. To justify it by saying that it preserves scale and rhythm is to misuse these concepts; it is far better to acknowledge that there are times when it is acceptable to be a little outrageous.

Paris is building a repertoire of entertaining inserts; another example is a little apartment block near the Pantheon by 'Cabinete de Paris' [Fig 12.2]. Its white tiles and bright red windows add sparkle and *joie de vivre* to the streetscape. In the publication referred to above, the ambitious multipurpose development at Ivry [Fig 12.3] is described as having 'fine grain'. What *is* fine grain? It implies delicacy and finesse, but Ivry is the epitome of *coarse* grain, with its profusion of triangular shapes on plan and elevation.

Fig 12.2
Apartments near the
Pantheon, Paris

Fig 12.3
Ivry, Paris

However, this is not necessarily an adverse criticism: in the rather colourless Parisian suburbs these 'hanging gardens' are an injection of life. Assertiveness succeeds because there is very little for it to be in scale with.

Finally, let us take the case of Princes Street in Edinburgh [Fig 12.4]. A special panel was set up by the City to establish guidelines for its redevelopment. However, the panel exceeded its brief and prescribed a fundamental design programme which provided for shopping at ground floor, a pedestrian deck at first floor level (an updated version of the Chester Rows) and above this a two-storey elevation capped by a penthouse or dormer storey. Had this policy been carried through, it would have drained Princes Street of all aesthetic value.

One new development in this prescribed mould is the New Club designed by Alan Reiach to replace a classical facade. In defending his design against a rebuke by Sir John Pilcher, Reiach declared[15]: 'Whatever coherence Princes Street may have had in the past has long since gone . . . the design for the New Club conforms to what was at the time an attempt to bring back some coherence to the facades on a bigger scale than most of the earlier developments'.

This kind of misconception has led to the destruction of countless acres of valuable townscape throughout Britain. Of course Princes Street has coherence – the coherence of scale. There is enormous variation in building type; the ugly and the beautiful mingle with the nondescript, but they all combine to form a memorable townscape because of the unifying effect of scale. Very little remains of the original New Town architecture, but the way Princes Street evolved in the nineteenth century has resulted in a variegated collection of buildings which greatly adds to the aesthetic resources of the City. Unity clearly emerges from diversity because the incidence or rate of information is relatively constant. Variety and change are kept within the critical band width which defines scale. Ironically, the only buildings which violate this scale are the new inserts which have been forced to conform to a bland typology. It is amazing that anyone could have thought that Princes Street would have been improved by the inevitably vapid architecture spawned by a committee.

Fig 12.4
Princes Street,
Edinburgh

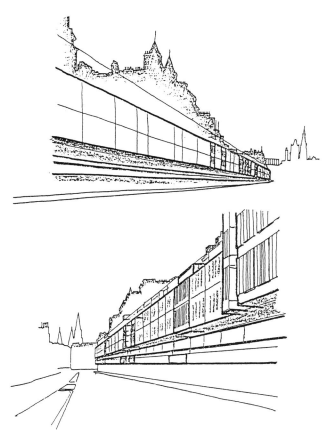

When architects and planners make an emotional commitment to a new image or ideal, they often develop a kind of 'culture blindness' which causes them to devalue anything which stands in its way – a psychological phenomenon to which dreamers and Utopianists are particularly prone. Any interstitial redevelopment in Princes Street must respect the scale of the street by maintaining the consensus rate of information, the aggregate ratio of complexity to redundancy, but this does not necessarily mean conforming with the existing style; it is quite possible for architecture which is wholly contemporary to respect the scale of the street on this abstract level of information.

To arrive at a working definition of scale, we need first to establish what it is not. Uniformity has nothing to do with scale; an identical series of features merely establishes repetition. An awareness of scale derives from a significant level of variation between elements – a reasonably high rate of complexity which occurs at a reasonably consistent rate. At the same time, there has to be an even higher level of correspondence. Out of the matrix of information the impression of pattern must be stronger than the sense of arbitrariness, and this concerns the way architectural features, colours, tones and textures aggregate to establish a kind of consensus. Each street and each town has its own consensus which we need to tune in to whenever we add to its stock of buildings. To observe the scale of a place may be a matter of conforming to the prevailing rate of likeness to difference – or even respecting the overall rate of idiosyncracy!

Chapter 13   The Last Chord

'The need of mankind is not for harmony, which is absurd, but for a profound understanding both of ordering and of clash, that will enable us to facilitate those ordering processes which are powerful enough to prevent clash from exceeding disastrous thresholds.'

This passage from the Aspen Papers[16] illustrates the classic misconception about harmony. Harmony is *not* the antithesis of ordering and clash, for it exists wherever the ordering processes are powerful enough to prevent clash from exceeding disastrous thresholds – a harmony which is strident and on the limit, but still harmony.

Harmony embraces a wide band of interactive conditions: at one end of the spectrum is the harmony of elegance when the contest between complexity is refined down to its essence; at the other, there is the harmony of romanticism where the pitch of the contest is often intensified by conscripting the forces of symbolism. Harmony is not confined to the tasteful and safe; it resides in romanticism as well as in classicism.

At this point, the unpersuaded reader might well ask what can the purity and reticence of Brunelleschi's Capella Pazzi, for example, possibly have in common with the effervescent eruptions of Neumann or Fischer. Is there any common denominator? A comprehensive aesthetic theory must demonstrate that there is.

Western art is manifestly dynamic in both a linear and cyclic sense. Initially there is steady progress towards higher complexity, expressed as multiplexity or novelty. Artists feel compelled to be innovative, architects in particular. Ultimately there is a reaction in favour of the ideal of restraint and simplicity; a new Classicism is born.

Several major phases in art have been comparatively self-contained and have demonstrated a progression from classical order and simplicity to complexity, most obviously the Renaissance. Filippo Brunelleschi was principally responsible for launching a new architectural era by re-synthesising elements from Greek and Roman architecture into a new style, delicate and restrained. He initiated a new Classicism which culminated in the high Renaissance.

The work of Michelangelo epitomised the pressure to achieve higher levels of complexity. His innovative and iconoclastic brilliance enhanced the whole scale of Classical architecture, inflating it to a size worthy of the mightiest basilica in Christendom. At times he flagrantly violated the rules of Classicism, most notably in the antechamber to the Laurenzian Library in Florence. Michelangelo injected new tension into Renaissance architecture, achieving a new dimension of intellectual complexity.

In the final phase of the Renaissance cycle, the emotions were the prime target. The church of Il Gesu in Rome by Vignola marks the beginning of an ascent into multiplexity and drama. The baroque phase of the cycle was shaped by the inventive minds of Maderna, Bernini, Rainaldi, Cortona, and Borromini who between them transformed the city of Rome. The architects of Germany and Austria finally took the baroque/rococo style to its limits of splendour and inventiveness, as noted in Neumann's church at Vierzehnheiligen [see Fig 11.6]. J M Fischer, the Assam brothers, Jakob Prandtauer and Dientzenhofer are among the leaders of this exuberant culmination of the Renaissance which expired in a shower of gold leaf.

The same progression can be identified in the Greco-Roman civilisation and in the Gothic era. The ideal gradually shifted from austere Classical simplicity and discipline to 'romantic' multiplexity.

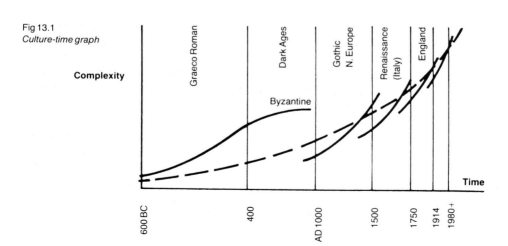

Fig 13.1
Culture-time graph

Complexity

Graeco Roman

Byzantine

Dark Ages

Gothic
N. Europe

Renaissance
(Italy)

England

Time

600 BC   400   AD 1000   1500   1750   1914   1980+

Thus we have identified a cyclic model of aesthetic change. And clearly such cycles have been occurring more and more frequently, perhaps even along an exponential curve [Fig 13.1], demonstrating that there is an organic continuity about art and architecture. In one sense it is a succession of reactions against previous norms – art developing by manageable 'catastrophes'. Yet there is a pattern to it all; the continuous thread which binds together all the phases of a cycle is the fact that each phase represents a different manifestation of the clash between complexity and orderliness.

Taste and fashion

The fickleness of taste and fashion causes some critics to believe that all attempts to arrive at the fundamental rationale behind the perception of harmony are doomed to failure. Taste and fashion are vulnerable to influences which have nothing to do with aesthetics (including the 'intervening variables' referred to in Chapter 1), and we must make due allowance for them. For example, an emotional philosophical commitment can distort aesthetic judgement, and did so in my own case.

During the early part of my architectural education it was fashionable to denigrate baroque architecture. It was 'vulgar', a deliberate counter-Reformation tactic to keep the simple peasantry of southern Europe loyal to Roman Catholicism. Thus aesthetic judgement was being conditioned by a Protestant reaction to so-called post-Tridentine propaganda. Then Niklaus Pevsner published his erudite *Outline of European Architecture*[12] (see Chapter 11). Pevsner was not a product of English Protestantism, he was from the central European tradition of scholarship and as such saw the baroque with different eyes. He rapidly infected others (myself included) with his enthusiasm for the genre.

I wasted no time in going to see the real thing. It was a breathtaking revelation, and it taught me to make myself vulnerable to the beauty inherent in all styles of architecture. It is a pity that critics of the calibre of Pevsner did not arrive in time to prevent the annihilation of so much of the legacy of the nineteenth century, perhaps the most maligned architectural period of all time.

So fashion may be defined as the adoption of values for other than aesthetic reasons, such as conforming to socially-agreed norms. It often seems more important to accept the social mores and so receive the badge of belonging than to stand out for our personal tastes and risk being ostracised. Ironically, the fashionable object then becomes a symbol of social acceptance and thus triggers emotional reward which may masquerade as aesthetic satisfaction.

Architects are particularly inclined to run before the winds of fashion, not so much because they must win clients to survive, but because they seek the acclaim of their peers or perhaps some fashion-forming critic. Yet within the broad movement of cultural values and the rapid fluctuations of fashion, there remains the infinite variety of individual taste. Only three variables are needed to ensure that no two human beings possess identical value systems: genetic endowment, acculturation, and experience.

Genes can mould our value systems in two ways. First, they can determine our tolerance of complexity. Each of us has a different 'redundancy threshold' or maximum point at which we can resolve complexity into orderliness. To some extent this can be changed by learning and experience, but in broad terms it will decide whether our musical 'taste' ends with Mozart or Schoenberg. Secondly, they determine our sensitivity towards particular classes of stimuli. Individuals vary in the extent to which they can discriminate between tones and hues and in the extent to which relationships between stimuli affect them emotionally.

The second variable is acculturation. Values instilled into us during the most impressionable years are hard to overturn; acculturation is a formidable arbiter of taste. And thirdly, there is the influence of experience. As I have already remarked, the ultimate orderliness threshold can be pushed steadily back by regular exposure to progressively higher rates of complexity. (So a taste for Schoenberg may be acquired after all – and without prejudice to Mozart.)

Finally, individual taste can undergo a reversal. This may not be as radical as it would seem, since any value judgement is the end product or resultant of a complex system of contrary forces, and although the difference between the respective values of the pros and cons may be slight, it may be sufficient to emerge into consciousness as a clear judgement. We could call it the 'watershed' principle. Just as extremely subtle variations in contour may decide whether a spring of water finally ends up in the Atlantic or the Pacific as a mighty river, so a relatively trivial event may alter the 'topography' of the mind and cause an apparently radical change of opinion. In reality this has simply been brought about by a minor shift in the disposition of mental forces. Indeed, much that is classified as 'personality' is the result of a contest of interior forces where victory has been won by the slenderest of margins.

Despite these formidable variables, my contention is that value judgements hinge upon the individual's preferred ratio of complexity to orderliness and the optimum acceptable level of complexity consistent with the ultimate assertion of order. And it is this principle which unites major cultural values first with fashion and ultimately with individual taste.

To sum up, beauty is a by-product of the search for certainty. Aesthetic perception is a mental stance where we seek out the unusual or the multiplex so as to extend our knowledge and assert the rule of order. In *Man's Race for Chaos: Biology, Behaviour and the Arts* Peckham observed: 'Art, as an adaptational mechanism, is a rehearsal for those real situations in which it is vital for our survival to endure cognitive tension . . . art is the reinforcement of the capacity to endure disorientation so that real and significant problems may emerge.'

We might adapt this observation and say that we endure disorientation (or complexity) so as to learn how to cope with more complex problems.

In this book I have tried to show how the eternal combat between order and anarchy is fought out on the architectural plane, from single buildings to whole cities. I believe we can now attach a broader significance to traditional proportional systems like *phi* and the Fibonacci series, translating them into interactions between complex systems of information. But whether or not *phi* and the Fibonacci series are confirmed as the datum of harmonic value, the main thrust of my argument is that the mind engages in the business of equating informational 'masses' so as to discover the harmony which can emerge from the most unlikely places. Because it is programmed to seek emotional reward through aesthetic pleasure, the mind is always on the alert to extract harmony from a continuous stream of sense impressions. It engages, often secretly, in synoptic perception whilst consciously focussing on a particular object or task. This is why an aesthetically satisfying composition of buildings can suddenly spring into consciousness, taking us by surprise. It has been picked up some time before by the minor cerebral hemisphere, which finally transmits a message to its dominant partner that it has something worthy of conscious attention. Perhaps the essence of *homo sapiens* lies in the asymmetry of the brain, another harmonic pairing between a dominant and a subordinate – likeness tempered with difference.

In the concluding chapter of *The Aesthetics of Architecture*[13], Roger Scruton claims that '. . . there is never any need, in the practice of aesthetic judgement, to say what proportion really means, in the sense of pinning down the term to some one property or set of properties which provide its true aesthetic sense'. I believe that this is what we *must* try to do if we are to carry the debate about aesthetics beyond the current stalemate. (Scruton has probably gone as far as such a philosophical approach will take him.) That is why I maintain that it is necessary to introduce biological and psychological determinants, new tools with which to construct an objective theory.

Scruton advocates a return to harmonic principles in architecture and urban design, associating this with the Classical approach. For my part, I have tried to show what harmonic principles are applicable to *all* ages, styles and scales of architecture. They can be identified in a medieval town of apparently fortuitous design as well as a carefully contrived Renaissance ensemble like the Capitol in Rome.

I further contend that fundamental relational reference standards constitute the basis of aesthetic perception, standards which are valid because they derive from the performance of the central nervous system and basic survival strategies. Because this is a broad principle rather than a specific value system, it can accommodate the infinite range of personality and experience. As I have tried to illustrate, aesthetic perception is based on the dynamics of informational weight; it relies upon concepts such as 'force' and 'energy', and that given phenomena have a significant level of consistency in terms of attributable weight. This is what enables us to talk representatively about harmony. Individual inheritance and experience generate variations, especially in respect of the informational weight of symbolism, but this divergence is not sufficient to overturn the broad consensus.

To see aesthetic perception as the product of evolutionary pressures linked to survival strategy is not to diminish its significance. On the contrary, it is to ascribe to it a real biological value which is becoming increasingly relevant to a society rushing headlong into micro-processed determinism.

In the heyday of the Modern Movement, Lethaby expressed its main axiom as follows[17]: 'We reject all esthetic (sic) speculation, all doctrine, all formalism. Architecture is the will of an epoch translated into space: living, changing, new.'

I have sought to show that there are powerful biological and philosophical reasons why Lethaby was wrong. Architecture may be one way in which the spirit of an age is expressed, but such expression has to use the current aesthetic agenda; formalism and architecture are inseparable. By looking at buildings through history, we see how each society has translated the primordial contest between order and anarchy. The idea that this contest has a biological connection may be distasteful to those who see art as the antithesis of the arbitrariness of nature. But nature is in fact the supreme affirmation of order defeating confusion. Art and nature are linked by much more than analogy.

Conclusion

Throughout history it has been possible to detect a moral aspect to architecture. If this book has a moral dimension, it must derive from the fact that creative and mind-enhancing stability is only possible where, in the tension between orderliness and arbitrariness, orderliness tips the scales. A second 'moral' factor is that mental performance improves, even if only by a fraction, whenever we rise to a challenge and attain a higher level of certainty. Architecture that achieves harmony on this principle constantly enlarges our capacity to recognise the order behind the chaos. On the other hand, buildings which fail to resolve into some kind of coherence are mentally debilitating; they promote atomised perception – a concentration on the parts in isolation. Any repeated mental strategy tends to become self-reinforcing, so buildings as the one unavoidable art form matter greatly. They affect our capacity to deal with complexity of any kind.

I have suggested that the mind engages in two kinds of information processing and classification, the analytical and the holistic. But nearly all the pressures in the contemporary world reinforce analytical perception *at the expense* of holism. Connectedness between objects and people is weakening, especially between ethnic divisions. The human mind is a dynamic universe continuously adapting according to environmental pressures, so that this apparent flight into wholly atomised perception must be halted. And in this respect the built environment has a crucial role to play.

Donald Berlyne was right to assert[2]: 'The aim of all intellectual pursuits, including science, philosophy and art (including the art of building well) is to seek unity in the midst of diversity or order in the midst of complexity. The ultimate task is to fit multifarious elements into some kind of compact, cohesive, apprehensible scheme.'

And Samuel Taylor Coleridge, discussing the power of imagination, said something very similar[18]: 'This power . . . reveals itself in the balance or reconciliation of opposite or discordant qualities: of sameness with difference; of the general with the concrete; the idea with the image; the individual with the representative; . . . the sense of novelty and freshness with old and familiar objects . . .'

This is what the creators of true art in all its forms have tried to do from earliest times. In an age of rapid change there is greater need than ever before to preserve a historical sense of beauty so as to be able to distil from each time and place its aesthetic essence. We must learn to identify the golden thread which binds good architecture of all ages from vernacular townscape to the high plane of the great monuments of architecture and urban design. As T S Eliot said, the historical sense is the only valid foundation upon which to build the future.

References

Chapter 1

[1] *Genes, Mind and Culture*
     C J Lumsden and E O Wilson
     pp 5, 89, 100 Harvard 1981

[2] *Aesthetics and Psychobiology*
     D E Berlyne
     Appleton-Century Crofts
     New York 1971

[3] *Future Shock*
     A Toffler
     Bodley Head and Pan Books 1972

Chapter 2

[4] *The Dynamics of Urbanism*
     P F Smith
     Ch 5 Hutchinson 1974

Chapter 3

[5] *Architectural Review*
     May 1978

Chapter 4

[6] *The Syntax of Cities*
     P F Smith
     Ch 19 Hutchinson 1977

[7] *Art and Visual Perception*
     R Arnheim
     Berkley, Calif 1954

Chapter 5

[6] P F Smith
     op cit

Chapter 6

[2] D E Berlyne
     op cit

Chapter 7

[1] Lumsden and Wilson
     op cit

Chapter 8

[8] *Architecture and the Human
     Dimension*
     P F Smith
     Godwin 1979

Chapter 9

[9] *Townscape*
     G Cullen
     Architectural Press 1960

Chapter 10

[10] *The Dynamics of Architectural
     Form*
     R Arnheim
     Univ of Calif 1977

[11] *Le inibizioni dell'architettura
     moderna*
     P Portoghesi
     Rome 1974

[6] P F Smith
     op cit

[8] P F Smith
     op cit

[10] *Albert Einstein*
     op cit R Arnheim

Chapter 11

[12] *An Outline of European
     Architecture*
     N Pevsner
     Harmondsworth 1943

[13] *Aesthetics in Architecture*
     R Scruton
     p 223 Methuen 1979

References

Chapter 12

[14] *Architectural Review*
      p 136 Sept 1979

[15] *Architectural Review*
      Oct 1978

Chapter 13

[16] *The Aspen Papers*
      Procs of the Aspen Conference

[12] N Pevsner
      op cit

[13] R Scruton
      op cit

[17] *Architecture*
      An introduction to the history and
      theory of the art of building
      W R Lethaby
      3rd ed OUP 1955

[2]   D E Berlyne
      op cit p296

[18] *Biographica Literaria*
      Samuel Taylor Coleridge

Appendix

An Analytical Programme for Aesthetic Assessment

There are persistent calls for an objective method of measuring the aesthetic quality of buildings and townscape. This is not it! At best, it is a programme for organising subjective assessments so as to arrive at a form of value judgement which will bear comparison with the observations of others.

The five sections correspond to the main analytical divisions of the book. The algebraic totals of the relevant sections (single buildings or urbanism) can be summarised on the final sheet. Where there is a positive result, this can be expressed as percentage success.

The first page provides a space for a quick, initial assessment which can later be compared with the sum of the detailed analyses.

This kind of programme is inevitably simplistic and is meant to suggest a strategy rather than provide an exhaustive critical check-list.

The copyright conditions which apply to the main text have been relaxed for this Appendix.

Analytical Programme

Location: Building or urban group

Map reference if applicable

General: Description

Investigator: Name and address

Details: Date   Time   Weather   Other factors

Initial assessment: On a scale of 1-100

Unity out of Particularity
Individual building

Value scale	Negative					0	Positive					Comments
	-5	-4	-3	-2	-1	0	$+1$	$+2$	$+3$	$+4$	$+5$	
Quality of unity over particularity via:												
Materials												
Disposition of principal architectural elements (e.g. tower and basilica)												
Secondary architectural elements (gables, dormers, windows, entrances etc.)												
Iconic features (e.g. stylistic features)												
Expression of structure												
Consistency in rate of visual incidents (abstract features, lines, curves etc.)												
Column totals												
Sub-totals												Maximum possible score 30
Algebraic sum												

159

Pattern out of Variety in Urbanism

Analysis Sheet No. 2
Page No. 1

Value scale	Negative					0	Positive					Comments
	−5	−4	−3	−2	−1		+1	+2	+3	+4	+5	
Prominence of pattern in respect of:												
Roofs												
Openings (windows/dormers, doors, arcades)												
Gables/eaves												
Materials												
Frequency and amplitude (change of plane) of visual incidents												
Column totals												
Sub-totals												Maximum possible score 25
Algebraic sum												

Discrete Binary Harmony
Individual building

Value scale	Negative						0	Positive					Comments
	−5	−4	−3	−2	−1			+1	+2	+3	+4	+5	
Harmonic success in terms of:													
Primary element 'a' to primary element 'b' (specify)													
Secondary element 'c' to secondary element 'd' (specify)													
Tertiary element 'e' to tertiary element 'f' (specify)													
Chunked elements 'g' to chunked elements 'h' (specify)													
Chunked elements 'i' to chunked elements 'j' (specify)													
Column totals													
Sub-totals													Maximum possible score 25
Algebraic sum													

Discrete Binary Harmony
Urban and landscape

Value scale	Negative						0	Positive						Comments
	−5	−4	−3	−2	−1			+1	+2	+3	+4	+5		
Harmony between:														
Sacred buildings and secular buildings														
Special object 'a' and special object 'b'														
New insterstitial building and wider architectural context														
Building(s) and natural setting														
Special building and chunked subordinate buildings														
Column totals														
Sub-totals														Maximum possible score 25
Algebraic sum														

Integral Binary Harmony
Individual building

Value scale	Negative						0	Positive					Comments
	−5	−4	−3	−2	−1			+1	+2	+3	+4	+5	
Harmonic success in terms of:													
Chunked weight of windows to wall													
Ratio of roof to wall													
Ratio of wall to base, plinth, rusticated ground storey													
Ratio of horizontal to vertical features													
Ratio of round to rectangular and curved to straight													
Column totals													
Sub-totals													

Continued

163

Integral Binary Harmony continued

Analysis Sheet No. 5
Page No. 2

Value scale	Negative					0	Positive					Comments
	−5	−4	−3	−2	−1	0	+1	+2	+3	+4	+5	
Column totals carried forward												
Harmonic success in terms of:												
Ratio of decoration to plain surfaces												
Solid to void (other than windows, doors etc)												
Frame to fenestration/curtain wall												
Material 'a' to material 'b' (specify)												
Elements 'a' to elements 'b' (specify)												
Column totals												
Sub-totals												Maximum possible score 50
Algebraic sum												

Summary to Cumulative Assessment

	Algebraic totals		Maximum possible score
	Negative	Positive	
Analysis Sheet No. 1 — **Unity out of Particularity** (individual building)			30
Analysis Sheet No. 2 — **Pattern out of Variety** (urban)			25
Analysis Sheet No. 3 — **Discrete Binary Harmony** (individual building)			25
Analysis Sheet No. 4 — **Discrete Binary Harmony** (urban)			25
Analysis Sheet No. 5 — **Integral Binary Harmony** (individual building)			50
Sub-totals			
Algebraic total			
Where there is a **positive** net total, then: $\dfrac{\text{Net total}}{\text{Maximum possible score}} \times 100 = \text{percentage success} =$			
Compare with initial assessment			

165